Quantitative Analysis
Interpreting Numerical Data

Pearson

At Pearson, we have a simple mission: to help people make more of their lives through learning.

We combine innovative learning technology with trusted content and educational expertise to provide engaging and effective learning experience that serve people wherever and whenever they are learning.

We enable our customers to access a wide and expanding range of market-leading content from world-renowned authors and develop their own tailor-made book. From classroom to boardroom, our curriculum materials, digital learning tools and testing programmes help to educate millions of people worldwide — more than any other private enterprise.

Every day our work helps learning flourish, and wherever learning flourishes, so do people.

To learn more, please visit us at: www.pearson.com/uk

Quantitative Analysis
Interpreting Numerical Data

Selected chapters from:

Elementary Statistics: Picturing the World
Seventh Edition, Global Edition
Ron Larson and Betsy Farber

Harlow, England • London • New York • Boston • San Francisco • Toronto • Sydney • Dubai • Singapore • Hong Kong
Tokyo • Seoul • Taipei • New Dehli • Cape Town • São Paulo • Mexico City • Madrid • Amsterdam • Munich • Paris • Milan

Pearson
KAO Two
KAO Park
Harlow
Essex CM17 9NA

And associated companies throughout the world

Visit us on the World Wide Web at:
www.pearson.com/uk

© Pearson Education Limited 2019

Compiled from:

Elementary Statistics: Picturing the World
Seventh Edition, Global Edition
Ron Larson and Betsy Farber
ISBN 978-1-292-26046-4
© Pearson Education Limited 2019

All rights reserved. No part of this publication may be reproduced, stored in a retrieval system, or transmitted in any form or by any means, electronic, mechanical, photocopying, recording or otherwise, without either the prior written permission of the publisher or a licence permitting restricted copying in the United Kingdom issued by the Copyright Licensing Agency Ltd, Barnard's Inn, 86 Fetter Lane, London, EC4A 1EN.

ISBN 978-1-787-64429-8

Printed and bound in Great Britain by CPI Group.

CONTENTS

Chapter 1 Introduction to Statistics — 2
Chapter 1 in *Elementary Statistics: Picturing the World*, Seventh Edition, Global Edition
Ron Larson and Betsy Farber

Chapter 2 Descriptive Statistics — 40
Chapter 2 in *Elementary Statistics: Picturing the World*, Seventh Edition, Global Edition
Ron Larson and Betsy Farber

Chapter 3 Confidence Intervals — 130
Chapter 6 in *Elementary Statistics: Picturing the World*, Seventh Edition, Global Edition
Ron Larson and Betsy Farber

Chapter 4 Correlation and Regression — 180
Chapter 9 in *Elementary Statistics: Picturing the World*, Seventh Edition, Global Edition
Ron Larson and Betsy Farber

Appendix B — A1
from Appendix B in *Elementary Statistics: Picturing the World*, Seventh Edition, Global Edition
Ron Larson and Betsy Farber

Try It Yourself Answers — A5
from Try It Yourself Answers in *Elementary Statistics: Picturing the World*, Seventh Edition, Global Edition
Ron Larson and Betsy Farber

Odd Answers — A9
from Odd Answers in *Elementary Statistics: Picturing the World*, Seventh Edition, Global Edition
Ron Larson and Betsy Farber

Quantitative Analysis
Interpreting Numerical Data

CHAPTER 1

Introduction to Statistics

For the first 10 months of 2016, construction completions of privately-owned housing units in the U.S. was greatest in the south.

1.1
An Overview of Statistics

1.2
Data Classification
Case Study

1.3
Data Collection and Experimental Design
Activity
Uses and Abuses
Real Statistics—Real Decisions
History of Statistics—Timeline
Technology

Where You've Been

You are already familiar with many of the practices of statistics, such as taking surveys, collecting data, and describing populations. What you may not know is that collecting accurate statistical data is often difficult and costly. Consider, for instance, the monumental task of counting and describing the entire population of the United States. If you were in charge of such a census, how would you do it? How would you ensure that your results are accurate? These and many more concerns are the responsibility of the United States Census Bureau, which conducts the census every decade.

Where You're Going

In Chapter 1, you will be introduced to the basic concepts and goals of statistics. For instance, statistics were used to construct the figures below, which show the numbers, by region in the U.S., of construction completions of privately-owned housing units for October of 2016 and for the first 10 months of 2016, as numbers in thousands and as percents of the total.

For the 2010 Census, the Census Bureau sent short forms to every household. Short forms ask all members of every household such things as their gender, age, race, and ethnicity. Previously, a long form, which covered additional topics, was sent to about 17% of the population. But for the first time since 1940, the long form was replaced by the American Community Survey, which surveys more than 3.5 million households a year throughout the decade. These households form a sample. In this course, you will learn how the data collected from a sample are used to infer characteristics about the entire population.

Housing Units Completed in the U.S. (October 2016)

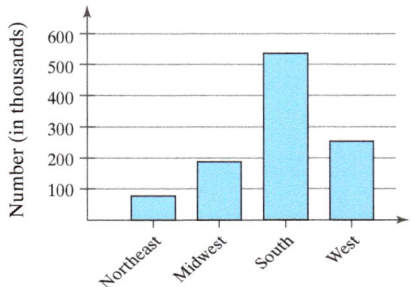

Housing Units Completed in the U.S. (October 2016)

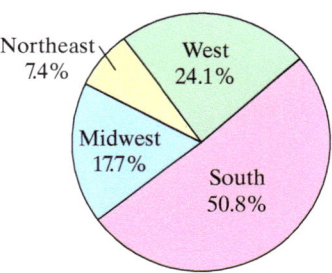

Housing Units Completed in the U.S. (January–October 2016)

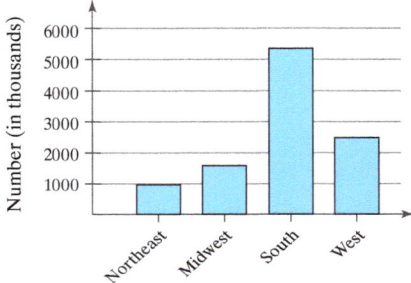

Housing Units Completed in the U.S. (January–October 2016)

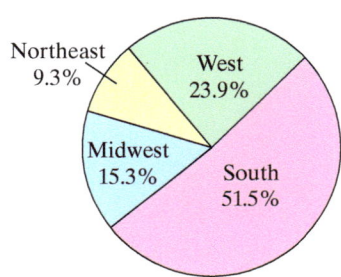

1.1 An Overview of Statistics

What You Should Learn

▶ A definition of statistics
▶ How to distinguish between a population and a sample and between a parameter and a statistic
▶ How to distinguish between descriptive statistics and inferential statistics

A Definition of Statistics ■ Data Sets ■ Branches of Statistics

A Definition of Statistics

Almost every day you are exposed to statistics. For instance, consider the next two statements.

- According to a survey, more than 7 in 10 Americans say a nursing career is a prestigious occupation. *(Source: The Harris Poll)*
- "Social media consumes kids today as well, as more score their first social media accounts at an average age of 11.4 years old." *(Source: Influence Central's 2016 Digital Trends Study)*

By learning the concepts in this text, you will gain the tools to become an informed consumer, understand statistical studies, conduct statistical research, and sharpen your critical thinking skills.

Many statistics are presented graphically. For instance, consider the figure shown below.

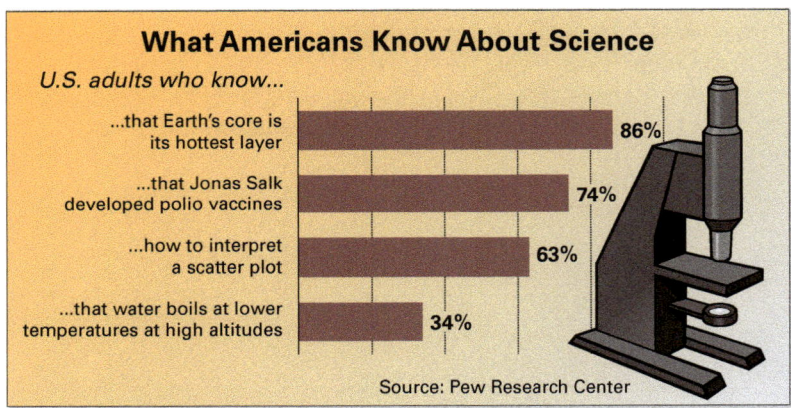

The information in the figure is based on the collection of **data.** In this instance, the data are based on the results of a science quiz given to 3278 U.S. adults.

> **DEFINITION**
>
> **Data** consist of information coming from observations, counts, measurements, or responses.

The use of statistics dates back to census taking in ancient Babylonia, Egypt, and later in the Roman Empire, when data were collected about matters concerning the state, such as births and deaths. In fact, the word *statistics* is derived from the Latin word *status*, meaning "state." The modern practice of statistics involves more than counting births and deaths, as you can see in the next definition.

> **DEFINITION**
>
> **Statistics** is the science of collecting, organizing, analyzing, and interpreting data in order to make decisions.

Data Sets

There are two types of data sets you will use when studying statistics. These data sets are called **populations** and **samples.**

Study Tip

A *census* consists of data from an entire population. But, unless a population is small, it is usually impractical to obtain all the population data. In most studies, information must be obtained from a random sample.

> **DEFINITION**
>
> A **population** is the collection of *all* outcomes, responses, measurements, or counts that are of interest. A **sample** is a subset, or part, of a population.

A sample is used to gain information about a population. For instance, to estimate the unemployment rate for the *population* of the United States, the U.S. Bureau of Labor uses a *sample* of about 60,000 households.

A sample should be representative of a population so that sample data can be used to draw conclusions about that population. Sample data must be collected using an appropriate method, such as *random sampling*. When sample data are collected using an *inappropriate* method, the data cannot be used to draw conclusions about the population. (You will learn more about random sampling and data collection in Section 1.3.)

EXAMPLE 1

Identifying Data Sets

In a survey, 834 employees in the United States were asked whether they thought their jobs were highly stressful. Of the 834 respondents, 517 said yes. Identify the population and the sample. Describe the sample data set. *(Source: CareerCast Job Stress Report)*

SOLUTION

The population consists of the responses of all employees in the United States. The sample consists of the responses of the 834 employees in the survey. In the Venn diagram below, notice that the sample is a subset of the responses of all employees in the United States. Also, the sample data set consists of 517 people who said yes and 317 who said no.

Responses of All Employees (population)

Responses of employees in survey (sample)

Responses of employees *not* in the survey

TRY IT YOURSELF 1

In a survey of 1501 ninth to twelfth graders in the United States, 1215 said "leaders today are more concerned with their own agenda than with achieving the overall goals of the organization they serve." Identify the population and the sample. Describe the sample data set. *(Source: National 4-H Council)*

Answer: Page A5

Whether a data set is a population or a sample usually depends on the context of the real-life situation. For instance, in Example 1, the population is the set of responses of all employees in the United States. Depending on the purpose of the survey, the population could have been the set of responses of all employees who live in California or who work in the healthcare industry.

Study Tip

To remember the terms parameter and statistic, try using the mnemonic device of matching the first letters in *population parameter* and the first letters in *sample statistic*.

Picturing the World

How accurate is the count of the U.S. population taken each decade by the Census Bureau? According to estimates, the net undercount of the U.S. population by the 1940 census was 5.4%. The accuracy of the census has improved greatly since then. The net undercount in the 2010 census was −0.01%. (This means that the 2010 census overcounted the U.S. population by 0.01%, which is about 36,000 people.) *(Source: U.S. Census Bureau)*

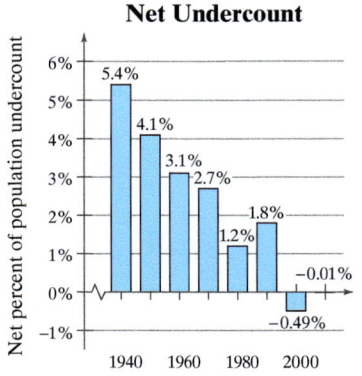

What are some difficulties in collecting population data?

Two important terms that are used throughout this course are **parameter** and **statistic.**

DEFINITION

A **parameter** is a numerical description of a *population* characteristic.

A **statistic** is a numerical description of a *sample* characteristic.

It is important to note that a sample statistic can differ from sample to sample, whereas a population parameter is constant for a population. For instance, consider the survey in Example 1. The results showed that 517 of 834 employees surveyed think their jobs are highly stressful. Another sample may have a different number of employees that say their jobs are highly stressful. For the population, however, the number of employees who think that their jobs are highly stressful does not change.

EXAMPLE 2

Distinguishing Between a Parameter and a Statistic

Determine whether each number describes a population parameter or a sample statistic. Explain your reasoning.

1. A survey of several hundred collegiate student-athletes in the United States found that, during the season of their sport, the average time spent on athletics by student-athletes is 50 hours per week. *(Source: Penn Schoen Berland)*
2. The freshman class at a university has an average SAT math score of 514.
3. In a random check of several hundred retail stores, the Food and Drug Administration found that 34% of the stores were not storing fish at the proper temperature.

SOLUTION

1. Because the average of 50 hours per week is based on a subset of the population, it is a sample statistic.
2. Because the average SAT math score of 514 is based on the entire freshman class, it is a population parameter.
3. Because 34% is based on a subset of the population, it is a sample statistic.

TRY IT YOURSELF 2

Determine whether each number describes a population parameter or a sample statistic. Explain your reasoning.

a. Last year, a small company spent a total of $5,150,694 on employees' salaries.
b. In the United States, a survey of a few thousand adults with hearing loss found that 43% have difficulty remembering conversations. *(Source: The Harris Poll)*

Answer: Page A5

In this course, you will see how the use of statistics can help you make informed decisions that affect your life. Consider the census that the U.S. government takes every decade. When taking the census, the Census Bureau attempts to contact everyone living in the United States. Although it is impossible to count everyone, it is important that the census be as accurate as it can be because public officials make many decisions based on the census information. Data collected in the census will determine how to assign congressional seats and how to distribute public funds.

Branches of Statistics

The study of statistics has two major branches: **descriptive statistics** and **inferential statistics.**

DEFINITION

Descriptive statistics is the branch of statistics that involves the organization, summarization, and display of data.

Inferential statistics is the branch of statistics that involves using a sample to draw conclusions about a population. A basic tool in the study of inferential statistics is probability. (You will learn more about probability in Chapter 3.)

EXAMPLE 3

Descriptive and Inferential Statistics

For each study, identify the population and the sample. Then determine which part of the study represents the descriptive branch of statistics. What conclusions might be drawn from the study using inferential statistics?

1. A study of 2560 U.S. adults found that of adults not using the Internet, 23% are from households earning less than $30,000 annually, as shown in the figure at the left. *(Source: Pew Research Center)*

2. A study of 300 Wall Street analysts found that the percentage who incorrectly forecasted high-tech earnings in a recent year was 44%. *(Adapted from Bloomberg News)*

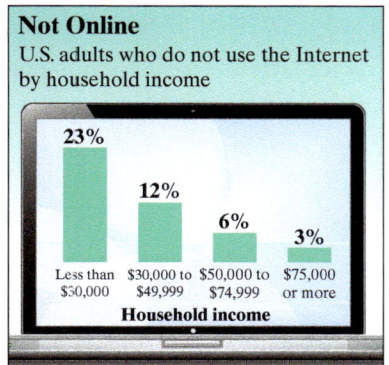

Not Online
U.S. adults who do not use the Internet by household income

SOLUTION

1. The population consists of the responses of all U.S. adults, and the sample consists of the responses of the 2560 U.S. adults in the study. The part of this study that represents the descriptive branch of statistics involves the statement "23% [of U.S. adults not using the Internet] are from households earning less than $30,000 annually." Also, the figure represents the descriptive branch of statistics. A possible inference drawn from the study is that lower-income households cannot afford access to the Internet.

2. The population consists of the high-tech earnings forecasts of all Wall Street analysts, and the sample consists of the forecasts of the 300 Wall Street analysts in the study. The part of this study that represents the descriptive branch of statistics involves the statement "the percentage [of Wall Street analysts] who incorrectly forecasted high-tech earnings in a recent year was 44%." A possible inference drawn from the study is that the stock market is difficult to forecast, even for professionals.

TRY IT YOURSELF 3

A study of 1000 U.S. adults found that when they have a question about their medication, three out of four adults will consult with their physician or pharmacist and only 8% visit a medication-specific website. *(Source: Finn Futures™ Health poll)*

a. Identify the population and the sample.
b. Determine which part of the study represents the descriptive branch of statistics.
c. What conclusions might be drawn from the study using inferential statistics?

Answer: Page A5

Study Tip

Throughout this course you will see applications of both branches of statistics. A major theme in this course will be how to use sample statistics to make inferences about unknown population parameters.

1.1 EXERCISES

For Extra Help: MyLab Statistics

Building Basic Skills and Vocabulary

1. How is a sample related to a population?
2. Why is a sample used more often than a population?
3. What is the difference between a parameter and a statistic?
4. What are the two main branches of statistics?

True or False? *In Exercises 5–10, determine whether the statement is true or false. If it is false, rewrite it as a true statement.*

5. A statistic is a numerical description of a population characteristic.
6. A sample is a subset of a population.
7. It is impossible to obtain all the census data about the U.S. population.
8. Inferential statistics involves using a population to draw a conclusion about a corresponding sample.
9. A population is the collection of some outcomes, responses, measurements, or counts that are of interest.
10. A sample statistic will not change from sample to sample.

Classifying a Data Set *In Exercises 11–20, determine whether the data set is a population or a sample. Explain your reasoning.*

11. A survey of 95 shopkeepers in a commercial complex with 550 shopkeepers
12. The amount of energy collected from every solar panel on a photovoltaic power plant
13. The height of each athlete participating in the Summer Olympics
14. The value of purchase by every sixth person entering a departmental store
15. The triglyceride levels of 10 patients in a clinic with 50 patients
16. The number of children in 25 households out of 75 households in a neighborhood
17. The final score of each gamer in a tournament
18. The ages at which all the presidents of a country were elected
19. The incomes of the top 10 taxpayers of a country
20. The air contamination levels at 20 locations near a factory

Graphical Analysis *In Exercises 21–24, use the Venn diagram to identify the population and the sample.*

21. **Parties of Registered Voters**

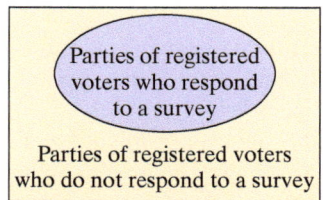

22. **Student Donations at a Food Drive**

23. **Ages of Adults in the United States Who Own Automobiles**

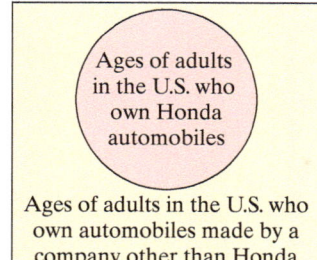

24. **Incomes of Home Owners in Massachusetts**

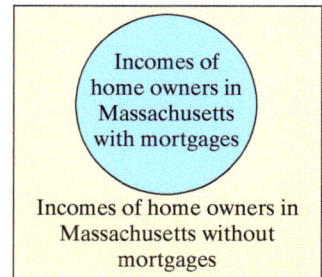

Using and Interpreting Concepts

Identifying Data Sets *In Exercises 25–34, identify the population and the sample. Describe the sample data set.*

25. A survey of 1020 U.S. adults found that 42% trust their political leaders. *(Source: Gallup)*

26. A study of 203 infants was conducted to find a link between fetal tobacco exposure and focused attention in infancy. *(Source: Infant Behavior and Development)*

27. A survey of 3301 U.S. adults found that 39% received an influenza vaccine for a recent flu season. *(Source: U.S. Centers for Disease Control and Prevention)*

28. A survey of 1500 employees worldwide found that 62% of the respondents working in a foreign country settle there.

29. A survey of 159 U.S. law firms found that the average hourly billing rate for partners was $604. *(Source: The National Law Journal)*

30. A survey of 328 children in a city in Belgium found that 86% planned to visit their grandparents during the summer vacation.

31. Of the 112.5 million blood donations collected globally, approximately 50% are collected from high-income countries. *(Source: World Health Organization)*

32. A survey of 1468 laptop users found that 81% preferred the use of mouse over touchpad.

33. To gather information about the best mutual funds listed on a recognized stock exchange website, a researcher collects data about 134 of the 1000 mutual funds.

34. A survey of 1060 parents of 13- to 17-year-olds found that 636 of the 1060 parents have checked their teen's social media profile. *(Source: Pew Research Center)*

Distinguishing Between a Parameter and a Statistic *In Exercises 35–42, determine whether the number describes a population parameter or a sample statistic. Explain your reasoning.*

35. Forty out of a high school's 500 students who took the midterm examination received a C grade.

36. A survey of 1058 college board members found that 56.3% think that college completion is a major priority or the most important priority for their board. *(Source: Association of Governing Boards of Universities and Colleges)*

37. Out of the 40 million casualties in the UK during World War II, two million were reported to be civilians.

38. In January 2016, 62% of the governors of the 50 states in the United States were Republicans. *(Source: National Governors Association)*

39. Employee records show that all the employees in an organization have received substantial increments over their joining salaries.

40. In a survey of 650 teachers, 16% reported that there have been instances of bullying in their class.

41. A survey of 2008 U.S. adults found that 80% think that the militant group known as ISIS is a major threat to the well-being of the United States. *(Source: Pew Research Center)*

42. In a recent year, the average math score on the ACT for all graduates was 20.6. *(Source: ACT, Inc.)*

43. **Descriptive and Inferential Statistics** Which part of the survey described in Exercise 31 represents the descriptive branch of statistics? What conclusions might be drawn from the survey using inferential statistics?

44. **Descriptive and Inferential Statistics** Which part of the survey described in Exercise 32 represents the descriptive branch of statistics? What conclusions might be drawn from the survey using inferential statistics?

Extending Concepts

45. **Identifying Data Sets in Articles** Find an article that describes a survey.
    (a) Identify the sample used in the survey.
    (b) What is the population?
    (c) Make an inference about the population based on the results of the survey.

46. **Writing** Write an essay about the importance of statistics for one of the following.
    - A study on the effectiveness of a new drug
    - An analysis of a manufacturing process
    - Drawing conclusions about voter opinions using surveys

47. **Exercise and Cognitive Ability** A study of 876 senior citizens shows that participants who exercise regularly exhibit less of a decline in cognitive ability than those who barely exercise at all. From this study, a researcher infers that your cognitive ability increases the more your exercise. What is wrong with this type of reasoning? *(Source: Neurology)*

48. **Increase in Obesity Rates** A study shows that the obesity rate among adolescents has steadily increased since 1988. From this study, a researcher infers that this trend will continue in future years. What is wrong with this type of reasoning? *(Source: Journal of the American Medical Association)*

49. **Sleep and Student Achievement** A study shows the closer that participants were to an optimal sleep duration target, the better they performed on a standardized test. *(Source: Eastern Economics Journal)*
    (a) Identify the sample used in the study.
    (b) What is the population?
    (c) Which part of the study represents the descriptive branch of statistics?
    (d) Make an inference about the population based on the results of the study.

1.2 Data Classification

What You Should Learn

▶ How to distinguish between qualitative data and quantitative data

▶ How to classify data with respect to the four levels of measurement: nominal, ordinal, interval, and ratio

Types of Data ■ Levels of Measurement

Types of Data

When conducting a study, it is important to know the kind of data involved. The type of data you are working with will determine which statistical procedures can be used. In this section, you will learn how to classify data by type and by level of measurement. Data sets can consist of two types of data: **qualitative data** and **quantitative data.**

> **DEFINITION**
>
> **Qualitative data** consist of attributes, labels, or nonnumerical entries.
>
> **Quantitative data** consist of numbers that are measurements or counts.

EXAMPLE 1

Classifying Data by Type

The table shows sports-related head injuries treated in U.S. emergency rooms during a recent five-year span for several sports. Which data are qualitative data and which are quantitative data? Explain your reasoning. *(Source: BMC Emergency Medicine)*

Sports-Related Head Injuries Treated in U.S. Emergency Rooms

Sport	Head injuries treated
Basketball	131,930
Baseball	83,522
Football	220,258
Gymnastics	33,265
Hockey	41,450
Soccer	98,710
Softball	41,216
Swimming	44,815
Volleyball	13,848

SOLUTION

The information shown in the table can be separated into two data sets. One data set contains the names of sports, and the other contains the numbers of head injuries treated. The names are nonnumerical entries, so these are qualitative data. The numbers of head injuries treated are numerical entries, so these are quantitative data.

TRY IT YOURSELF 1

The populations of several U.S. cities are shown in the table. Which data are qualitative data and which are quantitative data? Explain your reasoning. *(Source: U.S. Census Bureau)*

Answer: Page A5

City	Population
Baltimore, MD	621,849
Chicago, IL	2,720,546
Glendale, AZ	240,126
Miami, FL	441,003
Portland, OR	632,309
San Francisco, CA	864,816

Levels of Measurement

Another characteristic of data is its level of measurement. The level of measurement determines which statistical calculations are meaningful. The four levels of measurement, in order from lowest to highest, are **nominal, ordinal, interval,** and **ratio.**

> **DEFINITION**
>
> Data at the **nominal level of measurement** are qualitative only. Data at this level are categorized using names, labels, or qualities. No mathematical computations can be made at this level.
>
> Data at the **ordinal level of measurement** are qualitative or quantitative. Data at this level can be arranged in order, or ranked, but differences between data entries are not meaningful.

When numbers are at the nominal level of measurement, they simply represent a label. Examples of numbers used as labels include Social Security numbers and numbers on sports jerseys. For instance, it would not make sense to add the numbers on the players' jerseys for the Chicago Bears.

EXAMPLE 2

Classifying Data by Level

For each data set, determine whether the data are at the nominal level or at the ordinal level. Explain your reasoning. *(Source: U.S. Bureau of Labor Statistics)*

1.
Top five U.S. occupations with the most job growth (projected 2024)
1. Personal care aides
2. Registered nurses
3. Home health aides
4. Combined food preparation and serving workers, including fast food
5. Retail salespersons

2.
Movie genres
Action
Adventure
Comedy
Drama
Horror

SOLUTION

1. This data set lists the ranks of the five fastest-growing occupations in the U.S. over the next few years. The data set consists of the ranks 1, 2, 3, 4, and 5. Because the ranks can be listed in order, these data are at the ordinal level. Note that the difference between a rank of 1 and 5 has no mathematical meaning.

2. This data set consists of the names of movie genres. No mathematical computations can be made with the names, and the names cannot be ranked, so these data are at the nominal level.

TRY IT YOURSELF 2

For each data set, determine whether the data are at the nominal level or at the ordinal level. Explain your reasoning.

1. The final standings for the Pacific Division of the National Basketball Association
2. A collection of phone numbers

Answer: Page A5

Picturing the World

For more than 25 years, the Harris Poll has conducted an annual study to determine the strongest brands, based on consumer response, in several industries. A recent study determined the top five health nonprofit brands, as shown in the table. *(Source: Harris Poll)*

Top five health nonprofit brands
1. St Jude Children's Research Hospital
2. Shriners Hospital for Children
3. Make-A-Wish
4. The Jimmy Fund
5. American Cancer Society

In this list, what is the level of measurement?

The two highest levels of measurement consist of quantitative data only.

> **DEFINITION**
>
> Data at the **interval level of measurement** can be ordered, and meaningful differences between data entries can be calculated. At the interval level, a zero entry simply represents a position on a scale; the entry is not an inherent zero.
>
> Data at the **ratio level of measurement** are similar to data at the interval level, with the added property that a zero entry is an inherent zero. A ratio of two data entries can be formed so that one data entry can be meaningfully expressed as a multiple of another.

An *inherent zero* is a zero that implies "none." For instance, the amount of money you have in a savings account could be zero dollars. In this case, the zero represents no money; it is an inherent zero. On the other hand, a temperature of 0°C does not represent a condition in which no heat is present. The 0°C temperature is simply a position on the Celsius scale; it is not an inherent zero.

To distinguish between data at the interval level and at the ratio level, determine whether the expression "twice as much" has any meaning in the context of the data. For instance, $2 is twice as much as $1, so these data are at the ratio level. On the other hand, 2°C is not twice as warm as 1°C, so these data are at the interval level.

EXAMPLE 3

Classifying Data by Level

Two data sets are shown at the left. Which data set consists of data at the interval level? Which data set consists of data at the ratio level? Explain your reasoning. *(Source: Major League Baseball)*

SOLUTION

Both of these data sets contain quantitative data. Consider the dates of the Yankees' World Series victories. It makes sense to find differences between specific dates. For instance, the time between the Yankees' first and last World Series victories is

$$2009 - 1923 = 86 \text{ years.}$$

But it does not make sense to say that one year is a multiple of another. So, these data are at the interval level. However, using the home run totals, you can find differences *and* write ratios. For instance, Boston hit 23 more home runs than Cleveland hit because $208 - 185 = 23$ home runs. Also, Baltimore hit about 1.5 times as many home runs as Chicago hit because

$$\frac{253}{168} \approx 1.5.$$

So, these data are at the ratio level.

TRY IT YOURSELF 3

For each data set, determine whether the data are at the interval level or at the ratio level. Explain your reasoning.

1. The body temperatures (in degrees Fahrenheit) of an athlete during an exercise session
2. The heart rates (in beats per minute) of an athlete during an exercise session

Answer: Page A5

New York Yankees' World Series victories (years)

1923, 1927, 1928, 1932, 1936, 1937, 1938, 1939, 1941, 1943, 1947, 1949, 1950, 1951, 1952, 1953, 1956, 1958, 1961, 1962, 1977, 1978, 1996, 1998, 1999, 2000, 2009

2016 American League home run totals (by team)

Team	Home runs
Baltimore	253
Boston	208
Chicago	168
Cleveland	185
Detroit	211
Houston	198
Kansas City	147
Los Angeles	156
Minnesota	200
New York	183
Oakland	169
Seattle	223
Tampa Bay	216
Texas	215
Toronto	221

Quantitative Analysis: Interpreting Numerical Data

The tables below summarize which operations are meaningful at each of the four levels of measurement. When identifying a data set's level of measurement, use the highest level that applies.

Level of measurement	Put data in categories	Arrange data in order	Subtract data entries	Determine whether one data entry is a multiple of another
Nominal	Yes	No	No	No
Ordinal	Yes	Yes	No	No
Interval	Yes	Yes	Yes	No
Ratio	Yes	Yes	Yes	Yes

Summary of Four Levels of Measurement

	Example of a data set	Meaningful calculations
Nominal level (Qualitative data)	Types of Shows Televised by a Network Comedy Documentaries Drama Cooking Reality Shows Soap Operas Sports Talk Shows	*Put in a category.* For instance, a show televised by the network could be put into one of the eight categories shown.

Ordinal level (Qualitative or quantitative data)	Motion Picture Association of America Ratings
	Description
	  G General Audiences
	  PG Parental Guidance Suggested
	  PG-13 Parents Strongly Cautioned
	  R Restricted
	  NC-17 No One 17 and Under Admitted
		Put in a category and *put in order.*
		
		For instance, a PG rating has a stronger restriction than a G rating.

Interval level (Quantitative data)	Average Monthly Temperatures (in degrees Fahrenheit) for Denver, CO Jan 30.7 Jul 74.2 Feb 32.5 Aug 72.5 Mar 40.4 Sep 63.4 Apr 47.4 Oct 50.9 May 57.1 Nov 38.3 Jun 67.4 Dec 30.0 *(Source: National Climatic Data Center)*	Put in a category, put in order, and *find differences between data entries.* For instance, $72.5 - 63.4 = 9.1°F$. So, August is 9.1°F warmer than September.
Ratio level (Quantitative data)	Average Monthly Precipitation (in inches) for Orlando, FL Jan 2.35 Jul 7.27 Feb 2.38 Aug 7.13 Mar 3.77 Sep 6.06 Apr 2.68 Oct 3.31 May 3.45 Nov 2.17 Jun 7.58 Dec 2.58 *(Source: National Climatic Data Center)*	Put in a category, put in order, find differences between data entries, and *find ratios of data entries.* For instance, $$\frac{7.58}{3.77} \approx 2.$$ So, there is about twice as much precipitation in June as in March.

1.2 EXERCISES

For Extra Help: **MyLab Statistics**

Building Basic Skills and Vocabulary

1. Name each level of measurement for which data can be qualitative.

2. Name each level of measurement for which data can be quantitative.

True or False? *In Exercises 3–6, determine whether the statement is true or false. If it is false, rewrite it as a true statement.*

3. Data at the ordinal level are quantitative only.

4. For data at the interval level, you cannot calculate meaningful differences between data entries.

5. More types of calculations can be performed with data at the nominal level than with data at the interval level.

6. Data at the ratio level cannot be put in order.

Using and Interpreting Concepts

Classifying Data by Type *In Exercises 7–14, determine whether the data are qualitative or quantitative. Explain your reasoning.*

7. Breeds of horses participating in a horse race

8. American Standard Code for Information Interchange (ASCII) codes

9. Blood pressure levels of athletes participating in a race

10. Speeds of bullet trains

11. Colors of fabrics at a clothing store

12. Widths of veins in different species of leaves

13. Weights of bricks at a construction site

14. Marital statuses mentioned in an employment form

Classifying Data By Level *In Exercises 15–20, determine the level of measurement of the data set. Explain your reasoning.*

15. **China at Olympics** The ranks that China secured at the Summer Olympics in different years are listed. *(Source: International Olympic Committee)*

4	11	4	4	3
2	1	2	3	

16. **Business Schools** The top ten business schools in the United States for a recent year according to Forbes are listed. *(Source: Forbes Media LLC)*

    1. Stanford
    2. Harvard
    3. Northwestern (Kellogg)
    4. Columbia
    5. Dartmouth (Tuck)
    6. Chicago (Booth)
    7. Pennsylvania (Wharton)
    8. UC Berkeley (Haas)
    9. MIT (Sloan)
    10. Cornell (Johnson)

17. Flight Departures The flight numbers of 21 departing flights from Chicago O'Hare International Airport on an afternoon in October of 2016 are listed. *(Source: Chicago O'Hare International Airport)*

1785	5159	4509	1575	6827	3486	7676
1989	522	6868	1893	3133	3337	3266
3458	334	6320	8385	3112	2110	7664

18. Movie Times The times of the day when a multiplex shows a popular movie are listed:

9:00 A.M.	9:10 A.M.	9:25 A.M.	9:40 A.M.
10:35 A.M.	11:25 A.M.	2:30 P.M.	3:45 P.M.
4:45 P.M.	5:30 P.M.	6:00 P.M.	8:00 P.M.
9:30 P.M.	10:00 P.M.	10:20 P.M.	

19. Best Sellers List The top ten fiction books on The New York Times Best Sellers List on October 9, 2016, are listed. *(Source: The New York Times)*

1. The Girl on the Train
2. Home
3. The Kept Woman
4. Magic Binds
5. Commonwealth
6. The Light Between Oceans
7. Immortal Nights
8. A Man Called Ove
9. Thrice the Brinded Cat Hath Mew'd
10. The Woman in Cabin 10

20. Chapters The number of pages per chapter of a novel are listed.

45	50	52	61	39	41	52
55	43	28	36	44	48	39

Graphical Analysis *In Exercises 21–24, determine the level of measurement of the data listed on the horizontal and vertical axes in the figure.*

21.

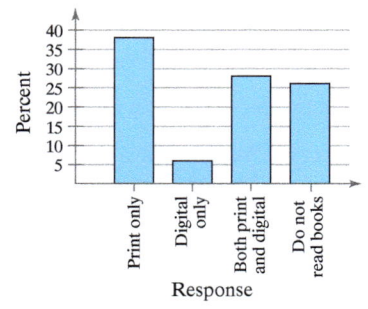

What is the Format of the Books You Read?

(Source: Pew Research Center)

22.

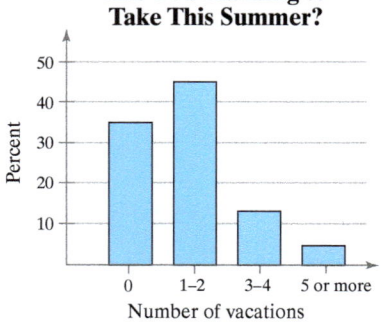

How Many Vacations Are You Planning to Take This Summer?

(Source: The Harris Poll)

23.

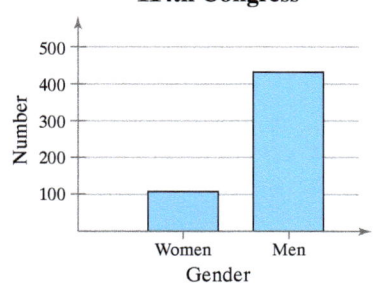

Gender Profile of the 114th Congress

(Source: Congressional Research Service)

24.

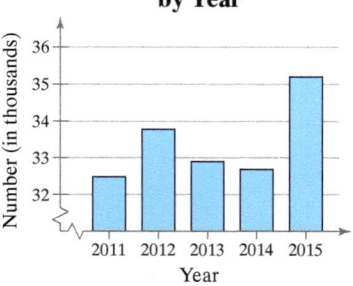

Motor Vehicle Fatalities by Year

(Source: National Highway Traffic Safety Administration)

25. The items below appear on a school's admission form. Determine the level of measurement of the data for each category.
   (a) Gender
   (b) Previous grade level completed
   (c) Religion
   (d) Month of birth

26. The items below appear on a movie rating website. Determine the level of measurement of the data for each category.
   (a) Year of release
   (b) Number of awards won
   (c) Genre
   (d) Star rating

Classifying Data by Type and Level *In Exercises 27–32, determine whether the data are qualitative or quantitative, and determine the level of measurement of the data set.*

27. Production The number of washing machines produced at six different manufacturing plants of a multinational company are listed.

10,000	25,000
14,000	19,000
21,000	12,000

28. Olympics The number of gold, silver, and bronze medals awarded at the 2008 Olympic Games are listed.

301   302   349

29. Chess The list of the top 10 chess players in the world released in March 2018 is given. *(Source: World Chess Federation)*

1. Carlsen
2. Mamedyarov
3. Kramnik
4. So
5. Aronion
6. Vachier-Lagrave
7. Nakamura
8. Caruana
9. Giri
10. Anand

30. Diving The scores for the gold medal winning diver in the men's 10-meter platform event from the 2016 Summer Olympics are listed. *(Source: International Olympic Committee)*

91.80	91.00	88.20
97.20	99.90	91.80

31. Concert Tours The top ten highest grossing worldwide concert tours for 2016 are listed. *(Source: Pollstar)*

1. Bruce Springsteen & the E Street Band
2. Beyoncé
3. Coldplay
4. Guns N' Roses
5. Adele
6. Justin Bieber
7. Paul McCartney
8. Garth Brooks
9. The Rolling Stones
10. Celine Dion

32. Numbers of Performances The numbers of performances for the 10 longest-running Broadway shows at the end of the 2016 season are listed. *(Source: The Broadway League)*

11,782	8107	7705	7485	6680
6137	5959	5758	5461	5238

Extending Concepts

33. Writing What is an inherent zero? Describe three examples of data sets that have inherent zeros and three that do not.

34. Describe two examples of data sets for each of the four levels of measurement. Justify your answer.

Quantitative Analysis: Interpreting Numerical Data

CASE STUDY: Reputations of Companies in the U.S.

For more than 50 years, The Harris Poll has conducted surveys using a representative sample of people in the United States. The surveys have been used to represent the opinions of people in the United States on many subjects, such as health, politics, the U.S. economy, and sports.

Since 1999, The Harris Poll has conducted an annual survey to measure the reputations of the most visible companies in the United States, as perceived by U.S. adults. The Harris Poll uses a sample of about 23,000 U.S. adults for the survey. The survey respondents rate companies according to 20 attributes that are classified into six categories: (1) social responsibility, (2) vision and leadership, (3) financial performance, (4) products and services, (5) emotional appeal, and (6) workplace environment. This information is used to determine the reputation of a company as Excellent, Very Good, Good, Fair, Poor, Very Poor, or Critical. The reputations (along with some additional information) of 10 companies are shown in the table.

All U.S. Adults

U.S. adults in The Harris Poll sample (about 23,000 U.S. adults)

U.S. adults *not* in The Harris Poll sample (about 242.8 million U.S. adults)

Reputations of 10 Companies in the U.S.

Company Name	Year Company Formed	Reputation	Industry	Number of Employees
Amazon.com	1994	Excellent	Retail	230,800
Apple, Inc.	1977	Excellent	Computers and peripherals	116,000
Netflix, Inc.	1999	Very Good	Internet television	4,700
The Kraft Heinz Co.	2015	Very Good	Food products	41,000
Facebook, Inc.	2004	Good	Internet	17,048
Ford Motor Co.	1903	Good	Automotive	201,000
Chipotle Mexican Grill, Inc.	1993	Fair	Restaurant	64,570
Comcast Corp.	1963	Poor	Cable television	136,000
Exxon Mobil Corp.	1999	Poor	Petroleum (integrated)	71,100
Wells Fargo & Co.	1998	Critical	Banking	265,000

(Source: The Harris Poll; Amazon.com; Apple, Inc.; Netflix, Inc.; The Kraft Heinz Co.; Facebook, Inc.; Ford Motor Co.; Chipotle Mexican Grill, Inc.; Comcast Corp.; Exxon Mobil Corp.; Wells Fargo & Co.)

EXERCISES

1. **Sampling Percent** What percentage of the total number of U.S. adults did The Harris Poll sample for its survey? (Assume the total number of U.S. adults is 242.8 million.)

2. **Nominal Level of Measurement** Identify any column in the table with data at the nominal level.

3. **Ordinal Level of Measurement** Identify any column in the table with data at the ordinal level. Describe two ways that the data can be ordered.

4. **Interval Level of Measurement** Identify any column in the table with data at the interval level. How can these data be ordered?

5. **Ratio Level of Measurement** Identify any column in the table with data at the ratio level.

6. **Inferences** What decisions can be made on the basis of The Harris Poll survey that measures the reputations of the most visible companies in the United States?

1.3 Data Collection and Experimental Design

What You Should Learn

- How to design a statistical study and how to distinguish between an observational study and an experiment
- How to collect data by using a survey or a simulation
- How to design an experiment
- How to create a sample using random sampling, simple random sampling, stratified sampling, cluster sampling, and systematic sampling and how to identify a biased sample

Design of a Statistical Study ■ Data Collection ■ Experimental Design ■ Sampling Techniques

Design of a Statistical Study

The goal of every statistical study is to collect data and then use the data to make a decision. Any decision you make using the results of a statistical study is only as good as the process used to obtain the data. When the process is flawed, the resulting decision is questionable.

Although you may never have to develop a statistical study, it is likely that you will have to interpret the results of one. Before interpreting the results of a study, however, you should determine whether the results are reliable. In other words, you should be familiar with how to design a statistical study.

GUIDELINES

Designing a Statistical Study

1. Identify the variable(s) of interest (the focus) and the population of the study.
2. Develop a detailed plan for collecting data. If you use a sample, make sure the sample is representative of the population.
3. Collect the data.
4. Describe the data, using descriptive statistics techniques.
5. Interpret the data and make decisions about the population using inferential statistics.
6. Identify any possible errors.

A statistical study can usually be categorized as an observational study or an experiment. In an **observational study,** a researcher does not influence the responses. In an **experiment,** a researcher deliberately applies a treatment before observing the responses. Here is a brief summary of these types of studies.

- In an **observational study,** a researcher observes and measures characteristics of interest of part of a population but does not change existing conditions. For instance, an observational study was conducted in which researchers measured the amount of time people spent doing various activities, such as paid work, childcare, and socializing. *(Source: U.S. Bureau of Labor Statistics)*

- In performing an **experiment,** a **treatment** is applied to part of a population, called a **treatment group,** and responses are observed. Another part of the population may be used as a **control group,** in which no treatment is applied. (The subjects in both groups are called **experimental units.**) In many cases, subjects in the control group are given a **placebo,** which is a harmless, fake treatment that is made to look like the real treatment. The responses of both groups can then be compared and studied. In most cases, it is a good idea to use the same number of subjects for each group. For instance, an experiment was performed in which overweight subjects in a treatment group were given the artificial sweetener sucralose to drink while a control group drank water. After performing a glucose test, researchers concluded that "sucralose affects the glycemic and insulin responses" in overweight people who do not normally consume artificial sweeteners. *(Source: Diabetes Care)*

EXAMPLE 1

Distinguishing Between an Observational Study and an Experiment

Determine whether each study is an observational study or an experiment.

1. Researchers study the effect of vitamin D_3 supplementation among patients with antibody deficiency or frequent respiratory tract infections. To perform the study, 70 patients receive 4000 IU of vitamin D_3 daily for a year. Another group of 70 patients receive a placebo daily for one year. *(Source: British Medical Journal)*

2. Researchers conduct a study to determine how confident Americans are in the U.S. economy. To perform the study, researchers call 3040 U.S. adults and ask them to rate current U.S. economic conditions and whether the U.S. economy is getting better or worse. *(Source: Gallup)*

SOLUTION

1. Because the study applies a treatment (vitamin D_3) to the subjects, the study is an experiment.

2. Because the study does not attempt to influence the responses of the subjects (there is no treatment), the study is an observational study.

TRY IT YOURSELF 1

The Pennsylvania Game Commission conducted a study to count the number of elk in Pennsylvania. The commission captured and released 636 elk, which included 350 adult cows, 125 calves, 110 branched bulls, and 51 spikes. Is this study an observational study or an experiment? *(Source: Pennsylvania Game Commission)*

Answer: Page A5

Data Collection

There are several ways to collect data. Often, the focus of the study dictates the best way to collect data. Here is a brief summary of two methods of data collection.

- A **simulation** is the use of a mathematical or physical model to reproduce the conditions of a situation or process. Collecting data often involves the use of computers. Simulations allow you to study situations that are impractical or even dangerous to create in real life, and often they save time and money. For instance, automobile manufacturers use simulations with dummies to study the effects of crashes on humans. Throughout this course, you will have the opportunity to use applets that simulate statistical processes on a computer.

- A **survey** is an investigation of one or more characteristics of a population. Most often, surveys are carried out on *people* by asking them questions. The most common types of surveys are done by interview, Internet, phone, or mail. In designing a survey, it is important to word the questions so that they do not lead to biased results, which are not representative of a population. For instance, a survey is conducted on a sample of female physicians to determine whether the primary reason for their career choice is financial stability. In designing the survey, it would be acceptable to make a list of reasons and ask each individual in the sample to select her first choice.

Experimental Design

To produce meaningful unbiased results, experiments should be carefully designed and executed. It is important to know what steps should be taken to make the results of an experiment valid. Three key elements of a well-designed experiment are *control*, *randomization*, and *replication*.

Because experimental results can be ruined by a variety of factors, being able to control these influential factors is important. One such factor is a **confounding variable.**

> **DEFINITION**
>
> A **confounding variable** occurs when an experimenter cannot tell the difference between the effects of different factors on the variable.

For instance, to attract more customers, a coffee shop owner experiments by remodeling the shop using bright colors. At the same time, a shopping mall nearby has its grand opening. If business at the coffee shop increases, it cannot be determined whether it is because of the new colors or the new shopping mall. The effects of the colors and the shopping mall have been confounded.

Another factor that can affect experimental results is the *placebo effect*. The **placebo effect** occurs when a subject reacts favorably to a placebo when in fact the subject has been given a fake treatment. To help control or minimize the placebo effect, a technique called **blinding** can be used.

> **DEFINITION**
>
> **Blinding** is a technique where the subjects do not know whether they are receiving a treatment or a placebo. In a **double-blind experiment,** neither the experimenter nor the subjects know whether the subjects are receiving a treatment or a placebo. The experimenter is informed after all the data have been collected. This type of experimental design is preferred by researchers.

Study Tip

The *Hawthorne effect* occurs in an experiment when subjects change their behavior simply because they know they are participating in an experiment.

One challenge for experimenters is assigning subjects to groups so the groups have similar characteristics (such as age, height, weight, and so on). When treatment and control groups are similar, experimenters can conclude that any differences between groups is due to the treatment. To form groups with similar characteristics, experimenters use **randomization.**

> **DEFINITION**
>
> **Randomization** is a process of randomly assigning subjects to different treatment groups.

In a **completely randomized design,** subjects are assigned to different treatment groups through random selection. In some experiments, it may be necessary for the experimenter to use **blocks,** which are groups of subjects with similar characteristics. A commonly used experimental design is a **randomized block design.** To use a randomized block design, the experimenter divides the subjects with similar characteristics into blocks, and then, within each block, randomly assign subjects to treatment groups. For instance, an experimenter who is testing the effects of a new weight loss drink may first divide the subjects into age categories such as 30–39 years old, 40–49 years old, and over 50 years old, and then, within each age group, randomly assign subjects to either the treatment group or the control group (see figure at the left).

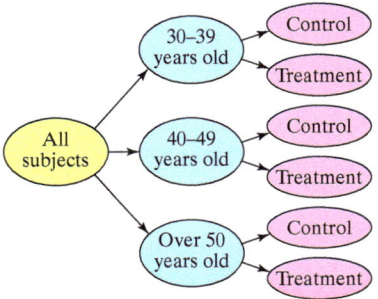

Randomized Block Design

Study Tip

The *validity* of an experiment refers to the accuracy and reliability of the experimental results. The results of a valid experiment are more likely to be accepted in the scientific community.

Another type of experimental design is a **matched-pairs design,** where subjects are paired up according to a similarity. One subject in each pair is randomly selected to receive one treatment while the other subject receives a different treatment. For instance, two subjects may be paired up because of their age, geographical location, or a particular physical characteristic.

Sample size, which is the number of subjects in a study, is another important part of experimental design. To improve the validity of experimental results, **replication** is required.

DEFINITION

Replication is the repetition of an experiment under the same or similar conditions.

For instance, suppose an experiment is designed to test a vaccine against a strain of influenza. In the experiment, 10,000 people are given the vaccine and another 10,000 people are given a placebo. Because of the sample size, the effectiveness of the vaccine would most likely be observed. But, if the subjects in the experiment are not selected so that the two groups are similar (according to age and gender), the results are of less value.

EXAMPLE 2

Analyzing an Experimental Design

A company wants to test the effectiveness of a new gum developed to help people quit smoking. Identify a potential problem with each experimental design and suggest a way to improve it.

1. The company identifies ten adults who are heavy smokers. Five of the subjects are given the new gum and the other five subjects are given a placebo. After two months, the subjects are evaluated and it is found that the five subjects using the new gum have quit smoking.

2. The company identifies one thousand adults who are heavy smokers. The subjects are divided into blocks according to gender. Females are given the new gum and males are given the placebo. After two months, a significant number of the female subjects have quit smoking.

SOLUTION

1. The sample size being used is not large enough to validate the results of the experiment. The experiment must be replicated to improve the validity.

2. The groups are not similar. The new gum may have a greater effect on women than on men, or vice versa. The subjects can be divided into blocks according to gender, but then, within each block, they should be randomly assigned to be in the treatment group or in the control group.

TRY IT YOURSELF 2

The company in Example 2 identifies 240 adults who are heavy smokers. The subjects are randomly assigned to be in a gum treatment group or in a control group. Each subject is also given a DVD featuring the dangers of smoking. After four months, most of the subjects in the treatment group have quit smoking. Identify a potential problem with the experimental design and suggest a way to improve it.

Answer: Page A5

Sampling Techniques

A **census** is a count or measure of an *entire* population. Taking a census provides complete information, but it is often costly and difficult to perform. A **sampling** is a count or measure of *part* of a population and is more commonly used in statistical studies. To collect unbiased data, a researcher must ensure that the sample is representative of the population. Appropriate sampling techniques must be used to ensure that inferences about the population are valid. Remember that when a study is done with faulty data, the results are questionable. Even with the best methods of sampling, a **sampling error** may occur. A sampling error is the difference between the results of a sample and those of the population. When you learn about inferential statistics, you will learn techniques of controlling sampling errors.

A **random sample** is one in which every member of the population has an equal chance of being selected. A **simple random sample** is a sample in which every possible sample of the same size has the same chance of being selected. One way to collect a simple random sample is to assign a different number to each member of the population and then use a random number table like Table 1 in Appendix B. Responses, counts, or measures for members of the population whose numbers correspond to those generated using the table would be in the sample. Calculators and computer software programs are also used to generate random numbers (see page 38).

> **Study Tip**
>
> A *biased sample* is one that is not representative of the population from which it is drawn. For instance, a sample consisting of only 18- to 22-year-old U.S. college students would not be representative of the entire 18- to 22-year-old population in the United States.

 To explore this topic further, see **Activity 1.3** on page 29.

Table 1—Random Numbers

92630	78240	19267	95457	53497	23894	37708	79862
79445	78735	71549	44843	26104	67318	00701	34986
59654	71966	27386	50004	05358	94031	29281	18544
31524	49587	76612	39789	13537	48086	59483	60680
06348	76938	90379	51392	55887	71015	09209	79157

Portion of Table 1 found in Appendix B

Consider a study of the number of people who live in West Ridge County. To use a simple random sample to count the number of people who live in West Ridge County households, you could assign a different number to each household, use a technology tool or table of random numbers to generate a sample of numbers, and then count the number of people living in each selected household.

> **Tech Tip**
>
> You can use technology such as Minitab, Excel, StatCrunch, or the TI-84 Plus to generate random numbers. (Detailed instructions for using Minitab, Excel, and the TI-84 Plus are shown in the technology manuals that accompany this text.) For instance, here are instructions for using the random integer generator on a TI-84 Plus for Example 3.
>
> MATH
>
> Choose the PRB menu.
>
> 5: randInt(
>
> 1 , 7 3 1 , 8)
>
> ENTER
>
> ```
> randInt(1,731,8)
>     {537 33 249 728…
> ```
>
> Continuing to press ENTER will generate more random samples of 8 integers.

EXAMPLE 3

Using a Simple Random Sample

There are 731 students currently enrolled in a statistics course at your school. You wish to form a sample of eight students to answer some survey questions. Select the students who will belong to the simple random sample.

SOLUTION

Assign numbers 1 to 731 to the students in the course. In the table of random numbers, choose a starting place at random and read the digits in groups of three (because 731 is a three-digit number). For instance, if you started in the third row of the table at the beginning of the second column, you would group the numbers as follows:

719 | 66   2 | 738 | 6   50 | 004 | 053 | 58   9 | 403 | 1   29 | 281 | 185 | 44

Ignoring numbers greater than 731, the first eight numbers are 719, 662, 650, 4, 53, 589, 403, and 129. The students assigned these numbers will make up the sample. To find the sample using a TI-84 Plus, follow the instructions shown at the left.

> **TRY IT YOURSELF 3**
>
> A company employs 79 people. Choose a simple random sample of five to survey.
>
> *Answer: Page A5*

When you choose members of a sample, you should decide whether it is acceptable to have the same population member selected more than once. If it is acceptable, then the sampling process is said to be *with replacement*. If it is not acceptable, then the sampling process is said to be *without replacement*.

There are several other commonly used sampling techniques. Each has advantages and disadvantages.

- *Stratified Sample* When it is important for the sample to have members from each segment of the population, you should use a stratified sample. Depending on the focus of the study, members of the population are divided into two or more subsets, called *strata*, that share a similar characteristic such as age, gender, ethnicity, or even political preference. A sample is then randomly selected from each of the strata. Using a stratified sample ensures that each segment of the population is represented. For instance, to collect a stratified sample of the number of people who live in West Ridge County households, you could divide the households into socioeconomic levels and then randomly select households from each level. In using a stratified sample, care must be taken to ensure that all strata are sampled in proportion to their actual percentages of occurrence in the population. For instance, if 40% of the people in West Ridge County belong to the low-income group, then the proportion of the sample should have 40% from this group.

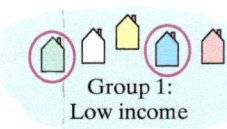
Group 1: Low income

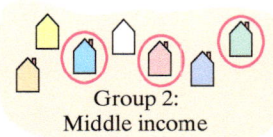
Group 2: Middle income

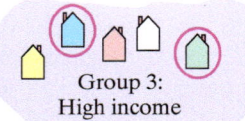
Group 3: High income

Stratified Sampling

Study Tip

Be sure you understand that stratified sampling randomly selects a *sample of members* from *all* strata. Cluster sampling uses *all members* from a randomly selected sample of *clusters* (but not all, so some clusters will not be part of the sample). For instance, in the figure for "Stratified Sampling" at the right, a *sample of households* in West Ridge County is randomly selected from *all* three income groups. In the figure for "Cluster Sampling," *all households* in a randomly selected *cluster* (Zone 1) are used. (Notice that the other zones are not part of the sample.)

- *Cluster Sample* When the population falls into naturally occurring subgroups, each having similar characteristics, a cluster sample may be the most appropriate. To select a cluster sample, divide the population into groups, called *clusters*, and select all of the members in one or more (but not all) of the clusters. Examples of clusters could be different sections of the same course or different branches of a bank. For instance, to collect a cluster sample of the number of people who live in West Ridge County households, divide the households into groups according to zip codes, then select all the households in one or more, but not all, zip codes and count the number of people living in each household. In using a cluster sample, care must be taken to ensure that all clusters have similar characteristics. For instance, if one of the zip code clusters has a greater proportion of high-income people, the data might not be representative of the population.

Zip Code Zones in West Ridge County

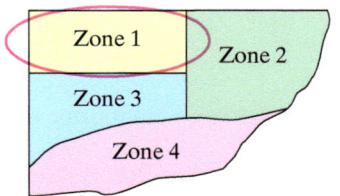

Cluster Sampling

- **Systematic Sample** A systematic sample is a sample in which each member of the population is assigned a number. The members of the population are ordered in some way, a starting number is randomly selected, and then sample members are selected at regular intervals from the starting number. (For instance, every 3rd, 5th, or 100th member is selected.) For instance, to collect a systematic sample of the number of people who live in West Ridge County households, you could assign a different number to each household, randomly choose a starting number, select every 100th household, and count the number of people living in each. An advantage of systematic sampling is that it is easy to use. In the case of any regularly occurring pattern in the data, however, this type of sampling should be avoided.

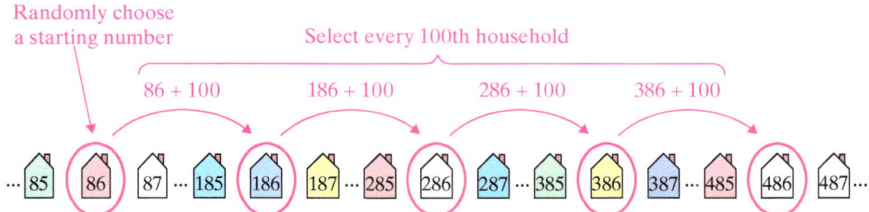

Systematic Sampling

A type of sample that often leads to biased studies (so it is not recommended) is a **convenience sample.** A convenience sample consists only of members of the population that are easy to get.

EXAMPLE 4

Identifying Sampling Techniques

You are doing a study to determine the opinions of students at your school regarding stem cell research. Identify the sampling technique you are using when you select the samples listed. Discuss potential sources of bias (if any).

1. You divide the student population with respect to majors and randomly select and question some students in each major.

2. You assign each student a number and generate random numbers. You then question each student whose number is randomly selected.

3. You select students who are in your biology class.

SOLUTION

1. Because students are divided into strata (majors) and a sample is selected from each major, this is a stratified sample.

2. Each sample of the same size has an equal chance of being selected and each student has an equal chance of being selected, so this is a simple random sample.

3. Because the sample is taken from students that are readily available, this is a convenience sample. The sample may be biased because biology students may be more familiar with stem cell research than other students and may have stronger opinions.

TRY IT YOURSELF 4

You want to determine the opinions of students regarding stem cell research. Identify the sampling technique you are using when you select these samples.

1. You select a class at random and question each student in the class.

2. You assign each student a number and, after choosing a starting number, question every 25th student.

Answer: Page A5

Picturing the World

The research firm Gallup conducts many polls (or surveys) regarding the president, Congress, and political and nonpolitical issues. A commonly cited Gallup poll is the public approval rating of the president. For instance, the approval ratings for President Barack Obama for selected months in 2016 are shown in the figure. (Each rating is from the poll conducted at the end of the indicated month.)

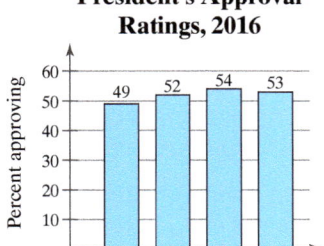

President's Approval Ratings, 2016

Discuss some ways that Gallup could select a biased sample to conduct a poll. How could Gallup select a sample that is unbiased?

1.3 EXERCISES

For Extra Help: **MyLab Statistics**

Building Basic Skills and Vocabulary

1. What is the difference between an observational study and an experiment?
2. What is the difference between a census and a sampling?
3. What is the difference between a random sample and a simple random sample?
4. What is replication in an experiment? Why is replication important?

True or False? *In Exercises 5–10, determine whether the statement is true or false. If it is false, rewrite it as a true statement.*

5. A placebo is an actual treatment.
6. A double-blind experiment is used to increase the placebo effect.
7. Using a systematic sample guarantees that members of each group within a population will be sampled.
8. A convenience sample is always representative of a population.
9. The method for selecting a stratified sample is to order a population in some way and then select members of the population at regular intervals.
10. To select a cluster sample, divide a population into groups and then select all of the members in at least one (but not all) of the groups.

Distinguishing Between an Observational Study and an Experiment

In Exercises 11–14, determine whether the study is an observational study or an experiment. Explain.

11. In a survey of 1033 U.S. adults, 51% said U.S. presidents should release all medical information that might affect their ability to serve. *(Source: Gallup)*
12. Researchers demonstrated that adults using an intensive program to lower systolic blood pressure to less than 120 millimeters of mercury reduce the risk of death from all causes by 27%. *(Source: American Heart Association)*
13. To study the effects of social media on teenagers' brains, researchers showed a few dozen teenagers photographs that had varying numbers of "likes" while scanning the reactions in their brains. *(Source: NPR)*
14. In a study designed to research the effect of music on driving habits, 1000 motorists ages 17–25 years old were asked whether the music they listened to influenced their driving. *(Source: More Th>n)*

15. **Random Number Table** Use the sixth row of Table 1 in Appendix B to generate 12 random numbers between 1 and 99.
16. **Random Number Table** Use the tenth row of Table 1 in Appendix B to generate 10 random numbers between 1 and 920.

Random Numbers *In Exercises 17 and 18, use technology to generate the random numbers.*

17. Fifteen numbers between 1 and 150
18. Nineteen numbers between 1 and 1000

Using and Interpreting Concepts

19. **Allergy Drug** A pharmaceutical company wants to test the effectiveness of a new drug used to treat migraine headaches. The company identifies 500 females ages 25 to 45 years old who suffer from migraine headaches. The subjects are randomly assigned into two groups. One group is given the drug and the other is given a placebo that looks exactly like the drug. After three months, the subjects' symptoms are studied and compared.

    (a) Identify the experimental units and treatments used in this experiment.

    (b) Identify a potential problem with the experimental design being used and suggest a way to improve it.

    (c) How could this experiment be designed to be double-blind?

20. **Dietary Supplement** Researchers in Germany tested the effect of a dietary supplement designed to control metabolism in patients with type 2 diabetes. Thirty-one patients with type 2 diabetes completed the study. The patients were assigned at random either the supplement or a placebo for 12 weeks. After a subsequent "wash-out" period of 12 weeks, the patients were assigned the other product. At the conclusion of the study, the patients' glycated hemoglobin, fasting blood glucose, and fructosamine levels were checked, as well as their lipid parameters. *(Source: Food and Nutrition Research)*

    (a) Identify the experimental units and treatments used in this experiment.

    (b) Identify a potential problem with the experimental design being used and suggest a way to improve it.

    (c) The experiment is described as a placebo-controlled, double-blind study. Explain what this means.

    (d) How could blocking be used in designing this experiment?

21. **Dieting** A researcher wants to study the effects of dieting on obesity. Eighteen people volunteer for the experiment: Lewis, Alice, Raj, William, Edwin, Mercer, Edgar, Bill, Zoya, Kate, Lara, Bertha, Dennis, Jennifer, Ahmed, Ronald, Harry, and Arthur. Use a random number generator to choose nine subjects for the treatment group. The other nine subjects will go into the control group. List the subjects in each group. Tell which method you used to generate the random numbers.

22. **Using a Simple Random Sample** Participants of an experiment are numbered from 1 to 80. The participants are to be randomly assigned to two different groups. Use a random number generator different from the one you used in Exercise 21 to choose 40 participants for the treatment group. The other 40 participants will go into the control group. List the participants, according to number, in each group. Tell which method you used to generate the random numbers.

Identifying Sampling Techniques *In Exercises 23–28, identify the sampling technique used, and discuss potential sources of bias (if any). Explain.*

23. After an election, a constituency is divided into 50 equal areas. Twelve of the areas are selected, and every occupied household in the area is interviewed to help focus political efforts on what residents require the most.

24. Questioning university students as they leave a fraternity party, a researcher asks 463 students about their study habits.

25. Selecting employees at random from an employee directory, researchers contact 300 people and ask what obstacles (such as computer problems) keep them from accomplishing tasks at work.

26. A sample executive is chosen from each department of an organization for a survey.

27. From visits made to randomly generated house numbers, 1638 residents are asked if they own a vehicle or not.

28. Every sixth customer entering an ice cream parlor is asked to name his or her favorite flavor of ice cream.

Choosing Between a Census and a Sampling *In Exercises 29 and 30, determine whether you would take a census or use a sampling. If you would use a sampling, determine which sampling technique you would use. Explain.*

29. The most popular model of mobile phone among 4,00,000 mobile phone purchasers

30. The average height of the 264 students of a high school.

Recognizing a Biased Question *In Exercises 31–34, determine whether the survey question is biased. If the question is biased, suggest a better wording.*

31. Why does eating whole-grain foods improve your health?

32. How much water do you drink on an average day?

33. Why does listening to music while studying increase the chances of retention?

34. What do you think about the battery backup of the mobile phone?

Extending Concepts

35. **Analyzing a Study** Find an article or a news story that describes a statistical study.
    (a) Identify the population and the sample.
    (b) Classify the data as qualitative or quantitative. Determine the level of measurement.
    (c) Is the study an observational study or an experiment? If it is an experiment, identify the treatment.
    (d) Identify the sampling technique used to collect the data.

36. **Designing and Analyzing a Study** Design a study for some subject that is of interest to you. Answer parts (a)–(d) of Exercise 35 for this study.

37. **Open and Closed Questions** Two types of survey questions are open questions and closed questions. An open question allows for any kind of response; a closed question allows for only a fixed response. An open question and a closed question with its possible choices are given below. List an advantage and a disadvantage of each question.

    Open Question What can be done to get students to eat healthier foods?
    Closed Question How would you get students to eat healthier foods?
    1. Mandatory nutrition course
    2. Offer only healthy foods in the cafeteria and remove unhealthy foods
    3. Offer more healthy foods in the cafeteria and raise the prices on unhealthy foods

38. **Natural Experiments** Observational studies are sometimes referred to as *natural experiments*. Explain, in your own words, what this means.

1.3 ACTIVITY: Random Numbers

You can find the interactive applet for this activity within **MyLab Statistics** or at *www.pearsonglobaleditions.com*.

The *random numbers* applet is designed to allow you to generate random numbers from a range of values. You can specify integer values for the minimum value, maximum value, and the number of samples in the appropriate fields. You should not use decimal points when filling in the fields. When SAMPLE is clicked, the applet generates random values, which are displayed as a list in the text field.

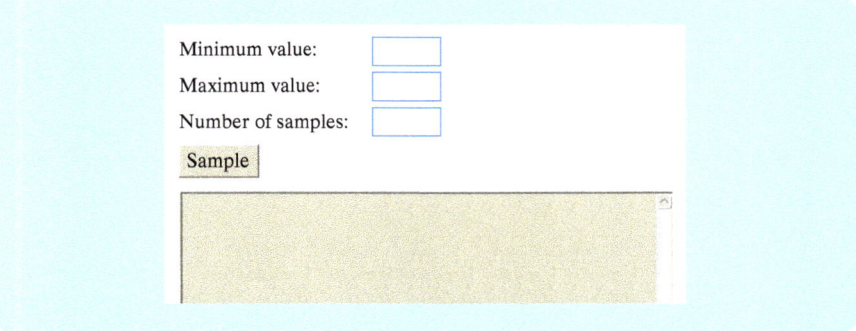

EXPLORE

Step 1 Specify a minimum value.
Step 2 Specify a maximum value.
Step 3 Specify the number of samples.
Step 4 Click SAMPLE to generate a list of random values.

DRAW CONCLUSIONS

1. Specify the minimum, maximum, and number of samples to be 1, 20, and 8, respectively, as shown. Run the applet. Continue generating lists until you obtain one that shows that the random sample is taken with replacement. Write down this list. How do you know that the list is a random sample taken with replacement?

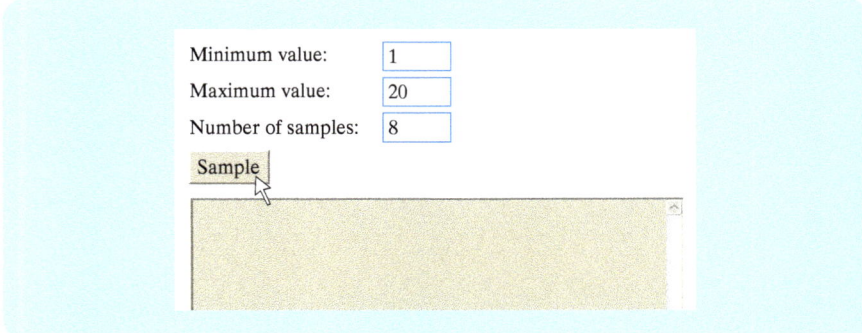

2. Use the applet to repeat Example 3 on page 23. What values did you use for the minimum, maximum, and number of samples? Which method do you prefer? Explain.

USES AND ABUSES

Statistics in the Real World

Uses

An experiment studied 321 women with advanced breast cancer. All of the women had been previously treated with other drugs, but the cancer had stopped responding to the medications. The women were then given the opportunity to take a new drug combined with a chemotherapy drug.

The subjects were divided into two groups, one that took the new drug combined with a chemotherapy drug, and one that took only the chemotherapy drug. After three years, results showed that the new drug in combination with the chemotherapy drug delayed the progression of cancer in the subjects. The results were so significant that the study was stopped, and the new drug was offered to all women in the study. The Food and Drug Administration has since approved use of the new drug in conjunction with a chemotherapy drug.

Abuses

For four years, one hundred eighty thousand teenagers in Norway were used as subjects to test a new vaccine against the deadly bacteria *meningococcus b*. A brochure describing the possible effects of the vaccine stated, "it is unlikely to expect serious complications," while information provided to the Norwegian Parliament stated, "serious side effects can not be excluded." The vaccine trial had some disastrous results: More than 500 side effects were reported, with some considered serious, and several of the subjects developed serious neurological diseases. The results showed that the vaccine was providing immunity in only 57% of the cases. This result was not sufficient for the vaccine to be added to Norway's vaccination program. Compensations have since been paid to the vaccine victims.

Ethics

Experiments help us further understand the world that surrounds us. But, in some cases, they can do more harm than good. In the Norwegian experiments, several ethical questions arise. Was the Norwegian experiment unethical if the best interests of the subjects were neglected? When should the experiment have been stopped? Should it have been conducted at all? When serious side effects are not reported and are withheld from subjects, there is no ethical question here, it is just wrong.

On the other hand, the breast cancer researchers would not want to deny the new drug to a group of patients with a life-threatening disease. But again, questions arise. How long must a researcher continue an experiment that shows better-than-expected results? How soon can a researcher conclude a drug is safe for the subjects involved?

EXERCISES

1. Find an example of a real-life experiment other than the one described above that may be considered an "abuse." What could have been done to avoid the outcome of the experiment?

2. *Stopping an Experiment* In your opinion, what are some problems that may arise when clinical trials of a new experimental drug or vaccine are stopped early and then the drug or vaccine is distributed to other subjects or patients?

1 Chapter Summary

What Did You Learn?	Example(s)	Review Exercises
Section 1.1		
▶ How to distinguish between a population and a sample	1	1–4
▶ How to distinguish between a parameter and a statistic	2	5–8
▶ How to distinguish between descriptive statistics and inferential statistics	3	9, 10
Section 1.2		
▶ How to distinguish between qualitative data and quantitative data	1	11–14
▶ How to classify data with respect to the four levels of measurement: nominal, ordinal, interval, and ratio	2, 3	15–18

Level of measurement	Put data in categories	Arrange data in order	Subtract data entries	Determine whether one data entry is a multiple of another
Nominal	Yes	No	No	No
Ordinal	Yes	Yes	No	No
Interval	Yes	Yes	Yes	No
Ratio	Yes	Yes	Yes	Yes

	Example(s)	Review Exercises
Section 1.3		
▶ How to design a statistical study and how to distinguish between an observational study and an experiment	1	19, 20
▶ How to design an experiment	2	21, 22
▶ How to create a sample using random sampling, simple random sampling, stratified sampling, cluster sampling, and systematic sampling and how to identify a biased sample	3, 4	23–29

Sampling Techniques
Random: A sample in which every member of a population has an equal chance of being selected.
Simple random: A sample in which every possible sample of the same size has the same chance of being selected from a population.
Stratified: Members of a population are divided into two or more subsets, called strata, that share a similar characteristic. A *sample* is then randomly selected from *each* of the strata. Using a stratified sample ensures that each segment of the population is represented.
Cluster: The population is divided into groups (or clusters) and *all of the members in one or more* (but not all) of the clusters are selected. To avoid a biased sample, care must be taken to ensure that all clusters have similar characteristics.
Systematic: Each member of a population is assigned a number. The members of the population are ordered in some way, a starting number is randomly selected, and then sample members are selected at regular intervals from the starting number. (For instance, every 3rd, 5th, or 100th member is selected.)

1 Review Exercises

Section 1.1

In Exercises 1–4, identify the population and the sample. Describe the sample data set.

1. A survey of 4787 U.S. adults found that 15% use ride-hailing applications. *(Source: Pew Research Center)*

2. Forty-two professors in Pennsylvania were surveyed concerning their opinions of the current education policy of the state.

3. A survey of 2223 U.S. adults found that 62% would encourage a child to pursue a career as a video game developer or designer. *(Source: The Harris Poll)*

4. A survey of 1601 U.S. children and adults ages 16 years and older found that 48% have visited a public library or a bookmobile over a recent span of 12 months. *(Source: Pew Research Center)*

In Exercises 5–8, determine whether the number describes a population parameter or a sample statistic. Explain your reasoning.

5. In 2016, the National Science Foundation announced $22.7 million in infrastructure-strengthening investments. *(Source: National Science Foundation)*

6. In a survey of 1000 likely U.S. voters, 29% trust media fact-checking of candidates' comments. *(Source: Rasmussen Reports)*

7. In a recent study of physics majors at a university, 12 students were minoring in math.

8. Thirty percent of a sample of 521 U.S. workers say that they worry about having their benefits reduced. *(Source: Gallup)*

9. Which part of the survey described in Exercise 3 represents the descriptive branch of statistics? Make an inference based on the results of the survey.

10. Which part of the survey described in Exercise 4 represents the descriptive branch of statistics? Make an inference based on the results of the survey.

Section 1.2

In Exercises 11–14, determine whether the data are qualitative or quantitative. Explain your reasoning.

11. The ages of a sample of 430 employees of a software company

12. The IQ levels of the students of a secondary school

13. The revenues of the companies on the Fortune 500 list

14. The genders of a sample of 1,000 students of a university

In Exercises 15–18, determine the level of measurement of the data set. Explain.

15. The daily high temperatures (in degrees Fahrenheit) for Sacramento, California, for a week in September are listed. *(Source: National Climatic Data Center)*

    90   80   76   84   91   94   97

16. The income groups for a sample of city residents are listed.

    Low   Middle   High

17. The four departments of a printing company are listed.

        Administration   Sales   Production   Billing

18. The total compensations (in millions of dollars) of the ten highest-paid CEOs at U.S. public companies are listed. *(Source: Equilar, Inc.)*

    94.6   56.4   54.1   53.2   53.2   51.6   47.5   43.5   39.2   37.0

Section 1.3

In Exercises 19 and 20, determine whether the study is an observational study or an experiment. Explain.

19. Researchers conduct a study to determine whether a drug used to treat hypertension in patients with obstructive sleep apnea works better when taken in the morning or in the evening. To perform the study, 78 patients are given one pill to take in the morning and one pill to take in the evening (one containing the drug and the other a placebo). After 6 weeks, researchers collected blood pressure information on the patients. *(Source: American Thoracic Society)*

20. Researchers conduct a study to determine the effect of coffee consumption on the development of multiple sclerosis. To perform the study, researchers asked 4408 adults in Sweden and 2331 adults in the United States how many cups of coffee they drink per day. *(Source: American Association for the Advancement of Science)*

In Exercises 21 and 22, two hundred students volunteer for an experiment to test the effects of sleep deprivation on memory recall. The students will be placed in one of five different treatment groups, including the control group.

21. Explain how you could design an experiment so that it uses a randomized block design.

22. Explain how you could design an experiment so that it uses a completely randomized design.

In Exercises 23–28, identify the sampling technique used, and discuss potential sources of bias (if any). Explain.

23. Using random digit dialing, researchers ask 1201 U.S. adults whether enough is being done to fight opioid addiction. *(Source: Kaiser Family Foundation)*

24. A professor asks 20 students to participate in a student reaction survey.

25. A study in a town in northwest Ethiopia designed to determine prevalence and predictors of depression among pregnant women randomly selects four districts of the town, then interviews all pregnant women in these districts. *(Source: Public Library of Science)*

26. A researcher surveys every tenth house for average family incomes.

27. Fifty voters are randomly selected from each religious group in a state and surveyed about their preferred political party.

28. A government official surveys 150 students of a school in Shanghai to study the eating habits of school-going children in the city.

29. Use the seventh row of Table 1 in Appendix B to generate 6 random numbers between 1 and 600.

1 Chapter Quiz

Take this quiz as you would take a quiz in class. After you are done, check your work against the answers given in the back of the book.

1. A study of the dietary habits of 359,264 Korean adolescents was conducted to find a link between dietary habits and school performance. Identify the population and the sample in the study. *(Source: Wolters Kluwer Health, Inc.)*

2. Determine whether each number describes a population parameter or a sample statistic. Explain your reasoning.

   (a) A survey of 1000 U.S. adults found that 52% think that the introduction of driverless cars will make roads less safe. *(Source: Rasmussen Reports)*

   (b) At a college, 90% of the members of the Board of Trustees approved the contract of the new president.

   (c) A survey of 727 small business owners found that 25% reported job openings they could not fill. *(Source: National Federation of Independent Business)*

3. Determine whether the data are qualitative or quantitative. Explain.

   (a) A list of debit card personal identification numbers

   (b) The final scores on a video game

4. Determine the level of measurement of the data set. Explain your reasoning.

   (a) A list of badge numbers of police officers at a precinct

   (b) The horsepowers of racing car engines

   (c) The top 10 grossing films released in a year

   (d) The years of birth for the runners in the Boston marathon

5. Determine whether the study is an observational study or an experiment. Explain.

   (a) Researchers conduct a study to determine whether body mass index (BMI) influences mortality. To conduct the study, researchers obtained the BMIs of 3,951,455 people. *(Source: Elsevier, Ltd.)*

   (b) Researchers conduct a study to determine whether taking a multivitamin daily affects cognitive health among men as they age. To perform the study, researchers studied 5947 male physicians ages 65 years or older and had one group take a multivitamin daily and had another group take a placebo daily. *(Source: American College of Physicians)*

6. An experiment is performed to test the effects of a new drug on high blood pressure. The experimenter identifies 320 people ages 35–50 years old with high blood pressure for participation in the experiment. The subjects are divided into equal groups according to age. Within each group, subjects are then randomly selected to be in either the treatment group or the control group. What type of experimental design is being used for this experiment?

7. Identify the sampling technique used in each study. Explain your reasoning.

   (a) A journalist asks people at a campground about air pollution.

   (b) For quality assurance, every tenth machine part is selected from an assembly line and measured for accuracy.

   (c) A study on attitudes about smoking is conducted at a college. The students are divided by class (freshman, sophomore, junior, and senior). Then a random sample is selected from each class and interviewed.

8. Which technique used in Exercise 7 could lead to a biased study? Explain.

1 Chapter Test

Take this test as you would take a test in class.

1. Determine whether you would take a census or use a sampling. If you would use a sampling, determine which sampling technique you would use. Explain.
   (a) The most popular type of investment among investors in New Jersey
   (b) The average age of the 30 employees of a company

2. Determine whether each number describes a population parameter or a sample statistic. Explain.
   (a) A survey of 1003 U.S. adults ages 18 years and older found that 72% own a smartphone. *(Source: Pew Research Center)*
   (b) In a recent year, the average evidence-based reading and writing score on the SAT was 543. *(Source: The College Board)*

3. Identify the sampling technique used, and discuss potential sources of bias (if any). Explain.
   (a) Chosen at random, 200 male and 200 female high school students are asked about their plans after high school.
   (b) Chosen at random, 625 customers at an electronics store are contacted and asked their opinions of the service they received.
   (c) Questioning teachers as they leave a faculty lounge, a researcher asks 45 of them about their teaching styles.

4. Determine whether the data are qualitative or quantitative, and determine the level of measurement of the data set. Explain your reasoning.
   (a) The numbers of employees at fast-food restaurants in a city are listed.

20	11	6	31	17	23	12	18	40	22
13	8	18	14	37	32	25	27	25	18

   (b) The grade point averages (GPAs) for a class of students are listed.

3.6	3.2	2.0	3.8	3.0	3.5	1.7	3.2
2.2	4.0	2.5	1.9	2.8	3.6	2.5	3.7

5. Determine whether the survey question is biased. If the question is biased, suggest a better wording.
   (a) How many hours of sleep do you get on a normal night?
   (b) Do you agree that the town's ban on skateboarding in parks is unfair?

6. Researchers surveyed 19,183 U.S. physicians, asking for the information below. *(Source: Medscape from WebMD)*

   location (region of the U.S.)   income (dollars)
   employment status (private practice or an employee)
   benefits received (health insurance, liability coverage, etc.)
   specialty (cardiology, family medicine, radiology, etc.)
   time spent seeing patients per week (hours)

   (a) Identify the population and the sample.
   (b) Is the data collected qualitative, quantitative, or both? Explain your reasoning.
   (c) Determine the level of measurement for each item above.
   (d) Determine whether the study is an observational study or an experiment. Explain.

REAL STATISTICS REAL DECISIONS
Putting it all together

You are a researcher for a professional research firm. Your firm has won a contract to conduct a study for a technology publication. The editors of the publication would like to know their readers' thoughts on using smartphones for making and receiving payments, for redeeming coupons, and as tickets to events. They would also like to know whether people are interested in using smartphones as digital wallets that store data from their drivers' licenses, health insurance cards, and other cards.

The editors have given you their readership database and 20 questions they would like to ask (two sample questions from a previous study are given at the right). You know that it is too expensive to contact all of the readers, so you need to determine a way to contact a representative sample of the entire readership population.

EXERCISES

1. *How Would You Do It?*
   (a) What sampling technique would you use to select the sample for the study? Why?
   (b) Will the technique you chose in part (a) give you a sample that is representative of the population?
   (c) Describe the method for collecting data.
   (d) Identify possible flaws or biases in your study.

2. *Data Classification*
   (a) What type of data do you expect to collect: qualitative, quantitative, or both? Why?
   (b) At what levels of measurement do you think the data in the study will be? Why?
   (c) Will the data collected for the study represent a population or a sample?
   (d) Will the numerical descriptions of the data be parameters or statistics?

3. *How They Did It*
   When The Harris Poll did a similar study, they used an Internet survey.
   (a) Describe some possible errors in collecting data by Internet surveys.
   (b) Compare your method for collecting data in Exercise 1 to this method.

When do you think smartphone payments will replace payment card transactions for a majority of purchases?

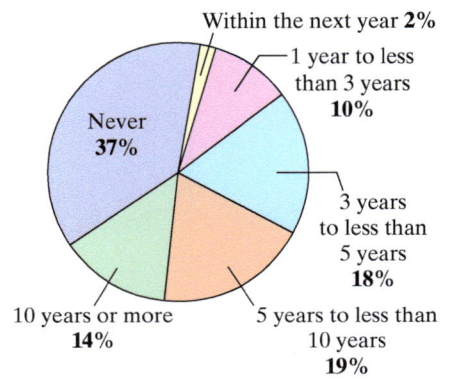

- Within the next year 2%
- 1 year to less than 3 years 10%
- 3 years to less than 5 years 18%
- 5 years to less than 10 years 19%
- 10 years or more 14%
- Never 37%

(Source: The Harris Poll)

How interested are you in being able to use your smartphone to make payments, rather than using cash or payment cards?

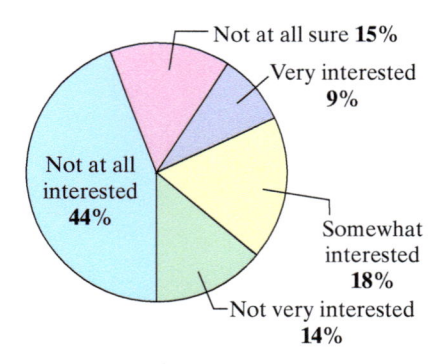

- Not at all sure 15%
- Very interested 9%
- Somewhat interested 18%
- Not very interested 14%
- Not at all interested 44%

(Source: The Harris Poll)

HISTORY OF STATISTICS-TIMELINE

17TH CENTURY

John Graunt (1620–1674)

Studied records of deaths in London in the early 1600s. The first to make extensive statistical observations from massive amounts of data (Chapter 2), his work laid the foundation for modern statistics.

Blaise Pascal (1623–1662)
Pierre de Fermat (1601–1665)

Pascal and Fermat corresponded about basic probability problems (Chapter 3)—especially those dealing with gaming and gambling.

18TH CENTURY

Pierre Laplace (1749–1827)

Studied probability (Chapter 3) and is credited with putting probability on a sure mathematical footing.

▶ **Carl Friedrich Gauss** (1777–1855)

Studied regression and the method of least squares (Chapter 9) through astronomy. In his honor, the normal distribution (Chapter 5) is sometimes called the Gaussian distribution.

19TH CENTURY

Lambert Quetelet (1796–1874)

Used descriptive statistics (Chapter 2) to analyze crime and mortality data and studied census techniques. Described normal distributions (Chapter 5) in connection with human traits such as height.

◀ **Florence Nightingale** (1820–1910)

A nurse during the Crimean War, she was one of the first to advocate the importance of sanitation in hospitals. One of the first statisticians to use descriptive statistics (Chapter 2) as a way to argue for social change and credited with having developed the Coxcomb chart.

Francis Galton (1822–1911)

Used regression and correlation (Chapter 9) to study genetic variation in humans. He is credited with the discovery of the Central Limit Theorem (Chapter 5).

20TH CENTURY

Karl Pearson (1857–1936)

Studied natural selection using correlation (Chapter 9). Formed first academic department of statistics and helped develop chi-square analysis (Chapter 6).

William Gosset (1876–1937)

Studied process of brewing and developed t-test to correct problems connected with small sample sizes (Chapter 6).

Charles Spearman (1863–1945)

British psychologist who was one of the first to develop intelligence testing using factor analysis (Chapter 10).

Ronald Fisher (1890–1962)

Studied biology and natural selection and developed ANOVA (Chapter 10), stressed the importance of experimental design (Chapter 1), and was the first to identify the null and alternative hypotheses (Chapter 7).

20TH CENTURY (later)

Frank Wilcoxon (1892–1965)

Biochemist who used statistics to study plant pathology. He introduced two-sample tests (Chapter 8), which led the way to the development of nonparametric statistics.

◀ **John Tukey** (1915–2000)

Worked at Princeton during World War II. Introduced exploratory data analysis techniques such as stem-and-leaf plots (Chapter 2). Also, worked at Bell Laboratories and is best known for his work in inferential statistics (Chapters 6–11).

David Kendall (1918–2007)

Worked at Princeton and Cambridge. Was a leading authority on applied probability and data analysis (Chapters 2 and 3).

TECHNOLOGY

MINITAB | EXCEL | TI-84 PLUS

Using Technology in Statistics

With large data sets, you will find that calculators or computer software programs can help perform calculations and create graphics. These calculations can be performed on many calculators and statistical software programs, such as Minitab, Excel, and the TI-84 Plus.

The following example shows a sample generated by each of these three technologies to generate a list of random numbers. This list of random numbers can be used to select sample members or perform simulations.

EXAMPLE

Generating a List of Random Numbers

A quality control department inspects a random sample of 15 of the 167 cars that are assembled at an auto plant. How should the cars be chosen?

SOLUTION

One way to choose the sample is to first number the cars from 1 to 167. Then you can use technology to form a list of random numbers from 1 to 167. Each of the technology tools shown requires different steps to generate the list. Each, however, does require that you identify the minimum value as 1 and the maximum value as 167. Check your user's manual for specific instructions.

MINITAB

↓	C1
1	167
2	11
3	74
4	160
5	18
6	70
7	80
8	56
9	37
10	6
11	82
12	126
13	98
14	104
15	137

EXCEL

	A
1	41
2	16
3	91
4	58
5	151
6	36
7	96
8	154
9	2
10	113
11	157
12	103
13	64
14	135
15	90

TI-84 PLUS

```
randInt (1, 167, 15)
{17 42 152 59 5 116
125 64 122 55 58 60
82 152 105}
```

Recall that when you generate a list of random numbers, you should decide whether it is acceptable to have numbers that repeat. If it is acceptable, then the sampling process is said to be *with replacement*. If it is not acceptable, then the sampling process is said to be *without replacement*.

With each of the three technology tools shown on page 38, you have the capability of sorting the list so that the numbers appear in order. Sorting helps you see whether any of the numbers in the list repeat. If it is not acceptable to have repeats, you should specify that the tool generate more random numbers than you need.

EXERCISES

1. The SEC (Securities and Exchange Commission) is investigating a financial services company. The company being investigated has 86 brokers. The SEC decides to review the records for a random sample of 10 brokers. Describe how this investigation could be done. Then use technology to generate a list of 10 random numbers from 1 to 86 and order the list.

2. A quality control department is testing 25 smartphones from a shipment of 300 smartphones. Describe how this test could be done. Then use technology to generate a list of 25 random numbers from 1 to 300 and order the list.

3. Consider the population of ten digits: 0, 1, 2, 3, 4, 5, 6, 7, 8, and 9. Select three random samples of five digits from this list. Find the average of each sample. Compare your results with the average of the entire population. Comment on your results. (Hint: To find the average, sum the data entries and divide the sum by the number of entries.)

4. Consider the population of 41 whole numbers from 0 to 40. What is the average of these numbers? Select three random samples of seven numbers from this list. Find the average of each sample. Compare your results with the average of the entire population. Comment on your results. (Hint: To find the average, sum the data entries and divide the sum by the number of entries.)

5. Use random numbers to simulate rolling a six-sided die 60 times. How many times did you obtain each number from 1 to 6? Are the results what you expected?

6. You rolled a six-sided die 60 times and got the following tally.

    20 ones
    20 twos
    15 threes
    3 fours
    2 fives
    0 sixes

    Does this seem like a reasonable result? What inference might you draw from the result?

7. Use random numbers to simulate tossing a coin 100 times. Let 0 represent heads, and let 1 represent tails. How many times did you obtain each number? Are the results what you expected?

8. You tossed a coin 100 times and got 77 heads and 23 tails. Does this seem like a reasonable result? What inference might you draw from the result?

9. A political analyst would like to survey a sample of the registered voters in a county. The county has 47 election districts. How could the analyst use random numbers to obtain a cluster sample?

CHAPTER 2
Descriptive Statistics

2.1
Frequency Distributions and Their Graphs

2.2
More Graphs and Displays

2.3
Measures of Central Tendency
Activity

2.4
Measures of Variation
Activity
Case Study

2.5
Measures of Position
Uses and Abuses
Real Statistics—Real Decisions
Technology

Since the 1966 season, the National Football League has determined its champion in the Super Bowl. The winning team receives the Lombardi Trophy.

Where You've Been

In Chapter 1, you learned that there are many ways to collect data. Usually, researchers must work with sample data in order to analyze populations, but occasionally it is possible to collect all the data for a given population. For instance, the data at the right represents the points scored by the winning teams in the first 51 Super Bowls. *(Source: NFL.com)*

35, 33, 16, 23, 16, 24, 14, 24, 16, 21, 32, 27, 35, 31, 27, 26, 27, 38, 38, 46, 39, 42, 20, 55, 20, 37, 52, 30, 49, 27, 35, 31, 34, 23, 34, 20, 48, 32, 24, 21, 29, 17, 27, 31, 31, 21, 34, 43, 28, 24, 34

Where You're Going

In Chapter 2, you will learn ways to organize and describe data sets. The goal is to make the data easier to understand by describing trends, averages, and variations. For instance, in the raw data showing the points scored by the winning teams in the first 51 Super Bowls, it is not easy to see any patterns or special characteristics. Here are some ways you can organize and describe the data.

Make a frequency distribution.

Class	Frequency, f
14–19	5
20–25	12
26–31	13
32–37	11
38–43	5
44–49	3
50–55	2

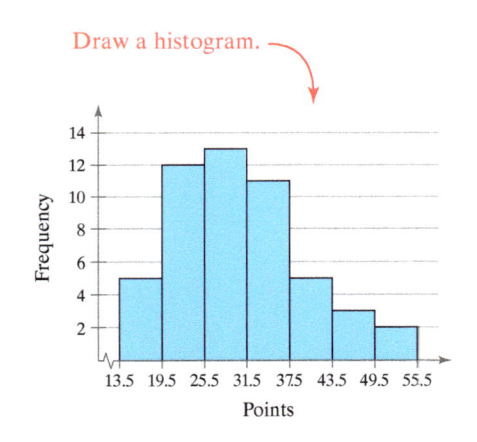

Draw a histogram.

$$\text{Mean} = \frac{35 + 33 + 16 + 23 + 16 + \cdots + 43 + 28 + 24 + 34}{51}$$

$$= \frac{1541}{51}$$

$$\approx 30.2 \text{ points} \quad \text{Find an average.}$$

$$\text{Range} = 55 - 14$$

$$= 41 \text{ points} \quad \text{Find how the data vary.}$$

2.1 Frequency Distributions and Their Graphs

What You Should Learn

▶ How to construct a frequency distribution, including limits, midpoints, relative frequencies, cumulative frequencies, and boundaries

▶ How to construct frequency histograms, frequency polygons, relative frequency histograms, and ogives

Frequency Distributions ■ Graphs of Frequency Distributions

Frequency Distributions

There are many ways to organize and describe a data set. Important characteristics to look for when organizing and describing a data set are its **center,** its **variability** (or spread), and its **shape.** Measures of center and shapes of distributions are covered in Section 2.3. Measures of variability are covered in Section 2.4.

When a data set has many entries, it can be difficult to see patterns. In this section, you will learn how to organize data sets by grouping the data into **intervals** called **classes** and forming a **frequency distribution.** You will also learn how to use frequency distributions to construct graphs.

> **DEFINITION**
>
> A **frequency distribution** is a table that shows **classes** or **intervals** of data entries with a count of the number of entries in each class. The **frequency** f of a class is the number of data entries in the class.

Example of a Frequency Distribution

Class	Frequency, f
1–5	5
6–10	8
11–15	6
16–20	8
21–25	5
26–30	4

In the frequency distribution shown at the left, there are six classes. The frequencies for each of the six classes are 5, 8, 6, 8, 5, and 4. Each class has a **lower class limit,** which is the least number that can belong to the class, and an **upper class limit,** which is the greatest number that can belong to the class. In the frequency distribution shown, the lower class limits are 1, 6, 11, 16, 21, and 26, and the upper class limits are 5, 10, 15, 20, 25, and 30. The **class width** is the distance between lower (or upper) limits of consecutive classes. For instance, the class width in the frequency distribution shown is $6 - 1 = 5$. Notice that the classes do not overlap.

The difference between the maximum and minimum data entries is called the **range.** In the frequency table shown, suppose the maximum data entry is 29, and the minimum data entry is 1. The range then is $29 - 1 = 28$. You will learn more about the range of a data set in Section 2.4.

Study Tip

In general, the frequency distributions shown in this text will use the minimum data entry for the lower limit of the first class. Sometimes it may be more convenient to choose a lower limit that is slightly less than the minimum data entry. The frequency distribution produced will vary slightly.

> **GUIDELINES**
>
> **Constructing a Frequency Distribution from a Data Set**
>
> 1. Decide on the number of classes to include in the frequency distribution. The number of classes should be between 5 and 20; otherwise, it may be difficult to detect any patterns.
> 2. Find the class width as follows. Determine the range of the data, divide the range by the number of classes, and *round up to the next convenient number.*
> 3. Find the class limits. You can use the minimum data entry as the lower limit of the first class. To find the remaining lower limits, add the class width to the lower limit of the preceding class. Then find the upper limit of the first class. Remember that classes cannot overlap. Find the remaining upper class limits.
> 4. Make a tally mark for each data entry in the row of the appropriate class.
> 5. Count the tally marks to find the total frequency f for each class.

EXAMPLE 1

Constructing a Frequency Distribution from a Data Set

The data set lists the out-of-pocket prescription medicine expenses (in dollars) for 30 U.S. adults in a recent year. Construct a frequency distribution that has seven classes. *(Adapted from: Health, United States, 2015)*

200	239	155	252	384	165	296	405	303	400
307	241	256	315	330	317	352	266	276	345
238	306	290	271	345	312	293	195	168	342

SOLUTION

1. The number of classes (7) is stated in the problem.

2. The minimum data entry is 155 and the maximum data entry is 405, so the range is 405 − 155 = 250. Divide the range by the number of classes and round up to find the class width.

$$\text{Class width} = \frac{250}{7} \quad \frac{\text{Range}}{\text{Number of classes}}$$

$$\approx 35.71 \quad \text{Round up to the next convenient number, 36.}$$

3. The minimum data entry is a convenient lower limit for the first class. To find the lower limits of the remaining six classes, add the class width of 36 to the lower limit of each previous class. So, the lower limits of the other classes are 155 + 36 = 191, 191 + 36 = 227, and so on. The upper limit of the first class is 190, which is one less than the lower limit of the second class. The upper limits of the other classes are 190 + 36 = 226, 226 + 36 = 262, and so on. The lower and upper limits for all seven classes are shown at the left.

4. Make a tally mark for each data entry in the appropriate class. For instance, the data entry 168 is in the 155–190 class, so make a tally mark in that class. Continue until you have made a tally mark for each of the 30 data entries.

5. The number of tally marks for a class is the frequency of that class.

The frequency distribution is shown below. The first class, 155–190, has three tally marks. So, the frequency of this class is 3. Notice that the sum of the frequencies is 30, which is the number of entries in the data set. The sum is denoted by Σf where Σ is the uppercase Greek letter **sigma**.

Frequency Distribution for Out-of-Pocket Prescription Medicine Expenses (in dollars)

Class	Tally	Frequency, f
155–190	|||	3
191–226	||	2
227–262	||||	5
263–298	||||		6
299–334	|||| ||	7
335–370	||||	4
371–406	|||	3
		$\Sigma f = 30$

Expenses → Class column
Number of adults → Frequency column
Check that the sum of the frequencies equals the number in the sample.

Study Tip

If you obtain a whole number when calculating the class width of a frequency distribution, use the next whole number as the class width. Doing this ensures that you will have enough space in your frequency distribution for all the data entries.

Lower limit	Upper limit
155	190
191	226
227	262
263	298
299	334
335	370
371	406

Study Tip

The uppercase Greek letter sigma (Σ) is used throughout statistics to indicate a summation of values.

Population of Iowa

Ages	Frequency
0–9	399,859
10–19	424,850
20–29	412,354
30–39	387,363
40–49	368,620
50–59	421,726
60–69	356,124
70–79	203,053
80 and older	143,699

The last class, 80 and older, is open-ended.

(Source: U.S. Census Bureau)

> **TRY IT YOURSELF 1**
> Construct a frequency distribution using the points scored by the 51 winning teams listed on page 41. Use six classes.
> *Answer: Page A5*

Note in Example 1 that the classes do not overlap, so each of the original data entries belongs to exactly one class. Also, the classes are of equal width. In general, all classes in a frequency distribution have the same width. However, this may not always be possible because a class can be *open-ended*. For instance, the frequency distribution for the population of Iowa shown at the left has an open-ended class, "80 and older."

After constructing a standard frequency distribution such as the one in Example 1, you can include several additional features that will help provide a better understanding of the data. These features (the **midpoint, relative frequency,** and **cumulative frequency** of each class) can be included as additional columns in your table.

DEFINITION

The **midpoint** of a class is the sum of the lower and upper limits of the class divided by two. The midpoint is sometimes called the *class mark*.

$$\text{Midpoint} = \frac{(\text{Lower class limit}) + (\text{Upper class limit})}{2}$$

The **relative frequency** of a class is the portion, or percentage, of the data that falls in that class. To find the relative frequency of a class, divide the frequency f by the sample size n.

$$\text{Relative frequency} = \frac{\text{Class frequency}}{\text{Sample size}} = \frac{f}{n} \qquad \text{Note that } n = \Sigma f.$$

The **cumulative frequency** of a class is the sum of the frequencies of that class and all previous classes. The cumulative frequency of the last class is equal to the sample size n.

You can use the formula shown above to find the midpoint of each class, or after finding the first midpoint, you can find the remaining midpoints by adding the class width to the previous midpoint. For instance, the midpoint of the first class in Example 1 is

$$\text{Midpoint} = \frac{155 + 190}{2} = 172.5. \qquad \text{Midpoint of first class.}$$

Using the class width of 36, the remaining midpoints are

$172.5 + 36 = 208.5$ Midpoint of second class.

$208.5 + 36 = 244.5$ Midpoint of third class.

$244.5 + 36 = 280.5$ Midpoint of fourth class.

and so on.

You can write the relative frequency as a fraction, decimal, or percent. The sum of the relative frequencies of all the classes should be equal to 1, or 100%. Due to rounding, the sum may be slightly less than or greater than 1. So, values such as 0.99 and 1.01 are sufficient.

EXAMPLE 2

Finding Midpoints, Relative Frequencies, and Cumulative Frequencies

Using the frequency distribution constructed in Example 1, find the midpoint, relative frequency, and cumulative frequency of each class. Describe any patterns.

SOLUTION

The midpoints, relative frequencies, and cumulative frequencies of the first five classes are calculated as follows.

Class	f	Midpoint	Relative frequency	Cumulative frequency
155–190	3	$\frac{155 + 190}{2} = 172.5$	$\frac{3}{30} = 0.1$	3
191–226	2	$\frac{191 + 226}{2} = 208.5$	$\frac{2}{30} \approx 0.07$	$3 + 2 = 5$
227–262	5	$\frac{227 + 262}{2} = 244.5$	$\frac{5}{30} \approx 0.17$	$5 + 5 = 10$
263–298	6	$\frac{263 + 298}{2} = 280.5$	$\frac{6}{30} = 0.2$	$10 + 6 = 16$
299–334	7	$\frac{299 + 334}{2} = 316.5$	$\frac{7}{30} \approx 0.23$	$16 + 7 = 23$

The remaining midpoints, relative frequencies, and cumulative frequencies are shown in the expanded frequency distribution below.

Frequency Distribution for Out-of-Pocket Prescription Medicine Expenses (in dollars)

Class	Frequency, f	Midpoint	Relative frequency	Cumulative frequency
155–190	3	172.5	0.1	3
191–226	2	208.5	0.07	5
227–262	5	244.5	0.17	10
263–298	6	280.5	0.2	16
299–334	7	316.5	0.23	23
335–370	4	352.5	0.13	27
371–406	3	388.5	0.1	30
	$\Sigma f = 30$		$\Sigma \frac{f}{n} = 1$	

Class → Expenses
Frequency, f → Number of adults
Cumulative frequency → Portion of adults

Interpretation There are several patterns in the data set. For instance, the most common range for the expenses is $299 to $334. Also, about half of the expenses are less than $299.

TRY IT YOURSELF 2

Using the frequency distribution constructed in Try It Yourself 1, find the midpoint, relative frequency, and cumulative frequency of each class. Describe any patterns.

Answer: Page A5

Graphs of Frequency Distributions

Sometimes it is easier to discover patterns in a data set by looking at a graph of the frequency distribution. One such graph is a **frequency histogram.**

> **DEFINITION**
>
> A **frequency histogram** uses bars to represent the frequency distribution of a data set. A histogram has the following properties.
>
> 1. The horizontal scale is quantitative and measures the data entries.
> 2. The vertical scale measures the frequencies of the classes.
> 3. Consecutive bars must touch.

Because consecutive bars of a histogram must touch, bars must begin and end at class boundaries instead of class limits. **Class boundaries** are the numbers that separate classes *without* forming gaps between them. For data that are integers, subtract 0.5 from each lower limit to find the lower class boundaries. To find the upper class boundaries, add 0.5 to each upper limit. The upper boundary of a class will equal the lower boundary of the next higher class.

EXAMPLE 3

Constructing a Frequency Histogram

Draw a frequency histogram for the frequency distribution in Example 2. Describe any patterns.

SOLUTION

First, find the class boundaries. Because the data entries are integers, subtract 0.5 from each lower limit to find the lower class boundaries and add 0.5 to each upper limit to find the upper class boundaries. So, the lower and upper boundaries of the first class are as follows.

First class lower boundary = 155 − 0.5 = 154.5
First class upper boundary = 190 + 0.5 = 190.5

Class	Class boundaries	Frequency, f
155–190	154.5–190.5	3
191–226	190.5–226.5	2
227–262	226.5–262.5	5
263–298	262.5–298.5	6
299–334	298.5–334.5	7
335–370	334.5–370.5	4
371–406	370.5–406.5	3

The boundaries of the remaining classes are shown in the table at the left. To construct the histogram, choose possible frequency values for the vertical scale. You can mark the horizontal scale either at the midpoints or at the class boundaries. Both histograms are shown below.

Study Tip
It is customary in bar graphs to have spaces between the bars, whereas with histograms, it is customary that the bars have no spaces between them.

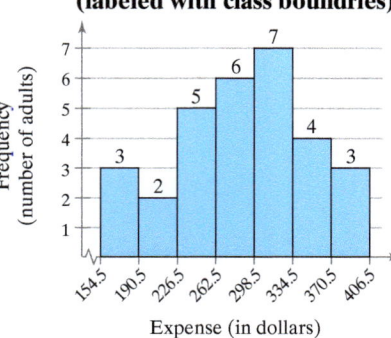

Interpretation From either histogram, you can see that two-thirds of the adults are paying more than $262.50 for out-of-pocket prescription medicine expenses.

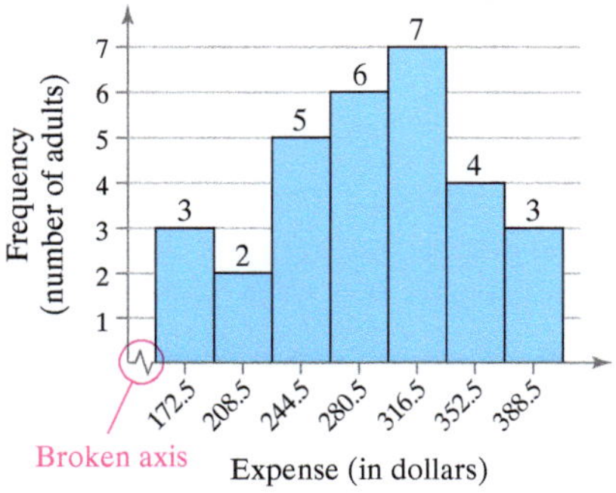

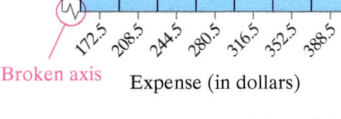

TRY IT YOURSELF 3

Use the frequency distribution from Try It Yourself 2 to construct a frequency histogram that represents the points scored by the 51 winning teams listed on page 41. Describe any patterns.   *Answer: Page A6*

Another way to graph a frequency distribution is to use a frequency polygon. A **frequency polygon** is a line graph that emphasizes the continuous change in frequencies.

EXAMPLE 4

Constructing a Frequency Polygon

Draw a frequency polygon for the frequency distribution in Example 2. Describe any patterns.

SOLUTION

To construct the frequency polygon, use the same horizontal and vertical scales that were used in the histogram labeled with class midpoints in Example 3. Then plot points that represent the midpoint and frequency of each class and connect the points in order from left to right with line segments. Because the graph should begin and end on the horizontal axis, extend the left side to one class width before the first class midpoint and extend the right side to one class width after the last class midpoint.

Out-of-Pocket Prescription Medicine Expenses

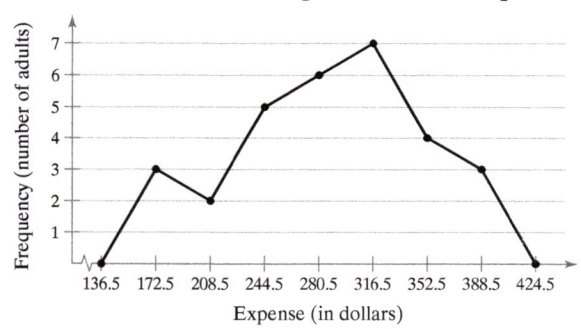

You can check your answer using technology, as shown below.

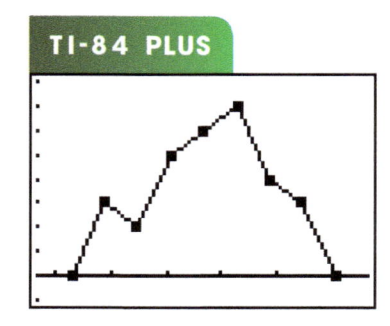

TI-84 PLUS

Interpretation You can see that the frequency of adults increases up to an expense of $316.50 and then the frequency decreases.

TRY IT YOURSELF 4

Use the frequency distribution from Try It Yourself 2 to construct a frequency polygon that represents the points scored by the 51 winning teams listed on page 41. Describe any patterns.   *Answer: Page A6*

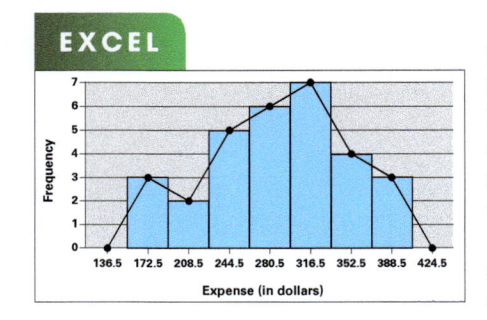

A histogram and its corresponding frequency polygon are often drawn together, as shown at the left using Excel. To do this by hand, first, construct the frequency polygon by choosing appropriate horizontal and vertical scales. The horizontal scale should consist of the class midpoints, and the vertical scale should consist of appropriate frequency values. Then plot the points that represent the midpoint and frequency of each class. After connecting the points with line segments, finish by drawing the bars for the histogram.

A **relative frequency histogram** has the same shape and the same horizontal scale as the corresponding frequency histogram. The difference is that the vertical scale measures the *relative* frequencies, not frequencies.

EXAMPLE 5

Constructing a Relative Frequency Histogram

Draw a relative frequency histogram for the frequency distribution in Example 2.

SOLUTION

The relative frequency histogram is shown. Notice that the shape of the histogram is the same as the shape of the frequency histogram constructed in Example 3. The only difference is that the vertical scale measures the relative frequencies.

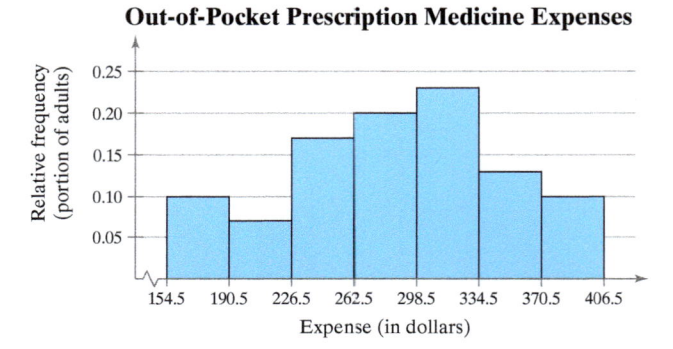

Interpretation From this graph, you can quickly see that 0.2, or 20%, of the adults have expenses between $262.50 and $298.50, which is not immediately obvious from the frequency histogram in Example 3.

TRY IT YOURSELF 5

Use the frequency distribution in Try It Yourself 2 to construct a relative frequency histogram that represents the points scored by the 51 winning teams listed on page 41.

Answer: Page A6

To describe the number of data entries that are less than or equal to a certain value, construct a **cumulative frequency graph**.

DEFINITION

A **cumulative frequency graph,** or **ogive** (pronounced ō′jīve), is a line graph that displays the cumulative frequency of each class at its upper class boundary. The upper boundaries are marked on the horizontal axis, and the cumulative frequencies are marked on the vertical axis.

Picturing the World

Old Faithful, a geyser at Yellowstone National Park, erupts on a regular basis. The time spans of a sample of eruptions are shown in the relative frequency histogram. (Source: Yellowstone National Park)

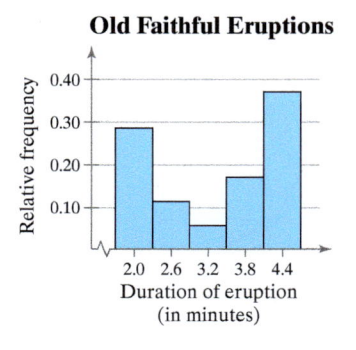

About 50% of the eruptions last less than how many minutes?

> **GUIDELINES**
>
> **Constructing an Ogive (Cumulative Frequency Graph)**
>
> 1. Construct a frequency distribution that includes cumulative frequencies as one of the columns.
> 2. Specify the horizontal and vertical scales. The horizontal scale consists of upper class boundaries, and the vertical scale measures cumulative frequencies.
> 3. Plot points that represent the upper class boundaries and their corresponding cumulative frequencies.
> 4. Connect the points in order from left to right with line segments.
> 5. The graph should start at the lower boundary of the first class (cumulative frequency is 0) and should end at the upper boundary of the last class (cumulative frequency is equal to the sample size).

EXAMPLE 6

Constructing an Ogive

Draw an ogive for the frequency distribution in Example 2.

SOLUTION

Using the cumulative frequencies, you can construct the ogive shown. The upper class boundaries, frequencies, and cumulative frequencies are shown in the table. Notice that the graph starts at 154.5, where the cumulative frequency is 0, and the graph ends at 406.5, where the cumulative frequency is 30.

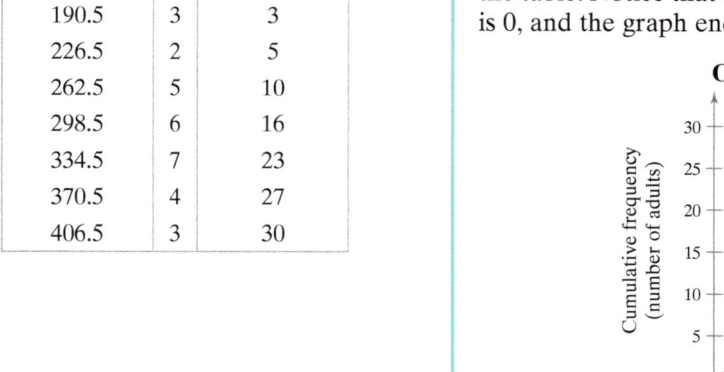

Upper class boundary	f	Cumulative frequency
190.5	3	3
226.5	2	5
262.5	5	10
298.5	6	16
334.5	7	23
370.5	4	27
406.5	3	30

Out-of-Pocket Prescription Medicine Expenses

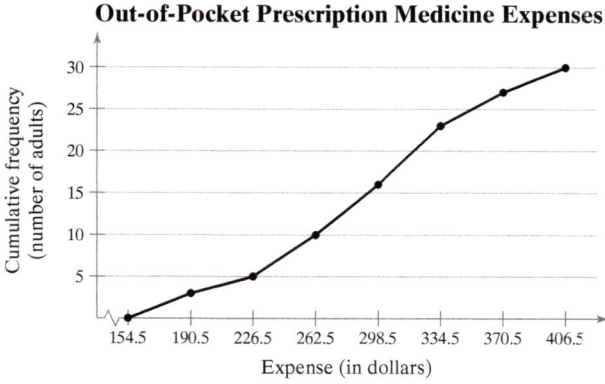

Interpretation From the ogive, you can see that 10 adults had expenses of $262.50 or less. Also, the greatest increase in cumulative frequency occurs between $298.50 and $334.50 because the line segment is steepest between these two class boundaries.

TRY IT YOURSELF 6

Use the frequency distribution from Try It Yourself 2 to construct an ogive that represents the points scored by the 51 winning teams listed on page 41.

Answer: Page A6

Another type of ogive uses percent as the vertical axis instead of frequency (see Example 5 in Section 2.5).

If you have access to technology such as Minitab, Excel, StatCrunch, or the TI-84 Plus, you can use it to draw the graphs discussed in this section.

EXAMPLE 7

Using Technology to Construct Histograms

Use technology to construct a histogram for the frequency distribution in Example 2.

SOLUTION

Using the instructions for a TI-84 Plus shown in the Tech Tip at the left, you can draw a histogram similar to the one below on the left. To investigate the graph, you can use the *trace* feature. After pressing TRACE, the midpoint and the frequency of the first class are displayed, as shown in the figure on the right. Use the right and left arrow keys to move through each bar.

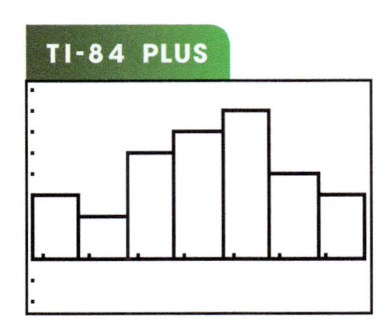

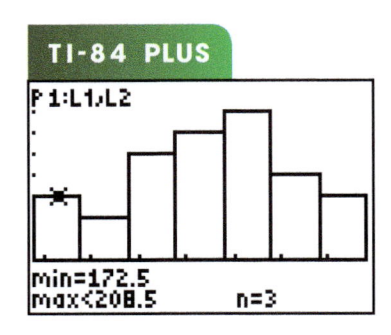

Tech Tip

You can use technology such as Minitab, Excel, StatCrunch, or the TI-84 Plus to create a histogram. (Detailed instructions for using Minitab, Excel, and the TI-84 Plus are shown in the technology manuals that accompany this text.) For instance, here are instructions for creating a histogram on a TI-84 Plus.

STAT ENTER

Enter midpoints in L1.
Enter frequencies in L2.

2nd STAT PLOT

Turn on Plot 1.
Highlight Histogram.

Xlist: L1
Freq: L2
ZOOM 9

Histograms made using Minitab, Excel, and StatCrunch are shown below.

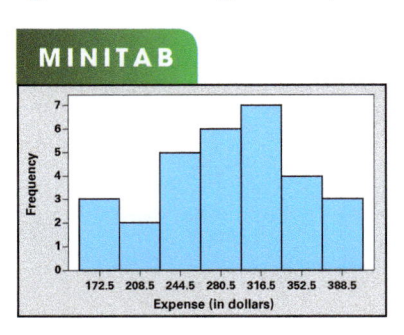

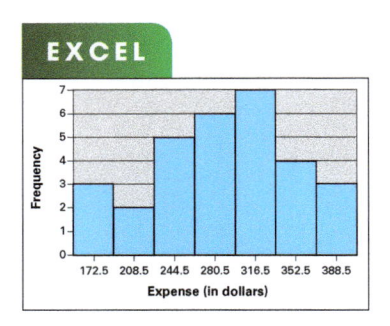

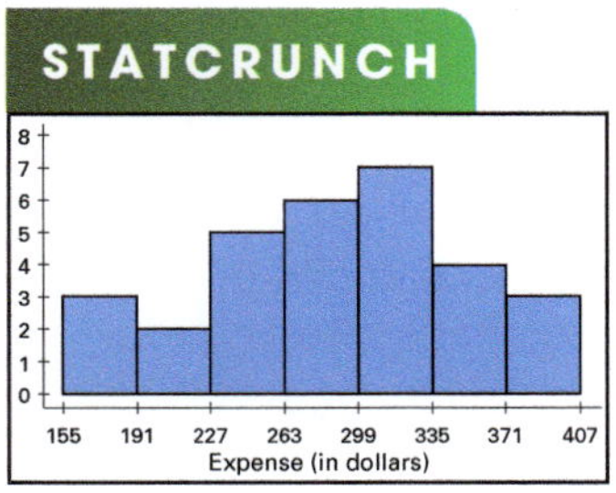

TRY IT YOURSELF 7

Use technology and the frequency distribution from Try It Yourself 2 to construct a frequency histogram that represents the points scored by the 51 winning teams listed on page 41.

Answer: Page A6

2.1 EXERCISES

For Extra Help: MyLab Statistics

Building Basic Skills and Vocabulary

1. What are some benefits of representing data sets using frequency distributions? What are some benefits of using graphs of frequency distributions?

2. Why should the number of classes in a frequency distribution be between 5 and 20?

3. What is the difference between class limits and class boundaries?

4. What is the difference between relative frequency and cumulative frequency?

5. After constructing an expanded frequency distribution, what should the sum of the relative frequencies be? Explain.

6. What is the difference between a frequency polygon and an ogive?

True or False? *In Exercises 7–10, determine whether the statement is true or false. If it is false, rewrite it as a true statement.*

7. In a frequency distribution, the class width is the distance between the lower and upper limits of a class.

8. The midpoint of a class is the sum of its lower and upper limits divided by two.

9. An ogive is a graph that displays relative frequencies.

10. Class boundaries ensure that consecutive bars of a histogram touch.

In Exercises 11–14, use the minimum and maximum data entries and the number of classes to find the class width, the lower class limits, and the upper class limits.

11. min = 9, max = 64, 7 classes
12. min = 12, max = 88, 6 classes
13. min = 17, max = 135, 8 classes
14. min = 54, max = 247, 10 classes

Reading a Frequency Distribution *In Exercises 15 and 16, use the frequency distribution to find the (a) class width, (b) class midpoints, and (c) class boundaries.*

15. **Travel Time to Work (in minutes)**

Class	Frequency, f
0–10	188
11–21	372
22–32	264
33–43	205
44–54	83
55–65	76
66–76	32

16. **Toledo, OH, Average Normal Temperatures (°F)**

Class	Frequency, f
25–32	86
33–40	39
41–48	41
49–56	48
57–64	43
65–72	68
73–80	40

17. Use the frequency distribution in Exercise 15 to construct an expanded frequency distribution, as shown in Example 2.

18. Use the frequency distribution in Exercise 16 to construct an expanded frequency distribution, as shown in Example 2.

Graphical Analysis *In Exercises 19 and 20, use the frequency histogram to*

(a) *determine the number of classes.*

(b) *estimate the greatest and least frequencies.*

(c) *determine the class width.*

(d) *describe any patterns with the data.*

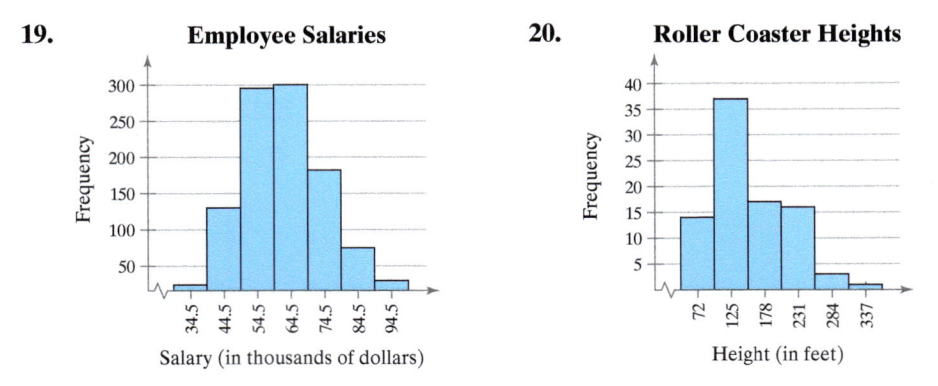

19. **Employee Salaries**

20. **Roller Coaster Heights**

Graphical Analysis *In Exercises 21 and 22, use the frequency polygon to identify the class with the greatest, and the class with the least, frequency.*

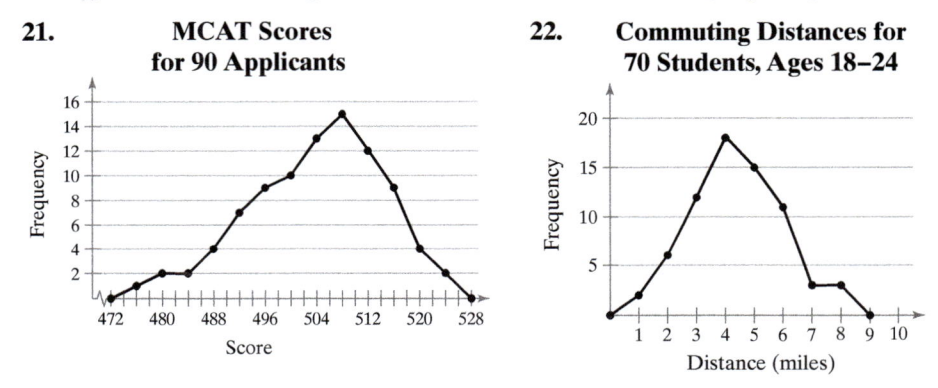

21. **MCAT Scores for 90 Applicants**

22. **Commuting Distances for 70 Students, Ages 18–24**

Graphical Analysis *In Exercises 23 and 24, use the relative frequency histogram to*

(a) *identify the class with the greatest, and the class with the least, relative frequency.*

(b) *approximate the greatest and least relative frequencies.*

(c) *describe any patterns with the data.*

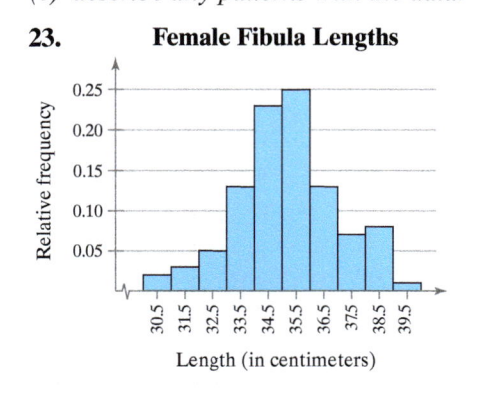

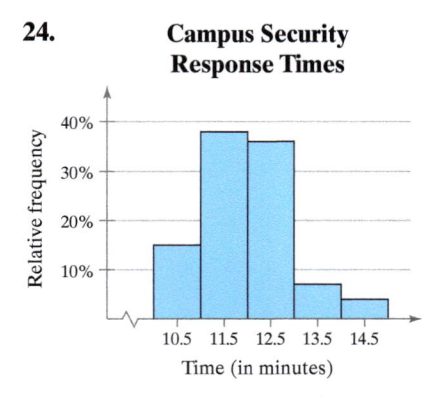

23. **Female Fibula Lengths**

24. **Campus Security Response Times**

Graphical Analysis *In Exercises 25 and 26, use the ogive to approximate*

(a) *the number in the sample.*

(b) *the location of the greatest increase in frequency.*

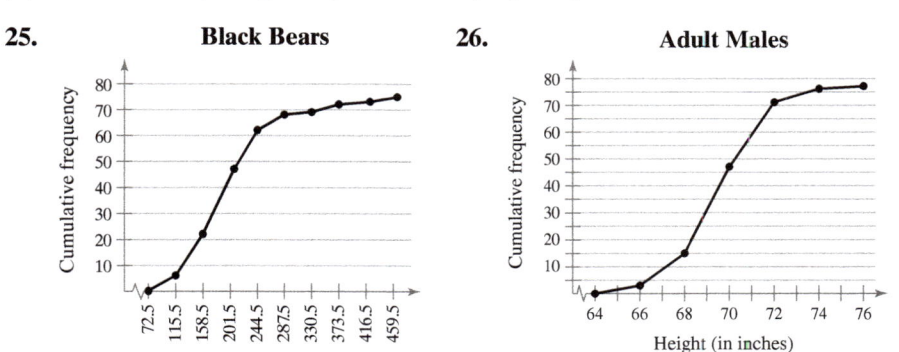

25. Black Bears

26. Adult Males

27. Use the ogive in Exercise 25 to approximate

(a) the cumulative frequency for a weight of 201.5 pounds.

(b) the weight for which the cumulative frequency is 68.

(c) the number of black bears that weigh between 158.5 pounds and 244.5 pounds.

(d) the number of black bears that weigh more than 330.5 pounds.

28. Use the ogive in Exercise 26 to approximate

(a) the cumulative frequency for a height of 72 inches.

(b) the height for which the cumulative frequency is 15.

(c) the number of adult males that are between 68 and 72 inches tall.

(d) the number of adult males that are taller than 70 inches.

Using and Interpreting Concepts

Constructing a Frequency Distribution *In Exercises 29 and 30, construct a frequency distribution for the data set using the indicated number of classes. In the table, include the midpoints, relative frequencies, and cumulative frequencies. Which class has the greatest class frequency and which has the least class frequency?*

29. Online Games Playing Times
Number of classes: 5
Data set: Times (in minutes) spent playing online games in a day

12	20	30	25	16	13	8	15	19	12	18	13
21	16	18	12	13	25	20	21	13	18	12	14

30. Conveyance Spending
Number of classes: 6
Data set: Amounts (in dollars) spent on conveyance for a quarter of a year

425	413	318	325	515	213	418	313	410	415
513	521	232	320	528	412	313	425	402	498
321	213	312	514	415	541	451	328	382	238

indicates that the data set for this exercise is available within MyStatLab or at *www.pearsonglobaleditions.com*.

Constructing a Frequency Distribution and a Frequency Histogram

In Exercises 31–34, construct a frequency distribution and a frequency histogram for the data set using the indicated number of classes. Describe any patterns.

31. Production

Number of classes: 6

Data set: January production (in units) for 21 manufacturing plants of a multinational company

1254	1248	2415	2697	1698	1387	985
2034	2169	1478	1312	2307	2802	2011
2804	1695	1489	1908	2707	1308	1566

32. Acid Strengths

Number of classes: 5

Data set: Strengths (in parts per thousands) of 24 acids

57	96	99	90	38	49	70	71	61	86	75	38
50	45	58	94	98	86	42	48	63	81	87	44

33. Response Times

Number of classes: 8

Data set: Response times (in days) of 30 males to a test drive survey

3	5	4	6	18	15	23	4	6	9
6	5	4	9	3	5	14	2	17	5
6	3	4	9	6	7	10	15	11	3

34. Bowling Speeds

Number of classes: 8

Data set: Bowling speeds (in kilometers per hour) of 21 bowlers in a cricket series

128	130	155	142	161	111	121
100	105	125	162	118	133	135
142	128	129	136	145	161	129

Constructing a Frequency Distribution and a Frequency Polygon

In Exercises 35 and 36, construct a frequency distribution and a frequency polygon for the data set using the indicated number of classes. Describe any patterns.

35. Ages of the Presidents

Number of classes: 6

Data set: Ages of the U.S. presidents at Inauguration *(Source: The White House)*

57	61	57	57	58	57	61	54	68	51	49	64	50	48	65
52	56	46	54	49	51	47	55	55	54	42	51	56	55	51
54	51	60	62	43	55	56	61	52	69	64	46	54	47	70

36. Regnal Years

Number of classes: 5

Data set: Regnal years of the monarchs of Great Britain *(Source: Britain Express)*

37	19	2	6	5	28	26	15	6	9	4	16	3
	34	2	1	1	19	5	2	14	1	21	13	35
	19	1	35	10	17	55	35	20	50	22	14	9
	39	22	1	2	24	38	6	1	5	45	22	24
	9	1	25	3	13	12	8					

Constructing a Frequency Distribution and a Relative Frequency Histogram
In Exercises 37–40, construct a frequency distribution and a relative frequency histogram for the data set using five classes. Which class has the greatest relative frequency and which has the least relative frequency?

37. Taste Test
Data set: Ratings from 1 (lowest) to 10 (highest) provided by 36 people after taste testing a new flavor of ice cream

```
1  3  5  6  9  10  2  5  6
6  5  6  9  4   2  3  6  4
6  5  9  8  7   4  5  7  1
1  2  5  6  7   1  3  6  9
```

38. Years of Driving
Data set: Years of service of 28 best drivers in a city in France

```
15  17  12  16  14  10  12
14  13  16  11  18  14  16
18  19  12   9  23  19  17
12  15  14  13  19  18  16
```

39. Polar Bears
Data set: Weights (in kilograms) of 28 adult male polar bears

```
450  420  489  456  417  413  499
456  418  436  459  475  429  415
436  425  469  468  412  436  491
402  409  473  496  463  417  420
```

40. Systolic Blood Pressures
Data set: Systolic blood pressure levels (in millimeters of mercury) of 28 patients

```
125  130  170  184   95  110  111
117  126  141  157  129  133  136
128  142  108  106  113  128  133
164  153  138  127  118  163  118
```

Constructing a Cumulative Frequency Distribution and an Ogive
In Exercises 41 and 42, construct a cumulative frequency distribution and an ogive for the data set using six classes. Then describe the location of the greatest increase in frequency.

41. Retirement Ages
Data set: Retirement ages of 35 Statistics professors

```
65  66  83  75  49  54  56
59  54  58  57  65  64  69
71  73  59  54  56  70  74
65  63  68  59  57  56  54
60  68  69  63  58  59  79
```

42. Calorie Intakes
Data set: Daily calorie intakes (in kilojoules) of 28 people

```
10500   9800   9500   9200  11000  13500  11500
14000   7800   9600  10800  10200  11000  11400
12400   8600   9900  10900  10000   9900  10600
14500  16900  14000  15500   9400  10800  10100
```

In Exercises 43 and 44, use the data set and the indicated number of classes to construct (a) an expanded frequency distribution, (b) a frequency histogram, (c) a frequency polygon, (d) a relative frequency histogram, and (e) an ogive.

43. Road Accidents
Data set: Number of accidents per day in a city

14	4	18	30	9	10	11	2	12	8	16	6
12	16	9	3	4	8	7	11	21	13	8	7

44. Constellations
Number of classes: 6
Data set: Number of stars in the Chinese Hellenistic constellations
(Source: Revolvy)

4	4	3	3	4	3	9
11	11	4	4	2	7	12
10	3	2	2	5	5	6
5	9					

Extending Concepts

45. What Would You Do? You work at a bank and are asked to recommend the amount of cash to put in an ATM each day. You do not want to put in too much (which would cause security concerns) or too little (which may create customer irritation). Here are the daily withdrawals (in hundreds of dollars) for 30 days.

72	84	61	76	104	76	86	92	80	88	98	76	97	82	84
67	70	81	82	89	74	73	86	81	85	78	82	80	91	83

(a) Construct a relative frequency histogram for the data. Use 8 classes.

(b) If you put $9000 in the ATM each day, what percent of the days in a month should you expect to run out of cash? Explain.

(c) If you are willing to run out of cash on 10% of the days, how much cash should you put in the ATM each day? Explain.

46. What Would You Do? The admissions department for a college is asked to recommend the minimum SAT scores that the college will accept for full-time students. Here are the SAT scores of 50 applicants.

1170	1000	910	870	1070	1290	920	1470	1080	1180
770	900	1120	1070	1370	1160	970	930	1240	1270
1250	1330	1010	1010	1410	1130	1210	1240	960	820
650	1010	1190	1500	1400	1270	1310	1050	950	1150
1450	1290	1310	1100	1330	1410	840	1040	1090	1080

(a) Construct a relative frequency histogram for the data. Use 10 classes.

(b) If you set the minimum score at 1070, what percent of the applicants will meet this requirement? Explain.

(c) If you want to accept the top 88% of the applicants, what should the minimum score be? Explain.

47. Writing Use the data set listed and technology to create frequency histograms with 5, 10, and 20 classes. Which graph displays the data best? Explain.

2	7	3	2	11	3	15	8	4	9	10	13	9
7	11	10	1	2	12	5	6	4	2	9	15	14

2.2 More Graphs and Displays

What You Should Learn

▶ How to graph and interpret quantitative data sets using stem-and-leaf plots and dot plots

▶ How to graph and interpret qualitative data sets using pie charts and Pareto charts

▶ How to graph and interpret paired data sets using scatter plots and time series charts

Graphing Quantitative Data Sets ■ Graphing Qualitative Data Sets ■ Graphing Paired Data Sets

Graphing Quantitative Data Sets

In Section 2.1, you learned several ways to display quantitative data graphically. In this section, you will learn more ways to display quantitative data, beginning with **stem-and-leaf plots.** Stem-and-leaf plots are examples of **exploratory data analysis (EDA),** which was developed by John Tukey in 1977.

In a stem-and-leaf plot, each number is separated into a **stem** (for instance, the entry's leftmost digits) and a **leaf** (for instance, the rightmost digit). You should have as many leaves as there are entries in the original data set and the leaves should be single digits. A stem-and-leaf plot is similar to a histogram but has the advantage that the graph still contains the original data. Another advantage of a stem-and-leaf plot is that it provides an easy way to sort data.

EXAMPLE 1

Constructing a Stem-and-Leaf Plot

The data set at the left lists the numbers of text messages sent in one day by 50 cell phone users. Display the data in a stem-and-leaf plot. Describe any patterns. *(Adapted from Pew Research)*

Number of Text Messages Sent

76	49	102	58	88
122	76	89	67	80
66	80	78	69	56
76	115	99	72	19
41	86	48	52	28
26	29	33	26	20
33	24	43	16	39
29	32	29	29	40
23	33	30	41	33
38	34	53	30	149

SOLUTION

Because the data entries go from a low of 16 to a high of 149, you should use stem values from 1 to 14. To construct the plot, list these stems to the left of a vertical line. For each data entry, list a leaf to the right of its stem. For instance, the entry 102 has a stem of 10 and a leaf of 2. Make the plot with the leaves in increasing order from left to right. Be sure to include a key.

Number of Text Messages Sent

```
 1 | 6 9                    Key: 10|2 = 102
 2 | 0 3 4 6 6 8 9 9 9 9
 3 | 0 0 2 3 3 3 3 4 8 9
 4 | 0 1 1 3 8 9
 5 | 2 3 6 8
 6 | 6 7 9
 7 | 2 6 6 6 8
 8 | 0 0 6 8 9
 9 | 9
10 | 2
11 | 5
12 | 2
13 |
14 | 9
```

Interpretation From the display, you can see that more than 50% of the cell phone users sent between 20 and 50 text messages.

Study Tip

It is important to include a key for a stem-and-leaf plot to identify the data entries. This is done by showing an entry represented by a stem and one leaf.

Tech Tip

You can use technology such as Minitab, StatCrunch, or Excel (with the XLSTAT add-in) to construct a stem-and-leaf plot. For instance, a StatCrunch stem-and-leaf plot for the data in Example 1 is shown below.

STATCRUNCH

Variable: Number of text messages sent

Decimal point is 1 digit(s) to the right of the colon.
Leaf unit = 1
```
 1 : 69
 2 : 0346689999
 3 : 0023333489
 4 : 011389
 5 : 2368
 6 : 679
 7 : 26668
 8 : 00689
 9 : 9
10 : 2
11 : 5
12 : 2
13 :
14 : 9
```

Study Tip

You can use stem-and-leaf plots to identify unusual data entries called *outliers*. In Examples 1 and 2, the data entry 149 is an outlier. You will learn more about outliers in Section 2.3.

TRY IT YOURSELF 1

Use a stem-and-leaf plot to organize the points scored by the 51 winning teams listed on page 41. Describe any patterns. *Answer: Page A6*

EXAMPLE 2

Constructing Variations of Stem-and-Leaf Plots

Organize the data set in Example 1 using a stem-and-leaf plot that has two rows for each stem. Describe any patterns.

SOLUTION

Use the stem-and-leaf plot from Example 1, except now list each stem twice. Use the leaves 0, 1, 2, 3, and 4 in the first stem row and the leaves 5, 6, 7, 8, and 9 in the second stem row. The revised stem-and-leaf plot is shown. Notice that by using two rows per stem, you obtain a more detailed picture of the data.

Number of Text Messages Sent

```
 1 |                    Key: 10|2 = 102
 1 | 6 9
 2 | 0 3 4
 2 | 6 6 8 9 9 9 9
 3 | 0 0 2 3 3 3 3 4
 3 | 8 9
 4 | 0 1 1 3
 4 | 8 9
 5 | 2 3
 5 | 6 8
 6 |
 6 | 6 7 9
 7 | 2
 7 | 6 6 6 8
 8 | 0 0
 8 | 6 8 9
 9 |
 9 | 9
10 | 2
10 |
11 |
11 | 5
12 | 2
12 |
13 |
13 |
14 |
14 | 9
```

Interpretation From the display, you can see that most of the cell phone users sent between 20 and 80 text messages.

TRY IT YOURSELF 2

Using two rows for each stem, revise the stem-and-leaf plot you constructed in Try It Yourself 1. Describe any patterns. *Answer: Page A6*

You can also use a dot plot to graph quantitative data. In a **dot plot,** each data entry is plotted, using a point, above a horizontal axis. Like a stem-and-leaf plot, a dot plot allows you to see how data are distributed, to determine specific data entries, and to identify unusual data entries.

EXAMPLE 3

Constructing a Dot Plot

Use a dot plot to organize the data set in Example 1. Describe any patterns.

Number of Text Messages Sent									
76	49	102	58	88	122	76	89	67	80
66	80	78	69	56	76	115	99	72	19
41	86	48	52	28	26	29	33	26	20
33	24	43	16	39	29	32	29	29	40
23	33	30	41	33	38	34	53	30	149

SOLUTION

So that each data entry is included in the dot plot, the horizontal axis should include numbers between 15 and 150. To represent a data entry, plot a point above the entry's position on the axis. When an entry is repeated, plot another point above the previous point.

Number of Text Messages Sent

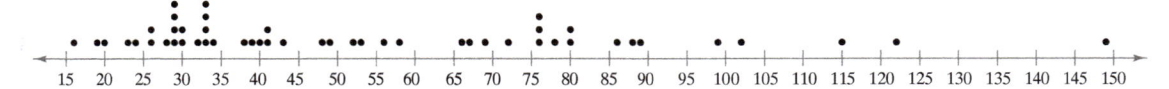

Interpretation From the dot plot, you can see that most entries occur between 20 and 80 and only 4 people sent more than 100 text messages. You can also see that 149 is an unusual data entry.

TRY IT YOURSELF 3

Use a dot plot to organize the points scored by the 51 winning teams listed on page 41. Describe any patterns.

Answer: Page A6

Technology can be used to construct dot plots. For instance, Minitab and StatCrunch dot plots for the text messaging data are shown below.

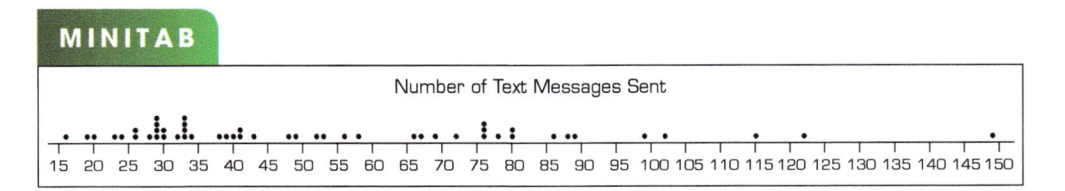

MINITAB

Number of Text Messages Sent

STATCRUNCH

Number of Text Messages Sent

Graphing Qualitative Data Sets

Pie charts provide a convenient way to present qualitative data graphically as percents of a whole. A **pie chart** is a circle that is divided into sectors that represent categories. The area of each sector is proportional to the frequency of each category. In most cases, you will be interpreting a pie chart or constructing one using technology. Example 4 shows how to construct a pie chart by hand.

EXAMPLE 4

Constructing a Pie Chart

The numbers of earned degrees conferred (in thousands) in 2014 are shown in the table at the right. Use a pie chart to organize the data. *(Source: U.S. National Center for Education Statistics)*

Earned Degrees Conferred in 2014

Type of degree	Number (in thousands)
Associate's	1003
Bachelor's	1870
Master's	754
Doctoral	178

SOLUTION

Begin by finding the relative frequency, or percent, of each category. Then construct the pie chart using the central angle that corresponds to each category. To find the central angle, multiply 360° by the category's relative frequency. For instance, the central angle for associate's degrees is 360°(0.264) ≈ 95°.

Type of degree	f	Relative frequency	Angle
Associate's	1003	0.264	95°
Bachelor's	1870	0.491	177°
Master's	754	0.198	71°
Doctoral	178	0.047	17°

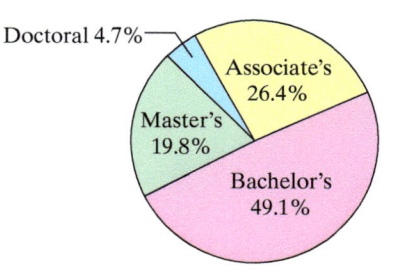

Interpretation From the pie chart, you can see that almost one-half of the degrees conferred in 2014 were bachelor's degrees.

TRY IT YOURSELF 4

The numbers of earned degrees conferred (in thousands) in 1990 are shown in the table. Use a pie chart to organize the data. Compare the 1990 data with the 2014 data. *(Source: U.S. National Center for Education Statistics)*

Earned Degrees Conferred in 1990

Type of degree	Number (in thousands)
Associate's	455
Bachelor's	1051
Master's	330
Doctoral	104

Answer: Page A6

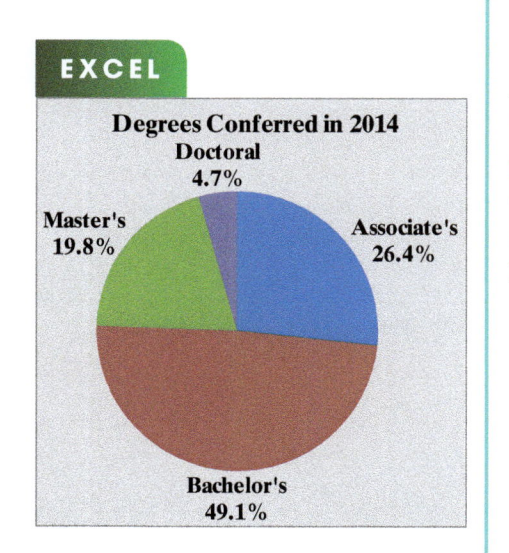

You can use technology to construct a pie chart. For instance, an Excel pie chart for the degrees conferred in 2014 is shown at the left.

Another way to graph qualitative data is to use a Pareto chart. A **Pareto chart** is a vertical bar graph in which the height of each bar represents frequency or relative frequency. The bars are positioned in order of decreasing height, with the tallest bar positioned at the left. Such positioning helps highlight important data and is used frequently in business.

EXAMPLE 5

Constructing a Pareto Chart

In 2014, these were the leading causes of death in the United States.

Accidents: 136,053

Cancer: 591,699

Chronic lower respiratory disease: 147,101

Heart disease: 614,348

Stroke (cerebrovascular diseases): 133,103

Use a Pareto chart to organize the data. What was the leading cause of death in the United States in 2014? *(Source: Health, United States, 2015, Table 19)*

SOLUTION

Using frequencies for the vertical axis, you can construct the Pareto chart as shown.

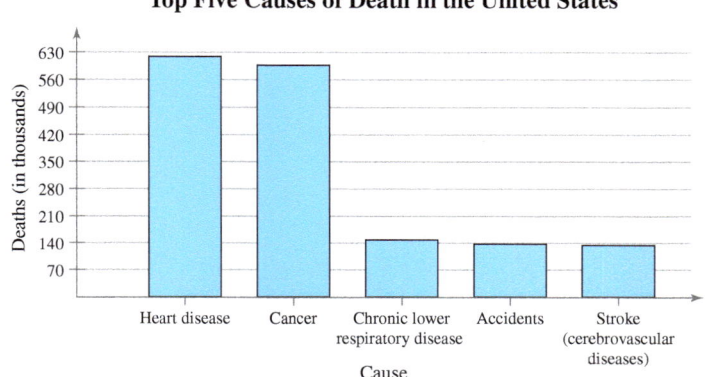

Top Five Causes of Death in the United States

Interpretation From the Pareto chart, you can see that the leading cause of death in the United States in 2014 was from heart disease. Also, heart disease and cancer caused more deaths than the other three causes combined.

TRY IT YOURSELF 5

Every year, the Better Business Bureau (BBB) receives complaints from customers. Here are some complaints the BBB received in a recent year.

16,281 complaints about auto dealers (used cars)

8384 complaints about insurance companies

3634 complaints about mortgage brokers

19,277 complaints about collection agencies

6985 complaints about travel agencies and bureaus

Use a Pareto chart to organize the data. Which industry is the greatest cause of complaints? *(Source: Council of Better Business Bureaus)*

Answer: Page A6

Picturing the World

According to data from the U.S. Bureau of Labor Statistics, earnings increase as educational attainment rises. The average weekly earnings data by educational attainment are shown in the Pareto chart. *(Source: Based on U.S. Bureau of Labor Statistics)*

Average Weekly Earnings by Educational Attainment

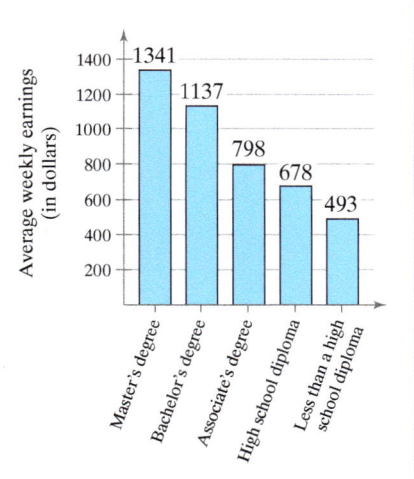

- Master's degree: 1341
- Bachelor's degree: 1137
- Associate's degree: 798
- High school diploma: 678
- Less than a high school diploma: 493

The average worker with an associate's degree makes how much more in a year (52 weeks) than the average worker with a high school diploma?

Graphing Paired Data Sets

When each entry in one data set corresponds to one entry in a second data set, the sets are called **paired data sets.** For instance, a data set contains the costs of an item and a second data set contains sales amounts for the item at each cost. Because each cost corresponds to a sales amount, the data sets are paired. One way to graph paired data sets is to use a **scatter plot,** where the ordered pairs are graphed as points in a coordinate plane. A scatter plot is used to show the relationship between two quantitative variables.

EXAMPLE 6

Interpreting a Scatter Plot

The British statistician Ronald Fisher (see page 37) introduced a famous data set called Fisher's Iris data set. This data set describes various physical characteristics, such as petal length and petal width (in millimeters), for three species of iris. In the scatter plot shown, the petal lengths form the first data set and the petal widths form the second data set. As the petal length increases, what tends to happen to the petal width? *(Source: Fisher, R. A., 1936)*

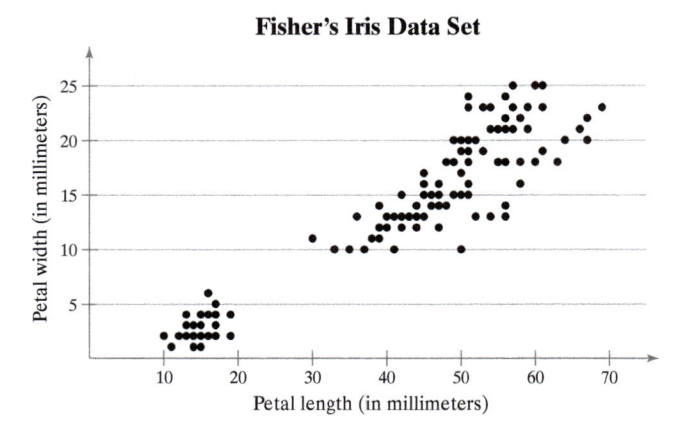

Fisher's Iris Data Set

SOLUTION

The horizontal axis represents the petal length, and the vertical axis represents the petal width. Each point in the scatter plot represents the petal length and petal width of one flower.

Interpretation From the scatter plot, you can see that as the petal length increases, the petal width also tends to increase.

TRY IT YOURSELF 6

The lengths of employment and the salaries of 10 employees are listed in the table below. Graph the data using a scatter plot. Describe any trends.

Length of employment (in years)	5	4	8	4	2
Salary (in dollars)	32,000	32,500	40,000	27,350	25,000

Length of employment (in years)	10	7	6	9	3
Salary (in dollars)	43,000	41,650	39,225	45,100	28,000

Answer: Page A7

You will learn more about scatter plots and how to analyze them in Chapter 9.

A data set that is composed of quantitative entries taken at regular intervals over a period of time is called a **time series.** For instance, the amount of precipitation measured each day for one month is a time series. You can use a **time series chart** to graph a time series.

EXAMPLE 7

> See Minitab and TI-84 Plus steps on pages 126 and 127.

Constructing a Time Series Chart

The table lists the number of motor vehicle thefts (in millions) and burglaries (in millions) in the United States for the years 2005 through 2015. Construct a time series chart for the number of motor vehicle thefts. Describe any trends. *(Source: Federal Bureau of Investigation, Crime in the United States)*

Year	Motor vehicle thefts (in millions)	Burglaries (in millions)
2005	1.24	2.16
2006	1.20	2.19
2007	1.10	2.19
2008	0.96	2.23
2009	0.80	2.20
2010	0.74	2.17
2011	0.72	2.19
2012	0.72	2.11
2013	0.70	1.93
2014	0.69	1.71
2015	0.71	1.58

SOLUTION

Let the horizontal axis represent the years and let the vertical axis represent the number of motor vehicle thefts (in millions). Then plot the paired data and connect them with line segments

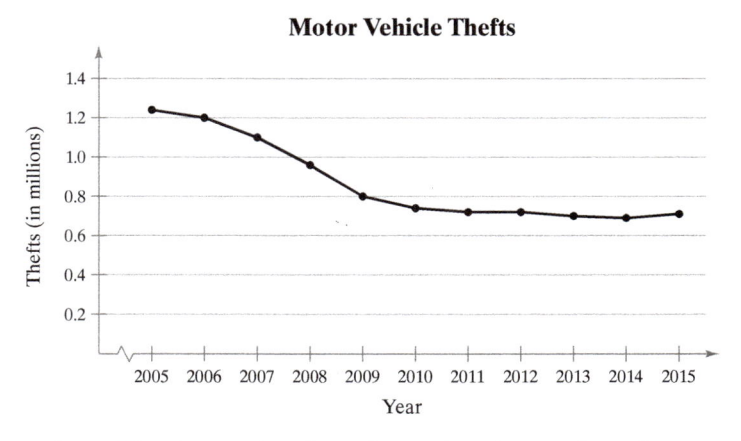

Interpretation The time series chart shows that the number of motor vehicle thefts decreased until 2011 and then remained about the same through 2015.

TRY IT YOURSELF 7

Use the table in Example 7 to construct a time series chart for the number of burglaries for the years 2005 through 2015. Describe any trends.

Answer: Page A7

2.2 EXERCISES

For Extra Help: MyLab Statistics

Building Basic Skills and Vocabulary

1. Name some ways to display quantitative data graphically. Name some ways to display qualitative data graphically.

2. What is an advantage of using a stem-and-leaf plot instead of a histogram? What is a disadvantage?

3. In terms of displaying data, how is a stem-and-leaf plot similar to a dot plot?

4. How is a Pareto chart different from a standard vertical bar graph?

Putting Graphs in Context *In Exercises 5–8, match the plot with the description of the sample.*

5. 0 | 8   Key: 0|8 = 0.8
    1 | 5 6 8
    2 | 1 3 4 5
    3 | 0 9
    4 | 0 0

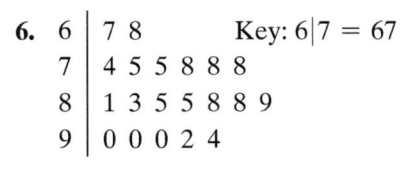

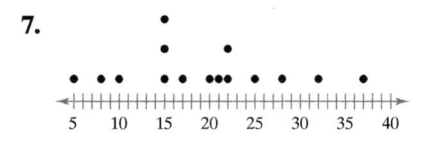

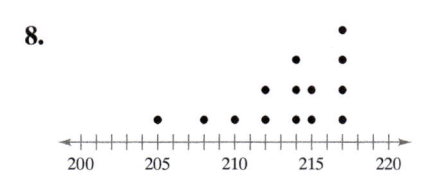

6. 6 | 7 8   Key: 6|7 = 67
    7 | 4 5 5 8 8 8
    8 | 1 3 5 5 8 8 9
    9 | 0 0 0 2 4

7. [dot plot from 5 to 40]

8. [dot plot from 200 to 220]

(a) Times (in minutes) it takes a sample of employees to drive to work
(b) Grade point averages of a sample of students with finance majors
(c) Top speeds (in miles per hour) of a sample of high-performance sports cars
(d) Ages (in years) of a sample of residents of a retirement home

Graphical Analysis *In Exercises 9–12, use the stem-and-leaf plot or dot plot to list the actual data entries. What is the maximum data entry? What is the minimum data entry?*

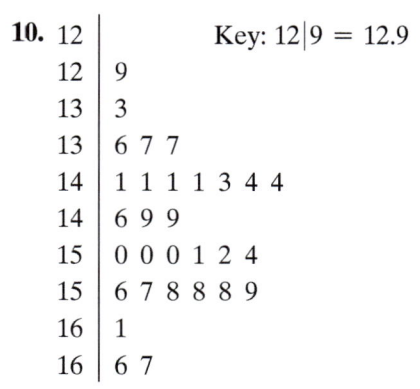

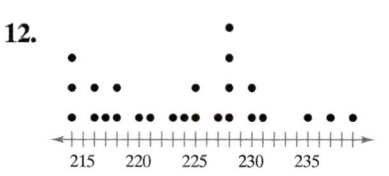

9. 2 | 7   Key: 2|7 = 27
    3 | 2
    4 | 1 3 3 4 7 7 8
    5 | 0 1 1 2 3 3 3 4 4 4 4 5 6 6 8 9
    6 | 8 8 8
    7 | 3 8 8
    8 | 5

10. 12 | Key: 12|9 = 12.9
    12 | 9
    13 | 3
    13 | 6 7 7
    14 | 1 1 1 1 3 4 4
    14 | 6 9 9
    15 | 0 0 0 1 2 4
    15 | 6 7 8 8 8 9
    16 | 1
    16 | 6 7

11. [dot plot from 13 to 19]

12. [dot plot from 215 to 235]

Using and Interpreting Concepts

Graphical Analysis *In Exercises 13–16, give three observations that can be made from the graph.*

13. Monthly Active Users on 5 Social Networking Sites as of September 2016

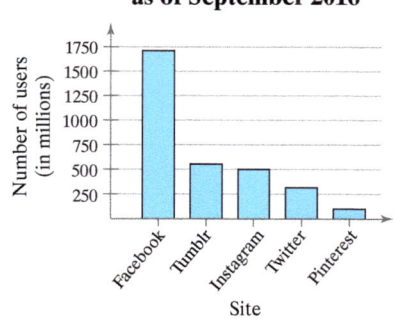

(Source: Statista)

14. Motor Vehicle Thefts at U.S. Universities and Colleges

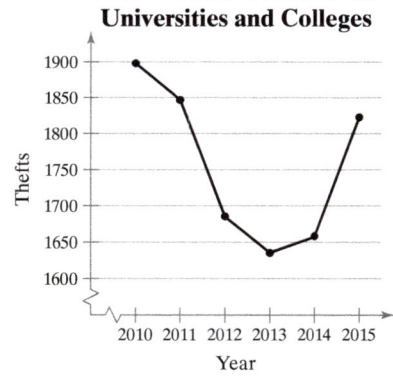

(Source: Federal Bureau of Investigation)

15. Least Popular American Drivers

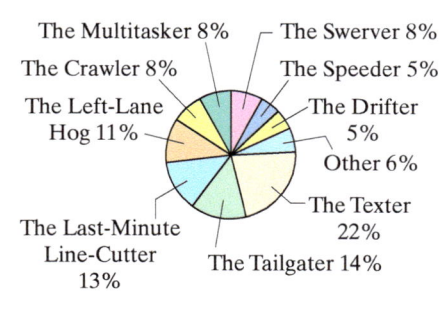

- The Multitasker 8%
- The Crawler 8%
- The Left-Lane Hog 11%
- The Last-Minute Line-Cutter 13%
- The Tailgater 14%
- The Texter 22%
- Other 6%
- The Drifter 5%
- The Speeder 5%
- The Swerver 8%

(Source: Expedia)

16. Amount Spent on Pet Care

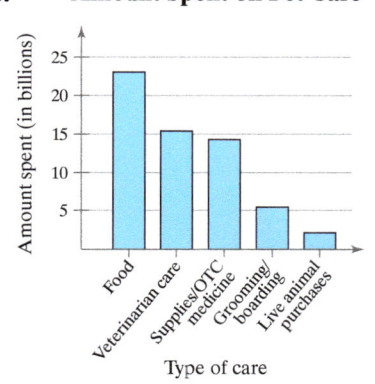

(Source: American Pet Products Association)

Graphing Data Sets *In Exercises 17–32, organize the data using the indicated type of graph. Describe any patterns.*

17. Humidity Use a stem-and-leaf plot to display the data, which represent the humidity (in percentages) in the atmosphere as measured in 20 different days in a city.

20.8 20.5 21.0 21.3 18.6 20.8 19.6 19.4 19.2 21.5
22.6 21.8 22.5 22.8 20.1 21.6 21.4 20.8 19.6 19.9

18. Studying Use a stem-and-leaf plot to display the data, which represent the numbers of hours 24 students study per week.

20 24 25 18 15 16 23 11 18 29 35 42
16 18 23 19 28 26 24 21 32 25 30 17

19. Runs scored Use a stem-and-leaf plot to display the data, which represent the runs scored by a batsman in a World Cup series.

70 75 71 73 78 70 90 91 94 85 87 99
75 88 86 82 78 79 81 77 90 73 91 98

20. Drunk Driving Use a stem-and-leaf plot to display the data shown in the table at the left, which represent the drunk driving cases registered at 30 strategic road intersections.

Drunk Driving Cases

30	32	28	36	25
40	28	27	25	10
19	16	36	42	41
28	26	11	13	15
23	17	32	31	30
18	34	28	22	20

TABLE FOR EXERCISE 20

21. **Highest-Paid Tech CEOs** Use a stem-and-leaf plot that has two rows for each stem to display the data, which represent the incomes (in millions) of the top 30 highest-paid tech CEOs. *(Source: Business Insider)*

   41 17 33 25 28 28 32 20 16 22 19 15 19
   14 13 25 14 41 20 19 20 33 25 20 22 18
   19 15 13 14

22. **Salaries** The salaries (in thousand dollars) of a sample of 10 employees

   225 410 368 310 228 298 361 159 486 296

23. **Blood Glucose Levels** Use a dot plot to display the data, which represent the blood glucose levels (in milligrams per deciliter) of 24 patients at a pathology laboratory.

   68 73 75 82 91 96 99 65 71 62 83 87
   101 94 82 96 100 78 73 78 94 63 85 97

24. **Weights of Adult Polar Bears** Use a dot plot to display the data, which represent the weights (in kilograms) of 20 polar bears.

   426 428 436 545 510 386 480 485 486 399
   525 501 425 442 369 510 525 408 399 403

25. **Student Loans** Use a pie chart to display the data, which represent the numbers of student loan borrowers (in millions) by balance owed in the fourth quarter of 2015. *(Source: Federal Reserve Bank of New York)*

$1 to $10,000	16.7	$10,001 to $25,000	12.4
$25,001 to $50,000	8.3	$50,001+	6.7

26. **New York City Marathon** Use a pie chart to display the data, which represent the number of men's New York City Marathon winners from each country through 2016. *(Source: New York Road Runners)*

United States	15	Tanzania	1	Great Britain	1
Italy	4	Kenya	12	Brazil	2
Ethiopia	2	Mexico	4	New Zealand	1
South Africa	2	Morocco	1	Eritrea	1

27. **FIFA World Cup** The five countries that have won the FIFA World cup more than once include Uruguay (2), Italy (4), Germany (4), Brazil (5), and Argentina (2). Use a Pareto chart to display the data. *(Source: FIFA)*

28. **Vehicle Costs** The average owning and operating costs for four types of vehicles in the United States in 2016 include small sedans ($6579), medium sedans ($8604), SUVs ($10,255), and minivans ($9262). Use a Pareto chart to display the data. *(Source: American Automobile Association)*

29. **Hourly Fees** Use a scatter plot to display the data shown in the table at the left. The data represent the numbers of coaching hours and the hourly fees (in dollars) of 12 cricket coaches.

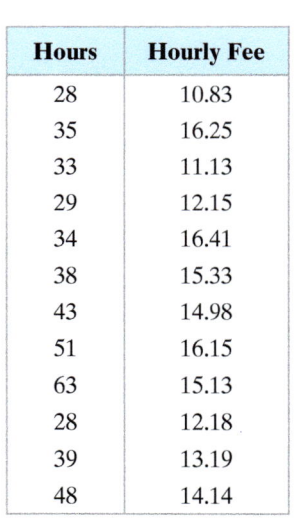

Hours	Hourly Fee
28	10.83
35	16.25
33	11.13
29	12.15
34	16.41
38	15.33
43	14.98
51	16.15
63	15.13
28	12.18
39	13.19
48	14.14

TABLE FOR EXERCISE 29

Hours	Hourly Fee
28	10.83
35	16.25
33	11.13
29	12.15
34	16.41
38	15.33
43	14.98
51	16.15
63	15.13
28	12.18
39	13.19
48	14.14

TABLE FOR EXERCISE 30

30. **Hourly Fees** Use a scatter plot to display the data shown in the table at the left. The data represent the numbers of coaching hours and the hourly fees (in dollars) of 12 cricket coaches.

31. **Engineering Degrees** Use a time series chart to display the data shown in the table. The data represent the numbers of bachelor's degrees in engineering (in thousands) conferred in the U.S. *(Source: American Society for Engineering Education)*

Year	2008	2009	2010	2011	2012	2013	2014	2015
Degrees	74.2	74.4	78.3	83.0	88.2	93.4	99.2	106.7

32. **Tourism** Use a time series chart to display the data shown in the table. The data represent the percentages of Egypt's gross domestic product (GDP) that come from the travel and tourism sector. *(Source: Knoema)*

Year	2005	2006	2007	2008	2009	2010
Percent	19.1%	19.0%	19.5%	19.0%	17.1%	16.7%

Year	2011	2012	2013	2014	2015	2016
Percent	12.8%	12.1%	9.2%	9.2%	8.6%	7.2%

33. **Basketball** Display the data below in a stem-and-leaf plot. Describe the differences in how the dot plot and the stem-and-leaf plot show patterns in the data.

Heights of Players on a College Basketball Team

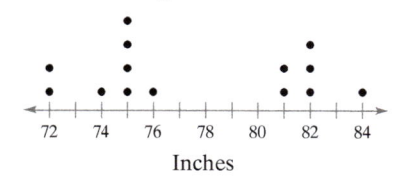

(dot plot showing heights in inches from 72 to 84)

34. **Phone Screen Sizes** Display the data below in a dot plot. Describe the differences in how the stem-and-leaf plot and the dot plot show patterns in the data.

Phone Screen Sizes (in inches)

```
5 | 0 0          Key: 5|0 = 5.0
5 | 5 5 5 6 7 8 8 9
6 | 0 0 0 1 2 3 4 4
6 | 5 5 6 8 8 9
7 | 0
7 |
```

35. **Favorite Season** Display the data below in a Pareto chart. Describe the differences in how the pie chart and the Pareto chart show patterns in the data. *(Source: Ipsos Public Affairs)*

Favorite Season of U.S. Adults Ages 18 and Older

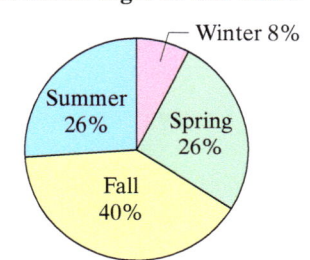

Winter 8%, Summer 26%, Spring 26%, Fall 40%

36. **Favorite Day of the Week** Display the data below in a pie chart. Describe the differences in how the Pareto chart and the pie chart show patterns in the data.

Favorite Day of the Week

(Pareto chart: Fri. 15, Sat. 14, Sun. 12, Thu. 4, Wed. 3, Tues. 1, Mon. 1)

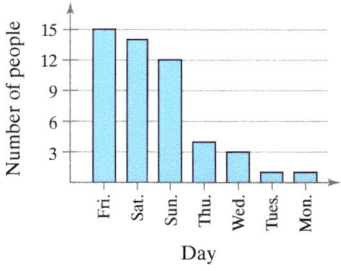

Extending Concepts

A Misleading Graph? *A misleading graph is not drawn appropriately, which can misrepresent data and lead to false conclusions. In Exercises 37–40, (a) explain why the graph is misleading, and (b) redraw the graph so that it is not misleading.*

37. Sales for Company A

38. Results of a Survey

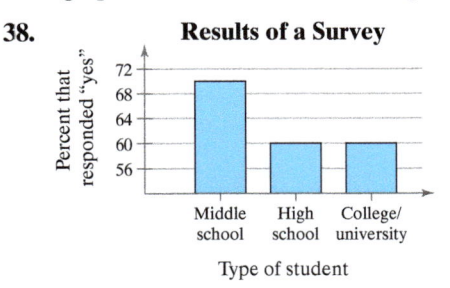

39. Sales for Company B
- 1st quarter 38%
- 2nd quarter 4%
- 3rd quarter 38%
- 4th quarter 20%

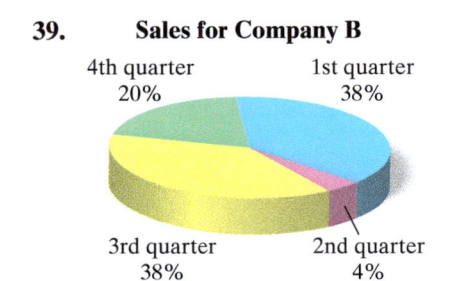

40. U.S. Crude Oil Imports by Country of Origin, January–August 2016

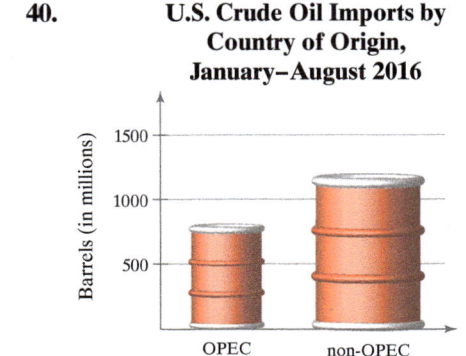

(Source: U.S. Energy Information Administration)

Law Firm A		Law Firm B
5 0	9	0 3
8 5 2 2 2	10	5 7
9 9 7 0 0	11	0 0 5
1 1	12	0 3 3 5
	13	2 2 5 9
	14	1 3 3 3 9
	15	5 5 5 6
	16	4 9 9
9 9 5 1 0	17	1 2 5
5 5 5 2 1	18	9
9 9 8 7 5	19	0
3	20	

Key: 5|19|0 = $195,000 for Law Firm A and $190,000 for Law Firm B

FIGURE FOR EXERCISE 41

41. Law Firm Salaries A **back-to-back stem-and-leaf plot** compares two data sets by using the same stems for each data set. Leaves for the first data set are on one side while leaves for the second data set are on the other side. The back-to-back stem-and-leaf plot at the left shows the salaries (in thousands of dollars) of all lawyers at two small law firms.

(a) What are the lowest and highest salaries at Law Firm A? at Law Firm B? How many lawyers are in each firm?

(b) Compare the distribution of salaries at each law firm. What do you notice?

42. Yoga Classes The data sets at the left show the ages of all participants in two yoga classes.

(a) Make a back-to-back stem-and-leaf plot as described in Exercise 41 to display the data.

(b) What are the lowest and highest ages of participants in the 3:00 P.M. class? in the 8:00 P.M. class? How many participants are in each class?

(c) Compare the distribution of ages in each class. What observation(s) can you make?

3:00 P.M. Class				8:00 P.M. Class			
40	60	73	77	19	18	20	29
51	68	68	35	39	43	71	56
68	53	64	75	44	44	18	19
76	69	59	55	19	18	18	20
38	57	68	84	25	29	25	22
75	62	73	75	31	24	24	23
85	77			19	19	18	28
				20	31		

TABLE FOR EXERCISE 42

43. Choosing an Appropriate Display Use technology to create (a) a stem-and-leaf plot, (b) a dot plot, (c) a pie chart, (d) a frequency histogram, and (e) an ogive for the data. Which graph displays the data best? Explain.

64 46 40 55 70 31 47 44 55 63
49 49 26 72 64 55 44 71 45 72

2.3 Measures of Central Tendency

What You Should Learn

▶ How to find the mean, median, and mode of a population and of a sample

▶ How to find a weighted mean of a data set, and how to estimate the sample mean of grouped data

▶ How to describe the shape of a distribution as symmetric, uniform, or skewed, and how to compare the mean and median for each

Mean, Median, and Mode ■ Weighted Mean and Mean of Grouped Data
■ The Shapes of Distributions

Mean, Median, and Mode

In Sections 2.1 and 2.2, you learned about the graphical representations of quantitative data. In Sections 2.3 and 2.4, you will learn how to supplement graphical representations with numerical statistics that describe the center and variability of a data set.

A **measure of central tendency** is a value that represents a typical, or central, entry of a data set. The three most commonly used measures of central tendency are the **mean,** the **median,** and the **mode.**

DEFINITION

The **mean** of a data set is the sum of the data entries divided by the number of entries. To find the mean of a data set, use one of these formulas.

$$\text{Population Mean: } \mu = \frac{\Sigma x}{N}$$

$$\text{Sample Mean: } \bar{x} = \frac{\Sigma x}{n}$$

The lowercase Greek letter μ (pronounced mu) represents the population mean and $\bar{x}$ (read as "x bar") represents the sample mean. Note that N represents the number of entries in a *population* and n represents the number of entries in a *sample*. Recall that the uppercase Greek letter sigma (Σ) indicates a summation of values.

EXAMPLE 1

Finding a Sample Mean

The weights (in pounds) for a sample of adults before starting a weight-loss study are listed. What is the mean weight of the adults?

274   235   223   268   290   285   235

SOLUTION The sum of the weights is

$$\Sigma x = 274 + 235 + 223 + 268 + 290 + 285 + 235 = 1810.$$

There are 7 adults in the sample, so $n = 7$. To find the mean weight, divide the sum of the weights by the number of adults in the sample.

$$\bar{x} = \frac{\Sigma x}{n} = \frac{1810}{7} \approx 258.6.$$ Round the last calculation to one more decimal place than the original data.

So, the mean weight of the adults is about 258.6 pounds.

TRY IT YOURSELF 1

Find the mean of the points scored by the 51 winning teams listed on page 41.

Answer: Page A7

Study Tip

Notice that the mean in Example 1 has one more decimal place than the original set of data entries. When the mean needs to be rounded, this *round-off rule* will be used in the text. Another important *round-off rule* is that rounding should not be done until the last calculation.

DEFINITION

The **median** of a data set is the value that lies in the middle of the data when the data set is ordered. The median measures the center of an ordered data set by dividing it into two equal parts. When the data set has an odd number of entries, the median is the middle data entry. When the data set has an even number of entries, the median is the mean of the two middle data entries.

Tech Tip

You can use technology such as Minitab, Excel, StatCrunch, or the TI-84 Plus to find the mean and median of a data set. For instance, to find the mean and median of the weights listed in Example 1 on a TI-84 Plus, enter the data in L1. Next, press [2nd] LIST and from the MATH menu choose *mean*. Then press [2nd] LIST and from the MATH menu choose *median*.

```
TI-84 PLUS
mean(L1)
         258.5714286
median(L1)
                 268
```

EXAMPLE 2

Finding the Median

Find the median of the weights listed in Example 1.

SOLUTION   To find the median weight, first order the data.

   223   235   235   268   274   285   290

Because there are seven entries (an odd number), the median is the middle, or fourth, entry. So, the median weight is 268 pounds.

TRY IT YOURSELF 2

Find the median of the points scored by the 51 winning teams listed on page 41.

Answer: Page A7

In a data set, the number of data entries above the median is the same as the number below the median. For instance, in Example 2, three of the weights are below 268 pounds and three are above 268 pounds.

EXAMPLE 3

Finding the Median

In Example 2, the adult weighing 285 pounds decides to not participate in the study. What is the median weight of the remaining adults?

SOLUTION   The remaining weights, in order, are

   223   235   235   268   274   290.

Because there are six entries (an even number), the median is the mean of the two middle entries.

$$\text{Median} = \frac{235 + 268}{2} = 251.5$$

So, the median weight of the remaining adults is 251.5 pounds. You can check your answer using technology, as shown below using Excel.

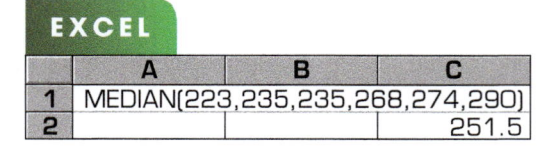

	A	B	C
1	MEDIAN(223,235,235,268,274,290)		
2			251.5

TRY IT YOURSELF 3

The points scored by the winning teams in the Super Bowls for the National Football League's 2001 through 2016 seasons are listed. Find the median.

   20   48   32   24   21   29   17   27
   31   31   21   34   43   28   24   34

Answer: Page A7

DEFINITION

The **mode** of a data set is the data entry that occurs with the greatest frequency. A data set can have one mode, more than one mode, or no mode. When no entry is repeated, the data set has no mode. When two entries occur with the same greatest frequency, each entry is a mode and the data set is called **bimodal.**

EXAMPLE 4

Finding the Mode

Find the mode of the weights listed in Example 1.

SOLUTION

To find the mode, first order the data.

   223   235   235   268   274   285   290

From the ordered data, you can see that the entry 235 occurs twice, whereas the other data entries occur only once. So, the mode of the weights is 235 pounds.

TRY IT YOURSELF 4

Find the mode of the points scored by the 51 winning teams listed on page 41.
Answer: Page A7

EXAMPLE 5

Finding the Mode

At a political debate, a sample of audience members were asked to name the political party to which they belonged. Their responses are shown in the table. What is the mode of the responses?

Political party	Frequency, f
Democrat	46
Republican	34
Independent	39
Other/don't know	5

SOLUTION

The response occurring with the greatest frequency is Democrat. So, the mode is Democrat.

Interpretation   In this sample, there were more Democrats than people of any other single affiliation.

TRY IT YOURSELF 5

In a survey, 1534 adults were asked, "How much do you, personally, care about the issue of global climate change?" Of those surveyed, 550 said "a great deal," 578 said "some," 274 said "not too much," 119 said "not at all," and 13 did not provide an answer. What is the mode of the responses? *(Adapted from Pew Research Center)*
Answer: Page A7

The mode is the only measure of central tendency that can be used to describe data at the nominal level of measurement. But when working with quantitative data, the mode is rarely used.

Although the mean, the median, and the mode each describe a typical entry of a data set, there are advantages and disadvantages of using each. The mean is a reliable measure because it takes into account every entry of a data set. The mean can be greatly affected, however, when the data set contains **outliers.**

DEFINITION

An **outlier** is a data entry that is far removed from the other entries in the data set. (You will learn a formal way for determining an outlier in Section 2.5.)

While some outliers are valid data, other outliers may occur due to data-recording errors. A data set can have one or more outliers, causing **gaps** in a distribution. Conclusions that are drawn from a data set that contains outliers may be flawed.

Ages in a class						
20	20	20	20	20	20	21
21	21	21	22	22	22	23
23	23	23	24	24	65	

EXAMPLE 6

Comparing the Mean, the Median, and the Mode

The table at the left shows the sample ages of students in a class. Find the mean, median, and mode of the ages. Are there any outliers? Which measure of central tendency best describes a typical entry of this data set?

SOLUTION

From the histogram below, it appears that the data entry 65 is an outlier because it is far removed from the other ages in the class.

Mean: $\bar{x} = \dfrac{\Sigma x}{n} = \dfrac{475}{20} \approx 23.8$ years

Median: Median $= \dfrac{21 + 22}{2} = 21.5$ years

Mode: The entry occurring with the greatest frequency is 20 years.

Interpretation The mean takes every entry into account but is influenced by the outlier of 65. The median also takes every entry into account, and it is not affected by the outlier. In this case the mode exists, but it does not appear to represent a typical entry. Sometimes a graphical comparison can help you decide which measure of central tendency best represents a data set. The histogram shows the distribution of the data and the locations of the mean, the median, and the mode. In this case, it appears that the median best describes the data set.

Picturing the World

The National Association of Realtors keeps track of existing-home sales. One list uses the *median* price of existing homes sold and another uses the *mean* price of existing homes sold. The sales for the third quarter of 2016 are shown in the double-bar graph. (Source: National Association of Realtors)

2016 U.S. Existing-Home Sales

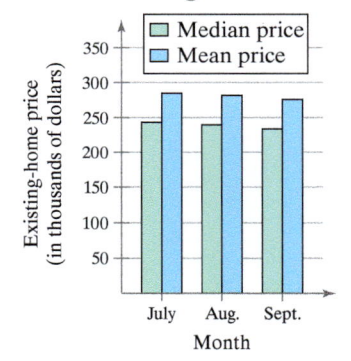

Notice in the graph that each month, the mean price is about $42,000 more than the median price. Identify a factor that would cause the mean price to be greater than the median price.

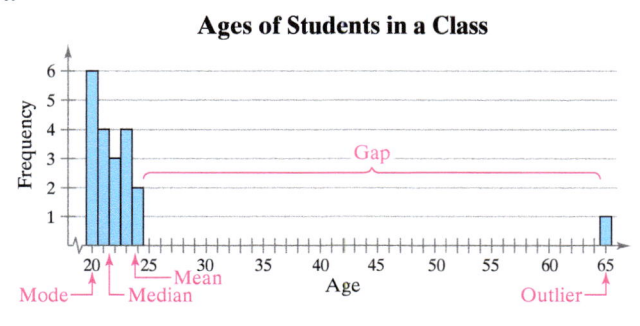

TRY IT YOURSELF 6

Remove the data entry 65 from the data set in Example 6. Then rework the example. How does the absence of this outlier change each of the measures?

Answer: Page A7

Weighted Mean and Mean of Grouped Data

Sometimes data sets contain entries that have a greater effect on the mean than do other entries. To find the mean of such a data set, you must find the **weighted mean**.

> **DEFINITION**
>
> A **weighted mean** is the mean of a data set whose entries have varying weights. The weighted mean is given by
>
> $$\bar{x} = \frac{\Sigma xw}{\Sigma w} \quad \frac{\text{Sum of the products of the entries and the weights}}{\text{Sum of the weights}}$$
>
> where w is the weight of each entry x.

Tech Tip

You can use technology such as Minitab, Excel, StatCrunch, or the TI-84 Plus to find the weighted mean. For instance, to find the weighted mean in Example 7 on a TI-84 Plus, enter the points in L1 and the credit hours in L2. Then, use the *1-Var Stats* feature with L1 as the list and L2 as the frequency list to calculate the mean (and other statistics), as shown below.

TI-84 PLUS

```
        1-Var Stats
x̄=2.5  ← Mean
Σx=40
Σx²=112
Sx=.894427191
σx=.8660254038
↓n=16
```

EXAMPLE 7

Finding a Weighted Mean

Your grades from last semester are in the table. The grading system assigns points as follows: A = 4, B = 3, C = 2, D = 1, F = 0. Determine your grade point average (weighted mean).

Final Grade	Credit Hours
C	3
C	4
D	1
A	3
C	2
B	3

SOLUTION

Let x be the points assigned to the letter grade and w be the credit hours. You can organize the points and hours in a table.

Points, x	Credit hours, w	xw
2	3	6
2	4	8
1	1	1
4	3	12
2	2	4
3	3	9
	$\Sigma w = 16$	$\Sigma(x \cdot w) = 40$

$$\bar{x} = \frac{\Sigma xw}{\Sigma w} = \frac{40}{16} = 2.5$$

Last semester, your grade point average was 2.5.

TRY IT YOURSELF 7

In Example 7, your grade in the two-credit course is changed to a B. What is your new weighted mean?

Answer: Page A7

Study Tip

For a frequency distribution that represents a population, the mean of the frequency distribution is estimated by

$$\mu = \frac{\Sigma xf}{N}$$

where $N = \Sigma f$.

For data presented in a frequency distribution, you can estimate the mean as shown in the next definition.

DEFINITION

The **mean of a frequency distribution** for a sample is estimated by

$$\bar{x} = \frac{\Sigma xf}{n} \qquad \text{Note that } n = \Sigma f.$$

where x and f are the midpoint and frequency of each class, respectively.

GUIDELINES

Finding the Mean of a Frequency Distribution

In Words	In Symbols
1. Find the midpoint of each class.	$x = \dfrac{(\text{Lower limit}) + (\text{Upper limit})}{2}$
2. Find the sum of the products of the midpoints and the frequencies.	Σxf
3. Find the sum of the frequencies.	$n = \Sigma f$
4. Find the mean of the frequency distribution.	$\bar{x} = \dfrac{\Sigma xf}{n}$

EXAMPLE 8

Finding the Mean of a Frequency Distribution

The frequency distribution at the left shows the out-of-pocket prescription medicine expenses (in dollars) for 30 U.S. adults in a recent year. Use the frequency distribution to estimate the mean expense. Using the sample mean formula from page 69 with the original data set (see Example 1 in Section 2.1), the mean expense is $285.50. Compare this with the estimated mean.

Class midpoint, x	Frequency, f	xf
172.5	3	517.5
208.5	2	417.0
244.5	5	1222.5
280.5	6	1683.0
316.5	7	2215.5
352.5	4	1410.0
388.5	3	1165.5
	$n = 30$	$\Sigma = 8631$

SOLUTION

$$\bar{x} = \frac{\Sigma xf}{n}$$

$$= \frac{8631}{30}$$

$$= 287.7$$

Interpretation The mean expense is $287.70. This value is an estimate because it is based on class midpoints instead of the original data set. Although it is not substantially different, the mean of $285.50 found using the original data set is a more accurate result.

TRY IT YOURSELF 8

Use a frequency distribution to estimate the mean of the points scored by the 51 winning teams listed on page 41. (See Try It Yourself 2 on page 45.) Using the population mean formula from page 69 with the original data set, the mean is about 30.2 points. Compare this with the estimated mean.

Answer: Page A7

Descriptive Statistics 75

The Shapes of Distributions

A graph reveals several characteristics of a frequency distribution. One such characteristic is the shape of the distribution.

> **DEFINITION**
>
> A frequency distribution is **symmetric** when a vertical line can be drawn through the middle of a graph of the distribution and the resulting halves are approximately mirror images.
>
> A frequency distribution is **uniform** (or **rectangular**) when all entries, or classes, in the distribution have equal or approximately equal frequencies. A uniform distribution is also symmetric.
>
> A frequency distribution is skewed when the "tail" of the graph elongates more to one side than to the other. A distribution is **skewed left (negatively skewed)** when its tail extends to the left. A distribution is **skewed right (positively skewed)** when its tail extends to the right.

Study Tip

The graph of a symmetric distribution is not always bell-shaped (see below). Some of the other possible shapes for the graph of a symmetric distribution are U-, M-, or W-shaped.

2.3 To explore this topic further, see **Activity 2.3** on page 83.

When a distribution is symmetric and unimodal, the mean, median, and mode are equal. When a distribution is skewed left, the mean is less than the median and the median is usually less than the mode. When a distribution is skewed right, the mean is greater than the median and the median is usually greater than the mode. Examples of these commonly occurring distributions are shown.

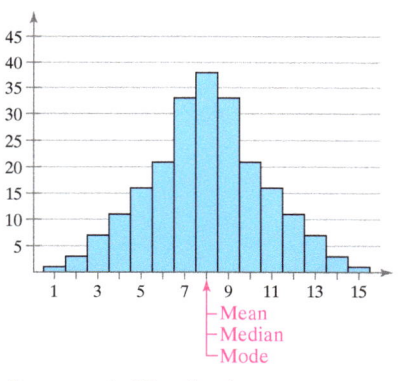

Symmetric Distribution

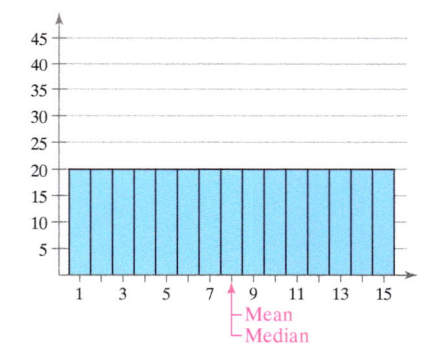

Uniform Distribution

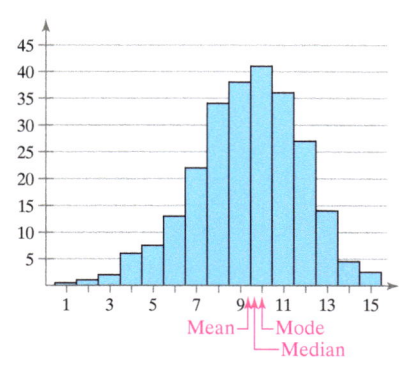

Study Tip

Be aware that there are many different shapes of distributions. In some cases, the shape cannot be classified as symmetric, uniform, or skewed. A distribution can have several gaps caused by outliers or *clusters* of data. Clusters may occur when several types of data entries are used in a data set. For instance, a data set of gas mileages for trucks (which get low gas mileage) and hybrid cars (which get high gas mileage) would have two clusters.

Skewed Left Distribution

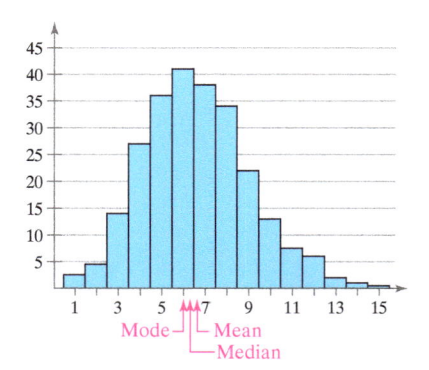

Skewed Right Distribution

The mean will always fall in the direction in which the distribution is skewed. For instance, when a distribution is skewed left, the mean is to the left of the median.

2.3 EXERCISES

For Extra Help: **MyLab Statistics**

Building Basic Skills and Vocabulary

True or False? *In Exercises 1–4, determine whether the statement is true or false. If it is false, rewrite it as a true statement.*

1. The mean is the measure of central tendency most likely to be affected by an outlier.

2. Some quantitative data sets do not have medians.

3. A data set can have the same mean, median, and mode.

4. When each data class has the same frequency, the distribution is symmetric.

Constructing Data Sets *In Exercises 5–8, construct the described data set. The entries in the data set cannot all be the same.*

5. Median and mode are the same.

6. Mean and mode are the same.

7. Mean is *not* representative of a typical number in the data set.

8. Mean, median, and mode are the same.

Graphical Analysis *In Exercises 9–12, determine whether the approximate shape of the distribution in the histogram is symmetric, uniform, skewed left, skewed right, or none of these. Justify your answer.*

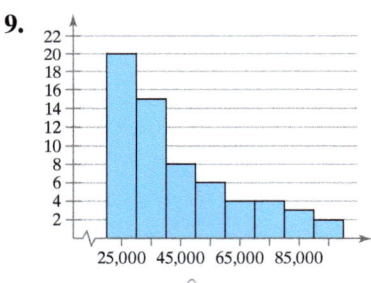

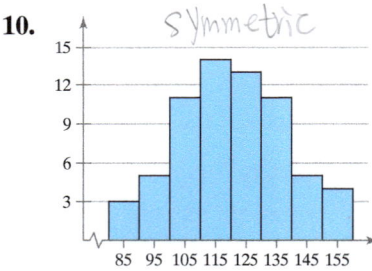

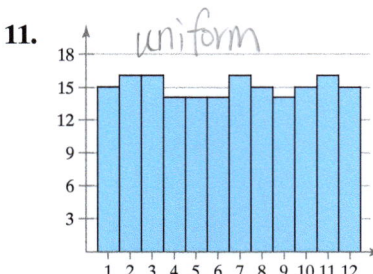

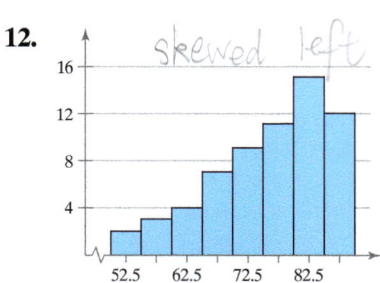

9.

10. symmetric

11. uniform

12. skewed left

Matching *In Exercises 13–16, match the distribution with one of the graphs in Exercises 9–12. Justify your decision.*

13. The frequency distribution of 180 rolls of a dodecagon (a 12-sided die) (11)

14. The frequency distribution of mileages of service vehicles at a business where a few vehicles have much higher mileages than the majority of vehicles

15. The frequency distribution of scores on a 90-point test where a few students scored much lower than the majority of students (12)

16. The frequency distribution of weights for a sample of seventh-grade boys

Using and Interpreting Concepts

Finding and Discussing the Mean, Median, and Mode *In Exercises 17–34, find the mean, the median, and the mode of the data, if possible. If any measure cannot be found or does not represent the center of the data, explain why.*

17. Subject Scores The English scores for a sample of 14 students

26 24 26 24 29 25 28
27 21 23 26 23 21 24

18. Salaries The salaries (in thousand dollars) of a sample of 10 employees

225 410 368 310 228 298 361 159 486 296

19. Idle Times The durations (in minutes) of idle times at a factory in the last 10 months

18 32 28 34 46 62 38
22 64 42 22 34 68 12
54 28 18 60 28 50 28

20. Leaders The ages (in completed years) of the youngest leaders at the time of assuming office *(Source: NinjaJournalist)*

33 37 37 39 39 41 43 43 44 45

21. Tuition The 2016–2017 tuition and fees (in thousands of dollars) for the top 14 universities in the U.S. *(Source: U.S. News & World Report)*

45 47 52 49 55 48 48
51 51 50 51 48 51 51

22. Cholesterol The cholesterol levels of a sample of 10 female employees

154 240 171 188 235 203 184 173 181 275

23. Ports of Entry The maximum numbers of passenger vehicle lanes at 16 Canadian border ports of entry *(Source: U.S. Customs and Border Protection)*

8 6 10 3 6 11 17 2
2 6 1 10 3 19 10 5

24. Power Failures The durations (in minutes) of power failures at a residence in the last 10 years

18 26 45 75 125 80 33
40 44 49 89 80 96 125
12 61 31 63 103 28 19

25. Treatment of Depression The numbers of patients who responded to various combinations of electroconvulsive therapy, medication, and cognitive-behavioral therapy to treat acute depression over different time periods *(Source: Adapted from Bipolar Network News)*

42 15 8 9 13 6 7

26. Number One Movies The numbers of weeks the 33 leading movies remained at number 1 as of March 2018. *(Source: BoxOfficeMojo)*

15 7 8 6 14 5 14 4 5 4 11 8
7 4 12 6 10 9 4 5 5 5 14 5
4 4 5 9 6 5 4 6 5

How purchases are made	Frequency, f
Research online and in store, buy in store	1173
Search and buy online	2238
Search and buy in store	1066
Research online and in store, buy online	853

TABLE FOR EXERCISE 27

Small Businesses

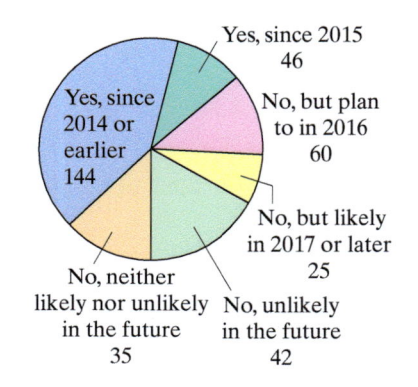

Pie chart data:
- Yes, since 2014 or earlier: 144
- Yes, since 2015: 46
- No, but plan to in 2016: 60
- No, but likely in 2017 or later: 25
- No, unlikely in the future: 42
- No, neither likely nor unlikely in the future: 35

FIGURE FOR EXERCISE 30

27. Online Shopping The responses of a sample of 5330 shoppers who were asked how their purchases are made are shown in the table at the left. *(Adapted from UPS)*

28. Criminal Justice The responses of a sample of 34 young adult United Kingdom males in custodial sentences who were asked what is affected by such sentences *(Adapted from User Voice)*

Mental health: 8
Trust: 3
Education: 8
Personal development: 5
Family: 3
Future opportunities: 3
Other: 4

29. Class Level The class levels of 25 students in a physics course

Freshman: 2   Junior: 10
Sophomore: 5   Senior: 8

30. Small Business Websites The pie chart at the left shows the responses of a sample of 352 small-business owners who were asked whether their business has a website. *(Source: Clutch)*

31. Weights (in pounds) of Packages on a Delivery Truck

```
0 | 5 8                Key: 3|0 = 30
1 | 0 1 3 6
2 | 1 3 3 3 6 7 7
3 | 0 1 2 4 4 4 5 7 8
4 | 3 4 5 6 9
5 | 2
```

32. Grade Point Averages of Students in a Class

```
0 | 8                  Key: 0|8 = 0.8
1 | 5 6 8
2 | 1 3 4 5
3 | 0 9
4 | 0 0
```

33. Times (in minutes) It Takes Employees to Drive to Work

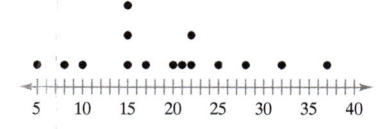

Dot plot on scale 5, 10, 15, 20, 25, 30, 35, 40

34. Prices (in dollars) of Flights from Chicago to Atlanta

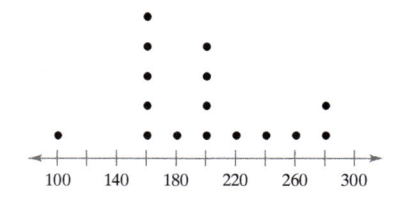

Dot plot on scale 100, 140, 180, 220, 260, 300

Graphical Analysis In Exercises 35 and 36, identify any clusters, gaps, or outliers.

35. Model Year 2017 Ethanol Flexible Fuel Vehicles

Histogram with Driving range (in miles) on x-axis (250, 300, 350, 400, 450, 500, 550, 600) and Frequency on y-axis (4, 8, 12, 16, 20)

(Source: United States Environmental Protection Agency)

36. Model Year 2017 Hybrid Electric Cars

Histogram with Annual fuel cost (in dollars) on x-axis (600, 900, 1200, 1500, 1800, 2100, 2400, 2700, 3000) and Frequency on y-axis (1–8)

(Source: Based on United States Environmental Protection Agency)

In Exercises 37–40, without performing any calculations, determine which measure of central tendency best represents the graphed data. Explain your reasoning.

37. How Often Do You Change Jobs?

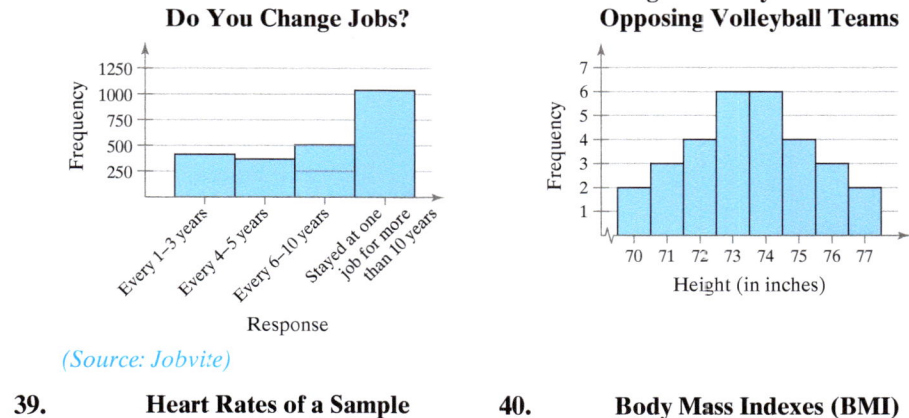

(Source: Jobvite)

38. Heights of Players on Two Opposing Volleyball Teams

39. Heart Rates of a Sample of Adults

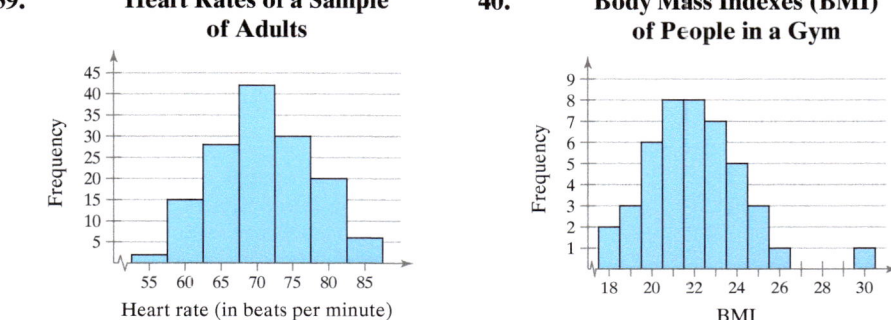

40. Body Mass Indexes (BMI) of People in a Gym

Finding a Weighted Mean *In Exercises 41–46, find the weighted mean of the data.*

41. Final Grade The scores and their percents of the final grade for a biology student are shown below. What is the student's mean score?

	Score	Percent of Final Grade
Assignment	75	10%
Class Participation	60	25%
Practical	90	25%
Theory Exam	85	40%

42. Final Grade The scores and their percents of the final grade for a statistics student are shown below. What is the student's mean score?

	Score	Percent of Final Grade
Assignment	75	10%
Class Participation	60	25%
Practical	90	25%
Theory Exam	85	40%

43. Account Balance For the month of April, a checking account has a balance of $523 for 24 days, $2415 for 2 days, and $250 for 4 days. What is the account's mean daily balance for April?

44. Credit Card Balance For the month of October, a credit card has a balance of $115.63 for 12 days, $637.19 for 6 days, $1225.06 for 7 days, $0 for 2 days, and $34.88 for 4 days. What is the account's mean daily balance for October?

45. Scores The mean scores for students in a statistics course (by major) are shown below. What is the mean score for the class?

9 engineering majors: 85   5 math majors: 90   13 business majors: 81

46. Grades A student receives the grades shown below, with an A worth 4 points, a B worth 3 points, a C worth 2 points, and a D worth 1 point. What is the student's grade point average?

A in 1 four-credit class   C in 1 three-credit class
B in 2 three-credit classes D in 1 two-credit class

47. Final Grade In Exercise 41, an error was made in grading your practical. Instead of getting 90, you scored 100. What is your new weighted mean?

48. Grades In Exercise 46, one of the student's B grades gets changed to an A. What is the student's new grade point average?

Finding the Mean of a Frequency Distribution *In Exercises 49–52, approximate the mean of the frequency distribution.*

49. Car Speeds The optimum speeds (in kilometers per hour) for 30 hatchbacks

Car Speeds (in kilometers per hour)	Frequency
20–24	15
25–29	8
30–34	4
35–39	3

50. Car Speeds The optimum speeds (in kilometers per hour) for 30 hatchbacks

Car Speeds (in kilometers per hour)	Frequency
20–24	8
25–29	16
30–34	5
35–39	1

51. Ages The ages (in years) of the residents of a small town in 2012

Age (in years)	Frequency
0–9	40
10–19	72
20–29	78
30–39	90
40–49	84
50–59	42
60–69	31
70–79	22
80–89	18
90–99	4

52. Populations The populations (in thousands) of the parishes of Louisiana in 2015 *(Source: U.S. Census Bureau)*

Population (in thousands)	Frequency
0–49	41
50–99	9
100–149	6
150–199	2
200–249	1
250–299	2
300–349	0
350–399	1
400–449	2

Identifying the Shape of a Distribution *In Exercises 53–56, construct a frequency distribution and a frequency histogram for the data set using the indicated number of classes. Describe the shape of the histogram as symmetric, uniform, negatively skewed, positively skewed, or none of these.*

53. Hospital Beds
Number of classes: 5
Data set: The number of beds in a sample of 20 hospitals

167 162 127 130 180 160 167 221 145 137
194 207 150 254 262 244 297 137 204 180

54. Emergency Room
Number of classes: 6
Data set: The numbers of patients visiting an emergency room per day over a two-week period

    256 317 237 182 382 106 162
    112 162 264 104 194 236 227

55. Weights of Females
Number of classes: 5
Data set: The weights (to the nearest kilograms) of 30 females

    46 48 40 58 56 60 42 43 49 52
    63 44 49 51 42 47 69 65 44 53
    50 51 47 41 64 62 54 49 70 68

56. Six-Sided Die
Number of classes: 6
Data set: The results of rolling a six-sided die 30 times

    1 4 6 1 5 3 2 5 4 6
    1 2 4 3 5 6 3 2 1 1
    5 6 2 4 4 3 1 6 2 4

57. Cement During a quality assurance check, the actual weights (in kilograms) of eight sacks of cement were recorded as 20.5, 19.4, 19.6, 18.0, 21.0, 20.2, 20.4, and 20.9.

(a) Find the mean and the median of the contents.

(b) The fifth value was incorrectly measured and is actually 20.0. Find the mean and the median of the contents again.

(c) Which measure of central tendency, the mean or the median, was affected more by the data entry error?

58. U.S. Trade Deficits The table at the left shows the U.S. trade deficits (in billions of dollars) with 18 countries in 2015. *(Source: U.S. Department of Commerce)*

(a) Find the mean and the median of the trade deficits.

(b) Find the mean and the median without the Chinese trade deficit. Which measure of central tendency, the mean or the median, was affected more by the elimination of the Chinese trade deficit?

(c) The Austrian trade deficit was $7.3 billion. Find the mean and the median with the Austrian trade deficit added to the original data set. Which measure of central tendency was affected more?

U.S. trade deficits (in billions of dollars)	
China: 367.2	Germany: 74.8
Japan: 68.9	Mexico: 60.7
Vietnam: 30.9	Ireland: 30.4
South Korea: 28.3	Italy: 28.0
India: 23.3	Malaysia: 21.7
France: 17.7	Thailand: 17.4
Canada: 15.5	Taiwan: 15.0
Indonesia: 12.5	Israel: 10.9
Russian Federation: 9.3	
Switzerland: 9.2	

TABLE FOR EXERCISE 58

Graphical Analysis *In Exercises 59 and 60, the letters A, B, and C are marked on the horizontal axis. Describe the shape of the data. Then determine which is the mean, which is the median, and which is the mode. Justify your answers.*

59. Sick Days Used by Employees

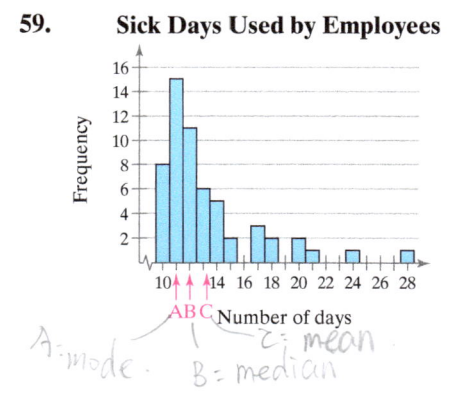

60. Hourly Wages of Employees

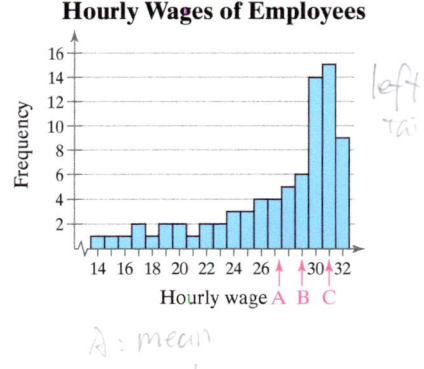

Extending Concepts

61. Writing In an academic year, a student receives the grades shown below, with an A worth 4 points, a B worth 3 points, and a C worth 2 points.

A in 2 four-credit classes and 3 three-credit classes
B in 2 three-credit classes and 2 two-credit classes
C in 1 two-credit class

The student can increase one of the Bs or Cs by one letter grade. Which one should the student choose? Explain your reasoning.

62. Golf The distances (in yards) for nine holes of a golf course are listed.

336 393 408 522 147 504 177 375 360

(a) Find the mean and the median of the data.
(b) Convert the distances to feet. Then rework part (a).
(c) Compare the measures you found in part (b) with those found in part (a). What do you notice?
(d) Use your results from part (c) to explain how to quickly find the mean and the median of the original data set when the distances are converted to inches.

63. Data Analysis A consumer testing service obtained the gas mileages (in miles per gallon) shown in the table at the left in five test runs performed with three types of compact cars.

(a) The manufacturer of Car A wants to advertise that its car performed best in this test. Which measure of central tendency—mean, median, or mode—should be used for its claim? Explain your reasoning.
(b) The manufacturer of Car B wants to advertise that its car performed best in this test. Which measure of central tendency—mean, median, or mode—should be used for its claim? Explain your reasoning.
(c) The manufacturer of Car C wants to advertise that its car performed best in this test. Which measure of central tendency—mean, median, or mode—should be used for its claim? Explain your reasoning.

64. Midrange Another measure of central tendency, which is rarely used, is the **midrange**. It can be found by using the formula

$$\text{Midrange} = \frac{(\text{Maximum data entry}) + (\text{Minimum data entry})}{2}.$$

Which of the manufacturers in Exercise 63 would prefer to use the midrange statistic in their ads? Explain your reasoning.

65. Data Analysis Students in an experimental psychology class did research on depression as a sign of stress. A test was administered to a sample of 30 students. The scores are shown in the table at the left.

(a) Find the mean and the median of the data.
(b) Draw a stem-and-leaf plot for the data using one row per stem. Locate the mean and the median on the display.
(c) Describe the shape of the distribution.

66. Trimmed Mean To find the 10% **trimmed mean** of a data set, order the data, delete the lowest 10% of the entries and the highest 10% of the entries, and find the mean of the remaining entries.

(a) Find the 10% trimmed mean for the data in Exercise 65.
(b) Compare the four measures of central tendency, including the midrange.
(c) What is the benefit of using a trimmed mean versus using a mean found using all data entries? Explain your reasoning.

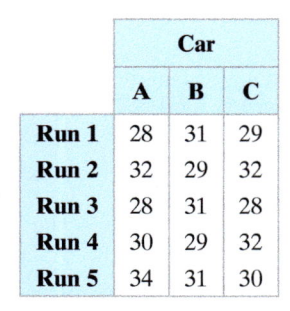

	Car		
	A	B	C
Run 1	28	31	29
Run 2	32	29	32
Run 3	28	31	28
Run 4	30	29	32
Run 5	34	31	30

TABLE FOR EXERCISE 63

Test scores							
44	51	11	90	76	36	64	37
43	72	53	62	36	74	51	72
37	28	38	61	47	63	36	41
22	37	51	46	85	13		

TABLE FOR EXERCISE 65

2.3 ACTIVITY — Mean Versus Median

The *mean versus median* applet is designed to allow you to investigate interactively the mean and the median as measures of the center of a data set. Points can be added to the plot by clicking the mouse above the horizontal axis. The mean of the points is shown as a green arrow and the median is shown as a red arrow. When the two values are the same, a single yellow arrow is displayed. Numeric values for the mean and the median are shown above the plot. Points on the plot can be removed by clicking on the point and then dragging the point into the trash can. All of the points on the plot can be removed by simply clicking inside the trash can. The range of values for the horizontal axis can be specified by inputting lower and upper limits and then clicking UPDATE.

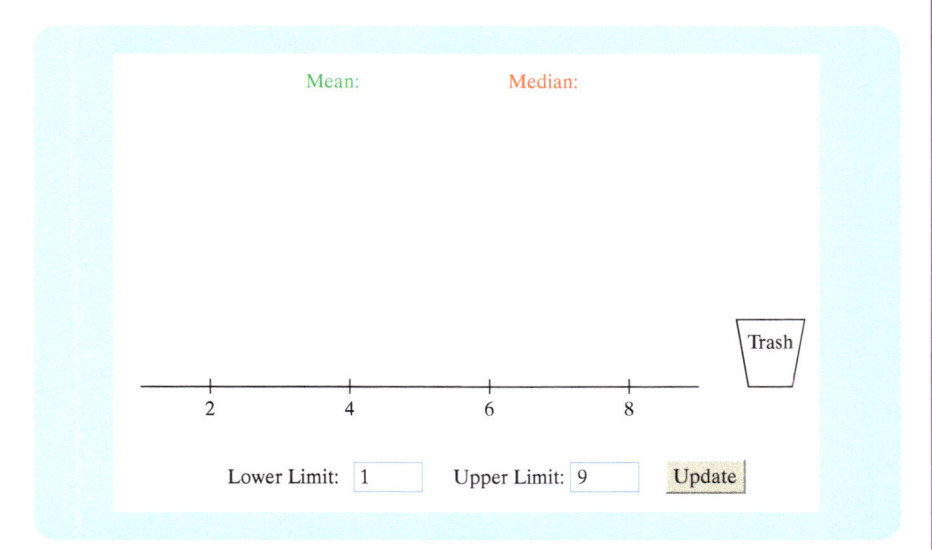

You can find the interactive applet for this activity within **MyLab Statistics** or at www.pearsonglobaleditions.com.

EXPLORE

Step 1 Specify a lower limit.
Step 2 Specify an upper limit.
Step 3 Add 15 points to the plot.
Step 4 Remove all of the points from the plot.

DRAW CONCLUSIONS

1. Specify the lower limit to be 1 and the upper limit to be 50. Add at least 10 points that range from 20 to 40 so that the mean and the median are the same. What is the shape of the distribution? What happens at first to the mean and the median when you add a few points that are less than 10? What happens over time as you continue to add points that are less than 10?

2. Specify the lower limit to be 0 and the upper limit to be 0.75. Place 10 points on the plot. Then change the upper limit to 25. Add 10 more points that are greater than 20 to the plot. Can the mean be any one of the points that were plotted? Can the median be any one of the points that were plotted? Explain.

2.4 Measures of Variation

What You Should Learn

▶ How to find the range of a data set
▶ How to find the variance and standard deviation of a population and of a sample
▶ How to use the Empirical Rule and Chebychev's Theorem to interpret standard deviation
▶ How to estimate the sample standard deviation for grouped data
▶ How to use the coefficient of variation to compare variation in different data sets

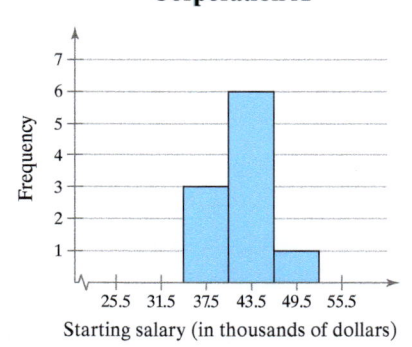

Range ■ Variance and Standard Deviation ■ Interpreting Standard Deviation ■ Standard Deviation for Grouped Data ■ Coefficient of Variation

Range

In this section, you will learn different ways to measure the variation (or spread) of a data set. The simplest measure is the **range** of the set.

DEFINITION

The **range** of a data set is the difference between the maximum and minimum data entries in the set. To find the range, the data must be quantitative.

Range = (Maximum data entry) − (Minimum data entry)

EXAMPLE 1

Finding the Range of a Data Set

Two corporations each hired 10 graduates. The starting salaries for each graduate are shown. Find the range of the starting salaries for Corporation A.

Starting Salaries for Corporation A (in thousands of dollars)

Salary	41	38	39	45	47	41	44	41	37	42

Starting Salaries for Corporation B (in thousands of dollars)

Salary	40	23	41	50	49	32	41	29	52	58

SOLUTION

Ordering the data helps to find the least and greatest salaries.

37   38   39   41   41   41   42   44   45   47

Minimum ⟵   ⟶ Maximum

Range = (Maximum salary) − (Minimum salary)
      = 47 − 37
      = 10

So, the range of the starting salaries for Corporation A is 10, or $10,000.

TRY IT YOURSELF 1

Find the range of the starting salaries for Corporation B. Compare the result to the one in Example 1.

Answer: Page A7

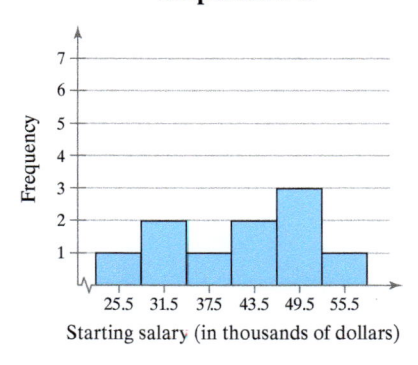

Both data sets in Example 1 have a mean of 41.5, or $41,500, a median of 41, or $41,000, and a mode of 41, or $41,000. And yet the two sets differ significantly. The difference is that the entries in the second set have greater variation. As you can see in the figures at the left, the starting salaries for Corporation B are more spread out than those for Corporation A.

Variance and Standard Deviation

As a measure of variation, the range has the advantage of being easy to compute. Its disadvantage, however, is that it uses only two entries from the data set. Two measures of variation that use all the entries in a data set are the *variance* and the *standard deviation*. Before you learn about these measures of variation, you need to know what is meant by the **deviation** of an entry in a data set.

> **DEFINITION**
>
> The **deviation** of an entry x in a population data set is the difference between the entry and the mean μ of the data set.
>
> Deviation of $x = x - \mu$

Deviations of Starting Salaries for Corporation A

Salary (in 1000s of dollars) x	Deviation (in 1000s of dollars) $x - \mu$
41	−0.5
38	−3.5
39	−2.5
45	3.5
47	5.5
41	−0.5
44	2.5
41	−0.5
37	−4.5
42	0.5
$\Sigma x = 415$	$\Sigma(x - \mu) = 0$

The sum of the deviations is 0.

Consider the starting salaries for Corporation A in Example 1. The mean starting salary is $\mu = 415/10 = 41.5$, or $41,500. The table at the left lists the deviation of each salary from the mean. For instance, the deviation of 41 is $41 - 41.5 = -0.5$. Notice that the sum of the deviations is 0. In fact, the sum of the deviations for *any* data set is 0. So, it does not make sense to find the average of the deviations. To overcome this problem, take the square of each deviation. The sum of the squares of the deviations, or **sum of squares**, is denoted by SS_x. In a population data set, the average of the squares of the deviations is the **population variance**.

> **DEFINITION**
>
> The **population variance** of a population data set of N entries is
>
> $$\text{Population variance} = \sigma^2 = \frac{\Sigma(x - \mu)^2}{N}.$$
>
> The symbol σ is the lowercase Greek letter sigma.

As a measure of variation, one disadvantage with the variance is that its units are different from the data set. For instance, the variance for the starting salaries (in thousands of dollars) in Example 1 is measured in "square thousands of dollars." To overcome this problem, take the square root of the variance to get the **standard deviation**.

> **DEFINITION**
>
> The **population standard deviation** of a population data set of N entries is the square root of the population variance.
>
> $$\text{Population standard deviation} = \sigma = \sqrt{\sigma^2} = \sqrt{\frac{\Sigma(x - \mu)^2}{N}}$$

Here are some observations about the standard deviation.

- The standard deviation measures the variation of the data set about the mean and has the same units of measure as the data set.

- The standard deviation is always greater than or equal to 0. When $\sigma = 0$, the data set has no variation and all entries have the same value.

- As the entries get farther from the mean (that is, more spread out), the value of σ increases.

To find the variance and standard deviation of a population data set, use these guidelines.

GUIDELINES

Finding the Population Variance and Standard Deviation

In Words	In Symbols
1. Find the mean of the population data set.	$\mu = \dfrac{\Sigma x}{N}$
2. Find the deviation of each entry.	$x - \mu$
3. Square each deviation.	$(x - \mu)^2$
4. Add to get the sum of squares.	$SS_x = \Sigma(x - \mu)^2$
5. Divide by N to get the population variance.	$\sigma^2 = \dfrac{\Sigma(x - \mu)^2}{N}$
6. Find the square root of the variance to get the population standard deviation.	$\sigma = \sqrt{\dfrac{\Sigma(x - \mu)^2}{N}}$

Sum of Squares of Starting Salaries for Corporation A

Salary x	Deviation $x - \mu$	Squares $(x - \mu)^2$
41	−0.5	0.25
38	−3.5	12.25
39	−2.5	6.25
45	3.5	12.25
47	5.5	30.25
41	−0.5	0.25
44	2.5	6.25
41	−0.5	0.25
37	−4.5	20.25
42	0.5	0.25
$\Sigma x = 415$		$SS_x = 88.5$

EXAMPLE 2

Finding the Population Variance and Standard Deviation

Find the population variance and standard deviation of the starting salaries for Corporation A listed in Example 1.

SOLUTION

For this data set, $N = 10$ and $\Sigma x = 415$. The mean is

$$\mu = \frac{415}{10} = 41.5. \qquad \text{Mean}$$

The table at the left summarizes the steps used to find SS_x. Because

$$SS_x = 88.5 \qquad \text{Sum of squares}$$

you can find the variance and standard deviation as shown.

$$\sigma^2 = \frac{88.5}{10} \approx 8.9 \qquad \text{Round to one more decimal place than the original data.}$$

$$\sigma = \sqrt{\frac{88.5}{10}} \approx 3.0 \qquad \text{Round to one more decimal place than the original data.}$$

So, the population variance is about 8.9, and the population standard deviation is about 3.0, or $3000.

TRY IT YOURSELF 2

Find the population variance and standard deviation of the starting salaries for Corporation B in Example 1.

Answer: Page A7

The formulas shown on the next page for the sample variance s^2 and sample standard deviation s of a sample data set differ slightly from those of a population. For instance, to find s, the formula uses $\bar{x}$. Also, SS_x is divided by $n - 1$. Why divide by one less than the number of entries? In many cases, a statistic is calculated to estimate the corresponding parameter, such as using $\bar{x}$ to estimate μ. Statistical theory has shown that the best estimates of σ^2 and σ are obtained when dividing SS_x by $n - 1$ in the formulas for s^2 and s.

Study Tip

Notice that the variance and standard deviation in Example 2 have one more decimal place than the original set of data entries. This is the same *round-off rule* that was used to calculate the mean.

DEFINITION

The **sample variance** and **sample standard deviation** of a sample data set of n entries are listed below.

$$\text{Sample variance} = s^2 = \frac{\Sigma(x - \bar{x})^2}{n - 1}$$

$$\text{Sample standard deviation} = s = \sqrt{s^2} = \sqrt{\frac{\Sigma(x - \bar{x})^2}{n - 1}}$$

Symbols in Variance and Standard Deviation Formulas

	Population	Sample
Variance	σ^2	s^2
Standard deviation	σ	s
Mean	μ	$\bar{x}$
Number of entries	N	n
Deviation	$x - \mu$	$x - \bar{x}$
Sum of squares	$\Sigma(x - \mu)^2$	$\Sigma(x - \bar{x})^2$

GUIDELINES

Finding the Sample Variance and Standard Deviation

In Words	In Symbols
1. Find the mean of the sample data set.	$\bar{x} = \dfrac{\Sigma x}{N}$
2. Find the deviation of each entry.	$x - \bar{x}$
3. Square each deviation.	$(x - \bar{x})^2$
4. Add to get the sum of squares.	$SS_x = \Sigma(x - \bar{x})^2$
5. Divide by $n - 1$ to get the sample variance.	$s^2 = \dfrac{\Sigma(x - \bar{x})^2}{n - 1}$
6. Find the square root of the variance to get the sample standard deviation.	$s = \sqrt{\dfrac{\Sigma(x - \bar{x})^2}{n - 1}}$

EXAMPLE 3

See Minitab and TI-84 Plus steps on pages 126 and 127.

Finding the Sample Variance and Standard Deviation

In a study of high school football players that suffered concussions, researchers placed the players in two groups. Players that recovered from their concussions in 14 days or less were placed in Group 1. Those that took more than 14 days were placed in Group 2. The recovery times (in days) for Group 1 are listed below. Find the sample variance and standard deviation of the recovery times. *(Adapted from The American Journal of Sports Medicine)*

4 7 6 7 9 5 8 10 9 8 7 10

SOLUTION

For this data set, $n = 12$ and $\Sigma x = 90$. The mean is $\bar{x} = 90/12 = 7.5$. To calculate s^2 and s, note that $n - 1 = 12 - 1 = 11$.

$SS_x = 39$ Sum of squares (see table at left)

$s^2 = \dfrac{39}{11} \approx 3.5$ Sample variance (divide SS_x by $n - 1$)

$s = \sqrt{\dfrac{39}{11}} \approx 1.9$ Sample standard deviation

So, the sample variance is about 3.5, and the sample standard deviation is about 1.9 days.

Time x	Deviation $x - \bar{x}$	Squares $(x - \bar{x})^2$
4	−3.5	12.25
7	−0.5	0.25
6	−1.5	2.25
7	−0.5	0.25
9	1.5	2.25
5	−2.5	6.25
8	0.5	0.25
10	2.5	6.25
9	1.5	2.25
8	0.5	0.25
7	−0.5	0.25
10	2.5	6.25
$\Sigma x = 90$		$SS_x = 39$

TRY IT YOURSELF 3

Refer to the study in Example 3. The recovery times (in days) for Group 2 are listed below. Find the sample variance and standard deviation of the recovery times.

43   57   18   45   47   33   49   24

Answer: Page A7

EXAMPLE 4

Using Technology to Find the Standard Deviation

Sample office rental rates (in dollars per square foot per year) for Los Angeles are shown in the table at the left. Use technology to find the mean rental rate and the sample standard deviation. *(Adapted from LoopNet.com)*

Office rental rates		
51	30	15
47	14	87
33	11	35
74	42	51
24	40	26
36	22	40
41	35	36
42	29	24

SOLUTION

Minitab, Excel, and the TI-84 Plus each have features that calculate the means and the standard deviations of data sets. Try using this technology to find the mean and the standard deviation of the office rental rates. From the displays, you can see that

$\bar{x} \approx 36.9$ and $s \approx 17.4$.

MINITAB

Descriptive Statistics: Office Rental Rates

Variable	N	Mean	SE Mean	StDev	Minimum
Rental Rates	24	36.88	3.55	17.39	11.00

Variable	Q1	Median	Q3	Maximum
Rental Rates	24.50	35.50	42.00	87.00

EXCEL

	A	B
1	Mean	36.875
2	Standard Error	3.550011
3	Median	35.5
4	Mode	51
5	Standard Deviation	17.39143
6	Sample Variance	302.462
7	Kurtosis	2.354212
8	Skewness	1.214477
9	Range	76
10	Minimum	11
11	Maximum	87
12	Sum	885
13	Count	24

TI-84 PLUS

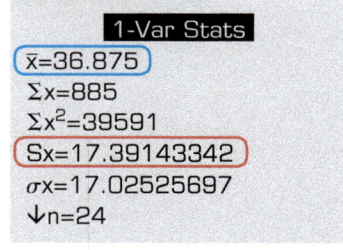

1-Var Stats
$\bar{x}=36.875$
$\Sigma x=885$
$\Sigma x^2=39591$
$Sx=17.39143342$
$\sigma x=17.02525697$
↓n=24

Sample Mean
Sample Standard Deviation

TRY IT YOURSELF 4

Sample office rental rates (in dollars per square foot per year) for Dallas are listed. Use technology to find the mean rental rate and the sample standard deviation. *(Adapted from LoopNet.com)*

18   27   21   14   20   20   24   11
16   7   12   22   10   15   21   34
23   13   38   16   18   30   15   30

Answer: Page A7

Interpreting Standard Deviation

When interpreting the standard deviation, remember that it is a measure of the typical amount an entry deviates from the mean. The more the entries are spread out, the greater the standard deviation.

Study Tip

You can use standard deviation to compare variation in data sets that use the same units of measure and have means that are about the same. For instance, in the data sets with $\bar{x} = 5$ shown at the right, the data set with $s \approx 3.0$ is more spread out than the other data sets. Not all data sets, however, use the same units of measure or have approximately equal means. To compare variation in these data sets, use the *coefficient of variation*, which is discussed later in this section.

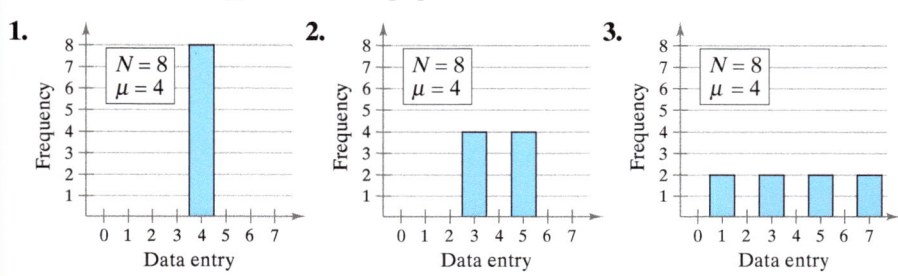

2.4 To explore this topic further, see **Activity 2.4** on page 102.

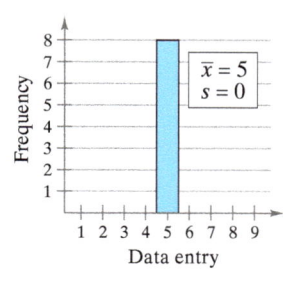

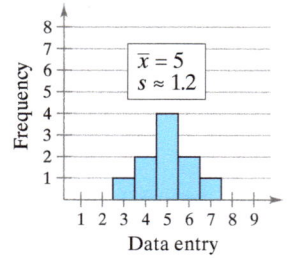

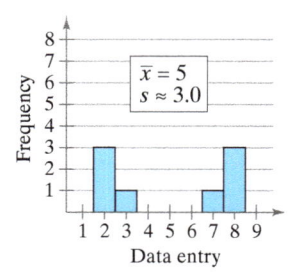

EXAMPLE 5

Estimating Standard Deviation

Without calculating, estimate the population standard deviation of each data set.

SOLUTION

1. Each of the eight entries is 4. The deviation of each entry is 0, so

   $\sigma = 0$.   Standard deviation

2. Each of the eight entries has a deviation of ± 1. So, the population standard deviation should be 1. By calculating, you can see that

   $\sigma = 1$.   Standard deviation

3. Each of the eight entries has a deviation of ± 1 or ± 3. So, the population standard deviation should be about 2. By calculating, you can see that σ is greater than 2, with

   $\sigma \approx 2.2$.   Standard deviation

TRY IT YOURSELF 5

Write a data set that has 10 entries, a mean of 10, and a population standard deviation that is approximately 3. (There are many correct answers.)

Answer: Page A7

Entry x	Deviation $x - \mu$	Squares $(x - \mu)^2$
1	−3	9
3	−1	1
5	1	1
7	3	9

Data entries that lie more than two standard deviations from the mean are considered unusual, while those that lie more than three standard deviations from the mean are very unusual. Unusual and very unusual entries have a greater influence on the standard deviation than entries closer to the mean. This happens because the deviations are squared. Consider the data entries from Example 5, part 3 (see table at the left). The squares of the deviations of the entries farther from the mean (1 and 7) have a greater influence on the value of the standard deviation than those closer to the mean (3 and 5).

Picturing the World

A survey was conducted by the National Center for Health Statistics to find the mean height of males in the United States. The histogram shows the distribution of heights for the sample of men examined in the 20–29 age group. In this group, the mean was 69.4 inches and the standard deviation was 2.9 inches. *(Adapted from National Center for Health Statistics)*

Heights of Men in the U.S. Ages 20–29

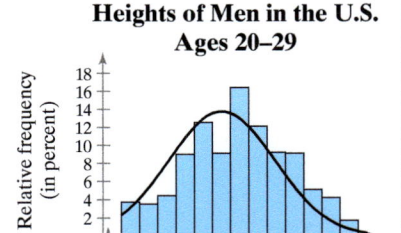

Estimate which two heights contain the middle 95% of the data. The height of a twenty-five-year-old male is 74 inches. Is this height unusual? Why or why not?

Many real-life data sets have distributions that are approximately symmetric and bell-shaped (see figure below). For instance, the distributions of men's and women's heights in the United States are approximately symmetric and bell-shaped (see the figures at the left and bottom left). Later in the text, you will study bell-shaped distributions in greater detail. For now, however, the **Empirical Rule** can help you see how valuable the standard deviation can be as a measure of variation.

Bell-Shaped Distribution

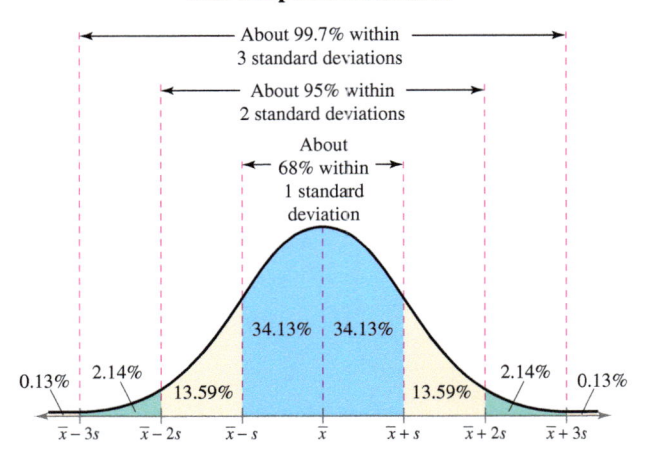

Empirical Rule (or 68-95-99.7 Rule)

For data sets with distributions that are approximately symmetric and bell-shaped (see figure above), the standard deviation has these characteristics.

1. About 68% of the data lie within one standard deviation of the mean.
2. About 95% of the data lie within two standard deviations of the mean.
3. About 99.7% of the data lie within three standard deviations of the mean.

EXAMPLE 6

Using the Empirical Rule

In a survey conducted by the National Center for Health Statistics, the sample mean height of women in the United States (ages 20–29) was 64.2 inches, with a sample standard deviation of 2.9 inches. Estimate the percent of women whose heights are between 58.4 inches and 64.2 inches. *(Adapted from National Center for Health Statistics)*

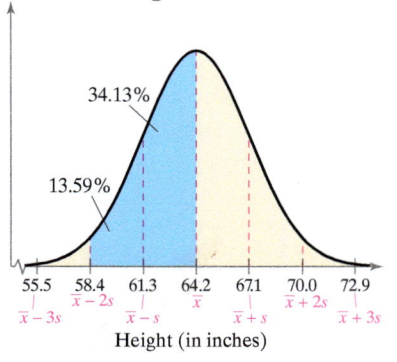

SOLUTION

The distribution of women's heights is shown at the left. Because the distribution is bell-shaped, you can use the Empirical Rule. The mean height is 64.2, so when you subtract two standard deviations from the mean height, you get

$$\bar{x} - 2s = 64.2 - 2(2.9) = 58.4.$$

Because 58.4 is two standard deviations below the mean height, the percent of the heights between 58.4 and 64.2 inches is about $13.59\% + 34.13\% = 47.72\%$.

Interpretation So, about 47.72% of women are between 58.4 and 64.2 inches tall.

Heights of Women in the U.S. Ages 20–29

TRY IT YOURSELF 6

Estimate the percent of women ages 20–29 whose heights are between 64.2 inches and 67.1 inches. *Answer: Page A7*

The Empirical Rule applies only to (symmetric) bell-shaped distributions. What if the distribution is not bell-shaped, or what if the shape of the distribution is not known? The next theorem gives an inequality statement that applies to *all* distributions. It is named after the Russian statistician Pafnuti Chebychev (1821–1894).

> ### Chebychev's Theorem
>
> The portion of any data set lying within k standard deviations ($k > 1$) of the mean is at least
>
> $$1 - \frac{1}{k^2}.$$
>
> - $k = 2$: In any data set, at least $1 - \frac{1}{2^2} = \frac{3}{4}$, or 75%, of the data lie within 2 standard deviations of the mean.
> - $k = 3$: In any data set, at least $1 - \frac{1}{3^2} = \frac{8}{9}$, or about 88.9%, of the data lie within 3 standard deviations of the mean.

EXAMPLE 7

Using Chebychev's Theorem

The age distributions for Georgia and Iowa are shown in the histograms. Apply Chebychev's Theorem to the data for Georgia using $k = 2$. What can you conclude? Is an age of 100 unusual for a Georgia resident? Explain. *(Source: Based on U.S. Census Bureau)*

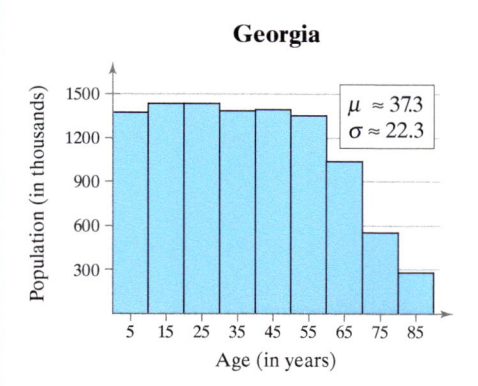

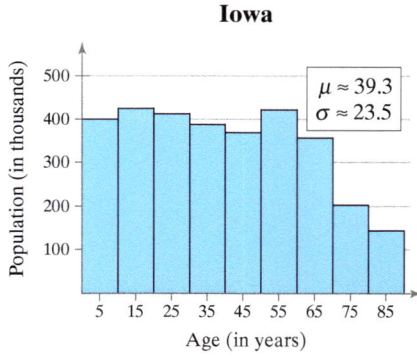

Georgia: $\mu \approx 37.3$, $\sigma \approx 22.3$

Iowa: $\mu \approx 39.3$, $\sigma \approx 23.5$

SOLUTION

The histogram on the left shows Georgia's age distribution. Moving two standard deviations to the left of the mean puts you below 0, because $\mu - 2\sigma \approx 37.3 - 2(22.3) = -7.3$. Moving two standard deviations to the right of the mean puts you at

$$\mu + 2\sigma \approx 37.3 + 2(22.3) = 81.9.$$

By Chebychev's Theorem, you can say that at least 75% of the population of Georgia is between 0 and 81.9 years old. Also, because $100 > 81.9$, an age of 100 lies more than two standard deviations from the mean. So, this age is unusual.

TRY IT YOURSELF 7

Apply Chebychev's Theorem to the data for Iowa using $k = 2$. What can you conclude? Is an age of 80 unusual for an Iowa resident? Explain.

Answer: Page A7

Study Tip

In Example 7, Chebychev's Theorem gives you an inequality statement that says at least 75% of the population of Georgia is under the age of 81.9. This is a true statement, but it is not nearly as strong a statement as could be made from reading the histogram.

In general, Chebychev's Theorem gives the minimum percent of data entries that fall within the given number of standard deviations of the mean. Depending on the distribution, there is probably a higher percent of data falling in the given range.

> **Study Tip**
>
> Remember that formulas for grouped data require you to multiply by the frequencies.

Standard Deviation for Grouped Data

In Section 2.1, you learned that large data sets are usually best represented by frequency distributions. The formula for the sample standard deviation for a frequency distribution is

$$\text{Sample standard deviation} = s = \sqrt{\frac{\Sigma(x - \bar{x})^2 f}{n - 1}}$$

where $n = \Sigma f$ is the number of entries in the data set.

EXAMPLE 8

Finding the Standard Deviation for Grouped Data

You collect a random sample of the number of children per household in a region. The results are listed below. Find the sample mean and the sample standard deviation of the data set.

```
1 3 1 1 1 1 2 2 1 0 1 1 0 0 0 1 5
0 3 6 3 0 3 1 1 1 1 6 0 1 3 6 6 1
2 2 3 0 1 1 4 1 1 2 2 0 3 0 2 4
```

SOLUTION

These data could be treated as 50 individual entries, and you could use the formulas for mean and standard deviation. Because there are so many repeated numbers, however, it is easier to use a frequency distribution.

x	f	xf	$x - \bar{x}$	$(x - \bar{x})^2$	$(x - \bar{x})^2 f$
0	10	0	−1.82	3.3124	33.1240
1	19	19	−0.82	0.6724	12.7756
2	7	14	0.18	0.0324	0.2268
3	7	21	1.18	1.3924	9.7468
4	2	8	2.18	4.7524	9.5048
5	1	5	3.18	10.1124	10.1124
6	4	24	4.18	17.4724	69.8896
	$\Sigma = 50$	$\Sigma = 91$			$\Sigma = 145.38$

$$\bar{x} = \frac{\Sigma xf}{n} = \frac{91}{50} = 1.82 \approx 1.8 \quad \text{Sample mean}$$

Use the sum of squares to find the sample standard deviation.

$$s = \sqrt{\frac{\Sigma(x - \bar{x})^2 f}{n - 1}} = \sqrt{\frac{145.38}{49}} \approx 1.7 \quad \text{Sample standard deviation}$$

So, the sample mean is about 1.8 children, and the sample standard deviation is about 1.7 children.

TRY IT YOURSELF 8

Change three of the 6's in the data set to 4's. How does this change affect the sample mean and sample standard deviation?

Answer: Page A7

When a frequency distribution has classes, you can estimate the sample mean and the sample standard deviation by using the midpoint of each class.

EXAMPLE 9

Using Midpoints of Classes

The figure below shows the results of a survey in which 1000 adults were asked how much they spend in preparation for personal travel each year. Make a frequency distribution for the data. Then use the table to estimate the sample mean and the sample standard deviation of the data set. *(Adapted from Travel Industry Association of America)*

Spending before traveling
What travelers spend in preparation for personal travel each year.

- $400 – $499: 60
- $500 or more: 70
- $300 – $399: 50
- Less than $100: 380
- $200 – $299: 210
- $100 – $199: 230

SOLUTION

Begin by using a frequency distribution to organize the data. Because the class of $500 or more is open-ended, you must choose a value to represent the midpoint, such as 599.5.

Class	x	f	xf	$x - \bar{x}$	$(x - \bar{x})^2$	$(x - \bar{x})^2 f$
0–99	49.5	380	18,810	−142.5	20,306.25	7,716,375.0
100–199	149.5	230	34,385	−42.5	1,806.25	415,437.5
200–299	249.5	210	52,395	57.5	3,306.25	694,312.5
300–399	349.5	50	17,475	157.5	24,806.25	1,240,312.5
400–499	449.5	60	26,970	257.5	66,306.25	3,978,375.0
500+	599.5	70	41,965	407.5	166,056.25	11,623,937.5
		$\Sigma = 1000$	$\Sigma = 192,000$			$\Sigma = 25,668,750.0$

$$\bar{x} = \frac{\Sigma xf}{n} = \frac{192,000}{1000} = 192 \quad \text{Sample mean}$$

Use the sum of squares to find the sample standard deviation.

$$s = \sqrt{\frac{\Sigma(x - \bar{x})^2 f}{n-1}} = \sqrt{\frac{25,668,750}{999}} \approx 160.3 \quad \text{Sample standard deviation}$$

So, an estimate for the sample mean is $192 per year, and an estimate for the sample standard deviation is $160.30 per year.

TRY IT YOURSELF 9

In the frequency distribution in Example 9, 599.5 was chosen as the midpoint for the class of $500 or more. How does the sample mean and standard deviation change when the midpoint of this class is 650?

Answer: Page A7

Coefficient of Variation

To compare variation in different data sets, you can use standard deviation when the data sets use the same units of measure and have means that are about the same. For data sets with different units of measure or different means, use the **coefficient of variation.**

> **DEFINITION**
>
> The **coefficient of variation (CV)** of a data set describes the standard deviation as a percent of the mean.
>
> Population: $CV = \dfrac{\sigma}{\mu} \cdot 100\%$ Sample: $CV = \dfrac{s}{\bar{x}} \cdot 100\%$

Note that the coefficient of variation measures the variation of a data set relative to the mean of the data.

EXAMPLE 10

Comparing Variation in Different Data Sets

The table below shows the population heights (in inches) and weights (in pounds) of the members of a basketball team. Find the coefficient of variation for the heights and the weights. Then compare the results.

Heights and Weights of a Basketball Team

Heights	72	74	68	76	74	69	72	79	70	69	77	73
Weights	180	168	225	201	189	192	197	162	174	171	185	210

SOLUTION

The mean height is $\mu \approx 72.8$ inches with a standard deviation of $\sigma \approx 3.3$ inches. The coefficient of variation for the heights is

$$CV_{\text{height}} = \dfrac{\sigma}{\mu} \cdot 100\%$$
$$= \dfrac{3.3}{72.8} \cdot 100\%$$
$$\approx 4.5\%.$$

The mean weight is $\mu \approx 187.8$ pounds with a standard deviation of $\sigma \approx 17.7$ pounds. The coefficient of variation for the weights is

$$CV_{\text{weight}} = \dfrac{\sigma}{\mu} \cdot 100\%$$
$$= \dfrac{17.7}{187.8} \cdot 100\%$$
$$\approx 9.4\%.$$

Interpretation   The weights (9.4%) are more variable than the heights (4.5%).

TRY IT YOURSELF 10

Find the coefficient of variation for the office rental rates in Los Angeles (see Example 4) and for those in Dallas (see Try It Yourself 4). Then compare the results.

Answer: Page A7

Descriptive Statistics 95

2.4 EXERCISES

For Extra Help: **MyLab Statistics**

Building Basic Skills and Vocabulary

1. Explain how to find the range of a data set. What is an advantage of using the range as a measure of variation? What is a disadvantage?
2. Explain how to find the deviation of an entry in a data set. What is the sum of all the deviations in any data set?
3. Why is the standard deviation used more frequently than the variance?
4. Explain the relationship between variance and standard deviation. Can either of these measures be negative? Explain.
5. Describe the difference between the calculation of population standard deviation and that of sample standard deviation.
6. Given a data set, how do you know whether to calculate σ or s?
7. Discuss the similarities and the differences between the Empirical Rule and Chebychev's Theorem.
8. What must you know about a data set before you can use the Empirical Rule?

Using and Interpreting Concepts

Finding the Range of a Data Set *In Exercises 9 and 10, find the range of the data set represented by the graph.*

9. Median Annual Income by State

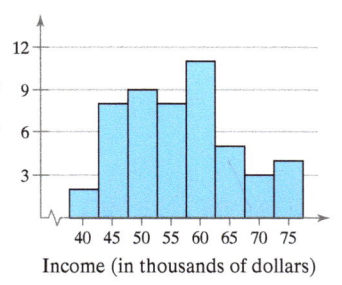

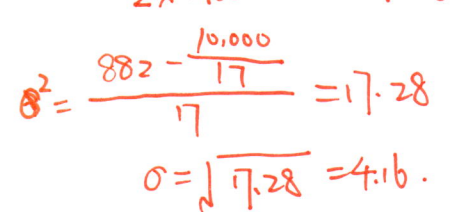

10.

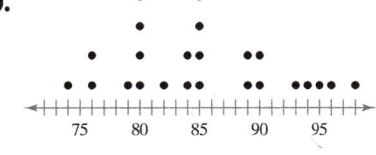

11. **Atmosphere** The altitudes (in kilometers) of atmosphere at which helium is found in majority in 10 different cities are listed.

    938.5 927.0 929.5 930.3 934.3 936.0 926.2 930.5 924.8 870.7

    (a) Find the range of the data set.
    (b) Change 870.7 to 807.7 and find the range of the new data set.

12. In Exercise 11, compare your answer to part (a) with your answer to part (b). How do outliers affect the range of a data set?

Finding Population Statistics *In Exercises 13 and 14, find the range, mean, variance, and standard deviation of the population data set.*

13. **Fire History** The numbers of deaths caused by fire per year from 1990 to 2005 in New South Wales *(Source: Australian Institute of Criminology)*

    8 13 2 11 5 5 14 1 6 3 13 3
    4 2 4 3 3

14. Density The densities (in kilograms per cubic meter) of the ten most abundant elements by weight in Earth's crust

1.4 2330 2700 7870 1500
970 900 1740 4500 0.09

Finding Sample Statistics *In Exercises 15 and 16, find the range, mean, variance, and standard deviation of the sample data set.*

15. Ages of Students The ages (in years) of a random sample of students in a campus dining hall

18 18 19 15 16 18 18 19 21 21
23 18 16 19 15 16 15 17 20 18

16. Germination The durations (in days) of germination for a random sample of seeds.

25 29 23 24 26 21 28
29 25 26 24 28 26 25
25 26 29 23 21 25 24

17. Estimating Standard Deviation Both data sets shown in the histograms have a mean of 50. One has a standard deviation of 2.4, and the other has a standard deviation of 5. By looking at the histograms, which is which? Explain your reasoning.

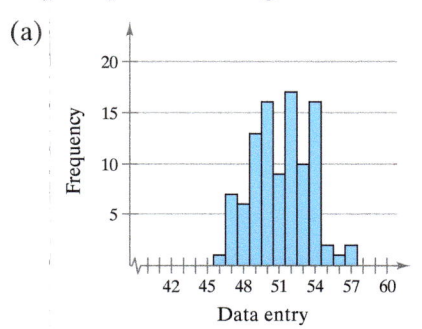

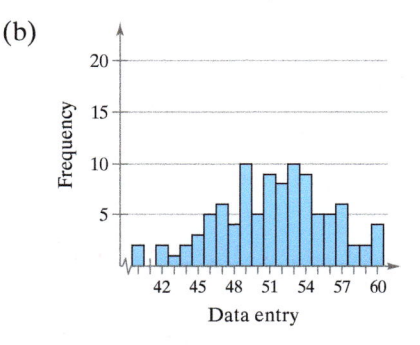

(a) [histogram with Data entry 42–60, Frequency 0–20]

(b) [histogram with Data entry 42–60, Frequency 0–20]

18. Estimating Standard Deviation Both data sets shown in the stem-and-leaf plots have a mean of 165. One has a standard deviation of 16, and the other has a standard deviation of 24. By looking at the stem-and-leaf plots, which is which? Explain your reasoning.

(a)
```
12 | 8 9        Key: 12|8 = 128
13 | 5 5 8
14 | 1 2
15 | 0 0 6 7
16 | 4 5 9
17 | 1 3 6 8
18 | 0 8 9
19 | 6
20 | 3 5 7
```

(b)
```
12 |           Key: 13|1 = 131
13 | 1
14 | 2 3 5
15 | 0 4 5 6 8
16 | 1 1 2 3 3 3
17 | 1 5 8 8
18 | 2 3 4 5
19 | 0 2
20 |
```

19. Salary Offers You are applying for jobs at two companies. Company A offers starting salaries with $\mu = \$30{,}000$ and $\sigma = \$4{,}000$. Company B offers starting salaries with $\mu = \$30{,}000$ and $\sigma = \$2{,}000$. From which company are you more likely to get an offer of $36,000 or more? Explain your reasoning.

20. Salary Offers You are applying for jobs at two companies. Company C offers starting salaries with $\mu = \$75{,}000$ and $\sigma = \$2{,}500$. Company D offers starting salaries with $\mu = \$75{,}000$ and $\sigma = \$5{,}000$. From which company are you more likely to get an offer of $85,000 or more? Explain your reasoning.

Graphical Analysis *In Exercises 21–24, you are asked to compare three data sets. (a) Without calculating, determine which data set has the greatest sample standard deviation and which has the least sample standard deviation. Explain your reasoning. (b) How are the data sets the same? How do they differ? (c) Estimate the sample standard deviations. Then determine how close each of your estimates is by finding the sample standard deviations.*

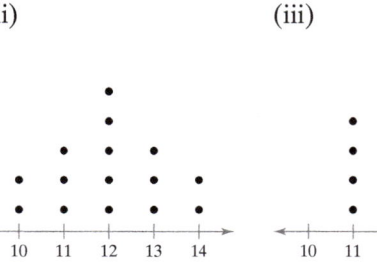

21. (i)   (ii)   (iii)

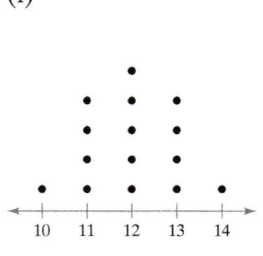

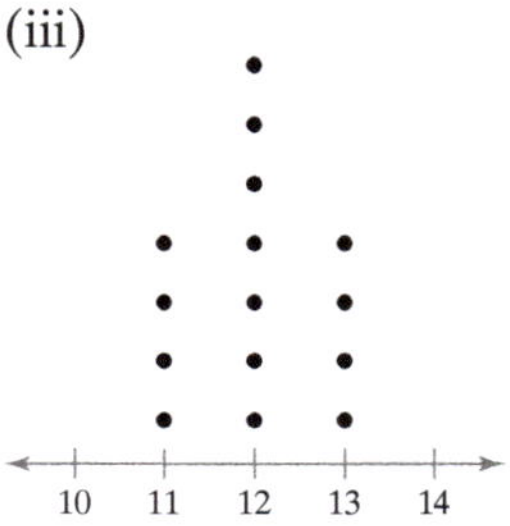

22. (i) 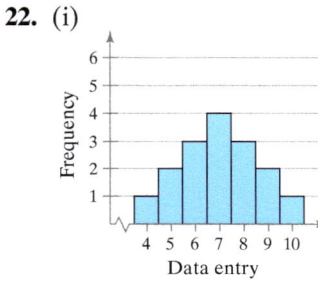   (ii) 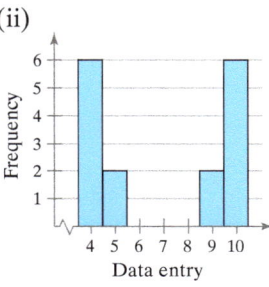   (iii)

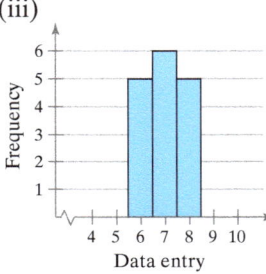

23.

(i)
0	9
1	5 8
2	3 3 7 7
3	2 5
4	1

Key: $1|5 = 15$

(ii)
0	9
1	5
2	3 3 3 7 7 7
3	5
4	1

Key: $1|5 = 15$

(iii)
0	
1	5
2	3 3 3 3 7 7 7 7
3	5
4	

Key: $1|5 = 15$

24. (i)   (ii) 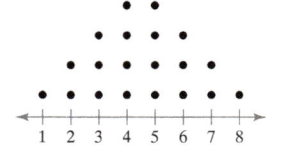   (iii)

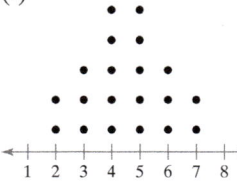

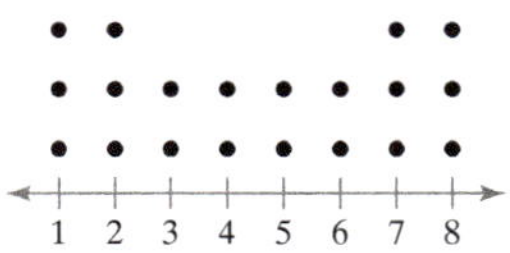

Constructing Data Sets *In Exercises 25–28, construct a data set that has the given statistics.*

25. $N = 6$
$\mu = 5$
$\sigma \approx 2$

26. $N = 9$
$\mu = 8$
$\sigma \approx 6$

27. $n = 5$
$\bar{x} = 12$
$s = 0$

28. $n = 5$
$\bar{x} = 8$
$s \approx 4$

Using the Empirical Rule *In Exercises 29–34, use the Empirical Rule.*

29. The mean speed of a sample of vehicles along a stretch of highway is 67 miles per hour, with a standard deviation of 4 miles per hour. Estimate the percent of vehicles whose speeds are between 63 miles per hour and 71 miles per hour. (Assume the data set has a bell-shaped distribution.)

30. The mean monthly utility bill for a sample of households in a city is $70, with a standard deviation of $8. Between what two values do about 95% of the data lie? (Assume the data set has a bell-shaped distribution.)

31. Use the sample statistics from Exercise 29 and assume the number of vehicles in the sample is 75.
    (a) Estimate the number of vehicles whose speeds are between 63 miles per hour and 71 miles per hour.
    (b) In a sample of 25 additional vehicles, about how many vehicles would you expect to have speeds between 63 miles per hour and 71 miles per hour?

32. Use the sample statistics from Exercise 30 and assume the number of households in the sample is 40.
    (a) Estimate the number of households whose monthly utility bills are between $54 and $86.
    (b) In a sample of 20 additional households, about how many households would you expect to have monthly utility bills between $54 and $86?

33. The speeds for eight vehicles are listed. Using the sample statistics from Exercise 29, determine which of the data entries are unusual. Are any of the data entries very unusual? Explain your reasoning.

    70, 78, 62, 71, 65, 76, 82, 64

34. The monthly utility bills for eight households are listed. Using the sample statistics from Exercise 30, determine which of the data entries are unusual. Are any of the data entries very unusual? Explain your reasoning.

    $65, $52, $63, $83, $77, $98, $84, $70

35. **Using Chebychev's Theorem** You are conducting a survey on the number of people per house in your region. From a sample with $n = 60$, the mean number of people per house is 3 and the standard deviation is 1 person. Using Chebychev's Theorem, determine at least how many of the households have 0 to 6 people.

36. **Using Chebychev's Theorem** Old Faithful is a famous geyser at Yellowstone National Park. From a sample with $n = 100$, the mean interval between Old Faithful's eruptions is 101.56 minutes and the standard deviation is 42.69 minutes. Using Chebychev's Theorem, determine at least how many of the intervals lasted between 16.18 minutes and 186.94 minutes. *(Adapted from Geyser Times)*

37. **Using Chebychev's Theorem** The mean height of students of a class is 125 centimeters, with a standard deviation of 4 centimeters. Apply Chebychev's Theorem to the data using $k = 2$. Interpret the results.

38. **Using Chebychev's Theorem** The mean number of runs per game scored by the Chicago Cubs during the 2016 World Series was 3.86 runs, with a standard deviation of 3.36 runs. Apply Chebychev's Theorem to the data using $k = 2$. Interpret the results. *(Adapted from Major League Baseball)*

Descriptive Statistics

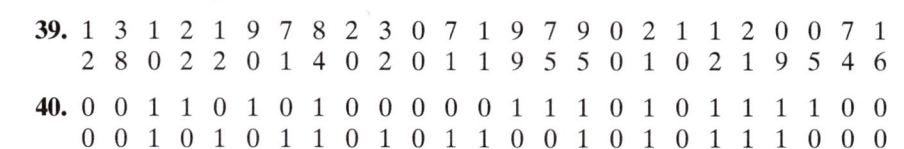

Finding the Sample Mean and Standard Deviation for Grouped Data *In Exercises 39 and 40, make a frequency distribution for the data. Then use the table to find the sample mean and the sample standard deviation of the data set.*

39. 1 3 1 2 1 9 7 8 2 3 0 7 1 9 7 9 0 2 1 1 2 0 0 7 1
2 8 0 2 2 0 1 4 0 2 0 1 1 9 5 5 0 1 0 2 1 9 5 4 6

40. 0 0 1 1 0 1 0 1 0 0 0 0 0 1 1 1 0 1 0 1 1 1 1 0 0
0 0 1 0 1 0 1 1 0 1 0 1 1 0 0 1 0 1 0 1 1 1 0 0 0

Estimating the Sample Mean and Standard Deviation for Grouped Data *In Exercises 41–44, make a frequency distribution for the data. Then use the table to estimate the sample mean and the sample standard deviation of the data set.*

41. College Expenses The distribution of the tuitions, fees, and room and board charges of a random sample of public 4-year degree-granting postsecondary institutions is shown in the pie chart. Use $26,249.50 as the midpoint for "$25,000 or more."

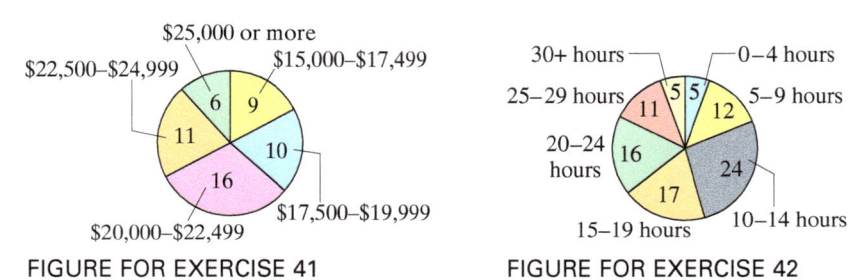

FIGURE FOR EXERCISE 41

FIGURE FOR EXERCISE 42

42. Weekly Study Hours The distribution of the numbers of hours that a random sample of college students study per week is shown in the pie chart. Use 32 as the midpoint for "30+ hours."

43. Teaching Load The numbers of courses taught per semester by a random sample of university professors are shown in the histogram.

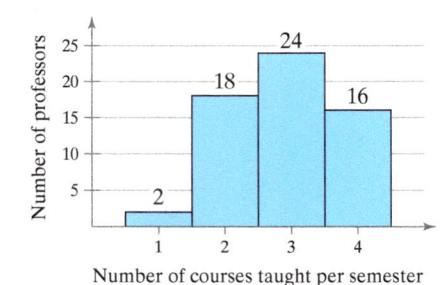

44. Amounts of Caffeine The amounts of caffeine in a sample of five-ounce servings of brewed coffee are shown in the histogram.

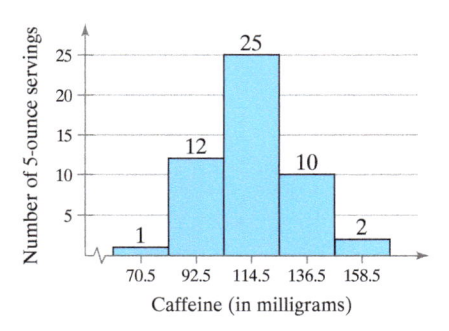

Comparing Variation in Different Data Sets *In Exercises 45–50, find the coefficient of variation for each of the two data sets. Then compare the results.*

45. **Annual Salaries** Sample annual salaries (in thousands of dollars) for entry level architects in Denver, CO, and Los Angeles, CA, are listed.

Denver	45.8	46.4	44.4	40.7	51.5	39.5
	44.2	53.1	44.8	51.6	41.3	49.0
Los Angeles	56.7	50.6	56.0	48.5	55.7	55.6
	47.6	56.3	48.1	46.3	51.9	61.2

46. **Wealth** Sample wealth (in billions of dollars) for billionaires in Africa and Asia are listed.

Africa	12.2	7.7	7.2	6.8	5.3	4	4	2.8	2.7
Asia	33.3	24.8	24.2	22.7	21.1	21	20.2	20	19.1

47. **Ages and Heights** The ages (in years) and heights (in inches) of all members of the 2016 Women's U.S. Olympic swimming team are listed. *(Source: USA Swimming)*

Ages	24	24	19	23	22	21	21	24	19	19	19
	24	25	21	20	26	21	21	28	30	19	21
Heights	70	70	68	66	69	67	74	68	69	71	71
	68	67	70	75	73	74	69	73	73	70	71

48. **Ages and Weights** The ages (in years) and weight classes (in kilograms) of all members of the 2016 Men's U.S. Olympic wrestling team are listed. *(Source: U.S. Olympic Committee)*

Ages	24	29	26	29	29	28	21	30	27	20
Weight Classes	59	75	85	130	57	74	86	125	65	97

49. **Sample Weight Averages** Sample weight averages (in kilograms) for 10 males and 10 females are listed.

Males	70	72	75	69	64	75	60	71	73	72
Females	65	66	68	61	64	69	65	63	62	65

50. **Sample Height Averages** Sample height averages (in centimeters) for 10 males and 10 females are listed.

Males	167	165	160	181	190	175	178	164	168	155
Females	145	170	138	140	151	171	142	151	153	157

Extending Concepts

51. **Alternative Formula** You used $SS_x = \Sigma(x - \bar{x})^2$ when calculating variance and standard deviation. An alternative formula that is sometimes more convenient for hand calculations is

    $$SS_x = \Sigma x^2 - \frac{(\Sigma x)^2}{n}.$$

    You can find the sample variance by dividing the sum of squares by $n - 1$ and the sample standard deviation by finding the square root of the sample variance.

    (a) Show how to obtain the alternative formula.

    (b) Use the alternative formula to calculate the sample standard deviation for the data set in Exercise 15.

    (c) Compare your result with the sample standard deviation obtained in Exercise 15.

52. **Mean Absolute Deviation** Another useful measure of variation for a data set is the **mean absolute deviation (MAD)**. It is calculated by the formula

$$MAD = \frac{\Sigma |x - \bar{x}|}{n}.$$

(a) Find the mean absolute deviation of the data set in Exercise 15. Compare your result with the sample standard deviation obtained in Exercise 15.

(b) Find the mean absolute deviation of the data set in Exercise 16. Compare your result with the sample standard deviation obtained in Exercise 16.

53. **Scaling Data** Sample annual salaries (in thousands of dollars) for employees at a company are listed.

42 36 48 51 39 39 42
36 48 33 39 42 45 50

(a) Find the sample mean and the sample standard deviation.

(b) Each employee in the sample receives a 5% raise. Find the sample mean and the sample standard deviation for the revised data set.

(c) Find each monthly salary. Then find the sample mean and the sample standard deviation for the monthly salaries.

(d) What can you conclude from the results of (a), (b), and (c)?

54. **Shifting Data** Sample annual salaries (in thousands of dollars) for employees at a company are listed.

40 35 49 53 38 39 40
37 49 34 38 43 47 35

(a) Find the sample mean and the sample standard deviation.

(b) Each employee in the sample receives a $1000 raise. Find the sample mean and the sample standard deviation for the revised data set.

(c) Each employee in the sample takes a pay cut of $2000 from their original salary. Find the sample mean and the sample standard deviation for the revised data set.

(d) What can you conclude from the results of (a), (b), and (c)?

55. **Pearson's Index of Skewness** The English statistician Karl Pearson (1857–1936) introduced a formula for the skewness of a distribution.

$$P = \frac{3(\bar{x} - \text{median})}{s} \quad \text{Pearson's index of skewness}$$

Most distributions have an index of skewness between -3 and 3. When $P > 0$, the data are skewed right. When $P < 0$, the data are skewed left. When $P = 0$, the data are symmetric. Calculate the coefficient of skewness for each distribution. Describe the shape of each.

(a) $\bar{x} = 17$, $s = 2.3$, median $= 19$
(b) $\bar{x} = 32$, $s = 5.1$, median $= 25$
(c) $\bar{x} = 9.2$, $s = 1.8$, median $= 9.2$
(d) $\bar{x} = 42$, $s = 6.0$, median $= 40$
(e) $x = 155$, $s = 20.0$, median $= 175$

56. **Chebychev's Theorem** At least 99% of the data in any data set lie within how many standard deviations of the mean? Explain how you obtained your answer.

2.4 ACTIVITY

Standard Deviation

APPLET

You can find the interactive applet for this activity within MyLab Statistics or at www.pearsonglobaleditions.com.

The *standard deviation* applet is designed to allow you to investigate interactively the standard deviation as a measure of spread for a data set. Points can be added to the plot by clicking the mouse above the horizontal axis. The mean of the points is shown as a green arrow. A numeric value for the standard deviation is shown above the plot. Points on the plot can be removed by clicking on the point and then dragging the point into the trash can. All of the points on the plot can be removed by simply clicking inside the trash can. The range of values for the horizontal axis can be specified by inputting lower and upper limits and then clicking UPDATE.

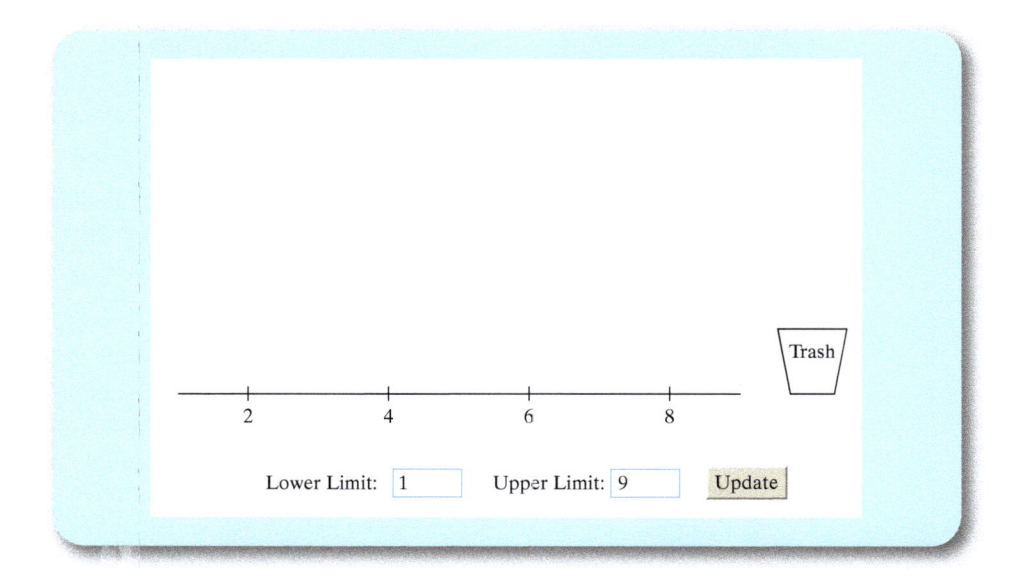

EXPLORE

Step 1 Specify a lower limit.
Step 2 Specify an upper limit.
Step 3 Add 15 points to the plot.
Step 4 Remove all of the points from the plot.

DRAW CONCLUSIONS

APPLET

1. Specify the lower limit to be 10 and the upper limit to be 20. Plot 10 points that have a mean of about 15 and a standard deviation of about 3. Write the estimates of the values of the points. Plot a point with a value of 15. What happens to the mean and standard deviation? Plot a point with a value of 20. What happens to the mean and standard deviation?

2. Specify the lower limit to be 30 and the upper limit to be 40. How can you plot eight points so that the points have the greatest possible standard deviation? Use the applet to plot the set of points and then use the formula for standard deviation to confirm the value given in the applet. How can you plot eight points so that the points have the least possible standard deviation? Explain.

CASE STUDY

Business Size

The numbers of employees at businesses can vary. A business can have anywhere from a single employee to more than 1000 employees. The data shown below are the numbers of manufacturing businesses for nine states in a recent year. *(Source: U.S. Census Bureau)*

State	Number of manufacturing businesses
California	38,293
Illinois	13,531
Indiana	8,036
Michigan	12,361
New York	16,076
Ohio	14,208
Pennsylvania	13,684
Texas	19,681
Wisconsin	8,858

Number of Manufacturing Businesses by Number of Employees

State	1–4	5–9	10–19	20–49	50–99	100–249	250–499	500–999	1000+
California	15,320	7,074	5,862	5,494	2,276	1,609	433	144	81
Illinois	4,683	2,234	2,103	2,165	1,123	852	241	96	34
Indiana	2,225	1,319	1,276	1,403	797	640	229	99	48
Michigan	4,055	2,103	2,008	2,044	974	800	254	76	47
New York	7,048	2,810	2,342	2,134	885	587	171	75	24
Ohio	4,274	2,469	2,281	2,495	1,233	982	311	112	51
Pennsylvania	4,505	2,292	2,185	2,335	1,125	860	268	79	35
Texas	7,019	3,409	2,994	3,078	1,501	1,114	358	145	63
Wisconsin	2,657	1,372	1,342	1,520	889	725	227	97	29

EXERCISES

Use the information given in the above tables.

1. **Employees** Which state has the greatest number of manufacturing employees? Explain your reasoning.

2. **Mean Business Size** Estimate the mean number of employees at a manufacturing business for each state. Use 1500 as the midpoint for "1000+."

3. **Employees** Which state has the greatest number of employees per manufacturing business? Explain your reasoning.

4. **Standard Deviation** Estimate the standard deviation for the number of employees at a manufacturing business for each state. Use 1500 as the midpoint for "1000+."

5. **Standard Deviation** Which state has the greatest standard deviation? Explain your reasoning.

6. **Distribution** Describe the distribution of the number of employees at manufacturing businesses for each state.

2.5 Measures of Position

What You Should Learn

▶ How to find the first, second, and third quartiles of a data set, how to find the interquartile range of a data set, and how to represent a data set graphically using a box-and-whisker plot

▶ How to interpret other fractiles such as percentiles, and how to find percentiles for a specific data entry

▶ How to find and interpret the standard score (z-score)

Quartiles ■ Percentiles and Other Fractiles ■ The Standard Score

Quartiles

In this section, you will learn how to use fractiles to specify the position of a data entry within a data set. **Fractiles** are numbers that partition, or divide, an ordered data set into equal parts (each part has the same number of data entries). For instance, the median is a fractile because it divides an ordered data set into two equal parts.

DEFINITION

The three **quartiles,** Q_1, Q_2, and Q_3, divide an ordered data set into four equal parts. About one-quarter of the data fall on or below the **first quartile** Q_1. About one-half of the data fall on or below the **second quartile** Q_2 (the second quartile is the same as the median of the data set). About three-quarters of the data fall on or below the **third quartile** Q_3.

EXAMPLE 1

Finding the Quartiles of a Data Set

Each year in the U.S., automobile commuters waste fuel due to traffic congestion. The amounts (in gallons per year) of fuel wasted by commuters in the 15 largest U.S. urban areas are listed. (Large urban areas have populations of at least 3 million.) Find the first, second, and third quartiles of the data set. What do you observe? *(Source: Based on 2015 Urban Mobility Scorecard)*

20 30 29 22 25 29 25 24 35 23 25 11 33 28 35

SOLUTION

First, order the data set and find the median Q_2. The first quartile Q_1 is the median of the data entries to the left of Q_2. The third quartile Q_3 is the median of the data entries to the right of Q_2.

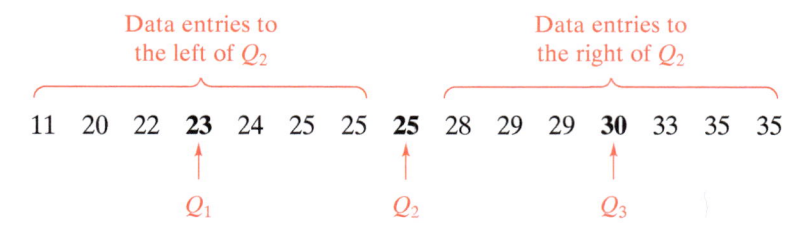

Data entries to the left of Q_2: 11 20 22 **23** 24 25 25
Q_2: **25**
Data entries to the right of Q_2: 28 29 29 **30** 33 35 35

$Q_1 = 23$, $Q_2 = 25$, $Q_3 = 30$

Interpretation In about one-quarter of the large urban areas, auto commuters waste 23 gallons of fuel or less, about one-half waste 25 gallons or less, and about three-quarters waste 30 gallons or less.

TRY IT YOURSELF 1

Find the first, second, and third quartiles for the points scored by the 51 winning teams using the data set listed on page 41. What do you observe?

Answer: Page A7

EXAMPLE 2

Using Technology to Find Quartiles

The tuition costs (in thousands of dollars) for 25 liberal arts colleges are listed. Use technology to find the first, second, and third quartiles. What do you observe? *(Source: U.S. News & World Report)*

50 52 51 49 52 51 25 41 47 36 30 44 40
35 40 45 34 33 23 34 27 16 18 18 35

SOLUTION

Minitab and the TI-84 Plus each have features that calculate quartiles. Try using this technology to find the first, second, and third quartiles of the tuition data. From the displays, you can see that

$Q_1 = 28.5$, $Q_2 = 36$, and $Q_3 = 48$.

MINITAB

Descriptive Statistics: Tuition

Variable	N	Mean	SE Mean	StDev	Minimum
Tuition	25	37.04	2.27	11.36	16.00

Variable	Q1	Median	Q3	Maximum
Tuition	28.50	36.00	48.00	52.00

TI-84 PLUS

1-Var Stats
↑n=25
minX=16
Q_1=28.5
Med=36
Q_3=48
maxX=52

STATCRUNCH

Summary statistics:

Column	Q1	Median	Q3
Tuition	30	36	47

EXCEL

	A	B
1	50	
2	52	Quartile.inc(A1:A25,1)
3	51	30
4	49	
5	52	Quartile.inc(A1:A25,2)
6	51	36
7	25	
8	41	Quartile.inc(A1:A25,3)
9	47	47
10	36	
11	30	
12	44	
13	40	
14	35	
15	40	
16	45	
17	34	
18	33	
19	23	
20	34	
21	27	
22	16	
23	18	
24	18	
25	35	

> **Tech Tip**
>
> Note that you may get results that differ slightly when comparing results obtained by different technology tools. For instance, in Example 2, the first quartile, as determined by Minitab and the TI-84 Plus, is 28.5, whereas the result using Excel is 30 (see below).

Interpretation About one-quarter of these colleges charge tuition of $28,500 or less; about one-half charge $36,000 or less; and about three-quarters charge $48,000 or less.

TRY IT YOURSELF 2

The tuition costs (in thousands of dollars) for 25 universities are listed. Use technology to find the first, second, and third quartiles. What do you observe? *(Source: U.S. News & World Report)*

44 30 38 23 20 29 19 44 29 17 45 39 29
18 43 45 39 24 44 26 34 20 35 30 36

Answer: Page A7

The median (the second quartile) is a measure of central tendency based on position. A measure of variation that is based on position is the **interquartile range**. The interquartile range tells you the spread of the middle half of the data, as shown in the next definition.

DEFINITION

The **interquartile range (IQR)** of a data set is a measure of variation that gives the range of the middle portion (about half) of the data. The IQR is the difference between the third and first quartiles.

$$IQR = Q_3 - Q_1$$

In Section 2.3, an outlier was described as a data entry that is far removed from the other entries in the data set. One way to identify outliers is to use the interquartile range.

GUIDELINES

Using the Interquartile Range to Identify Outliers

1. Find the first (Q_1) and third (Q_3) quartiles of the data set.
2. Find the interquartile range: $IQR = Q_3 - Q_1$.
3. Multiply IQR by 1.5: $1.5(IQR)$.
4. Subtract $1.5(IQR)$ from Q_1. Any data entry less than $Q_1 - 1.5(IQR)$ is an outlier.
5. Add $1.5(IQR)$ to Q_3. Any data entry greater than $Q_3 + 1.5(IQR)$ is an outlier.

EXAMPLE 3

Using the Interquartile Range to Identify an Outlier

Find the interquartile range of the data set in Example 1. Are there any outliers?

SOLUTION

From Example 1, you know that $Q_1 = 23$ and $Q_3 = 30$. So, the interquartile range is $IQR = Q_3 - Q_1 = 30 - 23 = 7$. To identify any outliers, first note that $1.5(IQR) = 1.5(7) = 10.5$. There is a data entry, 11, that is less than

$Q_1 - 1.5(IQR) = 23 - 10.5$ Subtract $1.5(IQR)$ from Q_1.
$= 12.5$ A data entry less than 12.5 is an outlier.

but there are no data entries greater than

$Q_3 + 1.5(IQR) = 30 + 10.5$ Add $1.5(IQR)$ from Q_3.
$= 40.5$.   A data entry greater than 40.5 is an outlier.

So, 11 is an outlier.

Interpretation In large urban areas, the amount of fuel wasted by auto commuters in the middle of the data set varies by at most 10.5 gallons. Notice that the outlier, 11, does not affect the IQR.

TRY IT YOURSELF 3

Find the interquartile range for the points scored by the 51 winning teams listed on page 41. Are there any outliers?

Answer: Page A7

Another important application of quartiles is to represent data sets using box-and-whisker plots. A **box-and-whisker plot** (or **boxplot**) is an exploratory data analysis tool that highlights the important features of a data set. To graph a box-and-whisker plot, you must know the values shown at the top of the next page.

Descriptive Statistics 107

1. The minimum entry
2. The first quartile Q_1
3. The median Q_2
4. The third quartile Q_3
5. The maximum entry

These five numbers are called the **five-number summary** of the data set.

Picturing the World

Since 1970, there have been 2845 fatalities in the United States attributed to lightning strikes. The box-and-whisker plot summarizes the fatalities for each year since 1970. (Source: National Weather Service)

Lightning Fatalities

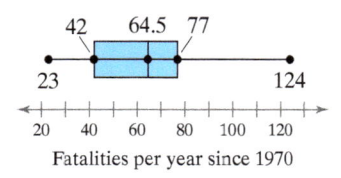

42 64.5 77
23   124
20 40 60 80 100 120
Fatalities per year since 1970

About how many fatalities are represented by the right whisker? There were 27 lightning fatalities in 2015. Into what quartile does this number of fatalities fall?

GUIDELINES

Drawing a Box-and-Whisker Plot

1. Find the five-number summary of the data set.
2. Construct a horizontal scale that spans the range of the data.
3. Plot the five numbers above the horizontal scale.
4. Draw a box above the horizontal scale from Q_1 to Q_3 and draw a vertical line in the box at Q_2.
5. Draw whiskers from the box to the minimum and maximum entries.

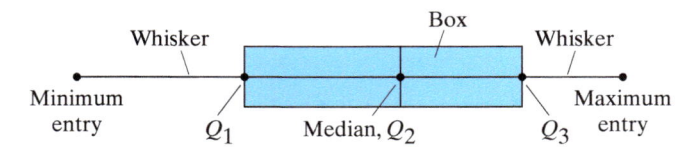

Whisker — Box — Whisker
Minimum entry — Q_1 — Median, Q_2 — Q_3 — Maximum entry

EXAMPLE 4

See Minitab and TI-84 Plus steps on pages 126 and 127.

Drawing a Box-and-Whisker Plot

Draw a box-and-whisker plot that represents the data set in Example 1. What do you observe?

SOLUTION Here is the five-number summary of the data set.

Minimum = 11 $Q_1 = 23$ $Q_2 = 25$ $Q_3 = 30$ Maximum = 35

Using these five numbers, you can construct the box-and-whisker plot shown.

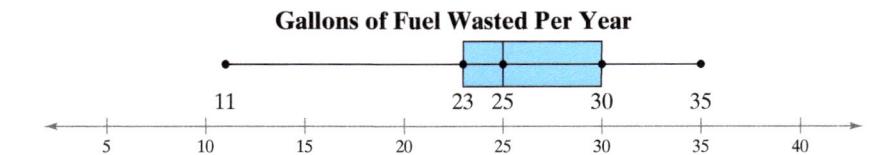

Gallons of Fuel Wasted Per Year

11   23 25   30   35
5 10 15 20 25 30 35 40

Interpretation The box represents about half of the data, which means about 50% of the data entries are between 23 and 30. The left whisker represents about one-quarter of the data, so about 25% of the data entries are less than 23. The right whisker represents about one-quarter of the data, so about 25% of the data entries are greater than 30. Also, the length of the left whisker is much longer than the right one. This indicates that the data set has a possible outlier to the left. (You already know from Example 3 that the data entry of 11 is an outlier).

TRY IT YOURSELF 4

Draw a box-and-whisker plot that represents the points scored by the 51 winning teams listed on page 41. What do you observe?

Answer: Page A7

Study Tip

For data sets that have outliers, you can represent them graphically using a modified box-and-whisker plot. A *modified box-and-whisker plot* is a box-and-whisker plot that uses symbols (such as an asterisk or a point) to indicate outliers. The horizontal line of a modified box-and-whisker plot extends as far as the minimum data entry that is not an outlier and the maximum data entry that is not an outlier. For instance, on pages 126 and 127, Minitab and the TI-84 Plus were used to draw modified box-and-whisker plots that represent the data set in Example 1. Compare these results with the one in Example 4.

You can use a box-and-whisker plot to determine the shape of a distribution. Notice that the box-and-whisker plot in Example 4 represents a distribution that is skewed left.

Percentiles and Other Fractiles

In addition to using quartiles to specify a measure of position, you can also use percentiles and deciles. Here is a summary of these common fractiles.

Fractiles	Summary	Symbols
Quartiles	Divide a data set into 4 equal parts.	Q_1, Q_2, Q_3
Deciles	Divide a data set into 10 equal parts.	$D_1, D_2, D_3, \ldots, D_9$
Percentiles	Divide a data set into 100 equal parts.	$P_1, P_2, P_3, \ldots, P_{99}$

Percentiles are often used in education and health-related fields to indicate how one individual compares with others in a group. Percentiles can also be used to identify unusually high or unusually low values. For instance, children's growth measurements are often expressed in percentiles. Measurements in the 95th percentile and above are unusually high, while those in the 5th percentile and below are unusually low.

Study Tip

Notice that the 25th percentile is the same as Q_1; the 50th percentile is the same as Q_2, or the median; and the 75th percentile is the same as Q_3.

Study Tip

Be sure you understand what a percentile means. For instance, the weight of a six-month-old infant is at the 78th percentile. This means the infant weighs the same as or more than 78% of all six-month-old infants. It does not mean that the infant weighs 78% of some ideal weight.

EXAMPLE 5

Interpreting Percentiles

The ogive at the right represents the cumulative frequency distribution for SAT scores of college-bound students in a recent year. What score represents the 80th percentile? *(Source: The College Board)*

SOLUTION

From the ogive, you can see that the 80th percentile corresponds to a score of 1250.

Interpretation This means that approximately 80% of the students had an SAT score of 1250 or less.

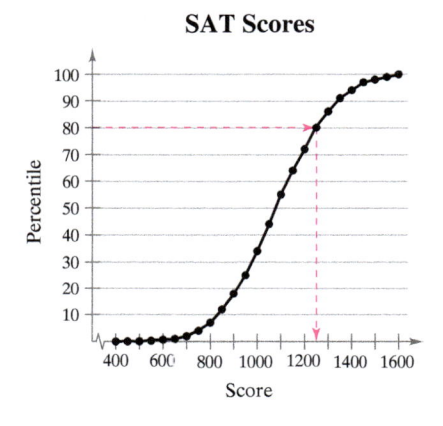

TRY IT YOURSELF 5

The points scored by the 51 winning teams in the Super Bowl (see page 41) are represented in the ogive at the left. What score represents the 10th percentile? How should you interpret this?

Answer: Page A7

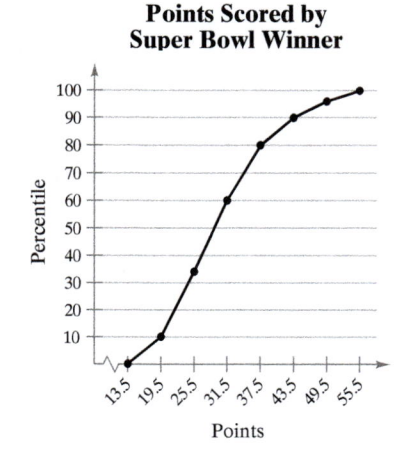

In Example 5, you used an ogive to approximate a data entry that corresponds to a percentile. You can also use an ogive to approximate a percentile that corresponds to a data entry. Another way to find a percentile is to use a formula.

DEFINITION

To find the **percentile that corresponds to a specific data entry** x, use the formula

$$\text{Percentile of } x = \frac{\text{number of data entries less than } x}{\text{total number of data entries}} \cdot 100$$

and then round to the nearest whole number.

EXAMPLE 6

Finding a Percentile

For the data set in Example 2, find the percentile that corresponds to $34,000.

SOLUTION

Recall that the tuition costs are in thousands of dollars, so $34,000 is the data entry 34. Begin by ordering the data.

16 18 18 23 25 27 30 33 34 34 35 35 36
40 40 41 44 45 47 49 50 51 51 52 52

There are 8 data entries less than 34 and the total number of data entries is 25.

$$\text{Percentile of } 34 = \frac{\text{number of data entries less than } 34}{\text{total number of entries}} \cdot 100$$

$$= \frac{8}{25} \cdot 100$$

$$= 32$$

The tuition cost of $34,000 corresponds to the 32nd percentile.

Interpretation The tuition cost of $34,000 is greater than 32% of the other tuition costs.

TRY IT YOURSELF 6

For the data set in Try It Yourself 2, find the percentile that corresponds to $26,000, which is the data entry 26.

Answer: Page A7

The Standard Score

When you know the mean and standard deviation of a data set, you can measure the position of an entry in the data set with a **standard score,** or **z-score.**

DEFINITION

The **standard score,** or **z-score,** represents the number of standard deviations a value x lies from the mean μ. To find the z-score for a value, use the formula

$$z = \frac{\text{Value} - \text{Mean}}{\text{Standard deviation}} = \frac{x - \mu}{\sigma}.$$

A z-score can be negative, positive, or zero. When z is negative, the corresponding x-value is less than the mean. When z is positive, the corresponding x-value is greater than the mean. For $z = 0$, the corresponding x-value is equal to the mean. A z-score can be used to identify an unusual value of a data set that is approximately bell-shaped.

When a distribution is approximately bell-shaped, you know from the Empirical Rule that about 95% of the data lie within 2 standard deviations of the mean. So, when this distribution's values are transformed to z-scores, about 95% of the z-scores should fall between -2 and 2. A z-score outside of this range will occur about 5% of the time and would be considered unusual. So, according to the Empirical Rule, a z-score less than -3 or greater than 3 would be very unusual, with such a score occurring about 0.3% of the time.

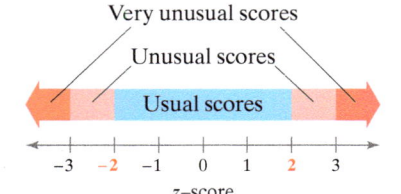

EXAMPLE 7

Finding z-Scores

The mean speed of vehicles along a stretch of highway is 56 miles per hour with a standard deviation of 4 miles per hour. You measure the speeds of three cars traveling along this stretch of highway as 62 miles per hour, 47 miles per hour, and 56 miles per hour. Find the z-score that corresponds to each speed. Assume the distribution of the speeds is approximately bell-shaped.

SOLUTION The z-score that corresponds to each speed is calculated below.

$x = 62$ mph
$$z = \frac{62 - 56}{4} = 1.5$$

$x = 47$ mph
$$z = \frac{47 - 56}{4} = -2.25$$

$x = 56$ mph
$$z = \frac{56 - 56}{4} = 0$$

Interpretation From the z-scores, you can conclude that a speed of 62 miles per hour is 1.5 standard deviations above the mean; a speed of 47 miles per hour is 2.25 standard deviations below the mean; and a speed of 56 miles per hour is equal to the mean. The car traveling 47 miles per hour is said to be traveling unusually slow, because its speed corresponds to a z-score of −2.25.

TRY IT YOURSELF 7

The monthly utility bills in a city have a mean of $70 and a standard deviation of $8. Find the z-scores that correspond to utility bills of $60, $71, and $92. Assume the distribution of the utility bills is approximately bell-shaped.

Answer: Page A7

EXAMPLE 8

Comparing z-Scores from Different Data Sets

The table shows the mean heights and standard deviations for a population of men and a population of women. Compare the z-scores for a 6-foot-tall man and a 6-foot-tall woman. Assume the distributions of the heights are approximately bell-shaped.

Men's heights	Women's heights
$\mu = 69.9$ in.	$\mu = 64.3$ in.
$\sigma = 3.0$ in.	$\sigma = 2.6$ in.

SOLUTION Note that 6 feet = 72 inches. Find the z-score for each height.

z-score for 6-foot-tall man
$$z = \frac{x - \mu}{\sigma} = \frac{72 - 69.9}{3.0} = 0.7$$

z-score for 6-foot-tall woman
$$z = \frac{x - \mu}{\sigma} = \frac{72 - 64.3}{2.6} \approx 3.0$$

Interpretation The z-score for the 6-foot-tall man is within 1 standard deviation of the mean (69.9 inches). This is among the typical heights for a man. The z-score for the 6-foot-tall woman is about 3 standard deviations from the mean (64.3 inches). This is an unusual height for a woman.

TRY IT YOURSELF 8

Use the information in Example 8 to compare the z-scores for a 5-foot-tall man and a 5-foot-tall woman.

Answer: Page A7

2.5 EXERCISES

For Extra Help: MyLab Statistics

Building Basic Skills and Vocabulary

1. The length of a guest lecturer's talk represents the third quartile for talks in a guest lecture series. Make an observation about the length of the talk.

2. A motorcycle's fuel efficiency represents the ninth decile of vehicles in its class. Make an observation about the motorcycle's fuel efficiency.

3. A student's score on the Fundamentals of Engineering exam is in the 89th percentile. Make an observation about the student's exam score.

4. A student's IQ score is in the 91st percentile on the Weschler Adult Intelligence Scale. Make an observation about the student's IQ score.

5. Explain how to identify outliers using the interquartile range.

6. Describe the relationship between quartiles and percentiles.

True or False? *In Exercises 7–10, determine whether the statement is true or false. If it is false, rewrite it as a true statement.*

7. About one-quarter of a data set falls below Q_1.

8. The second quartile is the mean of an ordered data set.

9. An outlier is any number above Q_3 or below Q_1.

10. It is impossible to have a z-score of 0.

Using and Interpreting Concepts

Finding Quartiles, Interquartile Range, and Outliers *In Exercises 11 and 12, (a) find the quartiles, (b) find the interquartile range, and (c) identify any outliers.*

11. 40 42 48 35 45 65 46 48 41 39 47 48 46 43 49

12. 31 48 39 40 37 49 46 34 32 30
    44 41 42 49 49 35 38 37 41 35

Graphical Analysis *In Exercises 13 and 14, use the box-and-whisker plot to identify the five-number summary.*

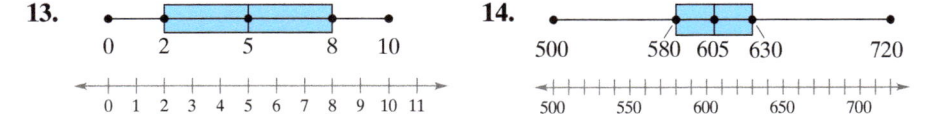

13. [Box-and-whisker plot with values 0, 2, 5, 8, 10 on scale 0 to 11]

14. [Box-and-whisker plot with values 500, 580, 605, 630, 720 on scale 500 to 700]

Drawing a Box-and-Whisker Plot *In Exercises 15–18, (a) find the five-number summary, and (b) draw a box-and-whisker plot that represents the data set.*

15. 55 65 69 64 52 75 79 45 48 64 63 51 59 56 52

16. 230 240 252 228 220 262 238 228 250 260 232 242

17. 4 7 7 5 2 9 7 6 8 5 8 4 1 5 2 8 7 6 6 9

18. 2 7 1 3 1 2 8 9 9 2 5 4 7 3 7 5 4
    2 3 5 9 5 6 3 9 3 4 9 8 8 2 3 9 5

Graphical Analysis *In Exercises 19–22, use the box-and-whisker plot to determine whether the shape of the distribution represented is symmetric, skewed left, skewed right, or none of these. Justify your answer.*

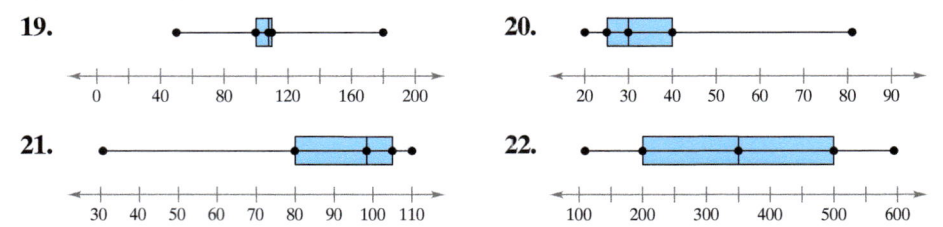

19.

20.

21.

22.

Using Technology to Find Quartiles and Draw Graphs *In Exercises 23–26, use technology to draw a box-and-whisker plot that represents the data set.*

23. **Studying** The numbers of extra classes taken per week by a sample of 32 students

   5 6 1 2 4 3 1 5 8 1 3 2 7 3 4 2
   8 7 6 5 1 2 8 1 9 3 2 1 2 2 4 1

24. **Leaves** The numbers of leaves availed by a sample of 20 executives in a recent year

   4 3 5 6 7 9 11 4 5 3
   9 6 15 2 6 4 7 11 5 9

25. **Hours worked** The numbers of working hours of a sample of 30 employees in a month

   160 182 195 196 174 185 135 169 168 154
   196 210 199 187 164 152 158 161 143 237
   131 211 238 132 147 195 184 164 145 191

26. **Annual Profits** The annual profits (in thousands of dollars) of a sample of 27 companies listed on a stock exchange

   12.86 51.11 13.84 15.96 23.81 45.11 63.22 29.13 13.12
   23.07 2.11 28.02 28.04 2.11 1.02 2.01 13.08 21.01
   12.09 18.04 16.12 18.11 9.11 22.01 11.04 16.14 22.04

27. **Studying** Refer to the data set in Exercise 23 and the box-and-whisker plot you drew that represents the data set.
   (a) About 25% of the students took no more than how many extra classes per week?
   (b) What percent of the students took less than three extra classes per week?
   (c) You randomly select one student from the sample. What is the likelihood that the student took more than 2 extra classes per week? Write your answer as a percent.

28. **Annual profits** Refer to the data set in Exercise 26 and the box-and-whisker plot you drew that represents the data set.
   (a) About 50% of the companies made less than what amount of annual profits?
   (b) What percent of the companies made profits of more than $12.09 thousand?
   (c) What percent of the companies made profits between $12.09 thousand and $23.81 thousand?
   (d) You randomly select one company from the sample. What is the likelihood that the company made an annual profit more than $23.81 thousand? Write your answer as a percent.

Interpreting Percentiles *In Exercises 29–32, use the ogive, which represents the cumulative frequency distribution for quantitative reasoning scores on the Graduate Record Examination in a recent range of years. (Adapted from Educational Testing Service)*

Quantitative Reasoning Scores

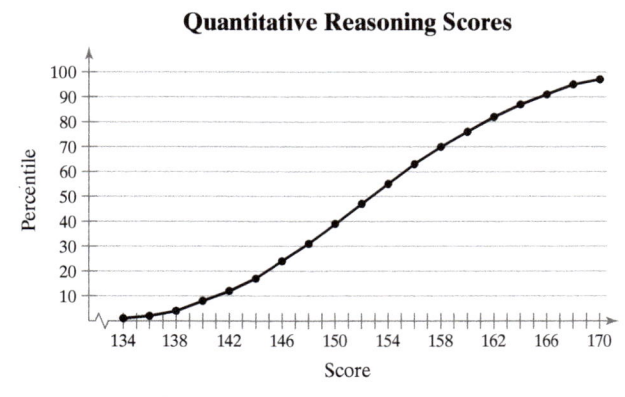

29. What score represents the 70th percentile? How should you interpret this?
30. Which score represents the 40th percentile? How should you interpret this?
31. What percentile is a score of 140? How should you interpret this?
32. What percentile is a score of 170? How should you interpret this?

Finding a Percentile *In Exercises 33–36, use the data set, which represents the ages of 30 executives.*

```
43  57  65  47  57  41  56  53  61  54
56  50  66  56  50  61  47  40  50  43
54  41  48  45  28  35  38  43  42  44
```

33. Find the percentile that corresponds to an age of 47 years old.
34. Find the percentile that corresponds to an age of 57 years old.
35. Which ages are below the 75th percentile?
36. Which ages are above the 25th percentile?

Finding and Interpreting Percentiles *In Exercises 37–40, use the data set, which represents wait times (in minutes) for various services at a state's Department of Motor Vehicles locations.*

```
6  10   1  22  23  10   6   7   2   1   6   6   2   4  14  15  16   4
19  3  19  26   5   3   4   7   6  10   9  10  20  18   3  20  10  13
14 11  14  17   4  27   4   8   4   3  26  18  21   1   3   3   5   5
```

37. Draw an ogive to show corresponding percentiles for the data.
38. Which wait time represents the 50th percentile? How would you interpret this?
39. Find the percentile that corresponds to a wait time of 20 minutes.
40. Which wait times are between the 25th and 75th percentiles?

Graphical Analysis *In Exercises 41 and 42, the midpoints A, B, and C are marked on the histogram at the left. Match them with the indicated z-scores. Which z-scores, if any, would be considered unusual?*

41. $z = 0$, $z = 2.14$, $z = -1.43$
42. $z = 0.77$, $z = 1.54$, $z = -1.54$

Applied Statistics Test Scores

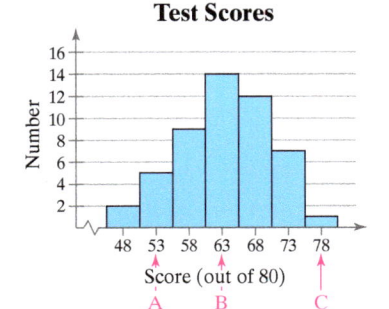

FIGURE FOR EXERCISE 41

Physics Test Scores

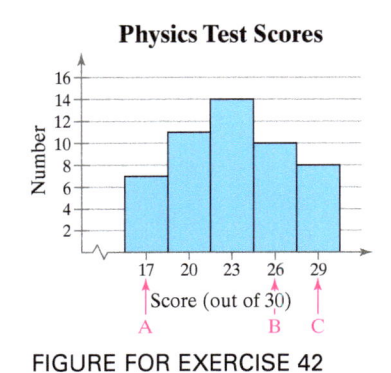

FIGURE FOR EXERCISE 42

Finding z-Scores *The distribution of the ages of the winners of the Tour de France from 1903 to 2016 is approximately bell-shaped. The mean age is 27.9 years, with a standard deviation of 3.3 years. In Exercises 43–48, use the corresponding z-score to determine whether the age is unusual. Explain your reasoning.* *(Source: Le Tour de France)*

	Winner	Year	Age
43.	Christopher Froome	2016	31
44.	Jan Ullrich	1997	24
45.	Antonin Magne	1931	27
46.	Firmin Lambot	1922	36
47.	Henri Cornet	1904	20
48.	Christopher Froome	2013	28

49. **Life Spans of Lady Bugs** The life spans of a species of lady bugs have a bell-shaped distribution, with a mean of 1000 days and a standard deviation of 100 days.
    (a) The life spans of three randomly selected lady bugs are 1250 days, 1175 days, and 950 days. Find the z-score that corresponds to each life span. Determine whether any of these life spans are unusual.
    (b) The life spans of three randomly selected lady bugs are 1150 days, 910 days, and 845 days. Using the Empirical Rule, find the percentile that corresponds to each life span.

50. **Life Spans of Bearings** A brand of bearings has a mean life span of 15,000 cycles, with a standard deviation of 1,250 cycles. Assume the life spans of the bearings have a bell-shaped distribution.
    (a) The life spans of three randomly selected bearings are 13,500 cycles, 17,000 cycles, and 18,500 cycles. Find the z-score that corresponds to each life span. Determine whether any of these life spans are unusual.
    (b) The life spans of three randomly selected bearings are 12,500 cycles, 14,750 cycles, and 19,000 cycles. Using the Empirical Rule, find the percentile that corresponds to each life span.

Comparing z-Scores from Different Data Sets *The table shows population statistics for the ages of Best Actor and Best Supporting Actor winners at the Academy Awards from 1929 to 2016. The distributions of the ages are approximately bell-shaped. In Exercises 51–54, compare the z-scores for the actors.*

Best actor	Best supporting actor
$\mu \approx 43.7$ yr	$\mu \approx 50.4$ yr
$\sigma \approx 8.7$ yr	$\sigma \approx 13.8$ yr

51. Best Actor 1984: Robert Duvall, Age: 53
    Best Supporting Actor 1984: Jack Nicholson, Age: 46

52. Best Actor 2005: Jamie Foxx, Age: 37
    Best Supporting Actor 2005: Morgan Freeman, Age: 67

53. Best Actor 1970: John Wayne, Age: 62
    Best Supporting Actor 1970: Gig Young, Age: 56

54. Best Actor 1982: Henry Fonda, Age: 76
    Best Supporting Actor 1982: John Gielgud, Age: 77

Extending Concepts

Midquartile Another measure of position is called the **midquartile**. You can find the midquartile of a data set by using the formula below.

$$\text{Midquartile} = \frac{Q_1 + Q_3}{2}$$

In Exercises 55 and 56, find the midquartile of the data set.

55. 5 7 1 2 3 10 8 7 5 3

56. 23 36 47 33 34 40 39 24 32 22 38 41

57. Song Lengths **Side-by-side box-and-whisker plots** can be used to compare two or more different data sets. Each box-and-whisker plot is drawn on the same number line to compare the data sets more easily. The lengths (in seconds) of songs played at two different concerts are shown.

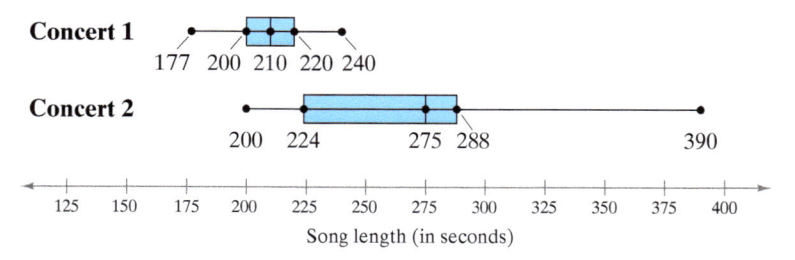

Concert 1: 177 200 210 220 240

Concert 2: 200 224 275 288 390

Song length (in seconds)

(a) Describe the shape of each distribution. Which concert has less variation in song lengths?

(b) Which distribution is more likely to have outliers? Explain.

(c) Which concert do you think has a standard deviation of 16.3? Explain.

(d) Can you determine which concert lasted longer? Explain.

58. Credit Card Purchases The credit card purchases (rounded to the nearest dollar) over the last three months for you and a friend are listed.

You   60 95 102 110 130 130 162 200 215 120 124 28
         58 40 102 105 141 160 130 210 145   90   46 76

Friend 100 125 132 90 85 75 140 160 180 190 160 105
          145 150 151 82 78 115 170 158 140 130 165 125

Use technology to draw side-by-side box-and-whisker plots that represent the data sets. Then describe the shapes of the distributions.

Modified Box-and-Whisker Plot *In Exercises 59–62, (a) identify any outliers and (b) draw a modified box-and-whisker plot that represents the data set. Use asterisks (*) to identify outliers.*

59. 16 9 11 12 8 10 12 13 11 10 24 9 2 15 7

60. 75 78 80 75 62 72 74 75 80 95 76 72

61. 47 29 59 83 46 1 46 23 52 53 35 37 49

62. 36 38 47 50 53 54 19 27 30 47 48 50 56 60 90 62

63. Project Find a real-life data set and use the techniques of Chapter 2, including graphs and numerical quantities, to discuss the center, variation, and shape of the data set. Describe any patterns.

USES AND ABUSES

Statistics in the Real World

Uses

Descriptive statistics help you see trends or patterns in a set of raw data. A good description of a data set consists of (1) a measure of the center of the data, (2) a measure of the variability (or spread) of the data, and (3) the shape (or distribution) of the data. When you read reports, news items, or advertisements prepared by other people, you are rarely given the raw data used for a study. Instead, you see graphs, measures of central tendency, and measures of variability. To be a discerning reader, you need to understand the terms and techniques of descriptive statistics.

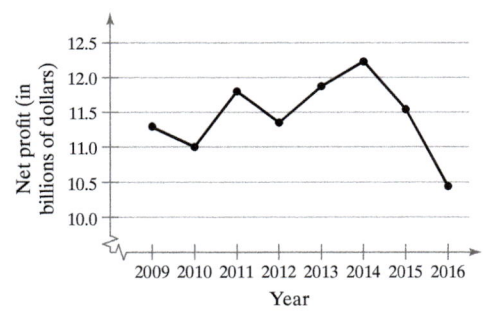

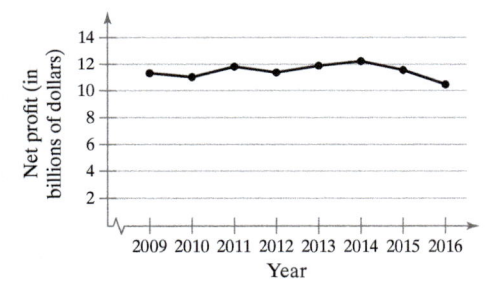

Abuses

Knowing how statistics are calculated can help you analyze questionable statistics. For instance, you are interviewing for a sales position and the company reports that the average yearly commission earned by the five people in its sales force is $60,000. This is a misleading statement if it is based on four commissions of $25,000 and one of $200,000. The median would more accurately describe the yearly commission, but the company used the mean because it is a greater amount.

Statistical graphs can also be misleading. Compare the two time series charts at the left, which show the net profits for the Procter & Gamble Corporation from 2009 through 2016. The data are the same for each chart. The first time series chart, however, has a cropped vertical axis, which makes it appear that the net profit decreased greatly from 2009 to 2010, from 2011 to 2012, and from 2014 to 2016, and increased greatly from 2010 to 2011 and from 2012 to 2014. In the second time series chart, the scale on the vertical axis begins at zero. This time series chart correctly shows that the net profit changed modestly during this time period. *(Source: Procter & Gamble Corporation)*

Ethics

Mark Twain helped popularize the saying, "There are three kinds of lies: lies, damned lies, and statistics." In short, even the most accurate statistics can be used to support studies or statements that are incorrect. Unscrupulous people can use misleading statistics to "prove" their point. Being informed about how statistics are calculated and questioning the data are ways to avoid being misled.

EXERCISES

1. Use the Internet or some other resource to find an example of a graph that might lead to incorrect conclusions.

2. You are publishing an article that discusses how drinking red wine can help prevent heart disease. Because drinking red wine might help people at risk for heart disease, you include a graph that exaggerates the effects of drinking red wine and preventing heart disease. Do you think it is ethical to publish this graph? Explain.

2 Chapter Summary

What Did You Learn?	Example(s)	Review Exercises
Section 2.1		
▸ How to construct a frequency distribution including limits, midpoints, relative frequencies, cumulative frequencies, and boundaries	1, 2	1
▸ How to construct frequency histograms, frequency polygons, relative frequency histograms, and ogives	3–7	2–6
Section 2.2		
▸ How to graph and interpret quantitative data sets using stem-and-leaf plots and dot plots	1–3	7, 8
▸ How to graph and interpret qualitative data sets using pie charts and Pareto charts	4, 5	9, 10
▸ How to graph and interpret paired data sets using scatter plots and time series charts	6, 7	11, 12
Section 2.3		
▸ How to find the mean, median, and mode of a population and of a sample	1–6	13, 14
▸ How to find a weighted mean of a data set, and how to estimate the sample mean of grouped data	7, 8	15–18
▸ How to describe the shape of a distribution as symmetric, uniform, or skewed, and how to compare the mean and median for each		19–24
Section 2.4		
▸ How to find the range of a data set, and how to find the variance and standard deviation of a population and of a sample	1–4	25–28
▸ How to use the Empirical Rule and Chebychev's Theorem to interpret standard deviation	5–7	29–32
▸ How to estimate the sample standard deviation for grouped data	8, 9	33, 34
▸ How to use the coefficient of variation to compare variation in different data sets	10	35, 36
Section 2.5		
▸ How to find the first, second, and third quartiles of a data set, how to find the interquartile range of a data set, and how to represent a data set graphically using a box-and-whisker plot	1–4	37–42
▸ How to interpret other fractiles such as percentiles, and how to find percentiles for a specific data entry	5, 6	43, 44
▸ How to find and interpret the standard score (z-score)	7, 8	45–48

2 Review Exercises

Section 2.1

In Exercises 1 and 2, use the data set, which represents the overall average class sizes for 20 national universities. (Adapted from Public University Honors)

37 34 42 44 39 40 41 51 49 31
55 26 31 40 30 27 36 43 49 35

1. Construct a frequency distribution for the data set using five classes. Include class limits, midpoints, boundaries, frequencies, relative frequencies, and cumulative frequencies.

2. Construct a relative frequency histogram using the frequency distribution in Exercise 1. Then determine which class has the greatest relative frequency and which has the least relative frequency.

In Exercises 3 and 4, use the data set shown in the table at the left, which represents the actual liquid volumes (in ounces) in 25 twelve-ounce cans.

3. Construct a frequency histogram for the data set using seven classes.

4. Construct a relative frequency histogram for the data set using seven classes.

In Exercises 5 and 6, use the data set, which represents the numbers of rooms reserved during one night's business at a sample of hotels.

153 104 118 166   89 104 100   79   93   96 116
 94 140   84   81   96 108 111   87 126 101 111
122 108 126   93 108   87 103   95 129   93 124

5. Construct a frequency distribution for the data set with six classes and draw a frequency polygon.

6. Construct an ogive for the data set using six classes.

Section 2.2

In Exercises 7 and 8, use the data set, which represents the pollution indices for 24 U.S. cities. (Adapted from Numbeo)

22 41 46 50 38 57 65 49 33 28 53 32
41 23 38 65 28 36 63 54 39 43 56 39

7. Use a stem-and-leaf plot to display the data set. Describe any patterns.

8. Use a dot plot to display the data set. Describe any patterns.

In Exercises 9 and 10, use the data set, which represents the results of a survey that asked U.S. full-time university and college students about their activities and time use on an average weekday. (Source: Bureau of Labor Statistics)

Response	Sleeping	Leisure and Sports	Working	Educational Activities	Other
Time (in hours)	8.8	4.0	2.3	3.5	5.4

9. Use a pie chart to display the data set. Describe any patterns.

10. Use a Pareto chart to display the data set. Describe any patterns.

Volumes (in ounces)

11.95	11.91	11.86	11.94	12.00
11.93	12.00	11.94	12.10	11.95
11.99	11.94	11.89	12.01	11.99
11.94	11.92	11.98	11.88	11.94
11.98	11.92	11.95	11.93	12.04

TABLE FOR EXERCISES 3 AND 4

11. The heights (in feet) and the numbers of stories of the ten tallest buildings in New York City are listed. Use a scatter plot to display the data. Describe any patterns. *(Source: Emporis)*

Height (in feet)	1776	1398	1250	1200	1079	1046	1046	1005	975	952
Stories	104	96	102	58	71	77	52	75	72	66

12. The U.S. real unemployment rates over a 12-year period are listed. Use a time series chart to display the data. Describe any patterns. *(Source: U.S. Bureau of Labor Statistics)*

Year	2005	2006	2007	2008	2009	2010
Rate	9.3%	8.4%	8.4%	9.2%	14.2%	16.7%

Year	2011	2012	2013	2014	2015	2016
Rate	16.2%	15.2%	14.5%	12.7%	11.3%	9.9%

Section 2.3

In Exercises 13 and 14, find the mean, the median, and the mode of the data, if possible. If any measure cannot be found or does not represent the center of the data, explain why.

13. The vertical jumps (in inches) of a sample of 10 college basketball players at the 2016 NBA Draft Combine *(Source: DraftExpress)*

    33.0 35.5 37.5 31.0 28.0 29.5 21.0 26.0 24.0 29.5

14. The responses of 1019 adults who were asked how much money they think they will spend on Christmas gifts in a recent year *(Adapted from Gallup)*

    $1000 or more: 306 $250–999: 336   Less than $250: 234
    Not sure: 51   None/do not celebrate Christmas: 92

15. Six test scores are shown below. The first 4 test scores are 15% of the final grade, and the last two test scores are 20% of the final grade. Find the weighted mean of the test scores.

    80 70 84 93 89 78

16. For the four test scores 96, 85, 91, and 86, the first 3 test scores are 20% of the final grade, and the last test score is 40% of the final grade. Find the weighted mean of the test scores.

17. Estimate the mean of the frequency distribution you made in Exercise 1.

18. The frequency distribution shows the numbers of magazine subscriptions per household for a sample of 60 households. Find the mean number of subscriptions per household.

Number of magazines	0	1	2	3	4	5	6
Frequency	13	9	19	8	5	2	4

19. Describe the shape of the distribution for the histogram you made in Exercise 3 as symmetric, uniform, skewed left, skewed right, or none of these.

20. Describe the shape of the distribution for the histogram you made in Exercise 4 as symmetric, uniform, skewed left, skewed right, or none of these.

In Exercises 21 and 22, determine whether the approximate shape of the distribution in the histogram is symmetric, uniform, skewed left, skewed right, or none of these.

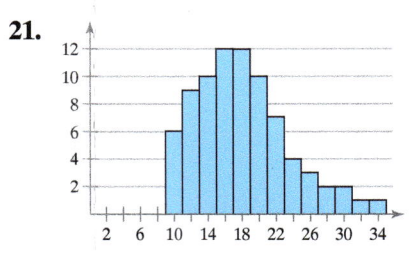

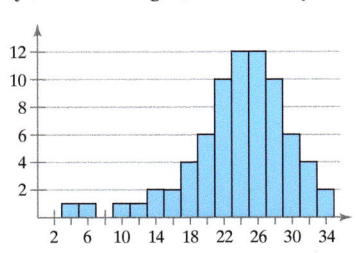

21.

22.

23. For the histogram in Exercise 21, which is greater, the mean or the median? Explain your reasoning.

24. For the histogram in Exercise 22, which is greater, the mean or the median? Explain your reasoning.

Section 2.4

In Exercises 25 and 26, find the range, mean, variance, and standard deviation of the population data set.

25. The weights (in lbs) of 14 newborn babies.

7 5 12 12 6 9 11 4 7 6 8 7 10 9

26. The ages of the Supreme Court justices as of December 22, 2016 *(Source: Supreme Court of the United States)*

61 80 68 83 78 66 62 56

In Exercises 27 and 28, find the range, mean, variance, and standard deviation of the sample data set.

27. The insurance claims (in dollars) from an auto insurance company.

1514 1473 1847 1746 1545 994 883 705
612 1204 612 585 936 1122 816

28. Annual household expenditures (in dollars) of a random sample of university professors:

37,224 40,964 43,724 36,188 38,882 38,157 39,914 37,443

In Exercises 29 and 30, use the Empirical Rule.

29. The mean wages for a sample of employees in a company was $18.00 per day with a standard deviation of $2.50 per day. Between what two values do 95% of the data lie? (Assume the data set has a bell-shaped distribution.)

30. The mean wages for a sample of employees in a company was $16.50 per day with a standard deviation of $1.50 per month. Estimate the percent of wages between $12.00 and $21.00 per day. (Assume the data set has a bell-shaped distribution.)

31. In a certain examination, the mean score per student for 20 students is 75 with a standard deviation of 8.5. Using Chebychev's Theorem, determine at least how many of the students scored between 58 and 92.

32. The mean duration of the 135 space shuttle flights was about 9.9 days, and the standard deviation was about 3.8 days. Using Chebychev's Theorem, determine at least how many of the flights lasted between 2.3 days and 17.5 days. *(Source: NASA)*

33. From a random sample of households, the numbers of televisions are listed. Find the sample mean and the sample standard deviation of the data.

    Number of televisions   0   1   2   3   4   5
    Number of households   1   8   13 10 5   3

34. From a random sample of airplanes, the numbers of defects found in their fuselages are listed. Find the sample mean and the sample standard deviation of the data.

    Number of defects   0   1   2   3   4   5   6
    Number of airplanes 4   5   2   9   1   3   1

In Exercises 35 and 36, find the coefficient of variation for each of the two data sets. Then compare the results.

35. Sample dividends (in %) paid by two companies are listed:

    Company A   2.3   2.9   3.9   3.1   2.2   1.5   2.2   2.7   1.8
    Company B   2.8   2.5   2.9   3.6   2.9   3.3   3.3   2.8   1.6

36. The heights (in inches) and weights (in lbs) of 8 students in a secondary school are listed.

    Heights   62   58   60   64   70   62   72   68
    Weights   92   80   82   106   136   96   146   138

Section 2.5

In Exercises 37–40, use the data set, which represents the model 2017 vehicles with the highest fuel economies (in miles per gallon) in the most popular classes. (Source: U.S. Environmental Protection Agency)

    35   35   112   34   124   35   107   46   136   56   58   119   50
    41   25   25   22   16   16   52   22   22   22   34   30   30

37. Find the five-number summary of the data set.

38. Find the interquartile range of the data set.

39. Draw a box-and-whisker plot that represents the data set.

40. About how many vehicles fall on or below the third quartile?

41. Find the interquartile range of the data set from Exercise 13.

42. The weights (in pounds) of the defensive players on a high school football team are shown below. Draw a box-and-whisker plot that represents the data set and describe the shape of the distribution.

    173   145   205   192   197   227   156   240   172
    208   185   190   167   212   228   190   184   195

43. A worker's income of $32 represents the 15th percentile of the incomes. What percentage of workers earns more than $32?

44. As of December 2016, there were 721 adult contemporary radio stations in the United States. One station finds that 115 stations have a larger daily audience than it has. What percentile does this station come closest to in the daily audience rankings? *(Source: Radio-Locator.com)*

The towing capacities (in pounds) of all the pickup trucks at a dealership have a bell-shaped distribution, with a mean of 11,830 pounds and a standard deviation of 2370 pounds. In Exercises 45–48, use the corresponding z-score to determine whether the towing capacity is unusual. Explain your reasoning.

45. 16,500 pounds   46. 5500 pounds   47. 18,000 pounds   48. 11,300 pounds

2 Chapter Quiz

Take this quiz as you would take a quiz in class. After you are done, check your work against the answers given in the back of the book.

1. The data set represents the numbers of minutes a sample of 27 people exercise each week.

108	139	120	123	120	132	123	131	131
157	150	124	111	101	135	119	116	117
127	128	139	119	118	114	127	142	130

   (a) Construct a frequency distribution for the data set using five classes. Include class limits, midpoints, boundaries, frequencies, relative frequencies, and cumulative frequencies.
   (b) Display the data using a frequency histogram and a frequency polygon on the same axes.
   (c) Display the data using a relative frequency histogram.
   (d) Describe the shape of the distribution as symmetric, uniform, skewed left, skewed right, or none of these.
   (e) Display the data using an ogive.
   (f) Display the data using a stem-and-leaf plot. Use one line per stem.
   (g) Display the data using a box-and-whisker plot.

2. Use frequency distribution formulas to approximate the sample mean and the sample standard deviation of the data set in Exercise 1.

3. The elements with known properties can be classified as metals (57 elements), metalloids (7 elements), halogens (5 elements), noble gases (6 elements), rare earth elements (30 elements), and other nonmetals (7 elements). Display the data using (a) a pie chart and (b) a Pareto chart.

4. Weekly salaries (in dollars) for a sample of construction workers are listed.

1100	720	1384	1124	1255	976	718	1316
749	1062	1248	891	969	790	860	1100

   (a) Find the mean, median, and mode of the salaries. Which best describes a typical salary?
   (b) Find the range, variance, and standard deviation of the data set.
   (c) Find the coefficient of variation of the data set.

5. The mean price of new homes from a sample of houses is $180,000 with a standard deviation of $15,000. The data set has a bell-shaped distribution. Using the Empirical Rule, between what two prices do 95% of the houses fall?

6. Refer to the sample statistics from Exercise 5 and determine whether any of the house prices below are unusual. Explain your reasoning.
   (a) $225,000   (b) $80,000   (c) $200,000   (d) $147,000

7. The numbers of regular season wins for each Major League Baseball team in 2016 are listed. Display the data using a box-and-whisker plot. *(Source: Major League Baseball)*

93	89	89	84	68	94	86	81	78	59
95	86	84	74	69	95	87	79	71	68
103	86	78	73	68	91	87	75	69	68

2 Chapter Test

Take this test as you would take a test in class.

1. The overall averages of 12 students in a statistics class prior to taking the final exam are listed.

   67   72   88   73   99   85   81   87   63   94   68   87

   (a) Find the mean, median, and mode of the data set. Which best represents the center of the data?
   (b) Find the range, variance, and standard deviation of the sample data set.
   (c) Find the coefficient of variation of the data set.
   (d) Display the data in a stem-and-leaf plot. Use one line per stem.

2. The data set represents the numbers of movies that a sample of 20 people watched in a year.

   121   148   94   142   170   88   221   106   18   67
   149   28   60   101   134   168   92   154   53   66

   (a) Construct a frequency distribution for the data set using six classes. Include class limits, midpoints, boundaries, frequencies, relative frequencies, and cumulative frequencies.
   (b) Display the data using a frequency histogram and a frequency polygon on the same axes.
   (c) Display the data using a relative frequency histogram.
   (d) Describe the shape of the distribution as symmetric, uniform, skewed left, skewed right, or none of these.
   (e) Display the data using an ogive.

3. Use frequency distribution formulas to estimate the sample mean and the sample standard deviation of the data set in Exercise 2.

4. For the data set in Exercise 2, find the percentile that corresponds to 149 movies watched in a year.

5. The table lists the numbers of albums by The Beatles that received sales certifications. Display the data using (a) a pie chart and (b) a Pareto chart. *(Source: Recording Industry Association of America)*

6. The numbers of minutes it took 12 students in a statistics class to complete the final exam are listed. Use a scatter plot to display this data set and the data set in Exercise 1. The data sets are in the same order. Describe any patterns.

   61   85   67   48   54   61   59   80   67   55   88   84

7. The data set represents the ages of 15 college professors.

   46   51   60   58   37   65   40   55   30   68   28   62   56   42   59

   (a) Display the data in a box-and-whisker plot.
   (b) About what percent of the professors are over the age of 40?

8. The mean gestational length of a sample of 208 horses is 343.7 days, with a standard deviation of 10.4 days. The data set has a bell-shaped distribution.

   (a) Estimate the number of gestational lengths between 333.3 and 354.1 days.
   (b) Determine whether a gestational length of 318.4 days feet is unusual.

Certification	Number of albums
Diamond	6
Multi-Platinum	26
Platinum	42
Gold	48

TABLE FOR EXERCISE 5

REAL STATISTICS REAL DECISIONS
Putting it all together

You are a member of your local apartment association. The association represents rental housing owners and managers who operate residential rental property throughout the greater metropolitan area. Recently, the association has received several complaints from tenants in a particular area of the city who feel that their monthly rental fees are much higher compared to other parts of the city.

You want to investigate the rental fees. You gather the data shown in the table at the right. Area A represents the area of the city where tenants are unhappy about their monthly rents. The data represent the monthly rents paid by a random sample of tenants in Area A and three other areas of similar size. Assume all the apartments represented are approximately the same size with the same amenities.

The Monthly Rents (in dollars) Paid by 12 Randomly Selected Apartment Tenants in 4 Areas of Your City

Area A	Area B	Area C	Area D
1435	1265	1221	1044
1249	1074	931	1234
1097	917	893	970
970	1213	1317	827
1171	949	1034	898
1122	839	1061	914
1259	896	851	1387
1022	918	861	1166
1002	1056	911	1123
1187	1218	1148	1029
968	844	799	1131
1097	791	872	1047

EXERCISES

1. **How Would You Do It?**
   (a) How would you investigate the complaints from renters who are unhappy about their monthly rents?
   (b) Which statistical measure do you think would best represent the data sets for the four areas of the city?
   (c) Calculate the measure from part (b) for each of the four areas.

2. **Displaying the Data**
   (a) What type of graph would you choose to display the data? Explain your reasoning.
   (b) Construct the graph from part (a).
   (c) Based on your data displays, does it appear that the monthly rents in Area A are higher than the rents in the other areas of the city? Explain.

3. **Measuring the Data**
   (a) What other statistical measures in this chapter could you use to analyze the monthly rent data?
   (b) Calculate the measures from part (a).
   (c) Compare the measures from part (b) with the graph you constructed in Exercise 2. Do the measurements support your conclusion in Exercise 2? Explain.

4. **Discussing the Data**
   (a) Do you think the complaints in Area A are legitimate? How do you think they should be addressed?
   (b) What reasons might you give as to why the rents vary among different areas of the city?

Highest Monthly Rents For Two-Bedroom Apartments
MEDIAN PER CITY

San Francisco, CA	$4570
New York, NY	$4310
Boston, MA	$3200
Jersey City, NJ	$3200
Washington, DC	$3000

(Source: Apartment List)

TECHNOLOGY

MINITAB · EXCEL · TI-84 PLUS

Parking Tickets

According to data from the city of Toronto, Ontario, Canada, there were more than 180,000 parking infractions in the city for December 2015, with fines totaling over 8,500,000 Canadian dollars.

The fines (in Canadian dollars) for a random sample of 105 parking infractions in Toronto, Ontario, Canada, for December 2015 are listed below. *(Source: City of Toronto)*

30	30	30	30	40	60	40
15	50	150	40	30	30	30
40	30	40	30	30	30	40
40	40	30	60	60	30	150
40	30	250	40	30	30	30
30	30	30	40	30	40	30
50	15	40	40	30	40	30
40	30	30	40	30	30	30
100	30	40	30	30	30	40
30	30	30	40	100	30	40
30	40	30	40	40	40	40
30	30	30	60	30	40	40
30	40	15	60	30	15	150
150	40	40	30	30	150	60
30	40	60	30	40	40	30

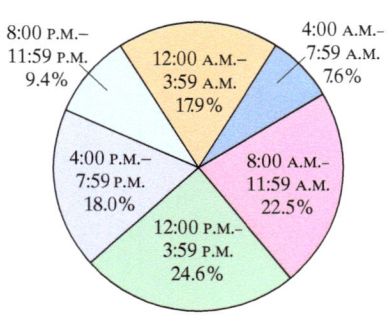

Parking Infractions by Time of Day

- 8:00 P.M.–11:59 P.M. 9.4%
- 12:00 A.M.–3:59 A.M. 17.9%
- 4:00 A.M.–7:59 A.M. 7.6%
- 8:00 A.M.–11:59 A.M. 22.5%
- 12:00 P.M.–3:59 P.M. 24.6%
- 4:00 P.M.–7:59 P.M. 18.0%

(Source: City of Toronto)

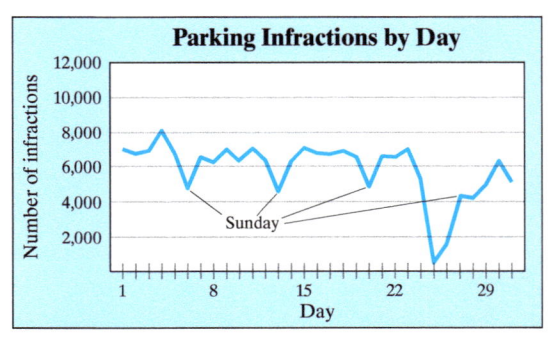

Parking Infractions by Day

(Source: City of Toronto)

The figures above show parking infractions in Toronto, Ontario, Canada, for December 2015 by time of day and by day.

EXERCISES

In Exercises 1–5, use technology. If possible, print your results.

1. Find the sample mean of the data.
2. Find the sample standard deviation of the data.
3. Find the five-number summary of the data.
4. Make a frequency distribution for the data. Use a class width of 15.
5. Draw a histogram for the data. Does the distribution appear to be bell-shaped?
6. What percent of the distribution lies within one standard deviation of the mean? Within two standard deviations of the mean? Within three standard deviations of the mean?
7. Do the results of Exercise 6 agree with the Empirical Rule? Explain.
8. Do the results of Exercise 6 agree with Chebychev's Theorem? Explain.
9. Use the frequency distribution in Exercise 4 to estimate the sample mean and sample standard deviation of the data. Do the formulas for grouped data give results that are as accurate as the individual entry formulas? Explain.
10. **Writing** Do you think the mean or the median better represents the data? Explain your reasoning.

Extended solutions are given in the technology manuals that accompany this text. Technical instruction is provided for Minitab, Excel, and the TI-84 Plus.

2 Using Technology to Determine Descriptive Statistics

Here are some Minitab and TI-84 Plus printouts for three examples in this chapter.

See Example 7, page 63.

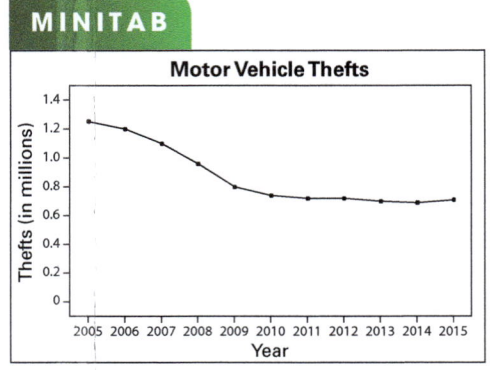

MINITAB

Bar Chart...
Pie Chart...
Time Series Plot...
Area Graph...
Contour Plot...
3D Scatterplot...
3D Surface Plot...

Motor Vehicle Thefts — Thefts (in millions) vs. Year (2005–2015), declining from about 1.25 to about 0.7.

See Example 3, page 87.

MINITAB

Display Descriptive Statistics...
Store Descriptive Statistics...
Graphical Summary...
1-Sample Z...
1-Sample t...
2-Sample t...
Paired t...

Descriptive Statistics: Recovery times

Variable	N	Mean	SE Mean	StDev	Minimum
Recovery times	12	7.500	0.544	1.883	4.000

Variable	Q1	Median	Q3	Maximum
Recovery times	6.250	7.500	9.000	10.000

See Example 4, page 107.

MINITAB

Empirical CDF...
Probability Distribution Plot ...
Boxplot...
Interval Plot...
Individual Value Plot...
Line Plot...

Boxplot of Gallons of Fuel Wasted Per Year, with an outlier near 10.

Descriptive Statistics **127**

See Example 7, page 63.

TI-84 PLUS
STAT PLOTS
1: Plot1...Off
   L1 L2
2: Plot2...Off
   L1 L2
3: Plot3...Off
   L1 L2
4↓ PlotsOff

↓

TI-84 PLUS
Plot1 Plot2 Plot3
On Off
Type: [icons]
Xlist: L1
Ylist: L2
Mark: ■ + .

↓

TI-84 PLUS
ZOOM MEMORY
4↑ ZDecimal
5: ZSquare
6: ZStandard
7: ZTrig
8: ZInteger
9: ZoomStat
0↓ ZoomFit

↓

TI-84 PLUS
[scatter plot]

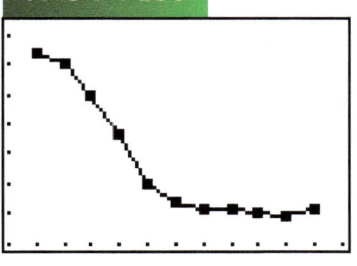

See Example 3, page 87.

TI-84 PLUS
EDIT CALC TESTS
1: 1-Var Stats
2: 2-Var Stats
3: Med-Med
4: LinReg(ax+b)
5: QuadReg
6: CubicReg
7↓ QuartReg

↓

TI-84 PLUS
1-Var Stats
List: L1
FreqList:
Calculate

↓

TI-84 PLUS
1-Var Stats
$\bar{x}=7.5$
$\Sigma x=90$
$\Sigma x^2=714$
$Sx=1.882937743$
$\sigma x=1.802775638$
↓$n=12$

See Example 4, page 107.

TI-84 PLUS
STAT PLOTS
1: Plot1...Off
   L1 L2
2: Plot2...Off
   L1 L2
3: Plot3...Off
   L1 L2
4↓ PlotsOff

↓

TI-84 PLUS
Plot1 Plot2 Plot3
On Off
Type: [icons]
Xlist: L1
Freq: 1
Mark: ■ + .

↓

TI-84 PLUS
ZOOM MEMORY
4↑ ZDecimal
5: ZSquare
6: ZStandard
7: ZTrig
8: ZInteger
9: ZoomStat
0↓ ZoomFit

↓

TI-84 PLUS
[box plot with outlier]

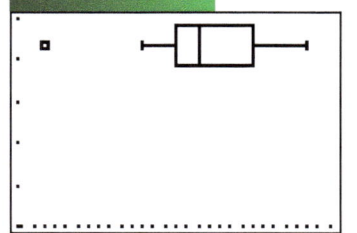

CHAPTERS 1 & 2
CUMULATIVE REVIEW

In Exercises 1 and 2, identify the sampling technique used, and discuss potential sources of bias (if any). Explain.

1. For quality assurance, every fortieth toothbrush is taken from each of four assembly lines and tested to make sure the bristles stay in the toothbrush.

2. Using random digit dialing, researchers asked 1090 U.S. adults their level of education.

3. In 2016, a worldwide study of workplace fraud found that initial detections of fraud resulted from a tip (39.1%), an internal audit (16.5%), management review (13.4%), detection by accident (5.6%), account reconciliation (5.5%), surveillance/monitoring (1.9%), confession (1.3%), or some other means (16.7%). Use a Pareto chart to organize the data. *(Source: Association of Certified Fraud Examiners)*

In Exercises 4 and 5, determine whether the number is a parameter or a statistic. Explain your reasoning.

4. In 2016, the median annual salary of a marketing account executive was $68,232.

5. In a survey of 1002 U.S. adults, 88% said that fake news has caused a great deal of confusion or some confusion. *(Source: Pew Research Center)*

6. The mean annual salary for a sample of electrical engineers is $86,500, with a standard deviation of $1500. The data set has a bell-shaped distribution.

   (a) Use the Empirical Rule to estimate the percent of electrical engineers whose annual salaries are between $83,500 and $89,500.

   (b) The salaries of three randomly selected electrical engineers are $93,500, $85,600, and $82,750. Find the z-score that corresponds to each salary. Determine whether any of these salaries are unusual.

In Exercises 7 and 8, identify the population and the sample.

7. A survey of 339 college and university admissions directors and enrollment officers found that 72% think their institution is losing potential applicants due to concerns about accumulating student loan debt. *(Source: Gallup)*

8. A survey of 67,901 Americans ages 12 years or older found that 1.6% had used pain relievers for nonmedical purposes. *(Source: Substance Abuse and Mental Health Services Administration)*

In Exercises 9 and 10, determine whether the study is an observational study or an experiment. Explain.

9. To study the effect of using digital devices in the classroom on exam performance, researchers divided 726 undergraduate students into three groups, including a group that was allowed to use digital devices, a group that had restricted access to tablets, and a control group that was "technology-free." *(Source: Massachusetts Institute of Technology)*

10. In a study of 7847 children in grades 1 through 5, 15.5% have attention deficit hyperactivity disorder. *(Source: Gallup)*

In Exercises 11 and 12, determine whether the data are qualitative or quantitative, and determine the level of measurement of the data set.

11. The numbers of stolen bases during the 2016 season for Chicago Cubs players who stole at least one base are listed. *(Source: Major League Baseball)*

    2   8   3   2   13   12   6   2   1   5   11   1

12. The six top-earning states in 2015 by median household income are listed. *(Source: U.S. Census Bureau)*

    1. New Hampshire   2. Alaska   3. Maryland
    4. Connecticut   5. Minnesota   6. New Jersey

13. The numbers of tornadoes by state in 2016 are listed. (a) Draw a box-and-whisker plot that represents the data set and (b) describe the shape of the distribution. *(Source: National Oceanic and Atmospheric Administration)*

87	0	3	23	7	45	0	0	48	27
0	1	50	40	46	99	32	31	2	2
2	15	44	67	23	4	47	0	2	2
3	1	16	32	31	55	4	9	0	3
16	11	90	3	0	12	6	6	11	1

14. Five test scores are shown below. The first 4 test scores are 15% of the final grade, and the last test score is 40% of the final grade. Find the weighted mean of the test scores.

    85   92   84   89   91

15. Tail lengths (in feet) for a sample of American alligators are listed.

    6.5   3.4   4.2   7.1   5.4   6.8   7.5   3.9   4.6

    (a) Find the mean, median, and mode of the tail lengths. Which best describes a typical American alligator tail length? Explain your reasoning.
    (b) Find the range, variance, and standard deviation of the data set.

16. A study shows that life expectancies for Americans have increased or remained stable every year for the past five years.

    (a) Make an inference based on the results of the study.
    (b) What is wrong with this type of reasoning?

In Exercises 17–19, use the data set, which represents the points scored by each player on the Montreal Canadiens in the 2015–2016 NHL season. (Source: National Hockey League)

17	10	0	19	2	18	9	5	1	29
5	26	0	12	20	10	56	40	2	6
0	2	0	0	2	44	1	2	19	64
7	16	54	0	4	12	51	2	0	26

17. Construct a frequency distribution for the data set using eight classes. Include class limits, midpoints, boundaries, frequencies, relative frequencies, and cumulative frequencies.

18. Describe the shape of the distribution.

19. Construct a relative frequency histogram using the frequency distribution in Exercise 17. Then determine which class has the greatest relative frequency and which has the least relative frequency.

CHAPTER 3
Confidence Intervals

3.1
Confidence Intervals for the Mean (σ Known)

3.2
Confidence Intervals for the Mean (σ Unknown)
Activity
Case Study

3.3
Confidence Intervals for Population Proportions
Activity

3.4
Confidence Intervals for Variance and Standard Deviation
Uses and Abuses
Real Statistics—Real Decisions
Technology

David Wechsler was one of the most influential psychologists of the 20th century. He is known for developing intelligence tests, such as the Wechsler Adult Intelligence Scale and the Wechsler Intelligence Scale for Children.

Where You've Been

In Chapters 1 and 2, you studied descriptive statistics (how to collect and describe data) and probability (how to find probabilities and analyze discrete and continuous probability distributions). For instance, psychologists use descriptive statistics to analyze the data collected during experiments and tests.

One of the most commonly administered psychological tests is the Wechsler Adult Intelligence Scale. It is an intelligence quotient (IQ) test that is standardized to have a normal distribution with a mean of 100 and a standard deviation of 15.

Where You're Going

In this chapter, you will begin your study of inferential statistics—the second major branch of statistics. For instance, a chess club wants to estimate the mean IQ of its members. The mean of a random sample of members is 115. Because this estimate consists of a single number represented by a point on a number line, it is called a *point estimate*. The problem with using a point estimate is that it is rarely equal to the exact parameter (mean, standard deviation, or proportion) of the population.

In this chapter, you will learn how to make a more meaningful estimate by specifying an interval of values on a number line, together with a statement of how confident you are that your interval contains the population parameter. Suppose the club wants to be 90% confident of its estimate for the mean IQ of its members. Here is an overview of how to construct an interval estimate.

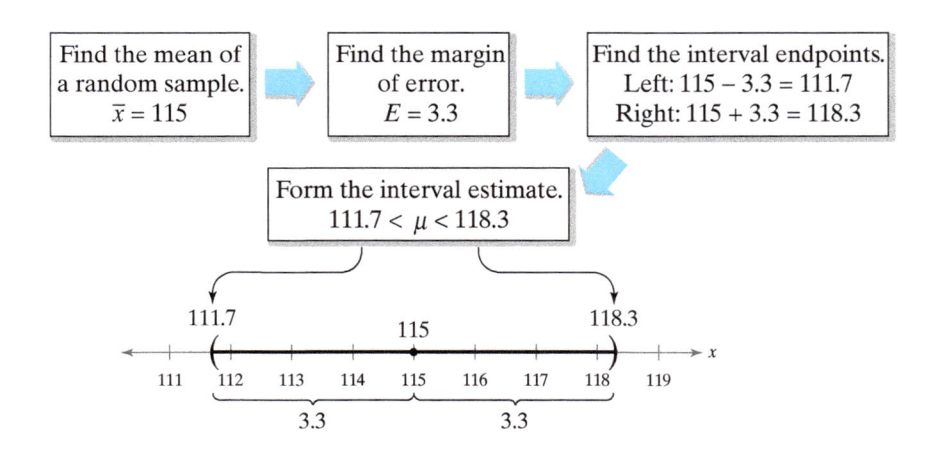

| Find the mean of a random sample. $\bar{x} = 115$ | → | Find the margin of error. $E = 3.3$ | → | Find the interval endpoints. Left: $115 - 3.3 = 111.7$ Right: $115 + 3.3 = 118.3$ |

Form the interval estimate.
$111.7 < \mu < 118.3$

So, the club can be 90% confident that the mean IQ of its members is between 111.7 and 118.3.

3.1 Confidence Intervals for the Mean (σ Known)

What You Should Learn

- How to find a point estimate and a margin of error
- How to construct and interpret confidence intervals for a population mean when σ is known
- How to determine the minimum sample size required when estimating a population mean

Estimating Population Parameters ■ Confidence Intervals for a Population Mean ■ Sample Size

Estimating Population Parameters

In this chapter, you will learn an important technique of statistical inference—to use sample statistics to estimate the value of an unknown population parameter. In this section and the next, you will learn how to use sample statistics to make an estimate of the population parameter μ when the population standard deviation σ is known (this section) or when σ is unknown (Section 3.2). To make such an inference, begin by finding a **point estimate.**

> **DEFINITION**
>
> A **point estimate** is a single value estimate for a population parameter. The most unbiased point estimate of the population mean μ is the sample mean $\bar{x}$.

The validity of an estimation method is increased when you use a sample statistic that is unbiased and has low variability. A statistic is unbiased if it does not overestimate or underestimate the population parameter. You learned that the mean of all possible sample means of the same size equals the population mean. As a result, $\bar{x}$ is an **unbiased estimator** of μ. When the standard error $\sigma/\sqrt{n}$ of a sample mean is decreased by increasing n, it becomes less variable.

EXAMPLE 1

Finding a Point Estimate

A researcher is collecting data about a college athletic conference and its student-athletes. A random sample of 40 student-athletes is selected and their numbers of hours spent on required athletic activities for one week are recorded (see table at left). Find a point estimate for the population mean μ, the mean number of hours spent on required athletic activities by all student-athletes in the conference. *(Adapted from Penn Schoen Berland)*

Number of hours

19	25	15	21	22	20	20	22
22	21	21	23	22	16	21	18
25	23	23	21	22	24	18	19
23	20	19	19	24	25	17	21
21	25	23	18	22	20	21	21

SOLUTION

The sample mean of the data is

$$\bar{x} = \frac{\Sigma x}{n} = \frac{842}{40} \approx 21.1.$$

So, the point estimate for the mean number of hours spent on required athletic activities by all student-athletes in the conference is about 21.1 hours.

TRY IT YOURSELF 1

In Example 1, the researcher selects a second random sample of 30 student-athletes and records their numbers of hours spent on required athletic activities (see table at left). Use this sample to find another point estimate of the population mean μ. *(Adapted from Penn Schoen Berland)*

Answer: Page A7

Number of hours

21	17	21	18	23	25
22	21	23	22	19	20
20	23	20	22	21	19
20	21	23	16	19	20
21	20	22	19	24	24

In Example 1, the probability that the population mean is exactly 21.1 is virtually zero. So, instead of estimating μ to be exactly 21.1 using a point estimate, you can estimate that μ lies in an interval. This is called making an **interval estimate**.

> **DEFINITION**
>
> An **interval estimate** is an interval, or range of values, used to estimate a population parameter.

Although you can assume that the point estimate in Example 1 is not equal to the actual population mean, it is probably close to it. To form an interval estimate, use the point estimate as the center of the interval, and then add and subtract a margin of error. For instance, if the margin of error is 0.6, then an interval estimate would be given by

$$21.1 \pm 0.6 \quad \text{or} \quad 20.5 < \mu < 21.7.$$

The point estimate and interval estimate are shown in the figure.

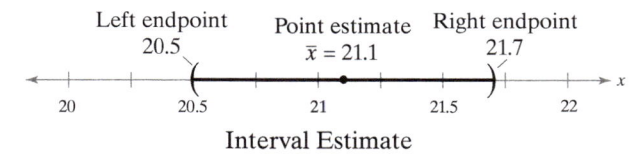

Interval Estimate

Before finding a margin of error for an interval estimate, you should first determine how confident you need to be that your interval estimate contains the population mean μ.

> **DEFINITION**
>
> The **level of confidence** c is the probability that the interval estimate contains the population parameter, assuming that the estimation process is repeated a large number of times.

You know from the Central Limit Theorem that when $n \geq 30$, the sampling distribution of sample means approximates a normal distribution. The level of confidence c is the area under the standard normal curve between the *critical values*, $-z_c$ and z_c. **Critical values** are values that separate sample statistics that are probable from sample statistics that are improbable, or unusual. You can see from the figure shown below that c is the percent of the area under the normal curve between $-z_c$ and z_c. The area remaining is $1 - c$, so the area in one tail is

$$\tfrac{1}{2}(1 - c). \quad \text{Area in one tail}$$

For instance, if $c = 90\%$, then 5% of the area lies to the left of $-z_c = -1.645$ and 5% lies to the right of $z_c = 1.645$, as shown in the table.

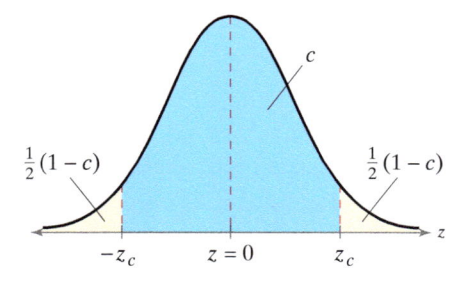

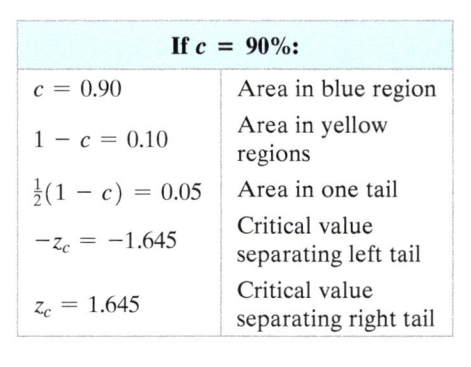

Study Tip

In this text, you will usually use 90%, 95%, and 99% levels of confidence. Here are the z-scores that correspond to these levels of confidence.

Level of Confidence	z_c
90%	1.645
95%	1.96
99%	2.575

If $c = 90\%$:	
$c = 0.90$	Area in blue region
$1 - c = 0.10$	Area in yellow regions
$\tfrac{1}{2}(1 - c) = 0.05$	Area in one tail
$-z_c = -1.645$	Critical value separating left tail
$z_c = 1.645$	Critical value separating right tail

Picturing the World

A survey of a random sample of 1000 smartphone owners found that the mean daily time spent communicating on a smartphone was 131.4 minutes. From previous studies, it is assumed that the population standard deviation is 21.2 minutes. Communicating on a smartphone includes text, email, social media, and phone calls. (Adapted from International Data Corporation)

Daily Time Spent on Smartphone

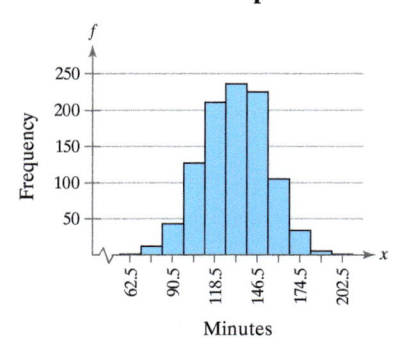

For a 95% confidence interval, what would be the margin of error for the population mean daily time spent communicating on a smartphone?

The difference between the point estimate and the actual parameter value is called the **sampling error.** When μ is estimated, the sampling error is the difference $\bar{x} - \mu$. In most cases, of course, μ is unknown, and $\bar{x}$ varies from sample to sample. However, you can calculate a maximum value for the error when you know the level of confidence and the sampling distribution.

DEFINITION

Given a level of confidence c, the **margin of error** E (sometimes also called the maximum error of estimate or error tolerance) is the greatest possible distance between the point estimate and the value of the parameter it is estimating. For a population mean μ where σ is known, the margin of error is

$$E = z_c \sigma_{\bar{x}} = z_c \frac{\sigma}{\sqrt{n}} \quad \text{Margin of error for } \mu \text{ (} \sigma \text{ known)}$$

when these conditions are met.

1. The sample is random.
2. At least one of the following is true: The population is normally distributed or $n \geq 30$. (Recall from the Central Limit Theorem that when $n \geq 30$, the sampling distribution of sample means approximates a normal distribution.)

EXAMPLE 2

Finding the Margin of Error

Use the data in Example 1 and a 95% confidence level to find the margin of error for the mean number of hours spent on required athletic activities by all student-athletes in the conference. Assume the population standard deviation is 2.3 hours.

SOLUTION

Because σ is known ($\sigma = 2.3$), the sample is random (see Example 1), and $n = 40 \geq 30$, use the formula for E given above. The z-score that corresponds to a 95% confidence level is 1.96. This implies that 95% of the area under the standard normal curve falls within 1.96 standard deviations of the mean, as shown in the figure below. (You can approximate the distribution of the sample means with a normal curve by the Central Limit Theorem because $n = 40 \geq 30$.)

Using the values $z_c = 1.96$, $\sigma = 2.3$, and $n = 40$,

$$E = z_c \frac{\sigma}{\sqrt{n}}$$
$$= 1.96 \cdot \frac{2.3}{\sqrt{40}}$$
$$\approx 0.7.$$

Interpretation You are 95% confident that the margin of error for the population mean is about 0.7 hour.

TRY IT YOURSELF 2

Use the data in Try It Yourself 1 and a 95% confidence level to find the margin of error for the mean number of hours spent on required athletic activities by all student-athletes in the conference. Assume the population standard deviation is 2.3 hours.

Answer: Page A7

Confidence Intervals for a Population Mean

Using a point estimate and a margin of error, you can construct an interval estimate of a population parameter such as μ. This interval estimate is called a **confidence interval**.

> **Study Tip**
>
> When you construct a confidence interval for a population mean, the general *round-off rule* is to round off to the same number of decimal places as the sample mean.

DEFINITION

A *c*-confidence interval for a population mean μ is

$$\bar{x} - E < \mu < \bar{x} + E.$$

The probability that the confidence interval contains μ is c, assuming that the estimation process is repeated a large number of times.

GUIDELINES

Constructing a Confidence Interval for a Population Mean (σ Known)

In Words	In Symbols
1. Verify that σ is known, the sample is random, and either the population is normally distributed or $n \geq 30$.	
2. Find the sample statistics n and $\bar{x}$.	$\bar{x} = \dfrac{\Sigma x}{n}$
3. Find the critical value z_c that corresponds to the given level of confidence.	Use Table 4 in Appendix B.
4. Find the margin of error E.	$E = z_c \dfrac{\sigma}{\sqrt{n}}$
5. Find the left and right endpoints and form the confidence interval.	Left endpoint: $\bar{x} - E$ Right endpoint: $\bar{x} + E$ Interval: $\bar{x} - E < \mu < \bar{x} + E$

EXAMPLE 3

See Minitab steps on page 178.

Constructing a Confidence Interval

Use the data in Example 1 to construct a 95% confidence interval for the mean number of hours spent on required athletic activities by all student-athletes in the conference.

SOLUTION

In Examples 1 and 2, you found that $\bar{x} \approx 21.1$ and $E \approx 0.7$. The confidence interval is constructed as shown.

Left Endpoint	Right Endpoint
$\bar{x} - E \approx 21.1 - 0.7$	$\bar{x} + E \approx 21.1 + 0.7$
$= 20.4$	$= 21.8$

$$20.4 < \mu < 21.8$$

> **Study Tip**
>
> Other ways to represent a confidence interval are $(\bar{x} - E, \bar{x} + E)$ and $\bar{x} \pm E$. For instance, in Example 3, you could write the confidence interval as (20.4, 21.8) or 21.1 ± 0.7.

Interpretation With 95% confidence, you can say that the population mean number of hours spent on required athletic activities is between 20.4 and 21.8 hours.

Study Tip

The width of a confidence interval is 2E. Examine the formula for E to see why a larger sample size tends to give you a narrower confidence interval for the same level of confidence.

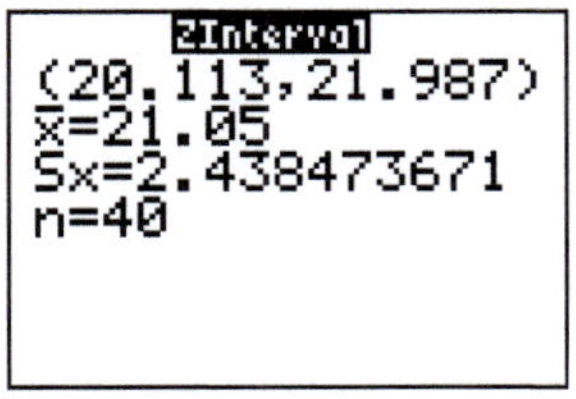

TRY IT YOURSELF 3

Use the data in Try It Yourself 1 to construct a 95% confidence interval for the mean number of hours spent on required athletic activities by all student-athletes in the conference. Compare your result with the interval found in Example 3.

Answer: Page A7

EXAMPLE 4

Constructing a Confidence Interval Using Technology

Use the data in Example 1 and technology to construct a 99% confidence interval for the mean number of hours spent on required athletic activities by all student-athletes in the conference.

SOLUTION

Minitab and StatCrunch each have features that allow you to construct a confidence interval. You can construct a confidence interval by entering the original data or by using the descriptive statistics. The original data was used to construct the confidence intervals shown below. From the displays, a 99% confidence interval for μ is (20.1, 22.0). Note that this interval is rounded to the same number of decimals places as the sample mean.

MINITAB

One-Sample Z: Hours

The assumed standard deviation = 2.3

Variable	N	Mean	StDev	SE Mean	99% CI
Hours	40	21.050	2.438	0.364	(20.113, 21.987)

STATCRUNCH

One sample Z confidence interval:
μ : Mean of variable
Standard deviation = 2.3

99% confidence interval results:

Variable	n	Sample Mean	Std. Err.	L. Limit	U. Limit
Hours	40	21.05	0.36366193	20.113269	21.986731

Interpretation With 99% confidence, you can say that the population mean number of hours spent on required athletic activities is between 20.1 and 22.0 hours.

TRY IT YOURSELF 4

Use the data in Example 1 and technology to construct 75%, 85%, and 90% confidence intervals for the mean number of hours spent on required athletic activities by all student-athletes in the conference. How does the width of the confidence interval change as the level of confidence increases?

Answer: Page A7

Tech Tip

Here are instructions for constructing a confidence interval on a TI-84 Plus. First, either enter the original data into a list or enter the descriptive statistics.

STAT

Choose the TESTS menu.

  7: ZInterval…

Select the *Data* input option when you use the original data. Select the *Stats* input option when you use the descriptive statistics. In each case, enter the appropriate values, then select *Calculate*. Your results may differ slightly depending on the method you use. For Example 4, the original data were entered.

```
ZInterval
(20.113,21.987)
x̄=21.05
Sx=2.438473671
n=40
```

In Examples 3 and 4, and Try It Yourself 4, the same sample data were used to construct confidence intervals with different levels of confidence. Notice that as the level of confidence increases, the width of the confidence interval also increases. In other words, when the same sample data are used, *the greater the level of confidence, the wider the interval.*

Tech Tip

Here are instructions for constructing a confidence interval in Excel. First, click *Formulas* at the top of the screen and click *Insert Function* in the *Function Library* group. Select the category *Statistical* and select the *Confidence.Norm* function. In the dialog box, enter the values of alpha, the standard deviation, and the sample size (see below). Then click OK. The value returned is the margin of error, which is used to construct the confidence interval.

	A	B
1	CONFIDENCE.NORM(0.1,1.5,20)	
2		0.551700678

Alpha is the *level of significance*. When using Excel in Chapter 3, you can think of alpha as the complement of the level of confidence. So, for a 90% confidence interval, alpha is equal to 1 − 0.90 = 0.10.

For a normally distributed population with σ known, you may use the normal sampling distribution for any sample size (even when $n < 30$), as shown in Example 5.

EXAMPLE 5

See TI-84 Plus steps on page 179.

Constructing a Confidence Interval

A college admissions director wishes to estimate the mean age of all students currently enrolled. In a random sample of 20 students, the mean age is found to be 22.9 years. From past studies, the standard deviation is known to be 1.5 years, and the population is normally distributed. Construct a 90% confidence interval for the population mean age.

SOLUTION

Because σ is known, the sample is random, and the population is normally distributed, use the formula for E given in this section. Using $n = 20$, $\bar{x} = 22.9$, $\sigma = 1.5$, and $z_c = 1.645$, the margin of error at the 90% confidence level is

$$E = z_c \frac{\sigma}{\sqrt{n}}$$

$$= 1.645 \cdot \frac{1.5}{\sqrt{20}}$$

$$\approx 0.6.$$

The 90% confidence interval can be written as $\bar{x} \pm E \approx 22.9 \pm 0.6$ or as shown below.

Left Endpoint
$\bar{x} - E \approx 22.9 - 0.6$
$= 22.3$

Right Endpoint
$\bar{x} + E \approx 22.9 + 0.6$
$= 23.5$

$$22.3 < \mu < 23.5$$

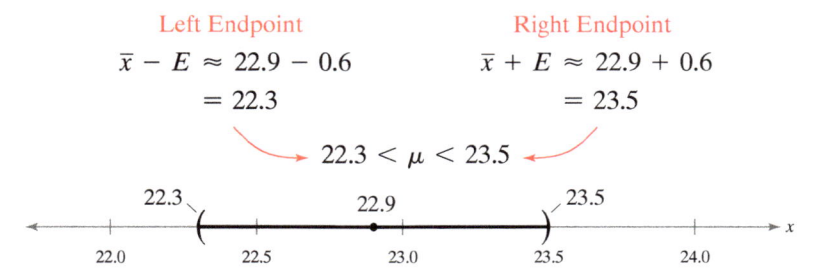

Interpretation With 90% confidence, you can say that the mean age of all the students is between 22.3 and 23.5 years.

TRY IT YOURSELF 5

Construct a 90% confidence interval for the population mean age for the college students in Example 5 with the sample size increased to 30 students. Compare your answer with Example 5.

Answer: Page A7

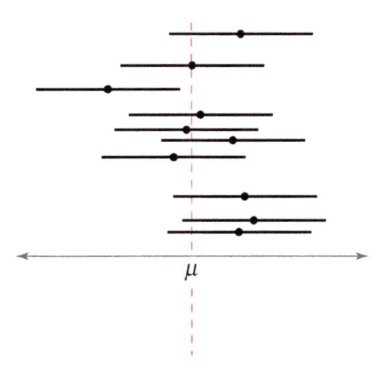

The horizontal segments represent 90% confidence intervals for different samples of the same size. In the long run, 9 of every 10 such intervals will contain μ.

After constructing a confidence interval, it is important that you interpret the results correctly. Consider the 90% confidence interval constructed in Example 5. Because μ is a fixed value predetermined by the population, it is either in the interval or not. It is *not* correct to say, "There is a 90% probability that the actual mean will be in the interval (22.3, 23.5)." This statement is wrong because it suggests that the value of μ can vary, which is not true. The correct way to interpret this confidence interval is to say, "With 90% confidence, the mean is in the interval (22.3, 23.5)." This means that when a large number of samples is collected and a confidence interval is created for each sample, approximately 90% of these intervals will contain μ, as shown in the figure at the left. This correct interpretation refers to the success rate of the process being used.

Sample Size

For the same sample statistics, as the level of confidence increases, the confidence interval widens. As the confidence interval widens, the precision of the estimate decreases. One way to improve the precision of an estimate without decreasing the level of confidence is to increase the sample size. But how large a sample size is needed to guarantee a certain level of confidence for a given margin of error? By using the formula for the margin of error

$$E = z_c \frac{\sigma}{\sqrt{n}}$$

a formula can be derived (see Exercise 59) to find the minimum sample size n, as shown in the next definition.

Finding a Minimum Sample Size to Estimate μ

Given a c-confidence level and a margin of error E, the minimum sample size n needed to estimate the population mean μ is

$$n = \left(\frac{z_c \sigma}{E}\right)^2.$$

If n is not a whole number, then round n up to the next whole number (see Example 6). Also, when σ is unknown, you can estimate it using s, provided you have a preliminary random sample with at least 30 members.

EXAMPLE 6

Determining a Minimum Sample Size

The researcher in Example 1 wants to estimate the mean number of hours spent on required athletic activities by all student-athletes in the conference. How many student-athletes must be included in the sample to be 95% confident that the sample mean is within 0.5 hour of the population mean?

SOLUTION

Using $c = 0.95$, $z_c = 1.96$, $\sigma = 2.3$ (from Example 2), and $E = 0.5$, you can solve for the minimum sample size n.

$$n = \left(\frac{z_c \sigma}{E}\right)^2$$
$$= \left(\frac{1.96 \cdot 2.3}{0.5}\right)^2$$
$$\approx 81.29.$$

Because n is not a whole number, round up to 82. So, the researcher needs at least 82 student-athletes in the sample.

Interpretation The researcher already has 40 student-athletes, so the sample needs 42 more members. Note that 82 is the *minimum* number of student-athletes to include in the sample. The researcher could include more, if desired.

TRY IT YOURSELF 6

In Example 6, how many student-athletes must the researcher include in the sample to be 95% confident that the sample mean is within 0.75 hour of the population mean? Compare your answer with Example 6.

Answer: Page A7

3.1 EXERCISES

For Extra Help: MyLab Statistics

Building Basic Skills and Vocabulary

1. When estimating a population mean, are you more likely to be correct when you use a point estimate or an interval estimate? Explain your reasoning.

2. Which statistic is the best unbiased estimator for μ?
   (a) s (b) $\bar{x}$ (c) the median   (d) the mode

3. For the same sample statistics, which level of confidence would produce the widest confidence interval? Explain your reasoning.
   (a) 90%   (b) 95%   (c) 98%   (d) 99%

4. You construct a 95% confidence interval for a population mean using a random sample. The confidence interval is $24.9 < \mu < 31.5$. Is the probability that μ is in this interval 0.95? Explain.

In Exercises 5–8, find the critical value z_c necessary to construct a confidence interval at the level of confidence c.

5. $c = 0.80$ 6. $c = 0.85$ 7. $c = 0.75$ 8. $c = 0.97$

Graphical Analysis *In Exercises 9–12, use the values on the number line to find the sampling error.*

9. $\bar{x} = 3.8 \quad \mu = 4.27$
   3.4 3.6 3.8 4.0 4.2 4.4 4.6

10. $\mu = 8.76 \quad \bar{x} = 9.5$
    8.6 8.8 9.0 9.2 9.4 9.6 9.8

11. $\mu = 24.67 \quad \bar{x} = 26.43$
    24 25 26 27

12. $\bar{x} = 46.56 \quad \mu = 48.12$
    46 47 48 49

In Exercises 13–16, find the margin of error for the values of c, σ, and n.

13. $c = 0.95, \sigma = 5.2, n = 30$
14. $c = 0.90, \sigma = 2.9, n = 50$
15. $c = 0.80, \sigma = 1.3, n = 75$
16. $c = 0.975, \sigma = 4.6, n = 100$

Matching *In Exercises 17–20, match the level of confidence c with the appropriate confidence interval. Assume each confidence interval is constructed for the same sample statistics.*

17. $c = 0.88$ 18. $c = 0.90$ 19. $c = 0.95$ 20. $c = 0.98$

(a) 54.9 — 57.2 — 59.5 (54–60)
(b) 55.2 — 57.2 — 59.2 (54–60)
(c) 55.6 — 57.2 — 58.8 (54–60)
(d) 55.5 — 57.2 — 58.9 (54–60)

In Exercises 21–24, construct the indicated confidence interval for the population mean μ.

21. $c = 0.90, \bar{x} = 12.3, \sigma = 1.5, n = 50$
22. $c = 0.95, \bar{x} = 31.39, \sigma = 0.80, n = 82$
23. $c = 0.99, \bar{x} = 10.50, \sigma = 2.14, n = 45$
24. $c = 0.80, \bar{x} = 20.6, \sigma = 4.7, n = 100$

In Exercises 25–28, use the confidence interval to find the margin of error and the sample mean.

25. (12.0, 14.8) **26.** (21.61, 30.15)

27. (1.71, 2.05) **28.** (3.144, 3.176)

In Exercises 29–32, determine the minimum sample size n needed to estimate μ for the values of c, σ, and E.

29. $c = 0.90, \sigma = 6.8, E = 1$ **30.** $c = 0.95, \sigma = 2.5, E = 1$

31. $c = 0.80, \sigma = 4.1, E = 2$ **32.** $c = 0.98, \sigma = 10.1, E = 2$

Using and Interpreting Concepts

Finding the Margin of Error *In Exercises 33 and 34, use the confidence interval to find the estimated margin of error. Then find the sample mean.*

33. Commute Times A government agency reports a confidence interval of (26.2, 30.1) when estimating the mean commute time (in minutes) for the population of workers in a city.

34. Book Prices A store manager reports a confidence interval of (244.07, 280.97) when estimating the mean price (in dollars) for the population of textbooks.

Constructing Confidence Intervals *In Exercises 35–38, you are given the sample mean and the population standard deviation. Use this information to construct 90% and 95% confidence intervals for the population mean. Interpret the results and compare the widths of the confidence intervals.*

35. Oil Prices From a random sample of 48 business days from November 14, 2017 through January 23, 2018, London's crude oil prices had a mean of $59.23. Assume the population standard deviation is $2.79. *(Source: Live Charts UK)*

36. Stock Prices From a random sample of 36 business days from January 12, 2017 through January 12, 2018, the mean closing price of Egyptian iron and steel stock was 5.62 Egyptian pound. Assume the population standard deviation is 1.91 EGP. *(Source: Cairo Stock Exchange)*

37. Maximum Daily Rainfall From a random sample of 64 dates, the mean record of high daily rainfall in Changi (Singapore) area has a mean of 10.22 mm. Assume the population standard deviation is 15.77 mm. *(Source: Meteorological Service Singapore)*

38. Fire Accidents per Year From a random sample of 24 years from 1923 through 2004, the mean number of fire accidents per year in Japan was about 43.202. Assume the population standard deviation is 20,469. *(Source: Statistics Bureau of Japan)*

39. In Exercise 35, does it seem possible that the population mean could equal the sample mean? Explain.

40. In Exercise 36, does it seem possible that the population mean could be within 1% of the sample mean? Explain.

41. In Exercise 37, does it seem possible that the population mean could be greater than 14 millimeters? Explain.

42. In Exercise 38, does it seem possible that the population mean could be less than 35,000? Explain.

43. When all other quantities remain the same, how does the indicated change affect the width of a confidence interval? Explain.
    (a) Increase in the level of confidence
    (b) Increase in the sample size
    (c) Increase in the population standard deviation

44. Describe how you would construct a 90% confidence interval to estimate the population mean age for students at your school.

Constructing Confidence Intervals *In Exercises 45 and 46, use the information to construct 90% and 99% confidence intervals for the population mean. Interpret the results and compare the widths of the confidence intervals.*

45. **Sodium in Branded Cereals** A group of researchers calculates the mean quantity of sodium (in milligrams) in selected branded cereals consumed by people in each serving. To do so, the group takes a random sample of 30 branded cereals and obtain the quantity (in milligrams) below.

    130 15 260 140 200 180 125 210 200 210 220 290 210 140 180
    280 290 90 180 140 80 220 140 190 125 200   0 160 240 135

    From past studies, the research council assumes that σ is 70.7 milligrams.
    (Adapted from the Startcrunch Surveys)

46. **Sodium Chloride Concentrations** The sodium chloride concentrations (in grams per liter) for 36 randomly selected seawater samples are listed. Assume that σ is 7.61 grams per liter.

    30.63 33.47 26.76 15.23 13.21 10.57
    16.57 27.32 27.06 15.07 28.98 34.66
    10.22 22.43 17.33 28.40 35.70 14.09
    11.77 33.60 27.09 26.78 22.39 30.35
    11.83 13.05 22.22 13.45 18.86 24.92
    32.86 31.10 18.84 10.86 15.69 22.35

47. **Determining a Minimum Sample Size** Determine the minimum sample size required when you want to be 95% confident that the sample mean is within one unit of the population mean and $\sigma = 4.8$. Assume the population is normally distributed.

48. **Determining a Minimum Sample Size** Determine the minimum sample size required when you want to be 99% confident that the sample mean is within two units of the population mean and $\sigma = 1.4$. Assume the population is normally distributed.

49. **Cholesterol Contents of Cheese** A cheese processing company wants to estimate the mean cholesterol content of all one-ounce servings of a type of cheese. The estimate must be within 0.75 milligram of the population mean.
    (a) Determine the minimum sample size required to construct a 95% confidence interval for the population mean. Assume the population standard deviation is 3.10 milligrams.
    (b) The sample mean is 29 milligrams. Using the minimum sample size with a 95% level of confidence, does it seem possible that the population mean could be within 3% of the sample mean? within 0.3% of the sample mean? Explain.

Error tolerance = 0.5 oz

Volume = 1 gal (128 oz)

FIGURE FOR EXERCISE 51

Error tolerance = 0.25 fl oz

Volume = 1/2 gal (64 fl oz)

FIGURE FOR EXERCISE 52

50. **Ages of College Students** An admissions director wants to estimate the mean age of all students enrolled at a college. The estimate must be within 1.5 years of the population mean. Assume the population of ages is normally distributed.

   (a) Determine the minimum sample size required to construct a 90% confidence interval for the population mean. Assume the population standard deviation is 1.6 years.

   (b) The sample mean is 20 years of age. Using the minimum sample size with a 90% level of confidence, does it seem possible that the population mean could be within 7% of the sample mean? within 8% of the sample mean? Explain.

51. **Paint Can Volumes** A paint manufacturer uses a machine to fill gallon cans with paint (see figure at the left). The manufacturer wants to estimate the mean volume of paint the machine is putting in the cans within 0.5 ounce. Assume the population of volumes is normally distributed.

   (a) Determine the minimum sample size required to construct a 90% confidence interval for the population mean. Assume the population standard deviation is 0.75 ounce.

   (b) The sample mean is 127.75 ounces. With a sample size of 8, a 90% level of confidence, and a population standard deviation of 0.75 ounce, does it seem possible that the population mean could be exactly 128 ounces? Explain.

52. **Juice Dispensing Machine** A beverage company uses a machine to fill half-gallon bottles with fruit juice (see figure at the left). The company wants to estimate the mean volume of water the machine is putting in the bottles within 0.25 fluid ounce.

   (a) Determine the minimum sample size required to construct a 95% confidence interval for the population mean. Assume the population standard deviation is 1 fluid ounce.

   (b) The sample mean is exactly 64 fluid ounces. With a sample size of 68, a 95% level of confidence, and a population standard deviation of 1 fluid ounce, does it seem possible that the population mean could be greater than 63.85 fluid ounces? Explain.

53. **Soccer Balls** A soccer ball manufacturer wants to estimate the mean circumference of soccer balls within 0.15 inch.

   (a) Determine the minimum sample size required to construct a 99% confidence interval for the population mean. Assume the population standard deviation is 0.5 inch.

   (b) The sample mean is 27.5 inches. With a sample size of 84, a 99% level of confidence, and a population standard deviation of 0.5 inch, does it seem possible that the population mean could be less than 27.6 inches? Explain.

54. **Tennis Balls** A tennis ball manufacturer wants to estimate the mean circumference of tennis balls within 0.05 inch. Assume the population of circumferences is normally distributed.

   (a) Determine the minimum sample size required to construct a 99% confidence interval for the population mean. Assume the population standard deviation is 0.10 inch.

   (b) The sample mean is 8.3 inches. With a sample size of 34, a 99% level of confidence, and a population standard deviation of 0.10 inch, does it seem possible that the population mean could be exactly 8.258 inches? Explain.

55. When estimating the population mean, why not construct a 99% confidence interval every time?

56. When all other quantities remain the same, how does the indicated change affect the minimum sample size requirement? Explain.

    (a) Increase in the level of confidence
    (b) Increase in the error tolerance
    (c) Increase in the population standard deviation

Extending Concepts

Finite Population Correction Factor *In Exercises 57 and 58, use the information below.*

In this section, you studied the construction of a confidence interval to estimate a population mean. In each case, the underlying assumption was that the sample size n was small in comparison to the population size N. When $n \geq 0.05N$, however, the formula that determines the standard error of the mean $\sigma_{\bar{x}}$ needs to be adjusted, as shown below.

$$\sigma_{\bar{x}} = \frac{\sigma}{\sqrt{n}}\sqrt{\frac{N-n}{N-1}}$$

The expression $\sqrt{(N-n)/(N-1)}$ is called a *finite population correction factor*. The margin of error is

$$E = z_c \frac{\sigma}{\sqrt{n}}\sqrt{\frac{N-n}{N-1}}.$$

57. Determine the finite population correction factor for each value of N and n.

    (a) $N = 1000$ and $n = 500$
    (b) $N = 1000$ and $n = 100$
    (c) $N = 1000$ and $n = 75$
    (d) $N = 1000$ and $n = 50$
    (e) $N = 100$ and $n = 50$
    (f) $N = 400$ and $n = 50$
    (g) $N = 700$ and $n = 50$
    (h) $N = 1200$ and $n = 50$

    What happens to the finite population correction factor as the sample size n decreases but the population size N remains the same? as the population size N increases but the sample size n remains the same?

58. Use the finite population correction factor to construct each confidence interval for the population mean.

    (a) $c = 0.99, \bar{x} = 8.6, \sigma = 4.9, N = 200, n = 25$
    (b) $c = 0.90, \bar{x} = 10.9, \sigma = 2.8, N = 500, n = 50$
    (c) $c = 0.95, \bar{x} = 40.3, \sigma = 0.5, N = 300, n = 68$
    (d) $c = 0.80, \bar{x} = 56.7, \sigma = 9.8, N = 400, n = 36$

59. **Sample Size** The equation for determining the sample size

    $$n = \left(\frac{z_c \sigma}{E}\right)^2$$

    can be obtained by solving the equation for the margin of error

    $$E = \frac{z_c \sigma}{\sqrt{n}}$$

    for n. Show that this is true and justify each step.

3.2 Confidence Intervals for the Mean (σ Unknown)

What You Should Learn

- How to interpret the *t*-distribution and use a *t*-distribution table
- How to construct and interpret confidence intervals for a population mean when σ is not known

The *t*-Distribution ■ Confidence Intervals and *t*-Distributions

The *t*-Distribution

In many real-life situations, the population standard deviation is unknown. So, how can you construct a confidence interval for a population mean when σ is *not* known? For a simple random sample that is drawn from a population that is normally distributed or has a sample size of 30 or more, you can use the sample standard deviation s to estimate the population standard deviation σ. However, when using s, the sampling distribution of $\bar{x}$ does not follow a normal distribution. In this case, the sampling distribution of $\bar{x}$ follows a ***t*-distribution.**

> **DEFINITION**
>
> If the distribution of a random variable x is approximately normal, then
>
> $$t = \frac{\bar{x} - \mu}{s/\sqrt{n}}$$
>
> follows a ***t*-distribution.** Critical values of t are denoted by t_c. Here are several properties of the *t*-distribution.
>
> 1. The mean, median, and mode of the *t*-distribution are equal to 0.
> 2. The *t*-distribution is bell-shaped and symmetric about the mean.
> 3. The total area under the *t*-distribution curve is equal to 1.
> 4. The tails in the *t*-distribution are "thicker" than those in the standard normal distribution.
> 5. The standard deviation of the *t*-distribution varies with the sample size, but it is greater than 1.
> 6. The *t*-distribution is a family of curves, each determined by a parameter called the *degrees of freedom.* The **degrees of freedom** (sometimes abbreviated as d.f.) are the number of free choices left after a sample statistic such as $\bar{x}$ is calculated. When you use a *t*-distribution to estimate a population mean, the degrees of freedom are equal to one less than the sample size.
>
>   d.f. = $n - 1$ Degrees of freedom
>
> 7. As the degrees of freedom increase, the *t*-distribution approaches the standard normal distribution, as shown in the figure. For 30 or more degrees of freedom, the *t*-distribution is close to the standard normal distribution.

Study Tip

Here is an example that illustrates the concept of degrees of freedom.

The number of chairs in a classroom equals the number of students: 25 chairs and 25 students. Each of the first 24 students to enter the classroom has a choice on which chair he or she will sit. There is no freedom of choice, however, for the 25th student who enters the room.

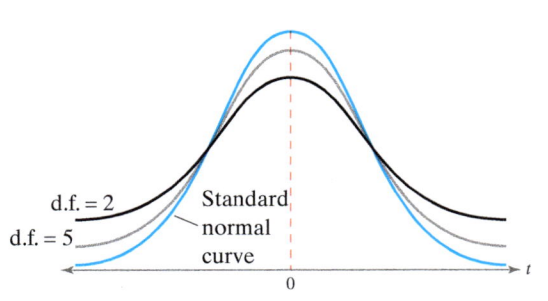

Table 5 in Appendix B lists critical values of t for selected confidence intervals and degrees of freedom.

EXAMPLE 1

Finding Critical Values of t

Find the critical value t_c for a 95% confidence level when the sample size is 15.

SOLUTION

Because $n = 15$, the degrees of freedom are d.f. $= n - 1 = 15 - 1 = 14$. A portion of Table 5 is shown. Using d.f. $= 14$ and $c = 0.95$, you can find the critical value t_c, as shown by the highlighted areas in the table.

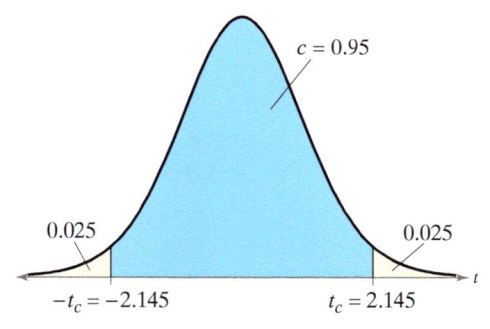

Study Tip

Critical values in the t-distribution table for a specific confidence interval can be found in the column headed by c in the appropriate d.f. row.

d.f.	Level of confidence, c	0.80	0.90	0.95	0.98	0.99
	One tail, α	0.10	0.05	0.025	0.01	0.005
	Two tails, α	0.20	0.10	0.05	0.02	0.01
1			3.078	6.314	12.706	31.821	63.657
2			1.886	2.920	4.303	6.965	9.925
3			1.638	2.353	3.182	4.541	5.841
12			1.356	1.782	2.179	2.681	3.055
13			1.350	1.771	2.160	2.650	3.012
14			1.345	1.761	2.145	2.624	2.977
15			1.341	1.753	2.131	2.602	2.947
16			1.337	1.746	2.120	2.583	2.921

From the table, you can see that $t_c = 2.145$. The figure shows the t-distribution for 14 degrees of freedom, $c = 0.95$, and $t_c = 2.145$.

You can use technology to find t_c. To use a TI-84 Plus, you need to know the area under the curve to the left of t_c, which is

$0.95 + 0.025 = 0.975$.   Area to the left of t_c

From the TI-84 Plus display at the left, $t_c \approx 2.145$.

TI-84 PLUS

```
invT(.975,14)
      2.144786681
```

Interpretation So, for a t-distribution curve with 14 degrees of freedom, 95% of the area under the curve lies between $t = \pm 2.145$.

TRY IT YOURSELF 1

Find the critical value t_c for a 90% confidence level when the sample size is 22.

Answer: Page A7

When the number of degrees of freedom you need is not in the table, use the closest number in the table that is *less than* the value you need (or use technology, as shown in Example 1). For instance, for d.f. $= 57$, use 50 degrees of freedom. This conservative approach will yield a larger confidence interval with a slightly higher level of confidence c.

Confidence Intervals and *t*-Distributions

Constructing a confidence interval for μ when σ is *not* known using the *t*-distribution is similar to constructing a confidence interval for μ when σ is known using the standard normal distribution—both use a point estimate $\bar{x}$ and a margin of error E. When σ is not known, the margin of error E is calculated using the sample standard deviation s and the critical value t_c. So, the formula for E is

$$E = t_c \frac{s}{\sqrt{n}}.$$ Margin of error for μ (σ unknown)

Before using this formula, verify that the sample is random, and either the population is normally distributed or $n \geq 30$.

Study Tip

Remember that you can calculate the sample standard deviation s using the formula

$$s = \sqrt{\frac{\Sigma(x - \bar{x})^2}{n - 1}}$$

or the alternate formula

$$s = \sqrt{\frac{\Sigma x^2 - (\Sigma x)^2 / n}{n - 1}}.$$

However, the most convenient way to find the sample standard deviation is to use technology.

GUIDELINES

Constructing a Confidence Interval for a Population Mean (σ Unknown)

In Words	In Symbols
1. Verify that σ is not known, the sample is random, and either the population is normally distributed or $n \geq 30$.	
2. Find the sample statistics n, $\bar{x}$, and s.	$\bar{x} = \frac{\Sigma x}{n}$, $s = \sqrt{\frac{\Sigma(x - \bar{x})^2}{n - 1}}$
3. Identify the degrees of freedom, the level of confidence c, and the critical value t_c.	d.f. $= n - 1$ Use Table 5 in Appendix B.
4. Find the margin of error E.	$E = t_c \frac{s}{\sqrt{n}}$
5. Find the left and right endpoints and form the confidence interval.	Left endpoint: $\bar{x} - E$ Right endpoint: $\bar{x} + E$ Interval: $\bar{x} - E < \mu < \bar{x} + E$

EXAMPLE 2

See Minitab steps on page 178.

Constructing a Confidence Interval

You randomly select 16 coffee shops and measure the temperature of the coffee sold at each. The sample mean temperature is 162.0°F with a sample standard deviation of 10.0°F. Construct a 95% confidence interval for the population mean temperature of coffee sold. Assume the temperatures are approximately normally distributed.

SOLUTION Because σ is unknown, the sample is random, and the temperatures are approximately normally distributed, use the *t*-distribution. Using $n = 16$, $\bar{x} = 162.0$, $s = 10.0$, $c = 0.95$, and d.f. $= 15$, you can use Table 5 to find that $t_c = 2.131$. The margin of error at the 95% confidence level is

$$E = t_c \frac{s}{\sqrt{n}} = 2.131 \cdot \frac{10.0}{\sqrt{16}} \approx 5.3.$$

The confidence interval is shown below and in the figure at the left.

Left Endpoint	Right Endpoint
$\bar{x} - E \approx 162 - 5.3 = 156.7$	$\bar{x} + E \approx 162 + 5.3 = 167.3$

$$156.7 < \mu < 167.3$$

Interpretation With 95% confidence, you can say that the population mean temperature of coffee sold is between 156.7°F and 167.3°F.

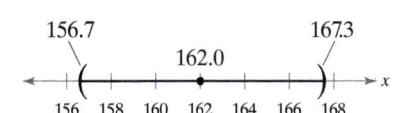

TRY IT YOURSELF 2

Construct 90% and 99% confidence intervals for the population mean temperature of coffee sold in Example 2.

Answer: Page A7

EXAMPLE 3

See TI-84 Plus steps on page 179.

Constructing a Confidence Interval

You randomly select 36 cars of the same model that were sold at a car dealership and determine the number of days each car sat on the dealership's lot before it was sold. The sample mean is 9.75 days, with a sample standard deviation of 2.39 days. Construct a 99% confidence interval for the population mean number of days the car model sits on the dealership's lot.

SOLUTION

Because σ is unknown, the sample is random, and $n = 36 \geq 30$, use the t-distribution. Using $n = 36$, $\bar{x} = 9.75$, $s = 2.39$, $c = 0.99$, and d.f. $= 35$, you can use Table 5 to find that $t_c = 2.724$. The margin of error at the 99% confidence level is

$$E = t_c \frac{s}{\sqrt{n}} = 2.724 \cdot \frac{2.39}{\sqrt{36}} \approx 1.09.$$

The confidence interval is constructed as shown.

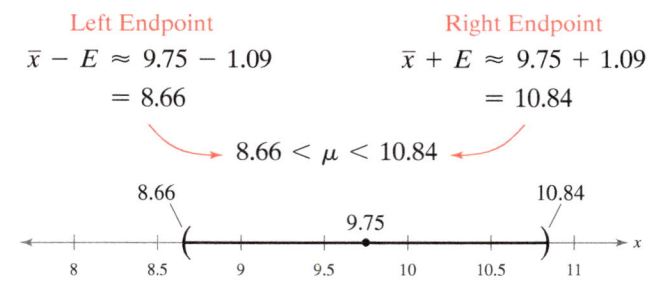

Left Endpoint	Right Endpoint
$\bar{x} - E \approx 9.75 - 1.09$	$\bar{x} + E \approx 9.75 + 1.09$
$= 8.66$	$= 10.84$

$$8.66 < \mu < 10.84$$

You can check this answer using technology, as shown below. (When using technology, your answers may differ slightly from those found using Table 5.)

STATCRUNCH

One sample T confidence interval:
μ : Mean of population

99% confidence interval results:

Mean	Sample Mean	Std. Err.	DF	L. Limit	U. Limit
μ	9.75	0.39833333	35	8.6650174	10.834983

Interpretation With 99% confidence, you can say that the population mean number of days the car model sits on the dealership's lot is between 8.66 and 10.84.

TRY IT YOURSELF 3

Construct 90% and 95% confidence intervals for the population mean number of days the car model sits on the dealership's lot in Example 3. Compare the widths of the confidence intervals.

Answer: Page A7

3.2 To explore this topic further, see **Activity 3.2** on page 152.

HISTORICAL REFERENCE

William S. Gosset (1876–1937)

Developed the *t*-distribution while employed by the Guinness Brewing Company in Dublin, Ireland. Gosset published his findings using the pseudonym Student. The *t*-distribution is sometimes referred to as Student's *t*-distribution. (See page 37 for others who were important in the history of statistics.)

Picturing the World

Two footballs, one filled with air and the other filled with helium, were kicked on a windless day at Ohio State University. The footballs were alternated with each kick. After 10 practice kicks, each football was kicked 29 more times. The distances (in yards) are listed. *(Source: The Columbus Dispatch)*

Air Filled

```
1 | 9
2 | 0 0 2 2 2
2 | 5 5 5 5 6 6
2 | 7 7 7 8 8 8 8 8 9 9 9
3 | 1 1 1 2
3 | 3 4        Key: 1|9 = 19
```

Helium Filled

```
1 | 1 2
1 | 4
1 |
2 | 2
2 | 3 4 6 6 6
2 | 7 8 8 8 9 9 9 9
3 | 0 0 0 0 1 1 2 2
3 | 3 4 5
3 | 9          Key: 1|1 = 11
```

Assume that the distances are normally distributed for each football. Apply the flowchart at the right to each sample. Construct a 95% confidence interval for the population mean distance each football traveled. Do the confidence intervals overlap? What does this result tell you?

The flowchart describes when to use the standard normal distribution and when to use the *t*-distribution to construct a confidence interval for a population mean.

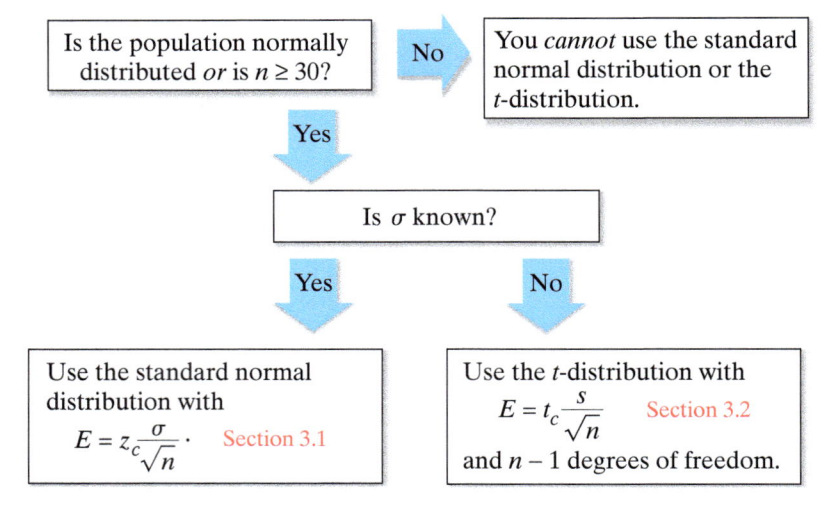

Is the population normally distributed *or* is $n \geq 30$?
→ **No**: You *cannot* use the standard normal distribution or the *t*-distribution.
→ **Yes**: **Is σ known?**
  → **Yes**: Use the standard normal distribution with
  $$E = z_c \frac{\sigma}{\sqrt{n}}.$$ *Section 3.1*
  → **No**: Use the *t*-distribution with
  $$E = t_c \frac{s}{\sqrt{n}}$$ *Section 3.2*
  and $n - 1$ degrees of freedom.

Notice in the flowchart that when both $n < 30$ and the population is *not* normally distributed, you *cannot* use the standard normal distribution or the *t*-distribution.

EXAMPLE 4

Choosing the Standard Normal Distribution or the *t*-Distribution

You randomly select 25 newly constructed houses. The sample mean construction cost is $181,000 and the population standard deviation is $28,000. Assuming construction costs are normally distributed, should you use the standard normal distribution, the *t*-distribution, or neither to construct a 95% confidence interval for the population mean construction cost? Explain your reasoning.

SOLUTION

Is the population normally distributed or is $n \geq 30$?
Yes, the population is normally distributed. Note that even though

$$n = 25 < 30$$

you can still use either the standard normal distribution or the *t*-distribution because the population is normally distributed.

Is σ known?
Yes.

Decision:
Use the standard normal distribution.

TRY IT YOURSELF 4

You randomly select 18 adult male athletes and measure the resting heart rate of each. The sample mean heart rate is 64 beats per minute, with a sample standard deviation of 2.5 beats per minute. Assuming the heart rates are normally distributed, should you use the standard normal distribution, the *t*-distribution, or neither to construct a 90% confidence interval for the population mean heart rate? Explain your reasoning.

Answer: Page A7

3.2 EXERCISES

For Extra Help: MyLab Statistics

Building Basic Skills and Vocabulary

Finding Critical Values of t *In Exercises 1–4, find the critical value t_c for the level of confidence c and sample size n.*

1. $c = 0.90, n = 10$
2. $c = 0.95, n = 12$
3. $c = 0.99, n = 16$
4. $c = 0.98, n = 40$

In Exercises 5–8, find the margin of error for the values of c, s, and n.

5. $c = 0.95, s = 5, n = 16$
6. $c = 0.99, s = 3, n = 6$
7. $c = 0.90, s = 2.4, n = 35$
8. $c = 0.98, s = 4.7, n = 9$

In Exercises 9–12, construct the indicated confidence interval for the population mean μ using the t-distribution. Assume the population is normally distributed.

9. $c = 0.90, \bar{x} = 12.5, s = 2.0, n = 6$
10. $c = 0.95, \bar{x} = 13.4, s = 0.85, n = 8$
11. $c = 0.98, \bar{x} = 4.3, s = 0.34, n = 14$
12. $c = 0.99, \bar{x} = 24.7, s = 4.6, n = 50$

In Exercises 13–16, use the confidence interval to find the margin of error and the sample mean.

13. (14.7, 22.1)
14. (6.17, 8.53)
15. (64.6, 83.6)
16. (16.2, 29.8)

Using and Interpreting Concepts

Constructing a Confidence Interval *In Exercises 17–20, you are given the sample mean and the sample standard deviation. Assume the population is normally distributed and use the t-distribution to find the margin of error and construct a 95% confidence interval for the population mean. Interpret the results.*

17. **Commute Time** In a random sample of eight people, the mean commute time to work was 35.5 minutes and the standard deviation was 7.2 minutes.

18. **Driving Distance** In a random sample of five people, the mean driving distance to work was 22.2 miles and the standard deviation was 5.8 miles.

19. **Cell Phone Prices** In a random sample of eight cell phones, the mean full retail price was $526.50 and the standard deviation was $184.00.

20. **Mobile Device Repair Costs** In a random sample of 12 mobile devices, the mean repair cost was $90.42 and the standard deviation was $33.61.

21. You research commute times to work and find that the population standard deviation is 9.3 minutes. Repeat Exercise 17 using the standard normal distribution with the appropriate calculations for a standard deviation that is known. Compare the results.

22. You research driving distances to work and find that the population standard deviation is 5.2 miles. Repeat Exercise 18 using the standard normal distribution with the appropriate calculations for a standard deviation that is known. Compare the results.

23. You research prices of cell phones and find that the population mean is $431.61. In Exercise 19, does the *t*-value fall between $-t_{0.95}$ and $t_{0.95}$?

24. You research repair costs of mobile devices and find that the population mean is $89.56. In Exercise 20, does the *t*-value fall between $-t_{0.95}$ and $t_{0.95}$?

Constructing a Confidence Interval *In Exercises 25–28, use the data set to (a) find the sample mean, (b) find the sample standard deviation, and (c) construct a 99% confidence interval for the population mean. Assume the population is normally distributed.*

25. **SAT Scores** The SAT scores of 12 randomly selected high school seniors

    1130 1290 1010 1320   950 1250
    1340 1100 1260 1180 1470   920

26. **Grade Point Averages** The grade point averages of 14 randomly selected college students

    2.3 3.3 2.6 1.8 3.1 4.0 0.7 2.3 2.0 3.1 3.4 1.3 2.6 2.6

27. **College Football** The weekly time (in hours) spent weight lifting for 16 randomly selected college football players

    7.4 5.8 7.3 7.0 8.9 9.4 8.3 9.3
    6.9 7.5 9.0 5.8 5.5 8.6 9.3 3.8

28. **Homework** The weekly time spent (in hours) on homework for 18 randomly selected high school students

    12.0 11.3 13.5 11.7 12.0 13.0 15.5 10.8 12.5
    12.3 14.0   9.5   8.8 10.0 12.8 15.0 11.8 13.0

29. In Exercise 25, the population mean SAT score is 1020. Does the *t*-value fall between $-t_{0.99}$ and $t_{0.99}$? *(Source: The College Board)*

30. In Exercise 28, the population mean weekly time spent on homework by students is 7.8 hours. Does the *t*-value fall between $-t_{0.99}$ and $t_{0.99}$?

Constructing a Confidence Interval *In Exercises 31 and 32, use the data set to (a) find the sample mean, (b) find the sample standard deviation, and (c) construct a 98% confidence interval for the population mean.*

31. **Earnings** The monthly earnings (in Yens) of 32 randomly selected teachers in Japan *(Adapted from Indeed.com)*

    240,833 308,333 380,456 296,364 199,980 332,325 269,654 212,294
    236,245 222,301 362,321 254,269 154,196 401,039 354,967 241,178
    264,531 297,813 213,546 221,239 230,280 249,236 297,246 315,218
    349,516 299,271 301,629 251,000 296,362 241,528 303,085 311,520

32. **Earnings** The annual earnings (in thousand Yens) of 40 randomly selected editors in Japan *(Adapted from Indeed.com)*

    3,614 4,284 3,548 3,694 4,182 5,142 4,568 3,954
    4,215 4,169 3,941 5,052 4,941 4,313 4,654 4,719
    3,845 3,964 4,418 3,874 3,674 3,224 5,248 5,920
    4,289 4,112 3,769 4,600 5,040 3,280 4,322 3,771
    4,758 5,920 3,691 5,178 2,120 3,040 2,940 2,949

33. In Exercise 31, the population mean salary is 305,046 Yen. Does the t-value fall between $-t_{0.98}$ and $t_{0.98}$? *(Source: Indeed.com)*

34. In Exercise 32, the population mean salary is 3,750 Yen. Does the t-value fall between $-t_{0.98}$ and $t_{0.98}$? *(Source: Indeed.com)*

Choosing a Distribution *In Exercises 35–38, use the standard normal distribution or the t-distribution to construct a 95% confidence interval for the population mean. Justify your decision. If neither distribution can be used, explain why. Interpret the results.*

35. **Body Mass Index** In a random sample of 50 people, the mean body mass index (BMI) was 27.7 and the standard deviation was 6.12.

36. **GDP Growth Rates** In a random sample of 18 quarters from 2008 through 2016, the mean GDP growth rate for Russia was 0.403 and the standard deviation was 1.306. Assume the growth rates are normally distributed. *(Source: Ieconomics.com)*

37. **Gas Mileage** The gas mileages (in miles per gallon) of 28 randomly selected sports cars are listed. Assume the mileages are not normally distributed.

    21 30 19 20 21 24 18 24 27 20 22 30 25 26
    22 17 21 24 22 20 24 21 20 18 20 21 20 27

38. **Deliveries per Fifty** In a recent Indian Premier League season, the population standard deviation of the deliveries faced to score fifty runs for all batsmen was 6.37. The deliveries per fifty of 10 randomly selected batsmen are listed. Assume the deliveries per fifty are normally distributed. *(Source: Indian Premiere League)*

    15 19 20 22 23 25 29 32 36 49

39. In Exercise 36, does it seem possible that the population mean could equal half the sample mean? Explain.

40. In Exercise 38, does it seem possible that the population mean could be within 10% of the sample mean? Explain.

Extending Concepts

41. **Tennis Ball Manufacturing** A company manufactures tennis balls. When its tennis balls are dropped onto a concrete surface from a height of 100 inches, the company wants the mean height the balls bounce upward to be 55.5 inches. This average is maintained by periodically testing random samples of 25 tennis balls. If the t-value falls between $-t_{0.99}$ and $t_{0.99}$, then the company will be satisfied that it is manufacturing acceptable tennis balls. For a random sample, the mean bounce height of the sample is 56.0 inches and the standard deviation is 0.25 inch. Assume the bounce heights are approximately normally distributed. Is the company making acceptable tennis balls? Explain.

42. **Light Bulb Manufacturing** A company manufactures light bulbs. The company wants the bulbs to have a mean life span of 1000 hours. This average is maintained by periodically testing random samples of 16 light bulbs. If the t-value falls between $-t_{0.99}$ and $t_{0.99}$, then the company will be satisfied that it is manufacturing acceptable light bulbs. For a random sample, the mean life span of the sample is 1015 hours and the standard deviation is 25 hours. Assume the life spans are approximately normally distributed. Is the company making acceptable light bulbs? Explain.

3.2 ACTIVITY: Confidence Intervals for a Mean

You can find the interactive applet for this activity within **MyLab Statistics** or at www.pearsonglobaleditions.com.

The *confidence intervals for a mean (the impact of not knowing the standard deviation)* applet allows you to visually investigate confidence intervals for a population mean. You can specify the sample size n, the shape of the distribution (Normal or Right-skewed), the population mean (Mean), and the true population standard deviation (Std. Dev.). When you click SIMULATE, 100 separate samples of size n will be selected from a population with these population parameters. For each of the 100 samples, a 95% Z confidence interval (known standard deviation) and a 95% T confidence interval (unknown standard deviation) are displayed in the plot at the right. The 95% Z confidence interval is displayed in green and the 95% T confidence interval is displayed in blue. When an interval does not contain the population mean, it is displayed in red. Additional simulations can be carried out by clicking SIMULATE multiple times. The cumulative number of times that each type of interval contains the population mean is also shown. Press CLEAR to clear existing results and start a new simulation.

EXPLORE

Step 1 Specify a value for n.
Step 2 Specify a distribution.
Step 3 Specify a value for the mean.
Step 4 Specify a value for the standard deviation.
Step 5 Click SIMULATE to generate the confidence intervals.

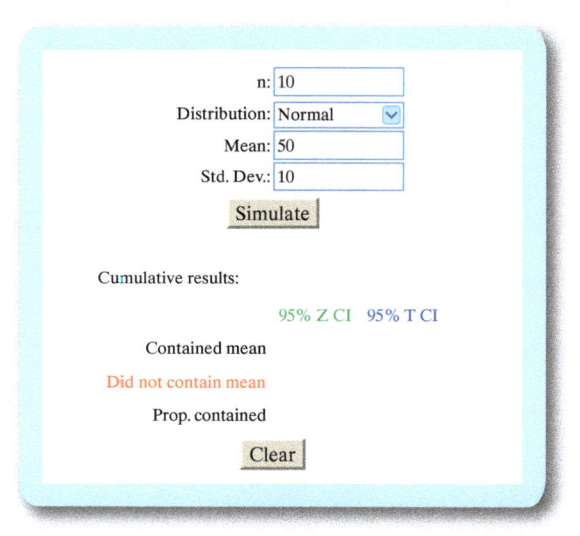

DRAW CONCLUSIONS

1. Set $n = 30$, Mean = 25, Std. Dev. = 5, and the distribution to Normal. Run the simulation so that at least 1000 confidence intervals are generated. Compare the proportion of the 95% Z confidence intervals and 95% T confidence intervals that contain the population mean. Is this what you would expect? Explain.

2. In a random sample of 24 high school students, the mean number of hours of sleep per night during the school week was 7.26 hours and the standard deviation was 1.19 hours. Assume the sleep times are normally distributed. Run the simulation for $n = 10$ so that at least 500 confidence intervals are generated. What proportion of the 95% Z confidence intervals and 95% T confidence intervals contain the population mean? Should you use a Z confidence interval or a T confidence interval for the mean number of hours of sleep? Explain.

CASE STUDY

Marathon Training

A marathon is a foot race with a distance of 26.22 miles. It was one of the original events of the modern Olympics, where it was a men's only event. The women's marathon became an Olympic event in 1984. The Olympic record for the men's marathon was set during the 2008 Olympics by Samuel Kamau Wanjiru of Kenya, with a time of 2 hours, 6 minutes, 32 seconds. The Olympic record for the women's marathon was set during the 2012 Olympics by Tiki Gelana of Ethiopa, with a time of 2 hours, 23 minutes, 7 seconds.

Training for a marathon typically lasts at least 6 months. The training is gradual, with increases in distance about every 2 weeks. About 1 to 3 weeks before the race, the distance run is decreased slightly. The stem-and-leaf plots below show the marathon training times (in minutes) for a random sample of 30 male runners and 30 female runners.

Training Times (in minutes) of Male Runners

```
15 | 5 8 9 9 9              Key: 15|5 = 155
16 | 0 0 0 0 1 2 3 4 4 5 8 9
17 | 0 1 1 3 5 6 6 7 7 9
18 | 0 1 5
```

Training Times (in minutes) of Female Runners

```
17 | 8 9 9                  Key: 17|8 = 178
18 | 0 0 0 0 1 2 3 4 6 6 7 9
19 | 0 0 0 1 3 4 5 5 6 6
20 | 0 0 1 2 3
```

EXERCISES

1. Use the sample to find a point estimate for the mean training time of the
   (a) male runners.
   (b) female runners.

2. Find the sample standard deviation of the training times for the
   (a) male runners.
   (b) female runners.

3. Use the sample to construct a 95% confidence interval for the population mean training time of the
   (a) male runners.
   (b) female runners.

4. Interpret the results of Exercise 3.

5. Use the sample to construct a 95% confidence interval for the population mean training time of all runners. How do your results differ from those in Exercise 3? Explain.

6. A trainer wants to estimate the population mean running times for both male and female runners within 2 minutes. Determine the minimum sample size required to construct a 99% confidence interval for the population mean training time of
   (a) male runners. Assume the population standard deviation is 8.9 minutes.
   (b) female runners. Assume the population standard deviation is 8.4 minutes.

3.3 Confidence Intervals for Population Proportions

What You Should Learn

- How to find a point estimate for a population proportion
- How to construct and interpret confidence intervals for a population proportion
- How to determine the minimum sample size required when estimating a population proportion

Point Estimate for a Population Proportion ■ Confidence Intervals for a Population Proportion ■ Finding a Minimum Sample Size

Point Estimate for a Population Proportion

The probability of success in a single trial of a binomial experiment is p. This probability is a **population proportion**. In this section, you will learn how to estimate a population proportion p using a confidence interval. As with confidence intervals for μ, you will start with a point estimate.

DEFINITION

The **point estimate for p,** the population proportion of successes, is given by the proportion of successes in a sample and is denoted by

$$\hat{p} = \frac{x}{n} \qquad \text{Sample proportion}$$

where x is the number of successes in the sample and n is the sample size. The point estimate for the population proportion of failures is $\hat{q} = 1 - \hat{p}$. The symbols $\hat{p}$ and $\hat{q}$ are read as "p hat" and "q hat."

EXAMPLE 1

Finding a Point Estimate for p

In a survey of 1550 U.S. adults, 1054 said that they use the social media website Facebook. Find a point estimate for the population proportion of U.S. adults who use Facebook. *(Adapted from Pew Research Center)*

SOLUTION

The number of successes is the number of adults who use Facebook, so $x = 1054$. The sample size is $n = 1550$. So, the sample proportion is

$$\hat{p} = \frac{x}{n} \qquad \text{Formula for sample proportion}$$

$$= \frac{1054}{1550} \qquad \text{Substitute 1054 for } x \text{ and 1550 for } n.$$

$$= 0.68 \qquad \text{Divide.}$$

$$= 68\%. \qquad \text{Write as a percent.}$$

So, the point estimate for the population proportion of U.S. adults who use Facebook is 0.68 or 68%.

TRY IT YOURSELF 1

A poll surveyed 4780 U.S. adults about how often they shop online. The results are shown in the table. Find a point estimate for the population proportion of U.S. adults who shop online at least once a week. *(Adapted from Pew Research Center)*

How often do you shop online?	Number responding yes
At least once a week	717
A few times a month	1338
Less often	1769
Never	956

Answer: Page A8

Study Tip

In Sections 3.1 and 3.2, estimates were made for quantitative data. In this section, sample proportions are used to make estimates for qualitative data.

Picturing the World

A poll surveyed 1519 U.S. adults about global climate change. Of those surveyed, 936 said that they expect to make major changes in their lives to address problems from climate change in the next 50 years. (Adapted from Pew Research Center)

In the Next 50 Years, Do You Think You Will Make Major Changes to Your Way of Life in Order to Address Problems from Global Climate Change?

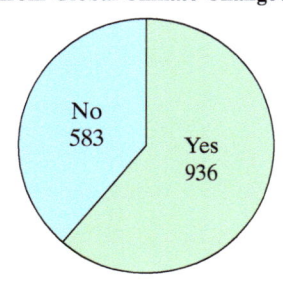

No 583
Yes 936

Find a 90% confidence interval for the population proportion of people who expect to make major changes in their lives to address problems from climate change in the next 50 years.

Tech Tip

Here are instructions for constructing a confidence interval for a population proportion on a TI-84 Plus.

STAT

Choose the TESTS menu.

A: 1-PropZInt . . .

Enter the values of x, n, and the level of confidence c (C-Level). Then select *Calculate*.

Confidence Intervals for a Population Proportion

Constructing a confidence interval for a population proportion p is similar to constructing a confidence interval for a population mean. You start with a point estimate and calculate a margin of error.

DEFINITION

A *c*-confidence interval for a population proportion p is

$$\hat{p} - E < p < \hat{p} + E$$

where

$$E = z_c \sqrt{\frac{\hat{p}\hat{q}}{n}}.$$ Margin of error for p

The probability that the confidence interval contains p is c, assuming that the estimation process is repeated a large number of times.

A binomial distribution can be approximated by a normal distribution when $np \geq 5$ and $nq \geq 5$. When $n\hat{p} \geq 5$ and $n\hat{q} \geq 5$, the sampling distribution of $\hat{p}$ is approximately normal with a mean of

$$\mu_{\hat{p}} = p$$ Mean of the sample proportions

and a standard error of

$$\sigma_{\hat{p}} = \sqrt{\frac{pq}{n}}.$$ Standard error of the sample proportions

$$\left(\text{Notice } \sigma_{\hat{p}} = \frac{\sigma}{n} = \frac{\sqrt{npq}}{n} = \frac{\sqrt{npq}}{\sqrt{n^2}} = \sqrt{\frac{npq}{n^2}} = \sqrt{\frac{pq}{n}}.\right)$$

GUIDELINES

Constructing a Confidence Interval for a Population Proportion

In Words	In Symbols
1. Identify the sample statistics n and x.	
2. Find the point estimate $\hat{p}$.	$\hat{p} = \dfrac{x}{n}$
3. Verify that the sampling distribution of $\hat{p}$ can be approximated by a normal distribution.	$n\hat{p} \geq 5, n\hat{q} \geq 5$
4. Find the critical value z_c that corresponds to the given level of confidence c.	Use Table 4 in Appendix B.
5. Find the margin of error E.	$E = z_c \sqrt{\dfrac{\hat{p}\hat{q}}{n}}$
6. Find the left and right endpoints and form the confidence interval.	Left endpoint: $\hat{p} - E$ Right endpoint: $\hat{p} + E$ Interval: $\hat{p} - E < p < \hat{p} + E$

In Step 4 above, note that the critical value z_c is found the same way it was found in Section 3.1, by either using Table 4 in Appendix B or using technology.

EXAMPLE 2

> Minitab and TI-84 Plus steps are shown on pages 178 and 179.

Constructing a Confidence Interval for p

Use the data in Example 1 to construct a 95% confidence interval for the population proportion of U.S. adults who use Facebook.

SOLUTION

From Example 1, $\hat{p} = 0.68$. So, the point estimate for the population proportion of failures is

$$\hat{q} = 1 - 0.68 = 0.32.$$

Using $n = 1550$, you can verify that the sampling distribution of $\hat{p}$ can be approximated by a normal distribution.

$$n\hat{p} = (1550)(0.68) = 1054 > 5$$

and

$$n\hat{q} = (1550)(0.32) = 496 > 5$$

Using $z_c = 1.96$, the margin of error is

$$E = z_c \sqrt{\frac{\hat{p}\hat{q}}{n}} = 1.96 \sqrt{\frac{(0.68)(0.32)}{1550}} \approx 0.023.$$

Next, find the left and right endpoints and form the 95% confidence interval.

Left Endpoint
$\hat{p} - E \approx 0.68 - 0.023$
$= 0.657$

Right Endpoint
$\hat{p} + E \approx 0.68 + 0.023$
$= 0.703$

$$0.657 < p < 0.703$$

> **Study Tip**
>
> Notice in Example 2 that the confidence interval for the population proportion p is rounded to three decimal places. This *round-off rule* will be used throughout the text.

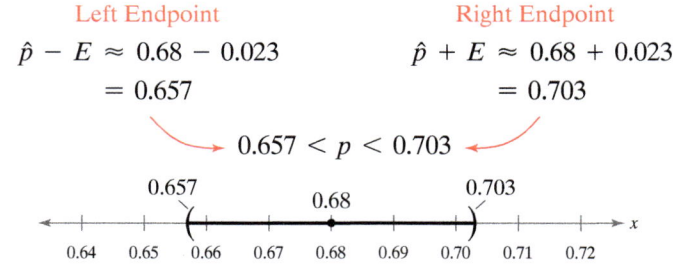

You can check this answer using technology, as shown below. (When using technology, your answers may differ slightly from those found using Table 4.)

STATCRUNCH

95% confidence interval results:

Proportion	Count	Total	Sample Prop.	Std. Err.	L. Limit	U. Limit
p	1054	1550	0.68	0.011849	0.65678	0.70322

Interpretation With 95% confidence, you can say that the population proportion of U.S. adults who use Facebook is between 65.7% and 70.3%.

TRY IT YOURSELF 2

Use the data in Try It Yourself 1 to construct a 90% confidence interval for the population proportion of U.S. adults who shop online at least once a week.

Answer: Page A8

The confidence level of 95% used in Example 2 is typical of opinion polls. The result, however, is usually not stated as a confidence interval. Instead, the result of Example 2 would be stated as shown.

> *A survey found that 68% of U.S. adults use Facebook. The margin of error for the survey is $\pm 2.3\%$.*

EXAMPLE 3

Constructing a Confidence Interval for p

The figure below is from a survey of 800 U.S. adults ages 18 to 29. Construct a 99% confidence interval for the population proportion of 18- to 29-year-olds who get their news on television. *(Adapted from Pew Research Center)*

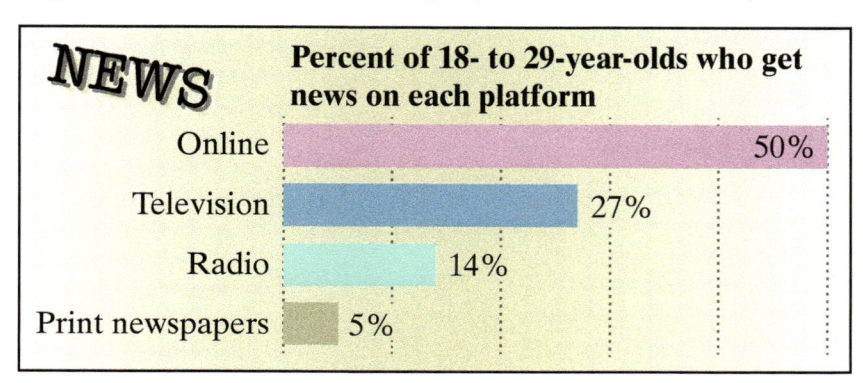

NEWS — Percent of 18- to 29-year-olds who get news on each platform

- Online: 50%
- Television: 27%
- Radio: 14%
- Print newspapers: 5%

SOLUTION

From the figure, $\hat{p} = 0.27$. So, $\hat{q} = 1 - 0.27 = 0.73$. Using $n = 800$, note that

$$n\hat{p} = (800)(0.27) = 216 > 5$$

and

$$n\hat{q} = (800)(0.73) = 584 > 5.$$

So, the sampling distribution of $\hat{p}$ is approximately normal. Using $z_c = 2.575$, the margin of error is

$$E = z_c \sqrt{\frac{\hat{p}\hat{q}}{n}}$$

$$\approx 2.575 \sqrt{\frac{(0.27)(0.73)}{800}}$$

$$\approx 0.040.$$

Use Table 4 in Appendix B to estimate that z_c is halfway between 2.57 and 2.58.

Next, find the left and right endpoints and form the 99% confidence interval.

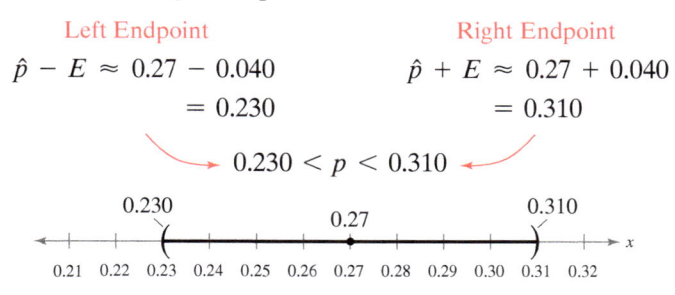

Left Endpoint	Right Endpoint
$\hat{p} - E \approx 0.27 - 0.040$	$\hat{p} + E \approx 0.27 + 0.040$
$= 0.230$	$= 0.310$

$$0.230 < p < 0.310$$

You can check this answer using technology, as shown at the left.

Interpretation With 99% confidence, you can say that the population proportion of 18- to 29-year-olds who get their news on television is between 23.0% and 31.0%.

TRY IT YOURSELF 3

Use the data in Example 3 to construct a 99% confidence interval for the population proportion of 18- to 29-year-olds who get their news online.

Answer: Page A8

3.3 To explore this topic further, see **Activity 3.3** on page 163.

TI-84 PLUS

```
1-PropZInt
(.22957,.31043)
p̂=.27
n=800
```

Finding a Minimum Sample Size

One way to increase the precision of a confidence interval without decreasing the level of confidence is to increase the sample size.

Finding a Minimum Sample Size to Estimate p

Given a c-confidence level and a margin of error E, the minimum sample size n needed to estimate the population proportion p is

$$n = \hat{p}\hat{q}\left(\frac{z_c}{E}\right)^2.$$

If n is not a whole number, then round n up to the next whole number (see Example 4). Also, note that this formula assumes that you have preliminary estimates of $\hat{p}$ and $\hat{q}$. If not, use $\hat{p} = 0.5$ and $\hat{q} = 0.5$.

> **Study Tip**
>
> The reason for using $\hat{p} = 0.5$ and $\hat{q} = 0.5$ when no preliminary estimate is available is that these values yield the maximum value of the product $\hat{p}\hat{q}$. (See Exercise 37.) In other words, without an estimate of $\hat{p}$, you must pay the penalty of using a larger sample.

EXAMPLE 4

Determining a Minimum Sample Size

You are running a political campaign and wish to estimate, with 95% confidence, the population proportion of registered voters who will vote for your candidate. Your estimate must be accurate within 3% of the population proportion. Find the minimum sample size needed when (1) no preliminary estimate is available and (2) a preliminary estimate gives $\hat{p} = 0.31$. Compare your results.

SOLUTION

1. Because you do not have a preliminary estimate of $\hat{p}$, use $\hat{p} = 0.5$ and $\hat{q} = 0.5$. Using $z_c = 1.96$ and $E = 0.03$, you can solve for n.

$$n = \hat{p}\hat{q}\left(\frac{z_c}{E}\right)^2 = (0.5)(0.5)\left(\frac{1.96}{0.03}\right)^2 \approx 1067.11$$

   Because n is not a whole number, round up to the next whole number, 1068.

2. You have a preliminary estimate of $\hat{p} = 0.31$. So, $\hat{q} = 0.69$. Using $z_c = 1.96$ and $E = 0.03$, you can solve for n.

$$n = \hat{p}\hat{q}\left(\frac{z_c}{E}\right)^2 = (0.31)(0.69)\left(\frac{1.96}{0.03}\right)^2 \approx 913.02$$

   Because n is not a whole number, round up to the next whole number, 914.

Interpretation With no preliminary estimate, the minimum sample size should be at least 1068 registered voters. With a preliminary estimate of $\hat{p} = 0.31$, the sample size should be at least 914 registered voters. So, you will need a larger sample size when no preliminary estimate is available.

TRY IT YOURSELF 4

A researcher is estimating the population proportion of people in the United States who delayed seeking medical care during the last 12 months due to costs. The estimate must be accurate within 2% of the population proportion with 90% confidence. Find the minimum sample size needed when (1) no preliminary estimate is available and (2) a previous survey found that 6.3% of people in the United States delayed seeking medical care during the last 12 months due to costs. *(Source: NCHS, National Health Interview Survey)*

Answer: Page A8

3.3 EXERCISES

For Extra Help: MyLab Statistics

Building Basic Skills and Vocabulary

True or False? *In Exercises 1 and 2, determine whether the statement is true or false. If it is false, rewrite it as a true statement.*

1. To estimate the value of p, the population proportion of successes, use the point estimate x.

2. The point estimate for the population proportion of failures is $1 - \hat{p}$.

Finding $\hat{p}$ and $\hat{q}$ *In Exercises 3–6, let p be the population proportion for the situation. Find point estimates of p and q.*

3. **Tax Fraud** In a survey of 1040 U.S. adults, 62 have had someone impersonate them to try to claim tax refunds. *(Adapted from Pew Research Center)*

4. **Investigating Crimes** In a survey of 1040 U.S. adults, 478 believe the government should be able to access encrypted communications when investigating crimes. *(Adapted from Pew Research Center)*

5. **Mainstream Media** In a survey of 2016 U.S. adults, 1310 think mainstream media is more interested in making money than in telling the truth. *(Adapted from Ipsos Public Affairs)*

6. **Terrorism** In a survey of 2016 U.S. adults, 665 believe America should stop terrorism at all costs. *(Adapted from Ipsos Public Affairs)*

In Exercises 7–10, use the confidence interval to find the margin of error and the sample proportion.

7. (0.905, 0.933)
8. (0.245, 0.475)
9. (0.512, 0.596)
10. (0.087, 0.263)

Using and Interpreting Concepts

Constructing Confidence Intervals *In Exercises 11 and 12, construct 90% and 95% confidence intervals for the population proportion. Interpret the results and compare the widths of the confidence intervals.*

11. **New Year's Resolutions** In a survey of 2241 U.S. adults in a recent year, 1322 say they have made a New Year's resolution. *(Adapted from The Harris Poll)*

12. **New Year's Resolutions** In a survey of 2241 U.S. adults in a recent year, 650 made a New Year's resolution to eat healthier. *(Adapted from The Harris Poll)*

Constructing Confidence Intervals *In Exercises 13 and 14, construct a 99% confidence interval for the population proportion. Interpret the results.*

13. **Police Body Cameras** In a survey of 1000 U.S. adults, 700 think police officers should be required to wear body cameras while on duty. *(Adapted from Rasmussen Reports)*

14. **Teacher Body Cameras** In a survey of 600 United Kingdom teachers, 226 say they would wear a body camera in school. *(Adapted from Times Education Supplement)*

15. **LGBT Identification** In a survey of 1,626,773 U.S. adults, 49,311 personally identify as lesbian, gay, bisexual, or transgender. Construct a 95% confidence interval for the population proportion of U.S. adults who personally identify as lesbian, gay, bisexual, or transgender. *(Source: Gallup)*

16. **Transgender Bathroom Policy** In a survey of 1000 U.S. adults, 490 oppose allowing transgender students to use the bathrooms of the opposite biological sex. Construct a 90% confidence interval for the population proportion of U.S. adults who oppose allowing transgender students to use the bathrooms of the opposite biological sex. *(Adapted from Rasmussen Reports)*

17. **Congress** You wish to estimate, with 95% confidence, the population proportion of U.S. adults who think Congress is doing a good or excellent job. Your estimate must be accurate within 4% of the population proportion.
    (a) No preliminary estimate is available. Find the minimum sample size needed.
    (b) Find the minimum sample size needed, using a prior survey that found that 25% of U.S. adults think Congress is doing a good or excellent job. *(Source: Rasmussen Reports)*
    (c) Compare the results from parts (a) and (b).

18. **Genetically Modified Organisms** You wish to estimate, with 99% confidence, the population proportion of U.S. adults who support labeling legislation for genetically modified organisms (GMOs). Your estimate must be accurate within 2% of the population proportion.
    (a) No preliminary estimate is available. Find the minimum sample size needed.
    (b) Find the minimum sample size needed, using a prior survey that found that 75% of U.S. adults support labeling legislation for GMOs. *(Source: The Harris Poll)*
    (c) Compare the results from parts (a) and (b).

19. **Fast Food** You wish to estimate, with 90% confidence, the population proportion of U.S. adults who eat fast food four to six times per week. Your estimate must be accurate within 3% of the population proportion.
    (a) No preliminary estimate is available. Find the minimum sample size needed.
    (b) Find the minimum sample size needed, using a prior study that found that 11% of U.S. adults eat fast food four to six times per week. *(Source: Statista)*
    (c) Compare the results from parts (a) and (b).

20. **Alcohol-Impaired Driving** You wish to estimate, with 95% confidence, the population proportion of motor vehicle fatalities that were caused by alcohol-impaired driving. Your estimate must be accurate within 5% of the population proportion.
    (a) No preliminary estimate is available. Find the minimum sample size needed.
    (b) Find the minimum sample size needed, using a prior study that found that 31% of motor vehicle fatalities were caused by alcohol-impaired driving. *(Source: WalletHub)*
    (c) Compare the results from parts (a) and (b).

21. In Exercise 11, does it seem possible that the population proportion could equal 0.59? Explain.

22. In Exercise 14, does it seem possible that the population proportion could be within 1% of the point estimate? Explain.

23. In Exercise 17(b), would a sample size of 200 be acceptable? Explain.

24. In Exercise 20(b), would a sample size of 600 be acceptable? Explain.

Constructing Confidence Intervals *In Exercises 25 and 26, use the figure, which shows the results of a survey in which 1003 adults from the United States, 1020 adults from Canada, 999 adults from France, 1000 adults from Japan, and 1000 adults from Australia were asked whether national identity is strongly tied to birthplace. (Source: Pew Research Center)*

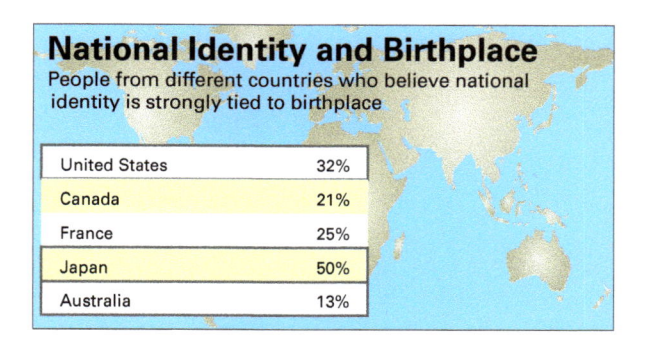

National Identity and Birthplace
People from different countries who believe national identity is strongly tied to birthplace

Country	Percent
United States	32%
Canada	21%
France	25%
Japan	50%
Australia	13%

25. **National Identity** Construct a 99% confidence interval for the population proportion of adults who say national identity is strongly tied to birthplace for each country listed.

26. In Exercise 25, does it seem possible that any of the population proportions could be equal? Explain.

Constructing Confidence Intervals *In Exercises 27 and 28, use the figure, which shows the results of a survey in which 2000 U.S. college graduates from the year 2016 were asked questions about employment. (Source: Accenture)*

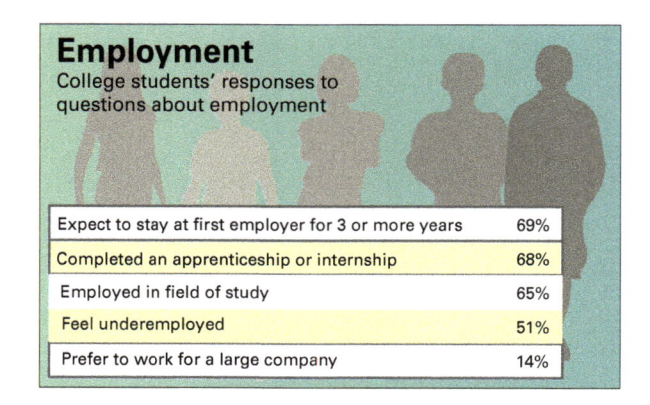

Employment
College students' responses to questions about employment

Response	Percent
Expect to stay at first employer for 3 or more years	69%
Completed an apprenticeship or internship	68%
Employed in field of study	65%
Feel underemployed	51%
Prefer to work for a large company	14%

27. **Employment** Construct (a) a 95% confidence interval and (b) a 99% confidence interval for the population proportion of college students who gave each response.

28. In Exercise 27, does it seem possible that any of the population proportions could be equal? Explain.

Extending Concepts

Translating Statements *In Exercises 29–34, translate the statement into a confidence interval. Approximate the level of confidence.*

29. In a survey of 1003 U.S. adults, 70% said being able to speak English is at the core of national identity. The survey's margin of error is $\pm 3.4\%$. *(Source: Pew Research Center)*

30. In a survey of 1503 U.S. adults, 79% say people have the right to nonviolent protest. The survey's margin of error is $\pm 2.9\%$. *(Source: Pew Research Center)*

31. In a survey of 1000 U.S. adults, 71% think teaching is one of the most important jobs in our country today. The survey's margin of error is $\pm 3\%$. *(Source: Rasmussen Reports)*

32. In a survey of 1035 U.S. adults, 37% say the U.S. spends too little on defense. The survey's margin of error is $\pm 4\%$. *(Source: Gallup)*

33. In a survey of 3539 U.S. adults, 47% believe the economy is getting better. Three weeks prior to this survey, 53% believed the economy was getting better. The survey's margin of error is $\pm 2\%$. *(Source: Gallup)*

34. In a survey of 1052 parents of children ages 8–14, 68% say they are willing to get a second or part-time job to pay for their children's college education, and 42% say they lose sleep worrying about college costs. The survey's margin of error is $\pm 3\%$. *(Source: T. Rowe Price Group, Inc.)*

35. **Why Check It?** Why is it necessary to check that $n\hat{p} \geq 5$ and $n\hat{q} \geq 5$?

36. **Sample Size** The equation for determining the sample size

$$n = \hat{p}\hat{q}\left(\frac{z_c}{E}\right)^2$$

can be obtained by solving the equation for the margin of error

$$E = z_c\sqrt{\frac{\hat{p}\hat{q}}{n}}$$

for n. Show that this is true and justify each step.

37. **Maximum Value of $\hat{p}\hat{q}$** Complete the tables for different values of $\hat{p}$ and $\hat{q} = 1 - \hat{p}$. From the tables, which value of $\hat{p}$ appears to give the maximum value of the product $\hat{p}\hat{q}$?

$\hat{p}$	$\hat{q} = 1 - \hat{p}$	$\hat{p}\hat{q}$
0.0	1.0	0.00
0.1	0.9	0.09
0.2	0.8	
0.3		
0.4		
0.5		
0.6		
0.7		
0.8		
0.9		
1.0		

$\hat{p}$	$\hat{q} = 1 - \hat{p}$	$\hat{p}\hat{q}$
0.45		
0.46		
0.47		
0.48		
0.49		
0.50		
0.51		
0.52		
0.53		
0.54		
0.55		

3.3 ACTIVITY Confidence Intervals for a Proportion

APPLET

You can find the interactive applet for this activity within **MyLab Statistics** or at *www.pearsonglobaleditions.com*.

The *confidence intervals for a proportion* applet allows you to visually investigate confidence intervals for a population proportion. You can specify the sample size n and the population proportion p. When you click SIMULATE, 100 separate samples of size n will be selected from a population with a proportion of successes equal to p. For each of the 100 samples, a 95% confidence interval (in green) and a 99% confidence interval (in blue) are displayed in the plot at the right. Each of these intervals is computed using the standard normal approximation. When an interval does not contain the population proportion, it is displayed in red. Note that the 99% confidence interval is always wider than the 95% confidence interval. Additional simulations can be carried out by clicking SIMULATE multiple times. The cumulative number of times that each type of interval contains the population proportion is also shown. Press CLEAR to clear existing results and start a new simulation.

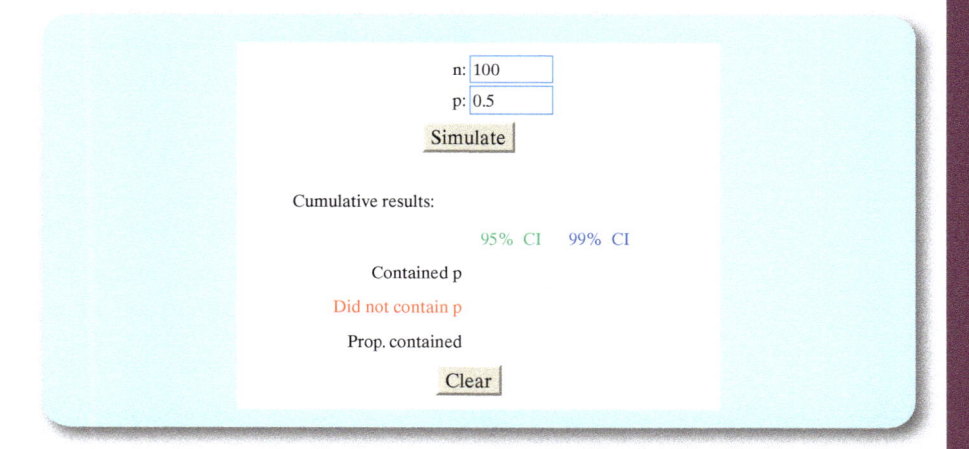

```
                    n: 100
                    p: 0.5
                   Simulate

           Cumulative results:
                              95% CI   99% CI
                Contained p
               Did not contain p
               Prop. contained
                    Clear
```

EXPLORE

Step 1 Specify a value for n.
Step 2 Specify a value for p.
Step 3 Click SIMULATE to generate the confidence intervals.

DRAW CONCLUSIONS

APPLET

1. Run the simulation for $p = 0.6$ and $n = 10, 20, 40,$ and 100. Clear the results after each trial. What proportion of the confidence intervals for each confidence level contains the population proportion? What happens to the proportion of confidence intervals that contains the population proportion for each confidence level as the sample size increases?

2. Run the simulation for $p = 0.4$ and $n = 100$ so that at least 1000 confidence intervals are generated. Compare the proportion of confidence intervals that contains the population proportion for each confidence level. Is this what you would expect? Explain.

3.4 Confidence Intervals for Variance and Standard Deviation

What You Should Learn

- How to interpret the chi-square distribution and use a chi-square distribution table
- How to construct and interpret confidence intervals for a population variance and standard deviation

The Chi-Square Distribution ■ Confidence Intervals for σ^2 and σ

The Chi-Square Distribution

In manufacturing, it is necessary to control the amount that a process varies. For instance, an automobile part manufacturer must produce thousands of parts to be used in the manufacturing process. It is important that the parts vary little or not at all. How can you measure, and consequently control, the amount of variation in the parts? You can start with a point estimate.

> **DEFINITION**
>
> The **point estimate for σ^2** is s^2 and the **point estimate for σ** is s. The most unbiased estimate for σ^2 is s^2.

You can use a **chi-square distribution** to construct a confidence interval for the variance and standard deviation.

> **DEFINITION**
>
> If a random variable x has a normal distribution, then the distribution of
>
> $$\chi^2 = \frac{(n-1)s^2}{\sigma^2}$$
>
> forms a **chi-square distribution** for samples of any size $n > 1$. Here are several properties of the chi-square distribution.
>
> 1. All values of χ^2 are greater than or equal to 0.
> 2. The chi-square distribution is a family of curves, each determined by the degrees of freedom. To form a confidence interval for σ^2, use the chi-square distribution with degrees of freedom equal to one less than the sample size.
>
>   d.f. $= n - 1$ Degrees of freedom
>
> 3. The total area under each chi-square distribution curve is equal to 1.
> 4. The chi-square distribution is positively skewed and therefore the distribution is not symmetric.
> 5. The chi-square distribution is different for each number of degrees of freedom, as shown in the figure. As the degrees of freedom increase, the chi-square distribution approaches a normal distribution.

Study Tip

The Greek letter χ is pronounced "*ki*," which rhymes with the more familiar Greek letter π.

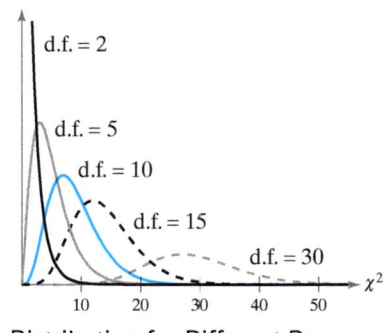

Chi-Square Distribution for Different Degrees of Freedom

Study Tip

For chi-square critical values with a c-confidence level, the values shown below, χ_L^2 and χ_R^2 are what you look up in Table 6 in Appendix B.

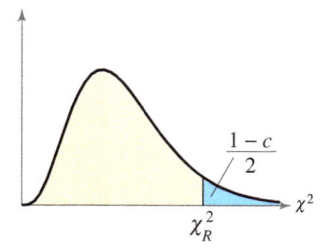

Area to the right of χ_R^2

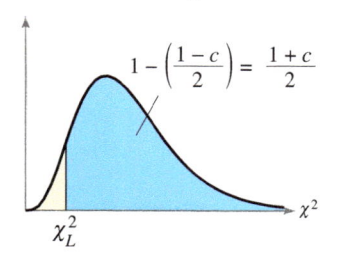

Area to the right of χ_L^2

The result is that you can conclude that the area between the left and right critical values is c.

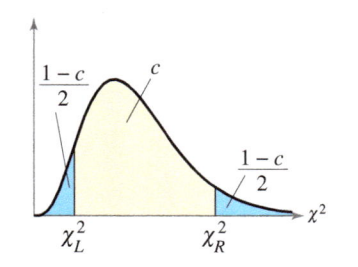

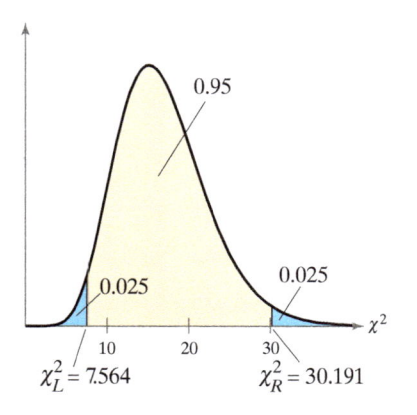

There are two critical values for each level of confidence. The value χ_R^2 represents the right-tail critical value and χ_L^2 represents the left-tail critical value. Table 6 in Appendix B lists critical values of χ^2 for various degrees of freedom and areas. Each area listed in the top row of the table represents the region under the chi-square curve to the *right* of the critical value.

EXAMPLE 1

Finding Critical Values for χ^2

Find the critical values χ_R^2 and χ_L^2 for a 95% confidence interval when the sample size is 18.

SOLUTION

Because the sample size is 18,

$$\text{d.f.} = n - 1 = 18 - 1 = 17. \quad \text{Degrees of freedom}$$

The area to the right of χ_R^2 is

$$\text{Area to the right of } \chi_R^2 = \frac{1-c}{2} = \frac{1-0.95}{2} = 0.025$$

and the area to the right of χ_L^2 is

$$\text{Area to the right of } \chi_L^2 = \frac{1+c}{2} = \frac{1+0.95}{2} = 0.975.$$

A portion of Table 6 is shown. Using d.f. = 17 and the areas 0.975 and 0.025, you can find the critical values, as shown by the highlighted areas in the table. (Note that the top row in the table lists areas to the right of the critical value. The entries in the table are critical values.)

Degrees of freedom	α							
	0.995	0.99	0.975	0.95	0.90	0.10	0.05	0.025
1	—	—	0.001	0.004	0.016	2.706	3.841	5.024
2	0.010	0.020	0.051	0.103	0.211	4.605	5.991	7.378
3	0.072	0.115	0.216	0.352	0.584	6.251	7.815	9.348
15	4.601	5.229	6.262	7.261	8.547	22.307	24.996	27.488
16	5.142	5.812	6.908	7.962	9.312	23.542	26.296	28.845
17	5.697	6.408	7.564	8.672	10.085	24.769	27.587	30.191
18	6.265	7.015	8.231	9.390	10.865	25.989	28.869	31.526
19	6.844	7.633	8.907	10.117	11.651	27.204	30.144	32.852
20	7.434	8.260	9.591	10.851	12.443	28.412	31.410	34.170

From the table, you can see that the critical values are

$$\chi_R^2 = 30.191 \quad \text{and} \quad \chi_L^2 = 7.564.$$

Interpretation So, for a chi-square distribution curve with 17 degrees of freedom, 95% of the area under the curve lies between 7.564 and 30.191, as shown in the figure at the left.

TRY IT YOURSELF 1

Find the critical values χ_R^2 and χ_L^2 for a 90% confidence interval when the sample size is 30.

Answer: Page A8

Picturing the World

The Florida panther is one of the most endangered mammals on Earth. In the southeastern United States, the only breeding population (with an estimated population of about 100 to 180 panthers) can be found on the southern tip of Florida. Most of the panthers live in (1) the Big Cypress National Preserve, (2) Everglades National Park, and (3) the Florida Panther National Wildlife Refuge, as shown on the map. In a study of 7 female panthers, it was found that the mean litter size was 2.14 kittens, with a standard deviation of 0.69. *(Source: Florida Fish and Wildlife Conservation Commission)*

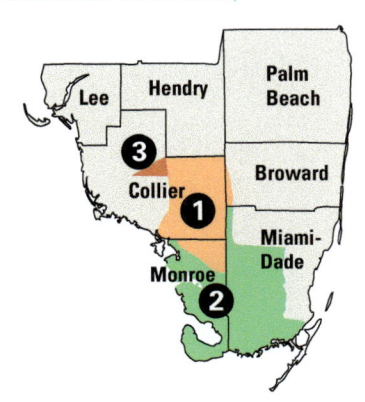

Construct a 90% confidence interval for the standard deviation of the litter size for female Florida panthers. Assume the litter sizes are normally distributed.

Confidence Intervals for σ^2 and σ

You can use the critical values χ^2_R and χ^2_L to construct confidence intervals for a population variance and standard deviation. The best point estimate for the variance is s^2 and the best point estimate for the standard deviation is s. Because the chi-square distribution is not symmetric, the confidence interval for σ^2 cannot be written as $s^2 \pm E$. You must do separate calculations for the endpoints of the confidence interval, as shown in the next definition.

DEFINITION

The c-confidence intervals for the population variance and standard deviation are shown.

Confidence Interval for σ^2:

$$\frac{(n-1)s^2}{\chi^2_R} < \sigma^2 < \frac{(n-1)s^2}{\chi^2_L}$$

Confidence Interval for σ:

$$\sqrt{\frac{(n-1)s^2}{\chi^2_R}} < \sigma < \sqrt{\frac{(n-1)s^2}{\chi^2_L}}$$

The probability that the confidence intervals contain σ^2 or σ is c, assuming that the estimation process is repeated a large number of times.

GUIDELINES

Constructing a Confidence Interval for a Variance and Standard Deviation

In Words	In Symbols
1. Verify that the population has a normal distribution.	
2. Identify the sample statistic n and the degrees of freedom.	d.f. $= n - 1$
3. Find the point estimate s^2.	$s^2 = \dfrac{\Sigma(x - \bar{x})^2}{n - 1}$
4. Find the critical values χ^2_R and χ^2_L that correspond to the given level of confidence c and the degrees of freedom.	Use Table 6 in Appendix B.
5. Find the left and right endpoints and form the confidence interval for the population variance.	Left Endpoint Right Endpoint $$\frac{(n-1)s^2}{\chi^2_R} < \sigma^2 < \frac{(n-1)s^2}{\chi^2_L}$$
6. Find the confidence interval for the population standard deviation by taking the square root of each endpoint.	Left Endpoint Right Endpoint $$\sqrt{\frac{(n-1)s^2}{\chi^2_R}} < \sigma < \sqrt{\frac{(n-1)s^2}{\chi^2_L}}$$

EXAMPLE 2

Constructing Confidence Intervals

You randomly select and weigh 30 samples of an allergy medicine. The sample standard deviation is 1.20 milligrams. Assuming the weights are normally distributed, construct 99% confidence intervals for the population variance and standard deviation.

SOLUTION

The area to the right of χ_R^2 is

$$\text{Area to the right of } \chi_R^2 = \frac{1-c}{2} = \frac{1-0.99}{2} = 0.005$$

and the area to the right of χ_L^2 is

$$\text{Area to the right of } \chi_L^2 = \frac{1+c}{2} = \frac{1+0.99}{2} = 0.995.$$

Using the values $n = 30$, d.f. $= 29$, and $c = 0.99$, the critical values χ_R^2 and χ_L^2 are

$$\chi_R^2 = 52.336 \quad \text{and} \quad \chi_L^2 = 13.121.$$

Using these critical values and $s = 1.20$, the confidence interval for σ^2 is

Left Endpoint

$$\frac{(n-1)s^2}{\chi_R^2} = \frac{(30-1)(1.20)^2}{52.336} \approx 0.80$$

Right Endpoint

$$\frac{(n-1)s^2}{\chi_L^2} = \frac{(30-1)(1.20)^2}{13.121} \approx 3.18$$

$$0.80 < \sigma^2 < 3.18.$$

The confidence interval for σ is

Left Endpoint

$$\sqrt{\frac{(30-1)(1.20)^2}{52.336}} < \sigma <$$

Right Endpoint

$$\sqrt{\frac{(30-1)(1.20)^2}{13.121}}$$

$$0.89 < \sigma < 1.78.$$

You can check your answer using technology, as shown below using Minitab.

MINITAB

Test and CI for One Variance
99% Confidence Intervals

Method	CI for StDev	CI for Variance
Chi-Square	(0.89, 1.78)	(0.80, 3.18)

Interpretation With 99% confidence, you can say that the population variance is between 0.80 and 3.18, and the population standard deviation is between 0.89 and 1.78 milligrams.

TRY IT YOURSELF 2

Construct the 90% and 95% confidence intervals for the population variance and standard deviation of the medicine weights. *Answer: Page A8*

> **Study Tip**
> When you construct a confidence interval for a population variance or standard deviation, the general *round-off rule* is to round off to the same number of decimal places as the sample variance or standard deviation.

Note in Example 2 that the confidence interval for the population standard deviation *cannot* be written as $s \pm E$ because the confidence interval does not have s as its center. (The same is true for the population variance.)

3.4 EXERCISES

For Extra Help: **MyLab Statistics**

Building Basic Skills and Vocabulary

1. Does a population have to be normally distributed in order to use the chi-square distribution?

2. What happens to the shape of the chi-square distribution as the degrees of freedom increase?

Finding Critical Values for χ^2 In Exercises 3–8, find the critical values χ^2_R and χ^2_L for the level of confidence c and sample size n.

3. $c = 0.90, n = 8$
4. $c = 0.99, n = 15$
5. $c = 0.95, n = 20$
6. $c = 0.98, n = 26$
7. $c = 0.99, n = 30$
8. $c = 0.80, n = 51$

In Exercises 9–12, construct the indicated confidence intervals for (a) the population variance σ^2 and (b) the population standard deviation σ. Assume the sample is from a normally distributed population.

9. $c = 0.95, s^2 = 11.56, n = 30$
10. $c = 0.99, s^2 = 0.64, n = 7$
11. $c = 0.90, s = 35, n = 18$
12. $c = 0.98, s = 278.1, n = 41$

Using and Interpreting Concepts

Constructing Confidence Intervals In Exercises 13–24, assume the sample is from a normally distributed population and construct the indicated confidence intervals for (a) the population variance σ^2 and (b) the population standard deviation σ. Interpret the results.

13. **Bottles** The heights (in centimeters) of 18 randomly selected bottles produced by a machine are listed. Use a 90% level of confidence.

    19.861 18.462 18.591 18.684 19.191 19.985 19.549
    19.631 18.909 19.101 19.845 19.863 18.645 19.111
    18.999 18.959 19.769 19.771

14. **Vitamin D Tablets** The quantity (in thousand IUs) of Vitamin D in 15 randomly selected supplement tablets are listed. Use a 95% level of confidence.

    5.256 5.218 5.236 4.813 4.998 5.011 5.861
    4.121 4.343 5.863 5.791 5.011 4.985 4.862
    5.682

15. **Earnings** The annual earnings (in thousands of dollars) of 21 randomly selected clinical pharmacists are listed. Use a 99% level of confidence. *(Adapted from Salary.com)*

    91.8   90.6   101.5 119.2 110.5 117.0 138.6
    112.1 136.6 123.6 111.4 80.5   105.7 99.9
    138.3 113.6 81.4   89.4   94.8   146.6 106.6

16. **Final Exam Scores** The final exam scores of 24 randomly selected students in a statistics class are shown in the table at the left. Use a 95% level of confidence.

17. **Space Shuttle Flights** The durations (in days) of 14 randomly selected space shuttle flights have a sample standard deviation of 3.54 days. Use a 99% level of confidence. *(Source: NASA)*

Final exam scores

61	73	59	99	83	60
68	69	97	43	61	87
55	40	67	48	87	64
55	90	59	71	65	59

TABLE FOR EXERCISE 16

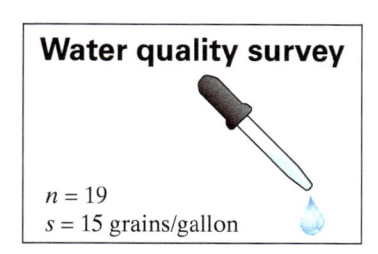

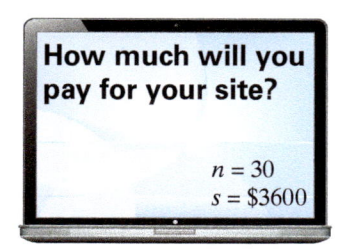

18. **College Football** The numbers of touchdowns scored by 11 randomly selected NCAA Division I Subdivision teams in a recent season have a sample standard deviation of 9.35. Use an 80% level of confidence. *(Source: National Collegiate Athletic Association)*

19. **Water Quality** As part of a water quality survey, you test the water hardness in several randomly selected streams. The results are shown in the figure at the left. Use a 95% level of confidence.

20. **Website Costs** As part of a survey, you ask a random sample of business owners how much they would be willing to pay for a website for their company. The results are shown in the figure at the left. Use a 90% level of confidence.

21. **Inverter Batteries** The reserve capacities (in hours) of 18 randomly selected inverter batteries have a sample standard deviation of 0.40 hour. Use a 90% level of confidence.

22. **Maximum Daily Temperature** The record high daily temperatures (in degrees Fahrenheit) of a random sample of 64 days of the year in Grand Junction, Colorado, have a sample standard deviation of 16.8°F. Use a 98% level of confidence. *(Source: NOAA)*

23. **Waiting Times** The waiting times (in minutes) of a random sample of 26 people at a book-signing event have a sample standard deviation of 4.9 minutes. Use a 99% level of confidence.

24. **Smartphones** The prices of a random sample of 23 new smartphones have a sample standard deviation of $1,200. Use an 80% level of confidence.

Extending Concepts

25. **Bottle Heights** You are analyzing the sample of bottles in Exercise 13. The population standard deviation of the bottles' heights should be less than 0.35 centimeter. Does the confidence interval you constructed for σ suggest that the variation in the bottles' heights is at an acceptable level? Explain your reasoning.

26. **Vitamin D Amounts** You are analyzing the sample of Vitamin D Tablets in Exercise 14. The population standard deviation of the amount of Vitamin D in the tablets should be less than 0.50 thousand IUs. Does the confidence interval you constructed for σ suggest that the variation in the amounts of Vitamin D in the tablets is at an acceptable level? Explain your reasoning.

27. **Battery Reserve Capacities** You are analyzing the sample of inverter batteries in Exercise 21. The population standard deviation of the batteries' reserve capacities should be less than 0.50 hour. Does the confidence interval you constructed for σ suggest that the variation in the batteries' reserve capacities is at an acceptable level? Explain your reasoning.

28. **Waiting Times** You are analyzing the sample of waiting times in Exercise 23. The population standard deviation of the waiting times should be less than 7.9 minutes. Does the confidence interval you constructed for σ suggest that the variation in the waiting times is at an acceptable level? Explain your reasoning.

29. In your own words, explain how finding a confidence interval for a population variance is different from finding a confidence interval for a population mean or proportion.

USES AND ABUSES: Statistics in the Real World

Uses

By now, you know that complete information about population parameters is often not available. The techniques of this chapter can be used to make interval estimates of these parameters so that you can make informed decisions.

From what you learned in this chapter, you know that point estimates (sample statistics) of population parameters are usually close but rarely equal to the actual values of the parameters they are estimating. Remembering this can help you make good decisions in your career and in everyday life. For instance, the results of a survey tell you that 52% of registered voters plan to vote in favor of the rezoning of a portion of a town from residential to commercial use. You know that this is only a point estimate of the actual proportion that will vote in favor of rezoning. If the margin of error is 3%, then the interval estimate is $0.49 < p < 0.55$ and it is possible that the item will not receive a majority vote.

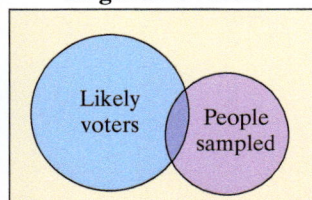

Abuses

Unrepresentative Samples There are many ways that surveys can result in incorrect predictions. When you read the results of a survey, remember to question the sample size, the sampling technique, and the questions asked. For instance, you want to know the proportion of people who will vote in favor of rezoning. From the diagram at the left, you can see that even when your sample is large enough, it may not consist of people who are likely to vote.

Biased Survey Questions In surveys, it is also important to analyze the wording of the questions. For instance, the question about rezoning might be presented as: "Knowing that rezoning will result in more businesses contributing to school taxes, would you support the rezoning?"

Misinterpreted Polls Some political pundits and voters vowed never to trust polls again after they failed to predict Donald Trump's win over Hillary Clinton in the 2016 U.S. presidential election. However, nationwide polls the week of the election were only off by about 1%—the polls showed Clinton ahead by about 3% and she ended up ahead in votes by about 2%.

Many state polls were inaccurate, most of them in the same direction, with Trump receiving up to 10% more of the vote than expected in some states. This was enough to give him the majority of electoral votes and the presidency. Analysts are still debating the reasons so many state polls were unrepresentative of the people who actually voted.

EXERCISES

1. *Unrepresentative Samples* Find an example of a survey that is reported in a newspaper, in a magazine, or on a website. Describe different ways that the sample could have been unrepresentative of the population.

2. *Biased Survey Questions* Find an example of a survey that is reported in a newspaper, in a magazine, or on a website. Describe different ways that the survey questions could have been biased.

3. *Misinterpreted Polls* Determine whether each state election poll below was misleading. Assume the margin of error is 4% for each poll.

    (a) Michigan poll leader: Clinton by 3.4%; Election winner: Trump by 0.3%

    (b) Wisconsin poll leader: Clinton by 6.5%; Election winner: Trump by 0.7%

3 Chapter Summary

What Did You Learn?	Example(s)	Review Exercises
Section 3.1		
▸ How to find a point estimate and a margin of error $$E = z_c \frac{\sigma}{\sqrt{n}} \quad \text{Margin of error}$$	1, 2	1, 2
▸ How to construct and interpret confidence intervals for a population mean when σ is known $$\bar{x} - E < \mu < \bar{x} + E$$	3–5	3–6
▸ How to determine the minimum sample size required when estimating a population mean	6	7, 8
Section 3.2		
▸ How to interpret the t-distribution and use a t-distribution table $$t = \frac{\bar{x} - \mu}{s/\sqrt{n}}, \quad \text{d.f.} = n - 1$$	1	9–12
▸ How to construct and interpret confidence intervals for a population mean when σ is not known $$\bar{x} - E < \mu < \bar{x} + E, \quad E = t_c \frac{s}{\sqrt{n}}$$	2–4	13–18
Section 3.3		
▸ How to find a point estimate for a population proportion $$\hat{p} = \frac{x}{n}$$	1	19–24
▸ How to construct and interpret confidence intervals for a population proportion $$\hat{p} - E < p < \hat{p} + E, \quad E = z_c \sqrt{\frac{\hat{p}\hat{q}}{n}}$$	2, 3	19–24
▸ How to determine the minimum sample size required when estimating a population proportion	4	25, 26
Section 3.4		
▸ How to interpret the chi-square distribution and use a chi-square distribution table $$\chi^2 = \frac{(n-1)s^2}{\sigma^2}, \quad \text{d.f.} = n - 1$$	1	27–30
▸ How to construct and interpret confidence intervals for a population variance and standard deviation $$\frac{(n-1)s^2}{\chi_R^2} < \sigma^2 < \frac{(n-1)s^2}{\chi_L^2}, \quad \sqrt{\frac{(n-1)s^2}{\chi_R^2}} < \sigma < \sqrt{\frac{(n-1)s^2}{\chi_L^2}}$$	2	31, 32

3 Review Exercises

Table for Exercise 1

Systolic blood pressures (in mmHg)						
125	80	118	130	95	128	155
108	96	134	92	103	97	142
93	104	140	124	131	93	107
98	123	97	132	145	133	98
155	162	87	99	154	137	122
155	123	129	96	122		

Section 3.1

1. The systolic blood pressures (in mmHg) of 40 persons are shown in the table. Assume the population standard deviation is 25 mmHg. Find (a) the point estimate of the population mean μ and (b) the margin of error for a 90% confidence interval.

2. The ages (in completed years) of 30 persons attending a course are shown below. Assume the population standard deviation is 10 years. Find (a) the point estimate of the population mean μ and (b) the margin of error for a 95% confidence interval.

   Ages (in completed years)

   15 16 16 14 21 22 19 29 30 14 34 32 43 52 32
   12 17 18 15 16 23 20 27 10 23 33 29 36 24 16

3. Construct a 90% confidence interval for the population mean in Exercise 1. Interpret the results.

4. Construct a 95% confidence interval for the population mean in Exercise 2. Interpret the results.

In Exercises 5 and 6, use the confidence interval to find the margin of error and the sample mean.

5. (30.25, 42.50)

6. (7.428, 7.562)

7. Determine the minimum sample size required to be 95% confident that the sample mean systolic blood pressure is within 8 mmHg of the population mean systolic blood pressure. Use the population standard deviation from Exercise 1.

8. Determine the minimum sample size required to be 99% confident that the sample mean age is within 3 years of the population mean age. Use the population standard deviation from Exercise 2.

Section 3.2

In Exercises 9–12, find the critical value t_c for the level of confidence c and sample size n.

9. $c = 0.90, n = 12$

10. $c = 0.95, n = 24$

11. $c = 0.80, n = 16$

12. $c = 0.99, n = 30$

In Exercises 13–16, (a) find the margin of error for the values of c, s, and n, and (b) construct the confidence interval for μ using the t-distribution. Assume the population is normally distributed.

13. $c = 0.80, s = 27.4, n = 36, \bar{x} = 81.6$

14. $c = 0.95, s = 1.1, n = 25, \bar{x} = 3.5$

15. $c = 0.90, s = 3.6, n = 20, \bar{x} = 20.6$

16. $c = 0.99, s = 16.5, n = 20, \bar{x} = 25.2$

17. In a random sample of 36 top-rated roller coasters, the average height is 165 feet and the standard deviation is 67 feet. Construct a 90% confidence interval for μ. Interpret the results. *(Source: POP World Media, LLC)*

18. You research the heights of top-rated roller coasters and find that the population mean is 160 feet. In Exercise 17, does the t-value fall between $-t_{0.95}$ and $t_{0.95}$?

Section 3.3

In Exercises 19–22, let p be the population proportion for the situation. (a) Find point estimates of p and q, (b) construct 90% and 95% confidence intervals for p, and (c) interpret the results of part (b) and compare the widths of the confidence intervals.

19. In a survey of 1035 U.S. adults, 745 say they want the U.S. to play a leading or major role in global affairs. *(Adapted from Gallup)*

20. In a survey of 1003 U.S. adults, 451 believe that for a person to be considered truly American, it is very important that he or she share American customs and traditions. *(Adapted from Pew Research Center)*

21. In a survey of 2202 U.S. adults, 1167 think antibiotics are effective against viral infections. *(Adapted from The Harris Poll)*

22. In a survey of 2223 U.S. adults, 1334 say an occupation as an athlete is prestigious. *(Adapted from The Harris Poll)*

23. In Exercise 19, does it seem possible that the population proportion could equal 0.75? Explain.

24. In Exercise 22, does it seem possible that the population proportion could be within 1% of the point estimate? Explain.

25. You wish to estimate, with 95% confidence, the population proportion of U.S. adults who have taken or planned to take a winter vacation in a recent year. Your estimate must be accurate within 5% of the population proportion.
    (a) No preliminary estimate is available. Find the minimum sample size needed.
    (b) Find the minimum sample size needed, using a prior study that found that 32% of U.S. adults have taken or planned to take a winter vacation in a recent year. *(Source: Rasmussen Reports)*
    (c) Compare the results from parts (a) and (b).

26. In Exercise 25(b), would a sample size of 369 be acceptable? Explain.

Section 3.4

In Exercises 27–30, find the critical values χ_R^2 and χ_L^2 for the level of confidence c and sample size n.

27. $c = 0.90, n = 15$
28. $c = 0.98, n = 25$
29. $c = 0.95, n = 20$
30. $c = 0.99, n = 10$

In Exercises 31 and 32, assume the sample is from a normally distributed population and construct the indicated confidence intervals for (a) the population variance σ^2 and (b) the population standard deviation σ. Interpret the results.

31. The maximum wind speeds (in knots) of 13 randomly selected hurricanes that have hit the U.S. mainland are listed. Use a 95% level of confidence. *(Source: National Oceanic & Atmospheric Administration)*

    70 85 70 75 100 100 110 105 130 75 85 75 70

32. The acceleration times (in seconds) from 0 to 60 miles per hour for 33 randomly selected sedans are listed. Use a 98% level of confidence. *(Source: Zero to 60 Times)*

    6.5   5.0   5.2   3.3   6.6   6.3   5.1   5.3   5.4   9.5   7.5
    4.5   5.8   8.6   6.9   8.1   6.0   6.7   7.9   8.8   7.1   7.9
    7.2 18.4   9.1   6.8 12.5   4.2   7.1   9.9   9.5   2.8   4.9

3 Chapter Quiz

Take this quiz as you would take a quiz in class. After you are done, check your work against the answers given in the back of the book.

Women's Open Division winning times (in hours)

3.36	3.45	3.50	3.14	2.79
2.79	2.75	2.59	2.45	2.38
2.57	2.42	2.41	2.42	2.41
2.42	2.45	2.44	2.39	2.44
2.40	2.35	2.41	2.39	2.49
2.42	2.54	2.44	2.44	2.49

TABLE FOR EXERCISE 1

1. The winning times (in hours) for a sample of 30 randomly selected Boston Marathon Women's Open Division champions are shown in the table at the left. *(Source: Boston Athletic Association)*

    (a) Find the point estimate of the population mean.

    (b) Find the margin of error for a 95% confidence level.

    (c) Construct a 95% confidence interval for the population mean. Interpret the results.

    (d) Does it seem possible that the population mean could be greater than 2.75 hours? Explain.

2. You wish to estimate the mean winning time for Boston Marathon Women's Open Division champions. The estimate must be within 0.13 hour of the population mean. Determine the minimum sample size required to construct a 99% confidence interval for the population mean. Use the population standard deviation from Exercise 1.

3. The data set represents the amounts of time (in minutes) spent checking email for a random sample of employees at a company.

    7.5   2.0   12.1   8.8   9.4   7.3   1.9   2.8   7.0   7.3

    (a) Find the sample mean and the sample standard deviation.

    (b) Construct a 90% confidence interval for the population mean. Interpret the results. Assume the times are normally distributed.

    (c) Repeat part (b), assuming $\sigma = 3.5$ minutes. Compare the results.

4. In a random sample of 12 senior-level chemical engineers, the mean annual earnings was $133,326 and the standard deviation was $36,729. Assume the annual earnings are normally distributed and construct a 95% confidence interval for the population mean annual earnings for senior-level chemical engineers. Interpret the results. *(Adapted from Salary.com)*

5. You research the salaries of senior-level chemical engineers and find that the population mean is $131,935. In Exercise 4, does the *t*-value fall between $-t_{0.95}$ and $t_{0.95}$?

6. In a survey of 1018 U.S. adults, 753 say that the energy situation in the United States is very or fairly serious. *(Adapted from Gallup)*

    (a) Find the point estimate for the population proportion.

    (b) Construct a 90% confidence interval for the population proportion. Interpret the results.

    (c) Does it seem possible that the population proportion could be between 90% and 95% of the point estimate? Explain.

    (d) Find the minimum sample size needed to estimate the population proportion at the 99% confidence level in order to ensure that the estimate is accurate within 4% of the population proportion.

7. Refer to the data set in Exercise 3. Assume the population of times spent checking email is normally distributed. Construct a 95% confidence interval for (a) the population variance and (b) the population standard deviation. Interpret the results.

3 Chapter Test

Take this test as you would take a test in class.

1. In a survey of 2096 U.S. adults, 1740 think football teams of all levels should require players who suffer a head injury to take a set amount of time off from playing to recover. *(Adapted from The Harris Poll)*
   (a) Find the point estimate for the population proportion.
   (b) Construct a 95% confidence interval for the population proportion. Interpret the results.
   (c) Does it seem possible that the population proportion could be within 99% of the point estimate? Explain.
   (d) Find the minimum sample size needed to estimate the population proportion at the 99% confidence level in order to ensure that the estimate is accurate within 3% of the population proportion.

2. The data set represents the weights (in pounds) of 10 randomly selected black bears from northeast Pennsylvania. Assume the weights are normally distributed. *(Source: Pennsylvania Game Commission)*

   170 225 183 137 287 191 268 185 211 284

   (a) Find the sample mean and the sample standard deviation.
   (b) Construct a 95% confidence interval for the population mean. Interpret the results.
   (c) Construct a 99% confidence interval for the population standard deviation. Interpret the results.

3. The data set represents the scores of 12 randomly selected students on the SAT Physics Subject Test. Assume the population test scores are normally distributed and the population standard deviation is 104. *(Adapted from The College Board)*

   590 450 490 680 380 500 570 620 640 530 780 720

   (a) Find the point estimate of the population mean.
   (b) Construct a 90% confidence interval for the population mean. Interpret the results.
   (c) Does it seem possible that the population mean could equal 667? Explain.
   (d) Determine the minimum sample size required to be 95% confident that the sample mean test score is within 10 points of the population mean test score.

4. Use the standard normal distribution or the *t*-distribution to construct the indicated confidence interval for the population mean of each data set. Justify your decision. If neither distribution can be used, explain why. Interpret the results.
   (a) In a random sample of 40 patients, the mean waiting time at a dentist's office was 20 minutes and the standard deviation was 7.5 minutes. Construct a 95% confidence interval for the population mean.
   (b) In a random sample of 15 cereal boxes, the mean weight was 11.89 ounces. Assume the weights of the cereal boxes are normally distributed and the population standard deviation is 0.05 ounce. Construct a 90% confidence interval for the population mean.

REAL STATISTICS REAL DECISIONS
Putting it all together

The Safe Drinking Water Act, which was passed in 1974, allows the Environmental Protection Agency (EPA) to regulate the levels of contaminants in drinking water. The EPA requires that water utilities give their customers water quality reports annually. These reports include the results of daily water quality monitoring, which is performed to determine whether drinking water is safe for consumption.

A water department tests for contaminants at water treatment plants and at customers' taps. These contaminants include microorganisms, organic chemicals, and inorganic chemicals, such as cyanide. Cyanide's presence in drinking water is the result of discharges from steel, plastics, and fertilizer factories. For drinking water, the maximum contaminant level of cyanide is 0.2 part per million.

As part of your job for your city's water department, you are preparing a report that includes an analysis of the results shown in the figure at the right. The figure shows the point estimates for the population mean concentration and the 95% confidence intervals for μ for cyanide over a three-year period. The data are based on random water samples taken by the city's three water treatment plants.

EXERCISES

1. *Interpreting the Results*

   Use the figure to determine whether there has been a change in the mean concentration level of cyanide for each time period. Explain your reasoning.

   (a) From Year 1 to Year 2   (b) From Year 2 to Year 3

   (c) From Year 1 to Year 3

2. *What Can You Conclude?*

   Using the results of Exercise 1, what can you conclude about the concentrations of cyanide in the drinking water?

3. *What Do You Think?*

   The confidence interval for Year 2 is much larger than the other years. What do you think may have caused this larger confidence level?

4. *How Can You Improve the Report?*

   What can the water department do to decrease the size of the confidence intervals, regardless of the amount of variance in cyanide levels?

5. *How Do You Think They Did It?*

   How do you think the water department constructed the 95% confidence intervals for the population mean concentration of cyanide in the water? Include answers to the questions below in your explanation.

   (a) What sampling distribution do you think they used? Why?

   (b) Do you think they used the population standard deviation in calculating the margin of error? Why or why not? If not, what could they have used?

TECHNOLOGY

MINITAB | EXCEL | TI-84 PLUS

United States Foreign Policy Polls

THE GALLUP ORGANIZATION
www.gallup.com

Since 1935, the Gallup Organization has conducted public opinion polls in the United States and around the world. The table shows the results of four polls of randomly selected U.S. adults from 2015 through 2017. The remaining percentages not shown in the results are adults who were not sure.

Question	Results	Number Polled
Do you think the U.S. made a mistake sending troops to Iraq?	Yes: 51% No: 46%	1527
In the Middle East situation, are your sympathies more with the Israelis or the Palestinians?	Israelis: 62% Palestinians: 19%	1035
Do you have a favorable or unfavorable opinion of Russian president Vladimir Putin?	Favorable: 22% Unfavorable: 72%	1035
Should the NATO alliance be maintained or is it not necessary anymore?	Should be maintained: 80% Not necessary: 16%	485

EXERCISES

1. Use technology to find a 95% confidence interval for the population proportion of adults who
   (a) think sending troops to Iraq was a mistake.
   (b) sympathize more with the Israelis than the Palestinians.
   (c) have a favorable opinion of Vladimir Putin.
   (d) think the NATO alliance is not necessary.
   (e) do not sympathize with either the Israelis or the Palestinians more than the other.

2. Find the minimum sample size needed to estimate, with 95% confidence, the population proportion of adults who have a favorable opinion of Vladimir Putin. Your estimate must be accurate within 2% of the population proportion.

3. Use technology to simulate a poll. Assume that the actual population proportion of adults who think the U.S. made a mistake sending troops to Iraq is 54%. Run the simulation several times using $n = 1527$.
   (a) What was the least value you obtained for $\hat{p}$?
   (b) What was the greatest value you obtained for $\hat{p}$?

EXCEL

Random Number Generation

Number of Variables: 1
Number of Random Numbers: 200
Distribution: Binomial
Parameters
p Value = 0.54
Number of trials = 1537

4. Is it probable that the population proportion of adults who think the U.S. made a mistake sending troops to Iraq is 54%? Explain your reasoning.

Extended solutions are given in the technology manuals that accompany this text. Technical instruction is provided for Minitab, Excel, and the TI-84 Plus.

3 Using Technology to Construct Confidence Intervals

Here are some Minitab and TI-84 Plus printouts for some examples in this chapter. Answers may be slightly different because of rounding.

See Example 3, page 135.

19	25	15	21	22	20	20	22	22	21
21	23	22	16	21	18	25	23	23	21
22	24	18	19	23	20	19	19	24	25
17	21	21	25	23	18	22	20	21	21

MINITAB

One-Sample Z: Hours

The assumed standard deviation = 2.3

Variable	N	Mean	StDev	SE Mean	95% CI
Hours	40	21.050	2.438	0.364	(20.337, 21.763)

See Example 2, page 146.

MINITAB

One-Sample T

N	Mean	StDev	SE Mean	95% CI
16	162.00	10.00	2.50	(156.67, 167.33)

See Example 2, page 156.

MINITAB

Test and CI for One Proportion

Sample	X	N	Sample p	95% CI
1	1054	1550	0.680000	(0.656130, 0.703186)

Confidence Intervals

See Example 5, page 137.

TI-84 PLUS
EDIT CALC **TESTS**
1: Z–Test...
2: T–Test...
3: 2–SampZTest...
4: 2–SampTTest...
5: 1–PropZTest...
6: 2–PropZTest...
7↓ ZInterval...

↓

TI-84 PLUS
ZInterval
Inpt: Data **Stats**
σ: 1.5
x̄: 22.9
n: 20
C–Level: .9
Calculate

↓

TI-84 PLUS
ZInterval
(22.348, 23.452)
x̄=22.9
n=20

See Example 3, page 147.

TI-84 PLUS
EDIT CALC **TESTS**
2↑ T–Test...
3: 2–SampZTest...
4: 2–SampTTest...
5: 1–PropZTest...
6: 2–PropZTest...
7: ZInterval...
8↓ TInterval...

↓

TI-84 PLUS
TInterval
Inpt: Data **Stats**
x̄: 9.75
Sx: 2.39
n: 36
C–Level: .99
Calculate

↓

TI-84 PLUS
TInterval
(8.665, 10.835)
x̄=9.75
Sx=2.39
n=36

See Example 2, page 156.

TI-84 PLUS
EDIT CALC **TESTS**
5↑ 1–PropZTest...
6: 2–PropZTest...
7: ZInterval...
8: TInterval...
9: 2–SampZInt...
0: 2–SampTInt...
A↓ 1–PropZInt...

↓

TI-84 PLUS
1-PropZInt
x: 1054
n: 1550
C–Level: .95
Calculate

↓

TI-84 PLUS
1-PropZInt
(.65678, .70322)
p̂=.68
n=1550

CHAPTER 4

Correlation and Regression

4.1
Correlation
Activity

4.2
Linear Regression
Activity
Case Study

4.3
Measures of Regression and Prediction Intervals

4.4
Multiple Regression
Uses and Abuses
Real Statistics—Real Decisions
Technology

In 2016, the Los Angeles Dodgers had the highest team salary in Major League Baseball at $231.3 million and the highest average attendance at 45,720. The Tampa Bay Rays had the lowest team salary at $48.2 million and the lowest average attendance at 15,879.

Where You've Been

In Chapters 1–3, you studied descriptive statistics, probability, and inferential statistics. One of the techniques you learned in descriptive statistics was graphing paired data with a scatter plot (see Section 2.2). For instance, the salaries and average attendances at home games for the teams in Major League Baseball in 2016 are shown in the scatter plot at the right and in the table below.

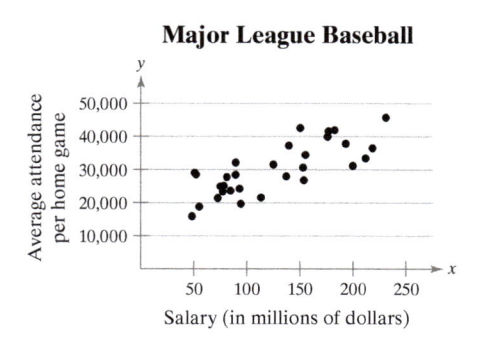

Salary (in millions of dollars)	78.4	75.0	153.7	218.7	176.1	113.4	77.3	94.5	89.7	199.9
Average attendance per home game	25,138	24,950	26,819	36,487	39,906	21,559	23,384	19,650	32,130	31,173

Salary (in millions of dollars)	89.5	125.1	139.7	231.3	72.5	52.1	93.3	155.2	193.2	55.0
Average attendance per home game	28,477	31,577	37,236	45,720	21,405	28,575	24,246	34,440	37,820	18,784

Salary (in millions of dollars)	84.8	81.2	50.7	137.2	177.0	150.4	48.2	212.1	182.7	153.0
Average attendance per home game	23,644	27,768	29,030	27,999	41,546	42,525	15,879	33,462	41,878	30,641

Where You're Going

In this chapter, you will study how to describe and test the significance of relationships between two variables when data are presented as ordered pairs. For instance, in the scatter plot above, it appears that higher team salaries tend to correspond to higher average attendances and lower team salaries tend to correspond to lower average attendances. This relationship is described by saying that the team salaries are positively correlated to the average attendances. Graphically, the relationship can be described by drawing a line, called a regression line, that fits the points as closely as possible, as shown below. The second scatter plot below shows the salaries and wins for the teams in Major League Baseball in 2016. From the scatter plot, it appears that there is a positive correlation between the team salaries and wins.

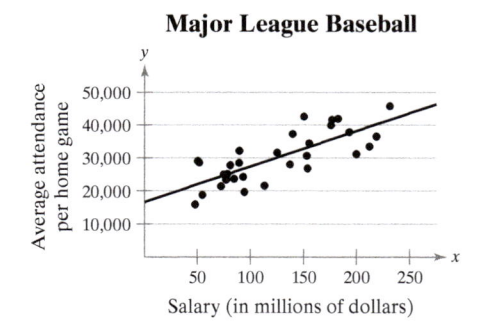

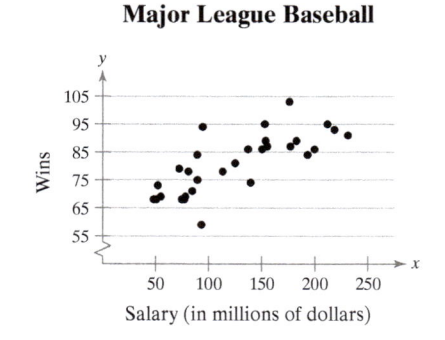

4.1 Correlation

What You Should Learn

- An introduction to linear correlation, independent and dependent variables, and the types of correlation
- How to find a correlation coefficient
- How to test a population correlation coefficient ρ using a table
- How to perform a hypothesis test for a population correlation coefficient ρ
- How to distinguish between correlation and causation

An Overview of Correlation ■ Correlation Coefficient ■ Using a Table to Test a Population Correlation Coefficient ρ ■ Hypothesis Testing for a Population Correlation Coefficient ρ ■ Correlation and Causation

An Overview of Correlation

Suppose a safety inspector wants to determine whether a relationship exists between the number of hours of training for an employee and the number of accidents involving that employee. Or suppose a psychologist wants to know whether a relationship exists between the number of hours a person sleeps each night and that person's reaction time. How would he or she determine if any relationship exists?

In this section, you will study how to describe what type of relationship, or correlation, exists between two quantitative variables and how to determine whether the correlation is significant.

> **DEFINITION**
>
> A **correlation** is a relationship between two variables. The data can be represented by the ordered pairs (x, y), where x is the **independent** (or **explanatory**) **variable** and y is the **dependent** (or **response**) **variable.**

In Section 2.2, you learned that the graph of ordered pairs (x, y) is called a *scatter plot*. In a scatter plot, the ordered pairs (x, y) are graphed as points in a coordinate plane. The independent (explanatory) variable x is measured on the horizontal axis, and the dependent (response) variable y is measured on the vertical axis. A scatter plot can be used to determine whether a linear (straight line) correlation exists between two variables. The scatter plots below show several types of correlation.

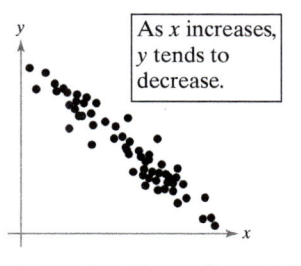

Negative Linear Correlation (As x increases, y tends to decrease.)

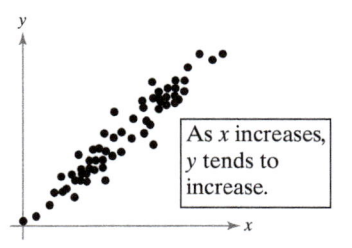

Positive Linear Correlation (As x increases, y tends to increase.)

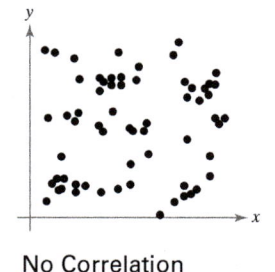

No Correlation

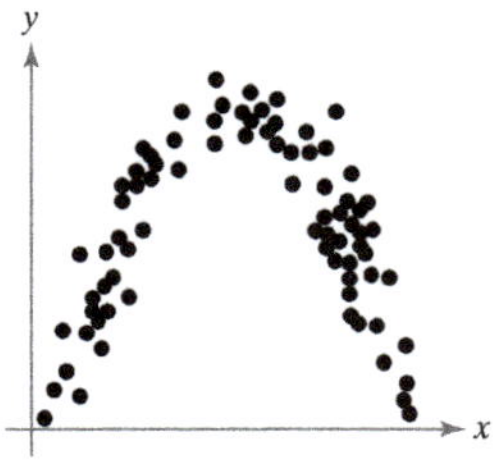

Nonlinear Correlation

GDP (in trillions of dollars), x	CO_2 emissions (in millions of metric tons), y
1.8	604.4
1.3	434.2
2.4	544.0
1.5	370.4
3.9	742.3
2.1	340.5
0.9	232.0
1.4	262.3
3.0	441.9
4.6	1157.7

Tech Tip

Remember that all data sets containing 20 or more entries are available electronically. Also, some of the data sets in this section are used throughout the chapter, so save any data that you enter. For instance, the data used in Example 1 is also used later in this section and in Sections 4.2 and 4.3.

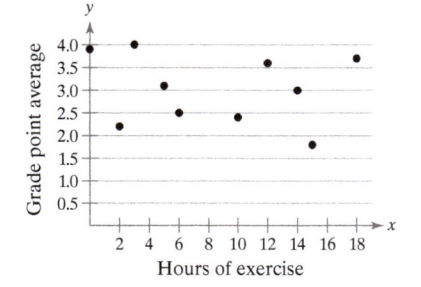

EXAMPLE 1

Constructing a Scatter Plot

An economist wants to determine whether there is a linear relationship between a country's gross domestic product (GDP) and carbon dioxide (CO_2) emissions. The data are shown in the table at the left. Display the data in a scatter plot and describe the type of correlation. *(Source: World Bank and U.S. Energy Information Administration)*

SOLUTION

The scatter plot is shown below. From the scatter plot, it appears that there is a positive linear correlation between the variables.

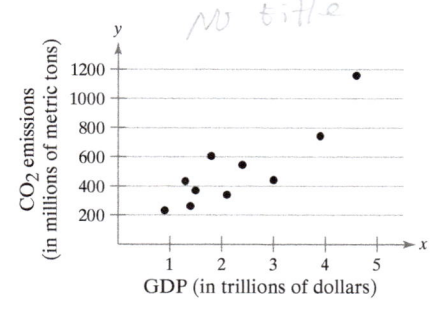

Interpretation Reading from left to right, as the gross domestic products increase, the carbon dioxide emissions tend to increase.

TRY IT YOURSELF 1

A director of alumni affairs at a small college wants to determine whether there is a linear relationship between the number of years alumni have been out of school and their annual contributions (in thousands of dollars). The data are shown in the table below. Display the data in a scatter plot and describe the type of correlation.

Number of years out of school, x	1	10	5	15	3	24	30
Annual contribution (in 1000s of \$), y	12.5	8.7	14.6	5.2	9.9	3.1	2.7

Answer: Page A8

EXAMPLE 2

Constructing a Scatter Plot

A student conducts a study to determine whether there is a linear relationship between the number of hours a student exercises each week and the student's grade point average (GPA). The data are shown in the table below. Display the data in a scatter plot and describe the type of correlation.

Hours of exercise, x	12	3	0	6	10	2	18	14	15	5
GPA, y	3.6	4.0	3.9	2.5	2.4	2.2	3.7	3.0	1.8	3.1

SOLUTION

The scatter plot is shown at the left. From the scatter plot, it appears that there is no linear correlation between the variables.

Interpretation The number of hours a student exercises each week does not appear to be related to the student's grade point average.

TRY IT YOURSELF 2

A researcher conducts a study to determine whether there is a linear relationship between a person's height (in inches) and pulse rate (in beats per minute). The data are shown in the table below. Display the data in a scatter plot and describe the type of correlation.

Height, x	68	72	65	70	62	75	78	64	68
Pulse rate, y	90	85	88	100	105	98	70	65	72

Answer: Page A8

Duration, x	Time, y	Duration, x	Time, y
1.80	56	3.78	79
1.82	58	3.83	85
1.90	62	3.88	80
1.93	56	4.10	89
1.98	57	4.27	90
2.05	57	4.30	89
2.13	60	4.43	89
2.30	57	4.47	86
2.37	61	4.53	89
2.82	73	4.55	86
3.13	76	4.60	92
3.27	77	4.63	91
3.65	77		

EXAMPLE 3

Constructing a Scatter Plot Using Technology

Old Faithful, located in Yellowstone National Park, is the world's most famous geyser. The durations (in minutes) of several of Old Faithful's eruptions and the times (in minutes) until the next eruption are shown in the table at the left. Use technology to display the data in a scatter plot. Describe the type of correlation.

SOLUTION

MINITAB, Excel, the TI-84 Plus, and StatCrunch each have features for graphing scatter plots. Try using this technology to draw the scatter plots shown. From the scatter plots, it appears that the variables have a positive linear correlation.

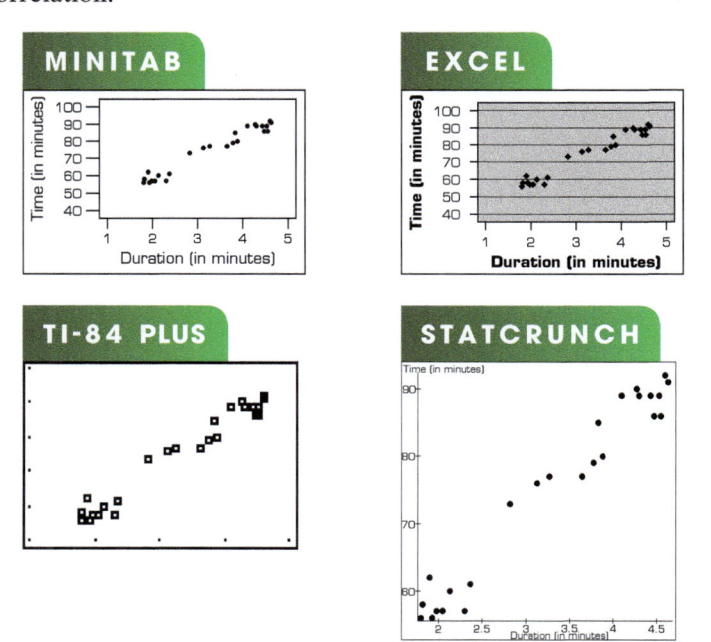

Interpretation Reading from left to right, as the durations of the eruptions increase, the times until the next eruption tend to increase.

TRY IT YOURSELF 3

Consider the data on page 181 on the salaries and average attendances at home games for the teams in Major League Baseball. Use technology to display the data in a scatter plot. Describe the type of correlation.

Answer: Page A8

Correlation Coefficient

Interpreting correlation using a scatter plot is subjective. A precise measure of the type and strength of a linear correlation between two variables is to calculate the **correlation coefficient**. A formula for the sample correlation coefficient is given, but it is more convenient to use technology to calculate this value.

> **Study Tip**
>
> The formal name for *r* is the *Pearson product moment correlation coefficient*. It is named after the English statistician Karl Pearson (1857–1936). (See page 37.)

DEFINITION

The **correlation coefficient** is a measure of the strength and the direction of a linear relationship between two variables. The symbol *r* represents the sample correlation coefficient. A formula for *r* is

$$r = \frac{n\Sigma xy - (\Sigma x)(\Sigma y)}{\sqrt{n\Sigma x^2 - (\Sigma x)^2}\sqrt{n\Sigma y^2 - (\Sigma y)^2}}$$ Sample correlation coefficient

where *n* is the number of pairs of data. The **population correlation coefficient** is represented by ρ (the lowercase Greek letter rho, pronounced "row").

The range of the correlation coefficient is -1 to 1, inclusive. When *x* and *y* have a strong positive linear correlation, *r* is close to 1. When *x* and *y* have a strong negative linear correlation, *r* is close to -1. When *x* and *y* have perfect positive linear correlation or perfect negative linear correlation, *r* is equal to 1 or -1, respectively. When there is no linear correlation, *r* is close to 0. It is important to remember that when *r* is close to 0, it does not mean that there is no relation between *x* and *y*, just that there is no *linear* relation. Several examples are shown below.

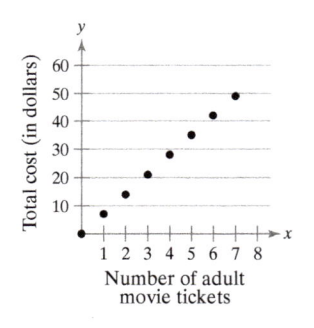

Perfect positive correlation
$r = 1$

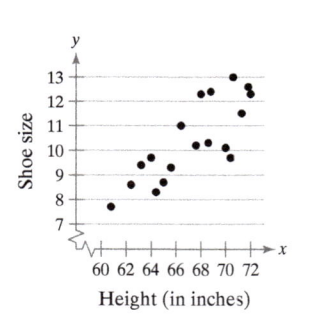

Strong positive correlation
$r = 0.81$

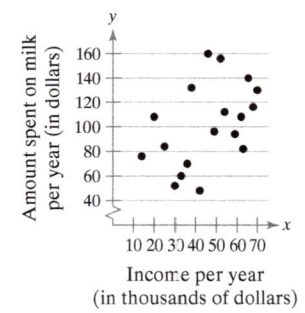

Weak positive correlation
$r = 0.45$

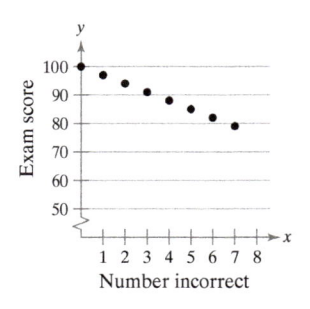

Perfect negative correlation
$r = -1$

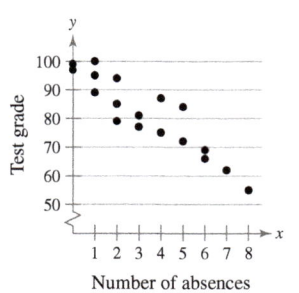

Strong negative correlation
$r = -0.92$

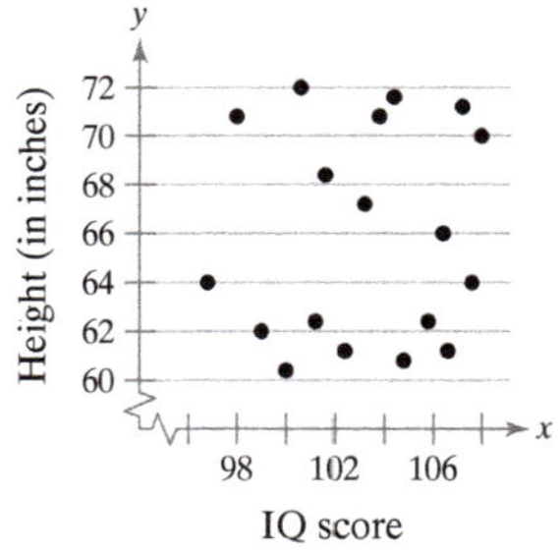

No correlation
$r = 0.04$

To use a correlation coefficient *r* to make an inference about a population, it is required that (1) the sample paired data (x, y) is random and (2) *x* and *y* have a *bivariate normal distribution* (you will learn more about this distribution in Section 4.3). In this text, unless stated otherwise, you can assume that these requirements are met.

Study Tip

The symbol Σx^2 means square each value and add the squares. The symbol $(\Sigma x)^2$ means add the values and square the sum.

GUIDELINES

Calculating a Correlation Coefficient

In Words	In Symbols
1. Find the sum of the x-values.	Σx
2. Find the sum of the y-values.	Σy
3. Multiply each x-value by its corresponding y-value and find the sum.	Σxy
4. Square each x-value and find the sum.	Σx^2
5. Square each y-value and find the sum.	Σy^2
6. Use these five sums to calculate the correlation coefficient.	$r = \dfrac{n\Sigma xy - (\Sigma x)(\Sigma y)}{\sqrt{n\Sigma x^2 - (\Sigma x)^2}\sqrt{n\Sigma y^2 - (\Sigma y)^2}}$

EXAMPLE 4

Calculating a Correlation Coefficient

Calculate the correlation coefficient for the gross domestic products and carbon dioxide emissions data in Example 1. Interpret the result in the context of the data.

SOLUTION Use a table to help calculate the correlation coefficient.

GDP (in trillions of dollars), x	CO_2 emissions (in millions of metric tons), y	xy	x^2	y^2
1.8	604.4	1087.92	3.24	365,299.36
1.3	434.2	564.46	1.69	188,529.64
2.4	544.0	1305.6	5.76	295,936
1.5	370.4	555.6	2.25	137,196.16
3.9	742.3	2894.97	15.21	551,009.29
2.1	340.5	715.05	4.41	115,940.25
0.9	232.0	208.8	0.81	53,824
1.4	262.3	367.22	1.96	68,801.29
3.0	441.9	1325.7	9	195,275.61
4.6	1157.7	5325.42	21.16	1,340,269.29
$\Sigma x = 22.9$	$\Sigma y = 5129.7$	$\Sigma xy = 14{,}350.74$	$\Sigma x^2 = 65.49$	$\Sigma y^2 = 3{,}312{,}080.89$

With these sums and $n = 10$, the correlation coefficient is

$$r = \dfrac{n\Sigma xy - (\Sigma x)(\Sigma y)}{\sqrt{n\Sigma x^2 - (\Sigma x)^2}\sqrt{n\Sigma y^2 - (\Sigma y)^2}}$$

$$= \dfrac{10(14{,}350.74) - (22.9)(5129.7)}{\sqrt{10(65.49) - (22.9)^2}\sqrt{10(3{,}312{,}080.89) - (5129.7)^2}}$$

$$= \dfrac{26{,}037.27}{\sqrt{130.49}\sqrt{6{,}806{,}986.81}}$$

$$\approx 0.874. \quad \text{Round to three decimal places.}$$

The result $r \approx 0.874$ suggests a strong positive linear correlation.

Interpretation As the gross domestic product increases, the carbon dioxide emissions tend to increase.

Study Tip

Notice that the correlation coefficient r in Example 4 is rounded to three decimal places. This *round-off rule* will be used throughout the text.

Number of years out of school, x	Annual contribution (in 1000s of $), y
1	12.5
10	8.7
5	14.6
15	5.2
3	9.9
24	3.1
30	2.7

4.1 To explore this topic further, see **Activity 4.1** on page 197.

Tech Tip

Before using the TI-84 Plus to calculate r, make sure the *diagnostics* feature is on. To turn on this feature, from the home screen, press [2nd] CATALOG and cursor to *DiagnosticOn*. Then press [ENTER] twice.

TRY IT YOURSELF 4

Calculate the correlation coefficient for the number of years out of school and annual contribution data in Try It Yourself 1. Interpret the result in the context of the data.

Answer: Page A8

EXAMPLE 5

Using Technology to Calculate a Correlation Coefficient

Use technology to calculate the correlation coefficient for the Old Faithful data in Example 3. Interpret the result in the context of the data.

SOLUTION

Minitab, Excel, the TI-84 Plus, and StatCrunch each have features that allow you to calculate a correlation coefficient for paired data sets. Try using this technology to find r. You should obtain results similar to the displays shown.

MINITAB

Correlations: Duration, Time

Pearson correlation of Duration and Time = 0.979 ← Correlation coefficient

EXCEL

	A	B	C
26	CORREL(A1:A25,B1:B25)		
27			0.978659213

← Correlation coefficient

TI-84 PLUS

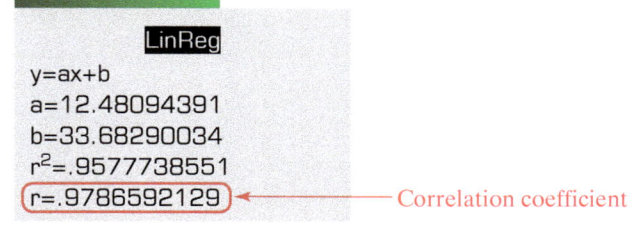

LinReg
y=ax+b
a=12.48094391
b=33.68290034
r²=.9577738551
r=.9786592129 ← Correlation coefficient

STATCRUNCH

Correlation between Duration and Time is:
0.97865921 ← Correlation coefficient

Rounded to three decimal places, the correlation coefficient is

$r \approx 0.979$.   *Round to three decimal places.*

This value of r suggests a strong positive linear correlation.

Interpretation As the duration of the eruptions increases, the time until the next eruption tends to increase.

TRY IT YOURSELF 5

Use technology to calculate the correlation coefficient for the data on page 181 on the salaries and average attendances at home games for the teams in Major League Baseball. Interpret the result in the context of the data.

Answer: Page A8

Using a Table to Test a Population Correlation Coefficient ρ

Once you have calculated r, the sample correlation coefficient, you will want to determine whether there is enough evidence to decide that the population correlation coefficient ρ is significant. In other words, based on a few pairs of data, can you make an inference about the population of all such data pairs? Remember that you are using sample data to make a decision about population data, so it is always possible that your inference may be wrong. In correlation studies, the small percentage of times when you decide that the correlation is significant when it is really not is called the *level of significance*. It is typically set at $\alpha = 0.01$ or 0.05. When $\alpha = 0.05$, you will probably decide that the population correlation coefficient is significant when it is really not 5% of the time. (Of course, 95% of the time, you will correctly determine that a correlation coefficient is significant.) When $\alpha = 0.01$, you will make this type of error only 1% of the time. When using a lower level of significance, however, you may fail to identify some significant correlations.

In order for a correlation coefficient to be significant, its absolute value must be close to 1. To determine whether the population correlation coefficient ρ is significant, use the critical values given in Table 11 in Appendix B. A portion of the table is shown below. If $|r|$ is greater than the critical value, then there is enough evidence to decide that the correlation is significant. Otherwise, there is *not* enough evidence to say that the correlation is significant. For instance, to determine whether ρ is significant for five pairs of data ($n = 5$) at a level of significance of $\alpha = 0.01$, you need to compare $|r|$ with a critical value of 0.959, as shown in the table.

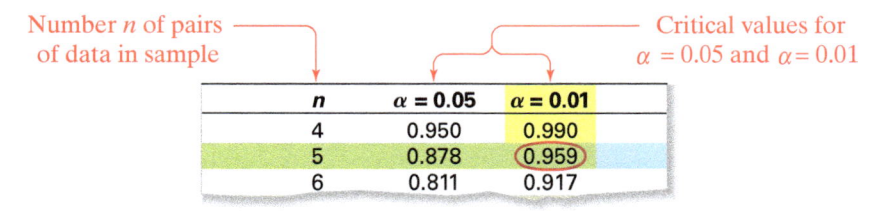

Number n of pairs of data in sample — Critical values for $\alpha = 0.05$ and $\alpha = 0.01$

n	α = 0.05	α = 0.01
4	0.950	0.990
5	0.878	0.959
6	0.811	0.917

If $|r| > 0.959$, then the correlation is significant. Otherwise, there is *not* enough evidence to conclude that the correlation is significant. Here are the guidelines for this process.

Study Tip
The level of significance is denoted by α, the lowercase Greek letter alpha.

Study Tip
The symbol $|r|$ represents the absolute value of r. Recall that the absolute value of a number is its value, disregarding its sign. For example, $|3| = 3$ and $|-7| = 7$.

Study Tip
If you determine that the linear correlation is significant, then you will be able to proceed to write the equation for the line that best describes the data. This line, called the *regression line*, can be used to predict the value of y when given a value of x. You will learn how to write this equation in the next section.

GUIDELINES

Using Table 11 for the Correlation Coefficient ρ

In Words	In Symbols
1. Determine the number of pairs of data in the sample.	Determine n.
2. Specify the level of significance.	Identify α.
3. Find the critical value.	Use Table 11 in Appendix B.
4. Decide whether the correlation is significant.	If $|r|$ is greater than the critical value, then the correlation is significant. Otherwise, there is *not* enough evidence to conclude that the correlation is significant.
5. Interpret the decision in the context of the original claim.	

EXAMPLE 6

Using Table 11 for a Correlation Coefficient

In Example 5, you used 25 pairs of data to find $r \approx 0.979$. Is the correlation coefficient significant? Use $\alpha = 0.05$.

SOLUTION

The number of pairs of data is 25, so $n = 25$. The level of significance is $\alpha = 0.05$. Using Table 11, find the critical value in the $\alpha = 0.05$ column that corresponds to the row with $n = 25$. The number in that column and row is 0.396.

Critical values for $\alpha = 0.05$

n	$\alpha = 0.05$	$\alpha = 0.01$
4	0.950	0.990
5	0.878	0.959
6	0.811	0.917
7	0.754	0.875
8	0.707	0.834
9	0.666	0.798
10	0.632	0.765
11	0.602	0.735
12	0.576	0.708
13	0.553	0.684
14	0.532	0.661
15	0.514	0.641
16	0.497	0.623
17	0.482	0.606
18	0.468	0.590
19	0.456	0.575
20	0.444	0.561
21	0.433	0.549
22	0.423	0.537
23	0.413	0.526
24	0.404	0.515
25	0.396	0.505
26	0.388	0.496
27	0.381	0.487
28	0.374	0.479
29	0.367	0.471

$n = 25$

Because $|r| \approx 0.979 > 0.396$, you can decide that the population correlation is significant.

Interpretation There is enough evidence at the 5% level of significance to conclude that there is a significant linear correlation between the duration of Old Faithful's eruptions and the time between eruptions.

TRY IT YOURSELF 6

In Try It Yourself 4, you calculated the correlation coefficient of the number of years out of school and annual contribution data to be $r \approx -0.908$. Is the correlation coefficient significant? Use $\alpha = 0.01$.

Answer: Page A8

In Table 11, notice that for fewer data pairs (smaller values of n), stronger evidence is needed to conclude that the correlation coefficient is significant.

Hypothesis Testing for a Population Correlation Coefficient ρ

You can also use a hypothesis test to determine whether the sample correlation coefficient r provides enough evidence to conclude that the population correlation coefficient ρ is significant. A hypothesis test for ρ can be one-tailed or two-tailed. The null and alternative hypotheses for these tests are listed below.

$\begin{cases} H_0: \rho \geq 0 \text{ (no significant negative correlation)} \\ H_a: \rho < 0 \text{ (significant negative correlation)} \end{cases}$ Left-tailed test

$\begin{cases} H_0: \rho \leq 0 \text{ (no significant positive correlation)} \\ H_a: \rho > 0 \text{ (significant positive correlation)} \end{cases}$ Right-tailed test

$\begin{cases} H_0: \rho = 0 \text{ (no significant correlation)} \\ H_a: \rho \neq 0 \text{ (significant correlation)} \end{cases}$ Two-tailed test

In this text, you will consider only two-tailed hypothesis tests for ρ.

The *t*-Test for the Correlation Coefficient

A *t*-test can be used to test whether the correlation between two variables is significant. The **test statistic** is r and the **standardized test statistic**

$$t = \frac{r}{\sigma_r} = \frac{r}{\sqrt{\frac{1-r^2}{n-2}}}$$

follows a *t*-distribution with $n - 2$ degrees of freedom, where n is the number of pairs of data. (Note that there are $n - 2$ degrees of freedom because one degree of freedom is lost for each variable.)

GUIDELINES

Using the *t*-Test for the Correlation Coefficient ρ

In Words	In Symbols
1. Identify the null and alternative hypotheses.	State H_0 and H_a.
2. Specify the level of significance.	Identify α.
3. Identify the degrees of freedom.	d.f. $= n - 2$
4. Determine the critical value(s) and the rejection region(s).	Use Table 5 in Appendix B.
5. Find the standardized test statistic.	$t = \dfrac{r}{\sqrt{\frac{1-r^2}{n-2}}}$
6. Make a decision to reject or fail to reject the null hypothesis.	If t is in the rejection region, then reject H_0. Otherwise, fail to reject H_0.
7. Interpret the decision in the context of the original claim.	

To use the *t*-test for a correlation coefficient, note that the requirements for calculating a correlation coefficient given on page 186 also apply to the test. In this text, unless stated otherwise, you can assume that these requirements are met.

EXAMPLE 7

The *t*-Test for a Correlation Coefficient

In Example 4, you used 10 pairs of data to find $r \approx 0.874$. Test the significance of this correlation coefficient. Use $\alpha = 0.05$.

SOLUTION

The null and alternative hypotheses are

$H_0: \rho = 0$ (no correlation)   and $H_a: \rho \neq 0$ (significant correlation).

Because there are 10 pairs of data in the sample, there are $10 - 2 = 8$ degrees of freedom. Because the test is a two-tailed test, $\alpha = 0.05$, and d.f. = 8, the critical values are $-t_0 = -2.306$ and $t_0 = 2.306$. The rejection regions are $t < -2.306$ and $t > 2.306$. Using the *t*-test, the standardized test statistic is

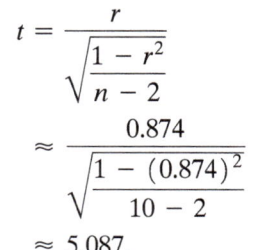

$$t = \frac{r}{\sqrt{\frac{1-r^2}{n-2}}}$$ Use the *t*-test for ρ.

$$\approx \frac{0.874}{\sqrt{\frac{1-(0.874)^2}{10-2}}}$$ Substitute 0.874 for r and 10 for n.

$\approx 5.087.$ Round to three decimal places.

You can check this result using technology. For instance, using a TI-84 Plus, you can find the standardized test statistic, as shown at the left. (Note that the result differs slightly due to rounding.) The figure below shows the location of the rejection regions and the standardized test statistic.

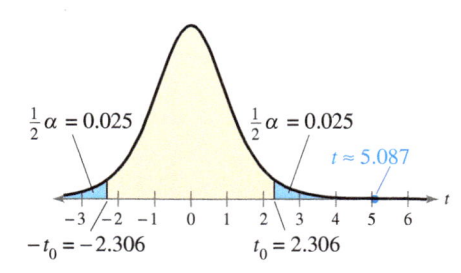

Because *t* is in the rejection region, you reject the null hypothesis.

Interpretation   There is enough evidence at the 5% level of significance to conclude that there is a significant linear correlation between gross domestic products and carbon dioxide emissions.

TRY IT YOURSELF 7

In Try It Yourself 5, you calculated the correlation coefficient of the salaries and average attendances at home games for the teams in Major League Baseball to be $r \approx 0.775$. Test the significance of this correlation coefficient. Use $\alpha = 0.01$.

Answer: Page A8

In Example 7, you can use Table 11 in Appendix B to test the population correlation coefficient ρ. Given $n = 10$ and $\alpha = 0.05$, the critical value from Table 11 is 0.632. Because $|r| \approx 0.874 > 0.632$, the correlation is significant. Note that this is the same result you obtained using a *t*-test for the population correlation coefficient ρ.

TI-84 PLUS

LinRegTTest
y=a+bx
β≠0 and ρ≠0
t=5.078276982
p=9.5516561E-4
df=8
↓a=56.03576519

Study Tip

Be sure you see in Example 7 that rejecting the null hypothesis means that there is enough evidence that the correlation is significant.

Picturing the World

The scatter plot shows the results of a survey conducted as a group project by students in a high school statistics class in the San Francisco area. In the survey, 125 high school students were asked their grade point average (GPA) and the number of caffeine drinks they consumed each day.

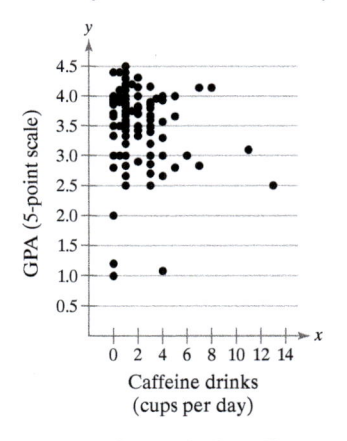

What type of correlation, if any, does the scatter plot show between caffeine consumption and GPA?

Correlation and Causation

The fact that two variables are strongly correlated does not in itself imply a cause-and-effect relationship between the variables. More in-depth study is usually needed to determine whether there is a causal relationship between the variables.

When there is a significant correlation between two variables, a researcher should consider these possibilities.

1. **Is there a direct cause-and-effect relationship between the variables?**

   That is, does x cause y? For instance, consider the relationship between gross domestic products and carbon dioxide emissions that has been discussed throughout this section. It is reasonable to conclude that an increase in a country's gross domestic product will result in higher carbon dioxide emissions.

2. **Is there a reverse cause-and-effect relationship between the variables?**

   That is, does y cause x? For instance, consider the Old Faithful data that have been discussed throughout this section. These variables have a positive linear correlation, and it is possible to conclude that the duration of an eruption affects the time before the next eruption. However, it is also possible that the time between eruptions affects the duration of the next eruption.

3. **Is it possible that the relationship between the variables can be caused by a third variable or perhaps a combination of several other variables?**

   For instance, consider the salaries and average attendances per home game for the teams in Major League Baseball listed on page 181. Although these variables have a positive linear correlation, it is doubtful that just because a team's salary decreases, the average attendance per home game will also decrease. The relationship is probably due to other variables, such as the economy, the players on the team, and whether or not the team is winning games. Variables that have an effect on the variables being studied but are not included in the study are called **lurking variables.**

4. **Is it possible that the relationship between two variables may be a coincidence?**

   For instance, although it may be possible to find a significant correlation between the number of animal species living in certain regions and the number of people who own more than two cars in those regions, it is highly unlikely that the variables are directly related. The relationship is probably due to coincidence.

Determining which of the cases above is valid for a data set can be difficult. For instance, consider this example. A person breaks out in a rash after eating shrimp at a certain restaurant. This happens every time the person eats shrimp at the restaurant. The natural conclusion is that the person is allergic to shrimp. However, upon further study by an allergist, it is found that the person is not allergic to shrimp, but to a type of seasoning the chef is putting into the shrimp.

4.1 EXERCISES

For Extra Help: MyLab Statistics

Building Basic Skills and Vocabulary

1. Two variables have a positive linear correlation. Does the dependent variable increase or decrease as the independent variable increases? What if the variables have a negative linear correlation?

2. Describe the range of values for the correlation coefficient.

3. What does the sample correlation coefficient r measure? Which value indicates a stronger correlation: $r = 0.918$ or $r = -0.932$? Explain your reasoning.

4. Give examples of two variables that have perfect positive linear correlation and two variables that have perfect negative linear correlation.

5. Explain how to determine whether a sample correlation coefficient indicates that the population correlation coefficient is significant.

6. Discuss the difference between r and ρ.

7. What are the null and alternate hypotheses for a two-tailed t-test for the population correlation coefficient ρ? When do you reject the null hypothesis?

8. In your own words, what does it mean to say "correlation does not imply causation"? List a pair of variables that have correlation but no cause-and-effect relationship.

Graphical Analysis *In Exercises 9–12, determine whether there is a perfect positive linear correlation, a strong positive linear correlation, a perfect negative linear correlation, a strong negative linear correlation, or no linear correlation between the variables.*

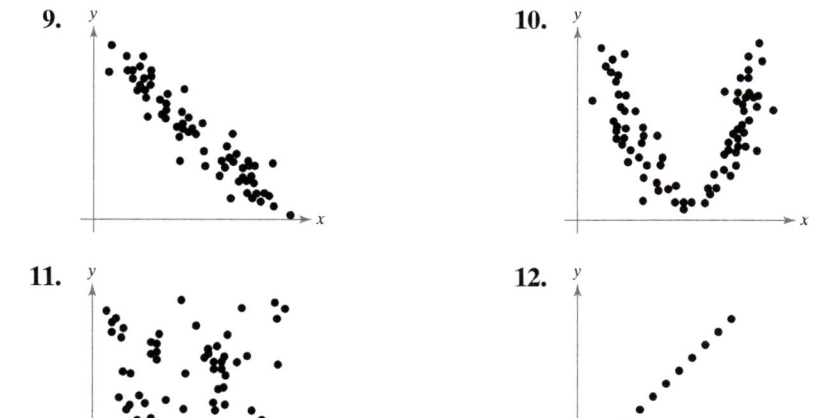

9.

10.

11.

12.

In Exercises 13 and 14, identify the explanatory variable and the response variable.

13. A nutritionist wants to determine whether the amounts of water consumed each day by persons of the same weight and on the same diet can be used to predict individual weight loss.

14. An actuary at an insurance company wants to determine whether the number of hours of safety driving classes can be used to predict the number of driving accidents for each driver.

Graphical Analysis *In Exercises 15–18, the scatter plots show the results of a survey of 20 randomly selected males ages 24–35. Using age as the explanatory variable, match each graph with the appropriate description. Explain your reasoning.*

(a) Age and body temperature
(b) Age and balance on student loans
(c) Age and income
(d) Age and height

15. [scatter plot: y in thousands of units vs Age; positive trend] — c

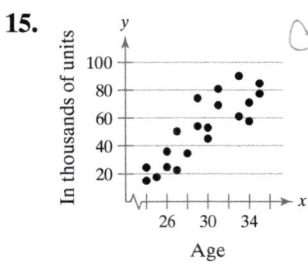

16. [scatter plot: y in units 60–80 vs Age; no trend] — d

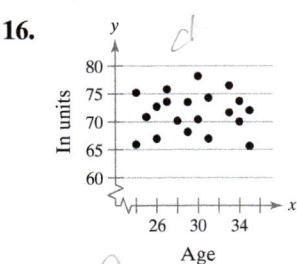

17. [scatter plot: y in thousands of units vs Age; negative trend] — b

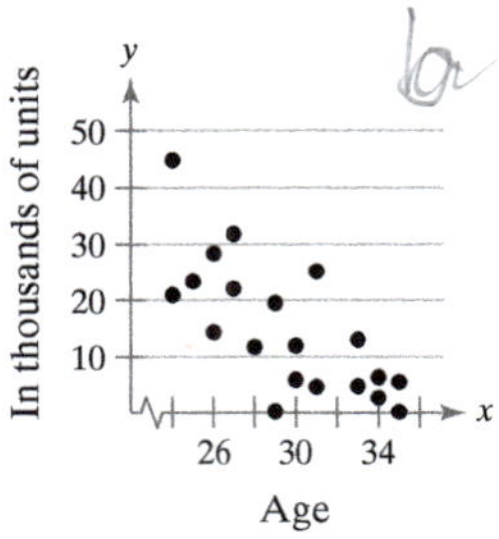

18. [scatter plot: y in units 70–110 vs Age; flat around 100] — a

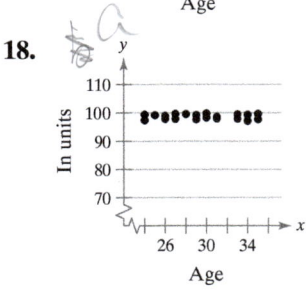

In Exercises 19–22, two variables are given that have been shown to have correlation but no cause-and-effect relationship. Describe at least one possible reason for the correlation.

19. Value of home and life span
20. Alcohol use and tobacco use
21. Ice cream sales and homicide rates
22. Marriage rate in Kentucky and number of deaths caused by falling out of a fishing boat

Using and Interpreting Concepts

Constructing a Scatter Plot and Determining Correlation *In Exercises 23–28, (a) display the data in a scatter plot, (b) calculate the sample correlation coefficient r, (c) describe the type of correlation, if any, and interpret the correlation in the context of the data, and (d) use Table 11 in Appendix B to make a conclusion about the correlation coefficient. If convenient, use technology. Let $\alpha = 0.01$.*

23. **Age and Vocabulary** The ages (in years) of 11 children and the numbers of words in their vocabulary

Age, x	1	2	3	4	5	6	3	5	2	4	6
Vocabulary size, y	3	220	540	1100	2100	2600	730	2200	260	1200	2500

24. **Weight and Waist** The weight (in kilograms) of 8 males and the circumference of their waists (in centimeters)

Weight, x	96.9	73.1	83.1	86.5	64.1	118.8	71.3	122.7
Waist, y	107.8	97.2	95.1	112.0	78.0	112.0	95.0	118.0

25. Maximal Strength and Jump Height The maximum weights (in kilograms) for which one repetition of a half squat can be performed and the jump heights (in centimeters) for 12 international soccer players *(Adapted from British Journal of Sports Medicine)*

Maximum weight, x	190	185	155	180	175	170
Jump height, y	60	57	54	60	56	64

Maximum weight, x	150	160	160	180	190	210
Jump height, y	52	51	49	57	59	64

26. Maximal Strength and Sprint Performance The maximum weights (in kilograms) for which one repetition of a half squat can be performed and the times (in seconds) to run a 10-meter sprint for 12 international soccer players *(Adapted from British Journal of Sports Medicine)*

Maximum weight, x	175	180	155	210	150	190
Time, y	1.80	1.77	2.05	1.42	2.04	1.61

Maximum weight, x	185	160	190	180	160	170
Time, y	1.70	1.91	1.60	1.63	1.98	1.90

27. Earnings and Dividends The earnings per share (in dollars) and the dividends per share (in dollars) for 6 companies in a recent year *(Source: The Value Line Investment Survey)*

Earnings per share, x	1.22	4.00	3.53	8.21	1.74	3.14
Dividends per share, y	0.90	0.31	2.10	1.00	0.55	1.48

28. Speed of Sound Eleven altitudes (in thousands of feet) and the speeds of sound (in feet per second) at these altitudes

Altitude, x	0	5	10	15	20	25
Speed of sound, y	1116.3	1096.9	1077.3	1057.2	1036.8	1015.8

Altitude, x	30	35	40	45	50
Speed of sound, y	994.5	969.0	967.7	967.7	967.7

29. In Exercise 23, remove data for a child who is 1 year old and has a vocabulary size of 3 words from the data set. Describe how this affects the correlation coefficient r.

30. In Exercise 24, add data for a male with a weight of 105.6 kilograms and a waist size of 98.3 centimeters to the data set. Describe how this affects the correlation coefficient r.

31. In Exercise 25, add data for an international soccer player with a maximum weight of 180 kilograms and a jump height of 50 centimeters to the data set. Describe how this affects the correlation coefficient r.

32. In Exercise 26, remove the data for the international soccer player who can perform the half squat with a maximum of 210 kilograms and can sprint 10 meters in 1.42 seconds from the data set. Describe how this affects the correlation coefficient r.

The *t*-Test for Correlation Coefficients *In Exercises 33–36, perform a hypothesis test using Table 5 in Appendix B to make a conclusion about the correlation coefficient.*

33. **Braking Distances: Dry Surface** The weights (in pounds) of eight vehicles and the variabilities of their braking distances (in feet) when stopping on a dry surface are shown in the table. At $\alpha = 0.01$, is there enough evidence to conclude that there is a significant linear correlation between vehicle weight and variability in braking distance on a dry surface? *(Adapted from National Highway Traffic Safety Administration)*

Weight, x	5940	5340	6500	5100	5850	4800	5600	5890
Variability, y	1.78	1.93	1.91	1.59	1.66	1.50	1.61	1.70

34. **Braking Distances: Wet Surface** The weights (in pounds) of eight vehicles and the variabilities of their braking distances (in feet) when stopping on a wet surface are shown in the table. At $\alpha = 0.05$, is there enough evidence to conclude that there is a significant linear correlation between vehicle weight and variability in braking distance on a wet surface? *(Adapted from National Highway Traffic Safety Administration)*

Weight, x	5890	5340	6500	4800	5940	5600	5100	5850
Variability, y	2.92	2.40	4.09	1.72	2.88	2.53	2.32	2.78

35. **Maximal Strength and Jump Height** The table in Exercise 25 shows the maximum weights (in kilograms) for which one repetition of a half squat can be performed and the jump heights (in centimeters) for 12 international soccer players. At $\alpha = 0.05$, is there enough evidence to conclude that there is a significant linear correlation between the data? (Use the value of *r* found in Exercise 25.)

36. **Maximal Strength and Sprint Performance** The table in Exercise 26 shows the maximum weights (in kilograms) for which one repetition of a half squat can be performed and the times (in seconds) to run a 10-meter sprint for 12 international soccer players. At $\alpha = 0.01$, is there enough evidence to conclude that there is a significant linear correlation between the data? (Use the value of *r* found in Exercise 26.)

Extending Concepts

37. **Interchanging *x* and *y*** In Exercise 26, let the time (in seconds) to sprint 10 meters represent the *x*-values and the maximum weight (in kilograms) for which one repetition of a half squat can be performed represent the *y*-values. Calculate the correlation coefficient *r*. What effect does switching the explanatory and response variables have on the correlation coefficient?

38. **Writing** Use your school's library, the Internet, or some other reference source to find a real-life data set with the indicated cause-and-effect relationship. Write a paragraph describing each variable and explain why you think the variables have the indicated cause-and-effect relationship.

   (a) *Direct Cause-and-Effect:* Changes in one variable cause changes in the other variable.
   (b) *Other Factors:* The relationship between the variables is caused by a third variable.
   (c) *Coincidence:* The relationship between the variables is a coincidence.

4.1 ACTIVITY Correlation by Eye

The *correlation by eye* applet allows you to guess the sample correlation coefficient r for a data set. When the applet loads, a data set consisting of 20 points is displayed. Points can be added to the plot by clicking the mouse. Points on the plot can be removed by clicking on the point and then dragging the point into the trash can. All of the points on the plot can be removed by simply clicking inside the trash can. You can enter your guess for r in the "Guess" field, and then click SHOW R! to see whether you are within 0.1 of the true value. When you click NEW DATA, a new data set is generated.

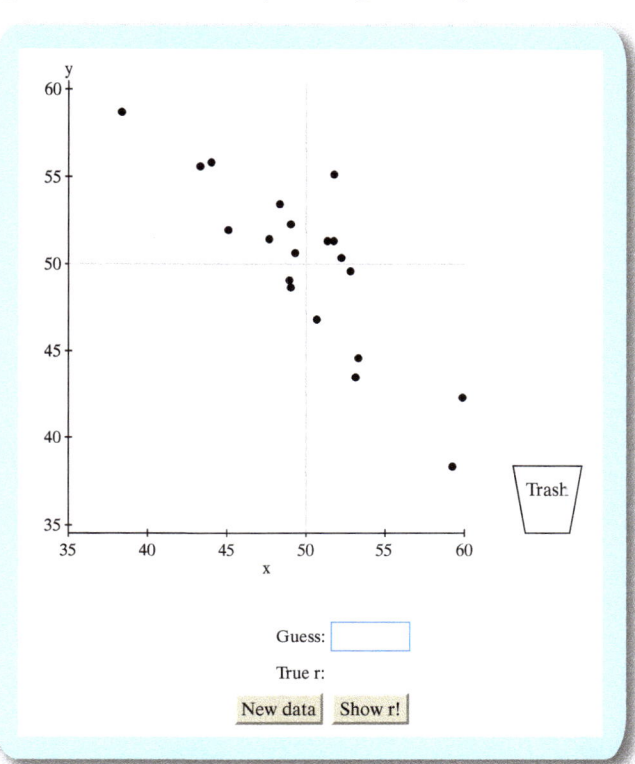

You can find the interactive applet for this activity within MyLab Statistics or at www.pearsonglobaleditions.com.

EXPLORE

Step 1 Add five points to the plot.
Step 2 Enter a guess for r.
Step 3 Click SHOW R!.
Step 4 Click NEW DATA.
Step 5 Remove five points from the plot.
Step 6 Enter a guess for r.
Step 7 Click SHOW R!.

DRAW CONCLUSIONS

1. Generate a new data set. Using your knowledge of correlation, try to guess the value of r for the data set. Repeat this 10 times. How many times were you correct? Describe how you chose each r value.

2. Describe how to create a data set with a value of r that is approximately 1.

3. Describe how to create a data set with a value of r that is approximately 0.

4. Try to create a data set with a value of r that is approximately -0.9. Then try to create a data set with a value of r that is approximately 0.9. What did you do differently to create the two data sets?

4.2 Linear Regression

What You Should Learn
- How to find the equation of a regression line
- How to predict y-values using a regression equation

Regression Lines ■ Applications of Regression Lines

Regression Lines

After verifying that the linear correlation between two variables is significant, the next step is to determine the equation of the line that best models the data. This line is called a **regression line,** and its equation can be used to predict the value of y for a given value of x. Although many lines can be drawn through a set of points, a regression line is determined by specific criteria.

Consider the scatter plot and the line shown below. For each data point, d_i represents the difference between the observed y-value and the predicted y-value for a given x-value. These differences are called **residuals** and can be positive, negative, or zero. When the point is above the line, d_i is positive. When the point is below the line, d_i is negative. When the observed y-value equals the predicted y-value, $d_i = 0$. Of all possible lines that can be drawn through a set of points, the regression line is the line for which the sum of the squares of all the residuals

Σd_i^2 Sum of the squares of the residuals

is a minimum.

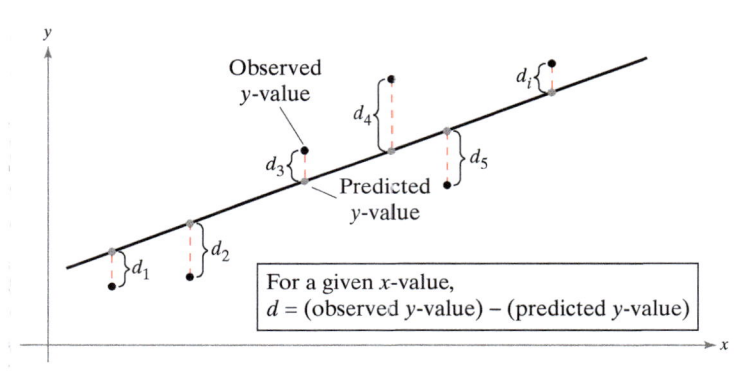

For a given x-value,
d = (observed y-value) − (predicted y-value)

> **DEFINITION**
>
> A **regression line,** also called a **line of best fit,** is the line for which the sum of the squares of the residuals is a minimum.

Study Tip

When determining the equation of a regression line, it is helpful to construct a scatter plot of the data to check for outliers, which can greatly influence a regression line. You should also check for gaps and clusters in the data.

In algebra, you learned that you can write an equation of a line by finding its slope m and y-intercept b. The equation has the form

$$y = mx + b.$$

Recall that the slope of a line is the ratio of its rise over its run and the y-intercept is the y-value of the point at which the line crosses the y-axis. It is the y-value when $x = 0$. For instance, the graph of $y = 2x + 1$ is shown in the figure at the right. The slope of the line is 2 and the y-intercept is 1.

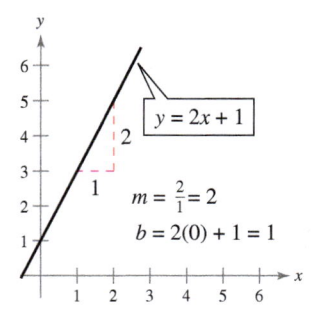

$y = 2x + 1$
$m = \frac{2}{1} = 2$
$b = 2(0) + 1 = 1$

In algebra, you used two points to determine the equation of a line. In statistics, you will use every point in the data set to determine the equation of the regression line.

Correlation and Regression

The equation of a regression line allows you to use the independent (explanatory) variable x to make predictions for the dependent (response) variable y.

The Equation of a Regression Line

The equation of a regression line for an independent variable x and a dependent variable y is

$$\hat{y} = mx + b$$

where $\hat{y}$ is the predicted y-value for a given x-value. The slope m and y-intercept b are given by

$$m = \frac{n\Sigma xy - (\Sigma x)(\Sigma y)}{n\Sigma x^2 - (\Sigma x)^2} \quad \text{and} \quad b = \bar{y} - m\bar{x} = \frac{\Sigma y}{n} - m\frac{\Sigma x}{n}$$

where $\bar{y}$ is the mean of the y-values in the data set, $\bar{x}$ is the mean of the x-values, and n is the number of pairs of data. The regression line always passes through the point $(\bar{x}, \bar{y})$.

Tech Tip

Although formulas for the slope and y-intercept are given, it is more convenient to use technology to calculate the equation of a regression line (see Example 2).

EXAMPLE 1

Finding the Equation of a Regression Line

Find the equation of the regression line for the gross domestic products and carbon dioxide emissions data used in Section 4.1. (See table at the left.)

GDP (in trillions of dollars), x	CO_2 emissions (in millions of metric tons), y
1.8	604.4
1.3	434.2
2.4	544.0
1.5	370.4
3.9	742.3
2.1	340.5
0.9	232.0
1.4	262.3
3.0	441.9
4.6	1157.7

SOLUTION

Recall from Example 7 of Section 4.1 that there is a significant linear correlation between gross domestic products and carbon dioxide emissions. Also, in Example 4 of Section 4.1, you found that $n = 10$, $\Sigma x = 22.9$, $\Sigma y = 5129.7$, $\Sigma xy = 14{,}350.74$, and $\Sigma x^2 = 65.49$. You can use these values to calculate the slope m of the regression line

$$m = \frac{n\Sigma xy - (\Sigma x)(\Sigma y)}{n\Sigma x^2 - (\Sigma x)^2} = \frac{10(14{,}350.74) - (22.9)(5129.7)}{10(65.49) - (22.9)^2} \approx 199.534600$$

and its y-intercept b.

$$b = \bar{y} - m\bar{x}$$
$$\approx \frac{5129.7}{10} - (199.534600)\left(\frac{22.9}{10}\right)$$
$$\approx 56.036$$

So, the equation of the regression line is

$$\hat{y} = 199.535x + 56.036.$$

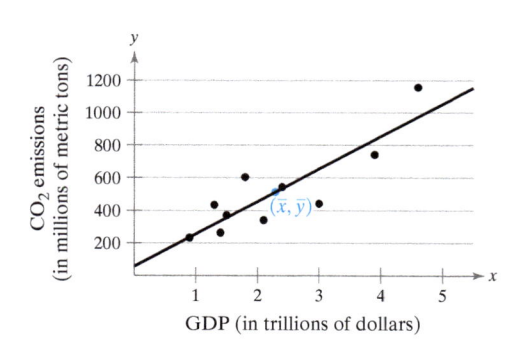

Study Tip

When writing the equation of a regression line, the slope m and the y-intercept b are rounded to three decimal places, as shown in Example 1. This *round-off rule* will be used throughout the text.

To sketch the regression line, first choose two x-values between the least and greatest x-values in the data set. Next, calculate the corresponding y-values using the regression equation. Then draw a line through the two points. The regression line and scatter plot of the data are shown at the right. Notice that the line passes through the point $(\bar{x}, \bar{y}) = (2.29, 512.97)$.

TRY IT YOURSELF 1

Find the equation of the regression line for the number of years out of school and annual contribution data used in Try It Yourself 4 in Section 4.1.

Answer: Page A8

Duration, x	Time, y	Duration, x	Time, y
1.80	56	3.78	79
1.82	58	3.83	85
1.90	62	3.88	80
1.93	56	4.10	89
1.98	57	4.27	90
2.05	57	4.30	89
2.13	60	4.43	89
2.30	57	4.47	86
2.37	61	4.53	89
2.82	73	4.55	86
3.13	76	4.60	92
3.27	77	4.63	91
3.65	77		

EXAMPLE 2

Using Technology to Find a Regression Equation

Use technology to find the equation of the regression line for the Old Faithful data used in Section 4.1. (See table at the left.)

SOLUTION

Recall from Example 6 of Section 4.1 that there is a significant linear correlation between the duration of Old Faithful's eruptions and the time between eruptions. Minitab, Excel, and the TI-84 Plus each have features that calculate a regression equation. Try using this technology to find the regression equation. You should obtain results similar to the displays shown below.

MINITAB

Regression Analysis: Time versus Duration

Coefficients

Term	Coef	SE Coef	T-Value	P-Value
Constant	33.68	1.89	17.79	0.000
Duration	12.481	0.546	22.84	0.000

Regression Equation

Time = 33.68 + 12.481 Duration

EXCEL

	A	B	C	D
26	Slope:			
27	SLOPE(B1:B25, A1:A25)			
28				12.48094
29				
30	Y-intercept:			
31	INTERCEPT(B1:B25, A1:A25)			
32				33.6829

TI-84 PLUS

LinReg
y=ax+b
a=12.48094391
b=33.68290034
r²=.9577738551
r=.9786592129

From the displays, you can see that the regression equation is

$$\hat{y} = 12.481x + 33.683.$$

The TI-84 Plus display at the right shows the regression line and a scatter plot of the data in the same viewing window. To do this, use the *Stat Plot* feature to construct the scatter plot and enter the regression equation as y_1.

4.2 To explore this topic further, see **Activity 4.2** on page 208.

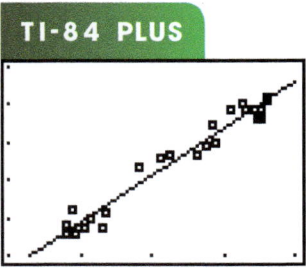

TRY IT YOURSELF 2

Use technology to find the equation of the regression line for the salaries and average attendances at home games for the teams in Major League Baseball listed on page 181.

Answer: Page A8

Applications of Regression Lines

When the correlation between x and y is *significant* (see Section 4.1), the equation of a regression line can be used to predict y-values for certain x-values. Prediction values are meaningful only for x-values in (or close to) the range of the observed x-values in the data. For instance, in Example 1 the observed x-values in the data range from $0.9 trillion to $4.6 trillion. So, it would not be appropriate to use the regression equation found in Example 1 to predict carbon dioxide emissions for gross domestic products such as $0.2 trillion or $14.5 trillion.

To predict y-values, substitute an x-value into the regression equation, then calculate $\hat{y}$, the predicted y-value. This process is shown in the next example.

EXAMPLE 3

Predicting *y*-Values Using Regression Equations

The regression equation for the gross domestic products (in trillions of dollars) and carbon dioxide emissions (in millions of metric tons) data is

$$\hat{y} = 199.535x + 56.036. \quad \text{See Example 1.}$$

Use this equation to predict the *expected* carbon dioxide emissions for each gross domestic product.

1. $1.2 trillion
2. $2.0 trillion
3. $2.6 trillion

SOLUTION

Recall from Section 4.1, Example 7, that x and y have a significant linear correlation. So, you can use the regression equation to predict y-values. Note that the given gross domestic products are in the range ($0.9 trillion to $4.6 trillion) of the observed x-values. To predict the expected carbon dioxide emissions, substitute each gross domestic product for x in the regression equation. Then calculate $\hat{y}$.

1. $\hat{y} = 199.535x + 56.036$
   $= 199.535(1.2) + 56.036$
   $= 295.478$

   Interpretation When the gross domestic product is $1.2 trillion, the predicted CO_2 emissions are 295.478 million metric tons.

2. $\hat{y} = 199.535x + 56.036$
   $= 199.535(2.0) + 56.036$
   $= 455.106$

   Interpretation When the gross domestic product is $2.0 trillion, the predicted CO_2 emissions are 455.106 million metric tons.

3. $\hat{y} = 199.535x + 56.036$
   $= 199.535(2.6) + 56.036$
   $= 574.827$

   Interpretation When the gross domestic product is $2.6 trillion, the predicted CO_2 emissions are 574.827 million metric tons.

TRY IT YOURSELF 3

The regression equation for the Old Faithful data is $\hat{y} = 12.481x + 33.683$. Use this to predict the time until the next eruption for each eruption duration. (Recall from Section 4.1, Example 6, that x and y have a significant linear correlation.)

1. 2 minutes
2. 3.32 minutes

Answer: Page A8

When the correlation between x and y is *not* significant, the best predicted y-value is $\bar{y}$, the mean of the y-values in the data.

Picturing the World

The scatter plot shows the relationship between the number of farms (in thousands) in a state and the total value of the farms (in billions of dollars). (Source: U.S. Department of Agriculture, National Agriculture Statistics Service)

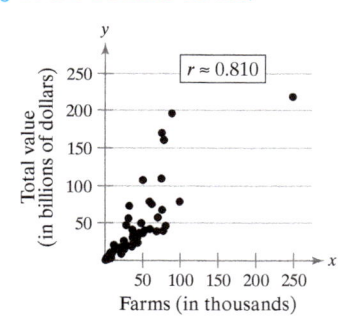

$r \approx 0.810$

Describe the correlation between these two variables in words. Use the scatter plot to predict the total value of farms in a state that has 150,000 farms. The regression line for this scatter plot is $\hat{y} = 1.014x + 2.611$. Use this equation to predict the total value in a state that has 150,000 farms ($x = 150$). (Assume x and y have a significant linear correlation.) How does your algebraic prediction compare with your graphical one?

4.2 EXERCISES

For Extra Help: MyLab Statistics

Building Basic Skills and Vocabulary

1. What is a residual? Explain when a residual is positive, negative, and zero.
2. Two variables have a positive linear correlation. Is the slope of the regression line for the variables positive or negative?
3. Explain how to predict y-values using the equation of a regression line.
4. For a set of data and a corresponding regression line, describe all values of x that provide meaningful predictions for y.
5. In order to predict y-values using the equation of a regression line, what must be true about the correlation coefficient of the variables?
6. Why is it not appropriate to use a regression line to predict y-values for x-values that are not in (or close to) the range of x-values found in the data?

In Exercises 7–12, match the description in the left column with its symbol(s) in the right column.

7. The y-value of a data point corresponding to x_i **a.** $\hat{y}_i$
8. The y-value for a point on the regression line corresponding to x_i **b.** y_i
    c. b
9. Slope
    d. $(\bar{x}, \bar{y})$
10. y-intercept
    e. m
11. The mean of the y-values
    f. $\bar{y}$
12. The point a regression line always passes through

Graphical Analysis *In Exercises 13–16, match the regression equation with the appropriate graph.*

13. $\hat{y} = -1.361x + 21.952$
14. $\hat{y} = 2.115x + 21.958$
15. $\hat{y} = 2.125x + 9.588$
16. $\hat{y} = -0.705x + 27.214$

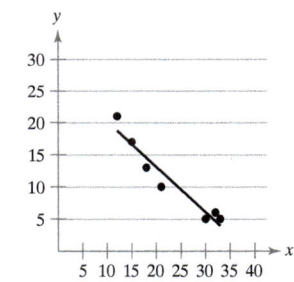

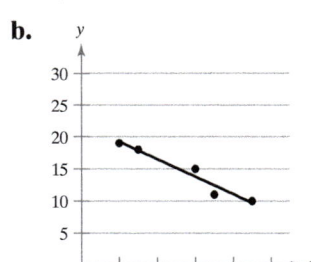

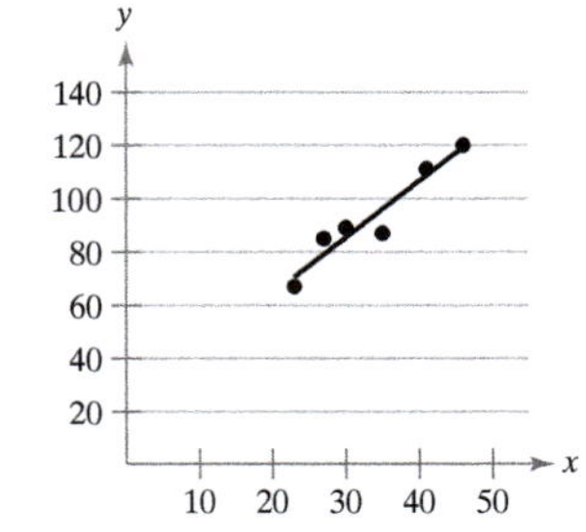

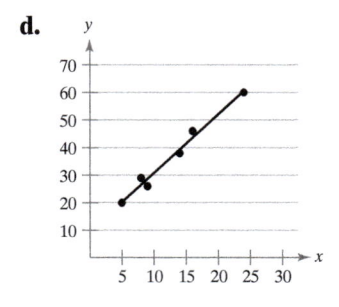

Using and Interpreting Concepts

Finding the Equation of a Regression Line *In Exercises 17–26, find the equation of the regression line for the data. Then construct a scatter plot of the data and draw the regression line. (Each pair of variables has a significant correlation.) Then use the regression equation to predict the value of y for each of the x-values, if meaningful. If the x-value is not meaningful to predict the value of y, explain why not. If convenient, use technology.*

17. Number of Athletes and Medals Won The number of athletes participating and the number of medals won in the Olympics by Japan through the last nine years *(Source: Olympian Database)*

Number of athletes, x	84	96	48	90	79	81	58	64	29
Medals won, y	13	41	8	38	5	25	1	37	2

(a) $x = 75$ athletes
(b) $x = 80$ athletes
(c) $x = 85$ athletes
(d) $x = 120$ athletes

18. Square Meters and Office Sale Price The square meters and sale prices (in thousands of Egyptian Pounds) of seven offices in Egypt are shown in the table at the left. *(Source: RE/MAX Egypt)*

(a) $x = 45$ square meters
(b) $x = 55$ square meters
(c) $x = 95$ square meters
(d) $x = 125$ square meters

19. Hours Studying and Test Scores The number of hours 9 students spent studying for a test and their scores on that test

Hours spent studying, x	0	1	1	2	4	6	7	7	8
Test scores, y	45	55	60	64	68	79	85	94	89

(e) $x = 3.5$ hours
(f) $x = 5$ hours
(g) $x = 7.5$ hours
(h) $x = 14$ hours

20. Goals and Wins The number of goals scored and the number of wins for the top 10 teams in the 2016–2017 English Premier League season *(Source: Premier League)*

Goals, x	85	86	80	78	77	54	62	41	55	43
Wins, y	30	26	23	22	23	18	17	12	12	12

(a) $x = 50$ goals
(b) $x = 70$ goals
(c) $x = 75$ goals
(d) $x = 95$ goals

21. Heart Rate and QT Interval The heart rates (in beats per minute) and QT intervals (in milliseconds) for 13 males (The figure at the left shows the QT interval of a heartbeat in an electrocardiogram.) *(Adapted from Chest)*

Heart rate, x	60	75	62	68	84	97	66
QT interval, y	403	363	381	367	341	317	401

Heart rate, x	65	86	78	93	75	88
QT interval, y	384	342	377	329	377	349

(a) $x = 120$ beats per minute
(b) $x = 67$ beats per minute
(c) $x = 90$ beats per minute
(d) $x = 83$ beats per minute

TABLE FOR EXERCISE 18

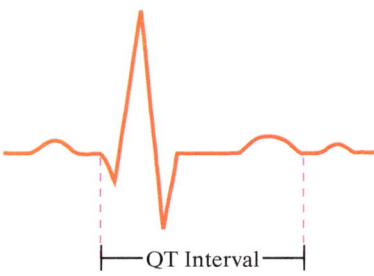

Square meters, x	Sale price, y
36	1782.5
71	380
100	450
40	525
65	750
90	900
85	1150

FIGURE FOR EXERCISE 21

The QT interval is a measure of electrical waves of the heart. A lengthened QT interval can indicate heart health problems.

22. Length and Girth of Harbor Seals The lengths (in centimeters) and girths (in centimeters) of 12 harbor seals *(Adapted from Moss Landing Marine Laboratories)*

Length, x	137	168	152	145	159	159
Girth, y	106	130	116	106	125	119

Length, x	124	137	155	148	147	146
Girth, y	103	104	120	110	107	109

(a) $x = 140$ centimeters (b) $x = 172$ centimeters
(c) $x = 164$ centimeters (d) $x = 158$ centimeters

23. Hot Dogs: Caloric and Sodium Content The caloric contents and the sodium contents (in milligrams) of 12 brands of beef hot dogs *(Source: Walmart)*

Calories, x	180	220	230	90	160	190
Sodium, y	510	740	740	280	530	580

Calories, x	150	110	110	160	140	150
Sodium, y	490	480	330	640	480	460

(a) $x = 170$ calories (b) $x = 100$ calories
(c) $x = 260$ calories (d) $x = 210$ calories

24. Employees and Revenue The number of employees and the 2016 revenue (in millions of dollars) of 13 hotel and gaming companies *(Source: Value Line)*

Employees, x	1800	8300	45,000	7300	52,000	10,000	20,200
Revenue, y	925	1271	4429	1006	9455	1811	4519

Employees, x	13,700	5200	24,600	19,900	4000	18,800
Revenue, y	1452	1601	4466	2184	1309	3034

(a) $x = 32,500$ employees (b) $x = 6000$ employees
(c) $x = 1350$ employees (d) $x = 47,000$ employees

25. Shoe Size and Height The shoe sizes and heights (in inches) of 14 men

Shoe size, x	8.5	9.0	9.0	9.5	10.0	10.0	10.5
Height, y	66.0	68.5	67.5	70.0	70.0	72.0	71.5

Shoe size, x	10.5	11.0	11.0	11.0	12.0	12.0	12.5
Height, y	69.5	71.5	72.0	73.0	73.5	74.0	74.0

(a) $x = $ size 11.5 (b) $x = $ size 8.0
(c) $x = $ size 15.5 (d) $x = $ size 10.0

26. Age and Hours Slept The ages (in years) of 10 infants and the numbers of hours each slept in a day

Age, x	0.1	0.2	0.4	0.7	0.6	0.9
Hours slept, y	14.5	14.3	14.1	13.9	13.9	13.7

Age, x	0.1	0.2	0.4	0.9
Hours slept, y	14.3	14.2	14.0	13.8

(a) $x = 0.3$ year
(b) $x = 3.9$ years
(c) $x = 0.6$ year
(d) $x = 0.8$ year

Registered Nurse Salaries In Exercises 27–30, use the table, which shows the years of experience of 14 registered nurses and their annual salaries (in thousands of dollars). *(Adapted from Payscale, Inc.)*

Years of experience, x	0.5	2	4	5	7	9	10
Annual salary (in thousands of dollars), y	45.2	49.9	54.7	59.3	61.4	62.9	66.0

Years of experience, x	12.5	13	16	18	20	22	25
Annual salary (in thousands of dollars), y	67.1	65.3	68.4	70.6	69.5	73.9	71.6

27. Correlation Using the scatter plot of the registered nurse salary data shown below, what type of correlation, if any, do you think the data have? Explain.

Registered Nurses

28. Regression Line Find an equation of the regression line for the data. Sketch a scatter plot of the data and draw the regression line.

29. Using the Regression Line An analyst used the regression line you found in Exercise 28 to predict the annual salary for a registered nurse with 28 years of experience. Is this a valid prediction? Explain your reasoning.

30. Significant Correlation? A salary analyst claims that the population has a significant correlation for $\alpha = 0.01$. Test this claim.

Extending Concepts

Interchanging x and y In Exercises 31 and 32, perform the steps below.

(a) Find the equation of the regression line for the data, letting Row 1 represent the x-values and Row 2 the y-values. Sketch a scatter plot of the data and draw the regression line.

(b) Find the equation of the regression line for the data, letting Row 2 represent the x-values and Row 1 the y-values. Sketch a scatter plot of the data and draw the regression line.

(c) Describe the effect of switching the explanatory and response variables on the regression line.

31.

Row 1	0	1	2	3	3	5	5	5	6	7
Row 2	96	85	82	74	95	68	76	84	58	65

32.

Row 1	16	25	39	45	49	64	70
Row 2	109	122	143	132	199	185	199

Residual Plots A *residual plot* allows you to assess correlation data and check for possible problems with a regression model. To construct a residual plot, make a scatter plot of $(x, y - \hat{y})$, where $y - \hat{y}$ is the residual of each y-value. If the resulting plot shows any type of pattern, then the regression line is not a good representation of the relationship between the two variables. If it does not show a pattern—that is, if the residuals fluctuate about 0—then the regression line is a good representation. Be aware that if a point on the residual plot appears to be outside the pattern of the other points, then it may be an outlier.

In Exercises 33 and 34, (a) find the equation of the regression line, (b) construct a scatter plot of the data and draw the regression line, (c) construct a residual plot, and (d) determine whether there are any patterns in the residual plot and explain what they suggest about the relationship between the variables.

33.

x	38	34	40	46	43	48	60	55	52
y	24	22	27	32	30	31	27	26	28

34.

x	8	4	15	7	6	3	12	10	5
y	18	11	29	18	14	8	25	20	12

Influential Points An *influential point* is a point in a data set that can greatly affect the graph of a regression line. An outlier may or may not be an influential point. To determine whether a point is influential, find two regression lines: one including all the points in the data set, and the other excluding the possible influential point. If the slope or y-intercept of the regression line shows significant changes, then the point can be considered influential. An influential point can be removed from a data set only when there is proper justification.

In Exercises 35 and 36, (a) construct a scatter plot of the data, (b) identify any possible outliers, and (c) determine whether the point is influential. Explain your reasoning.

35.

x	5	6	9	10	14	17	19	44
y	32	33	28	26	25	23	23	8

36.

x	1	3	6	8	12	14
y	4	7	10	9	15	3

Transformations to Achieve Linearity *When a linear model is not appropriate for representing data, other models can be used. In some cases, the values of x or y must be transformed to find an appropriate model. In a **logarithmic transformation**, the logarithms of the variables are used instead of the original variables when creating a scatter plot and calculating the regression line.*

In Exercises 37–40, use the data shown in the table at the left, which shows the number of bacteria present after a certain number of hours.

37. Find the equation of the regression line for the data. Then construct a scatter plot of (x, y) and sketch the regression line with it.

38. Replace each y-value in the table with its logarithm, $\log y$. Find the equation of the regression line for the transformed data. Then construct a scatter plot of $(x, \log y)$ and sketch the regression line with it. What do you notice?

39. An **exponential equation** is a nonlinear regression equation of the form $y = ab^x$. Use technology to find and graph the exponential equation for the original data. Include the original data in your graph. Note that you can also find this model by solving the equation $\log y = mx + b$ from Exercise 38 for y.

40. Compare your results in Exercise 39 with the equation of the regression line and its graph in Exercise 37. Which equation is a better model for the data? Explain.

Number of hours, x	Number of bacteria, y
1	165
2	280
3	468
4	780
5	1310
6	1920
7	4900

TABLE FOR EXERCISES 37–40

In Exercises 41–44, use the data shown in the table at the left.

41. Find the equation of the regression line for the data. Then construct a scatter plot of (x, y) and sketch the regression line with it.

42. Replace each x-value and y-value in the table with its logarithm. Find the equation of the regression line for the transformed data. Then construct a scatter plot of $(\log x, \log y)$ and sketch the regression line with it. What do you notice?

43. A **power equation** is a nonlinear regression equation of the form $y = ax^b$. Use technology to find and graph the power equation for the original data. Include a scatter plot in your graph. Note that you can also find this model by solving the equation $\log y = m(\log x) + b$ from Exercise 42 for y.

44. Compare your results in Exercise 43 with the equation of the regression line and its graph in Exercise 41. Which equation is a better model for the data? Explain.

x	y
1	695
2	410
3	256
4	110
5	80
6	75
7	68
8	74

TABLE FOR EXERCISES 41–44

Logarithmic Equation *The **logarithmic equation** is a nonlinear regression equation of the form $y = a + b \ln x$. In Exercises 45–48, use this information and technology.*

45. Find and graph the logarithmic equation for the data in Exercise 25.

46. Find and graph the logarithmic equation for the data in Exercise 26.

47. Compare your results in Exercise 45 with the equation of the regression line and its graph. Which equation is a better model for the data? Explain.

48. Compare your results in Exercise 46 with the equation of the regression line and its graph. Which equation is a better model for the data? Explain.

4.2 ACTIVITY — Regression by Eye

APPLET

You can find the interactive applet for this activity within **MyLab Statistics** or at www.pearsongloblaleditions.com.

The *regression by eye* applet allows you to interactively estimate the regression line for a data set. When the applet loads, a data set consisting of 20 points is displayed. Points on the plot can be added to the plot by clicking the mouse. Points on the plot can be removed by clicking on the point and then dragging the point into the trash can. All of the points on the plot can be removed by simply clicking inside the trash can. You can move the green line on the plot by clicking and dragging the endpoints. You should try to move the line in order to minimize the sum of the squares of the residuals, also known as the sum of square error (SSE). Note that the regression line minimizes the SSE. The SSE for the green line and for the regression line are shown below the plot. The equations of each line are shown above the plot. Click SHOW REGRESSION LINE! to see the regression line in the plot. Click NEW DATA to generate a new data set.

EXPLORE

Step 1 Move the endpoints of the green line to try to approximate the regression line.

Step 2 Click SHOW REGRESSION LINE!.

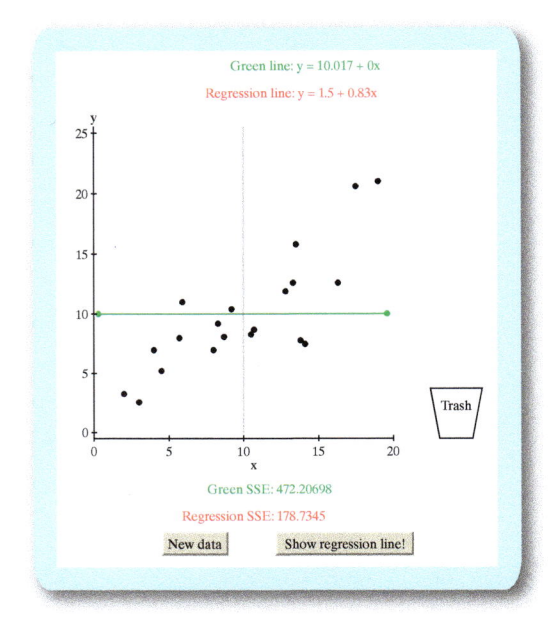

DRAW CONCLUSIONS

APPLET

1. Click NEW DATA to generate a new data set. Try to move the green line to where the regression line should be. Then click SHOW REGRESSION LINE!. Repeat this five times. Describe how you moved each green line.

2. On a blank plot, place 10 points so that they have a strong positive correlation. Record the equation of the regression line. Then, add a point in the upper left corner of the plot and record the equation of the regression line. How does the regression line change?

3. Remove the point from the upper-left corner of the plot. Add 10 more points so that there is still a strong positive correlation. Record the equation of the regression line. Add a point in the upper-left corner of the plot and record the equation of the regression line. How does the regression line change?

4. Use the results of Exercises 2 and 3 to describe what happens to the slope of the regression line when an outlier is added as the sample size increases.

CASE STUDY

Correlation of Body Measurements

In a study published in *Medicine and Science in Sports and Exercise* (volume 17, no. 2, page 211), the measurements of 252 men (ages 22–81) were taken. Of the 14 measurements taken of each man, some have significant correlations and others do not. For instance, the scatter plot at the right shows that the hip and abdomen circumferences of the men have a strong linear correlation ($r \approx 0.874$). The partial table shown here lists only the first nine rows of the data.

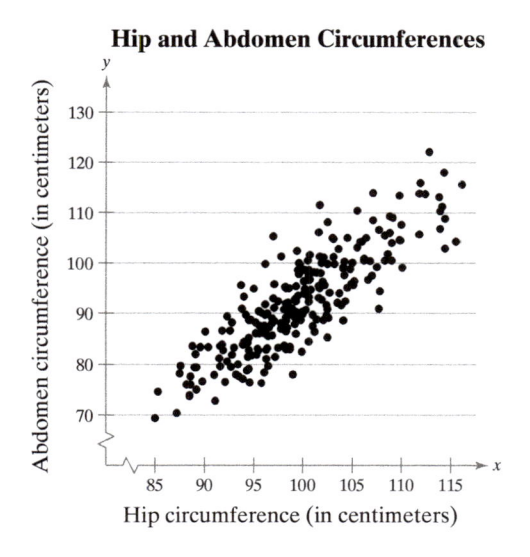

Hip and Abdomen Circumferences

Age (yr)	Weight (lb)	Height (in.)	Neck (cm)	Chest (cm)	Abdom. (cm)	Hip (cm)	Thigh (cm)	Knee (cm)	Ankle (cm)	Bicep (cm)	Forearm (cm)	Wrist (cm)	Body fat %
22	173.25	72.25	38.5	93.6	83.0	98.7	58.7	37.3	23.4	30.5	28.9	18.2	6.1
22	154.00	66.25	34.0	95.8	87.9	99.2	59.6	38.9	24.0	28.8	25.2	16.6	25.3
23	154.25	67.75	36.2	93.1	85.2	94.5	59.0	37.3	21.9	32.0	27.4	17.1	12.3
23	198.25	73.50	42.1	99.6	88.6	104.1	63.1	41.7	25.0	35.6	30.0	19.2	11.7
23	159.75	72.25	35.5	92.1	77.1	93.9	56.1	36.1	22.7	30.5	27.2	18.2	9.4
23	188.15	77.50	38.0	96.6	85.3	102.5	59.1	37.6	23.2	31.8	29.7	18.3	10.3
24	184.25	71.25	34.4	97.3	100.0	101.9	63.2	42.2	24.0	32.2	27.7	17.7	28.7
24	210.25	74.75	39.0	104.5	94.4	107.8	66.0	42.0	25.6	35.7	30.6	18.8	20.9
24	156.00	70.75	35.7	92.7	81.9	95.3	56.4	36.5	22.0	33.5	28.3	17.3	14.2

Source: "Generalized Body Composition Prediction Equation for Men Using Simple Measurement Techniques" by K.W. Penrose et al. (1985). MEDICINE AND SCIENCE IN SPORTS AND EXERCISE, vol. 17, no.2, p. 189.

EXERCISES

1. Using your intuition, classify each (x, y) pair as having a weak correlation ($0 < r < 0.5$), a moderate correlation ($0.5 < r < 0.8$), or a strong correlation ($0.8 < r < 1.0$).

    (a) (weight, neck)
    (b) (weight, height)
    (c) (age, body fat)
    (d) (chest, hip)
    (e) (age, wrist)
    (f) (ankle, wrist)
    (g) (forearm, height)
    (h) (bicep, forearm)
    (i) (weight, body fat)
    (j) (knee, thigh)
    (k) (hip, abdomen)
    (l) (abdomen, hip)

2. Use technology to find the correlation coefficient for each pair in Exercise 1. Compare your results with those obtained by intuition.

3. Use technology to find the regression line for each pair in Exercise 1 that has a strong correlation.

4. Use the results of Exercise 3 to predict the following.

    (a) The hip circumference of a man whose chest circumference is 95 centimeters
    (b) The height of a man whose forearm circumference is 28 centimeters

5. Are there pairs of measurements that have stronger correlation coefficients than 0.85? Use technology and intuition to reach a conclusion.

4.3 Measures of Regression and Prediction Intervals

What You Should Learn

- How to interpret the three types of variation about a regression line
- How to find and interpret the coefficient of determination
- How to find and interpret the standard error of estimate for a regression line
- How to construct and interpret a prediction interval for y

Variation about a Regression Line ■ The Coefficient of Determination ■ The Standard Error of Estimate ■ Prediction Intervals

Variation About a Regression Line

In this section, you will study two measures used in correlation and regression studies—the coefficient of determination and the standard error of estimate. You will also learn how to construct a prediction interval for y using a regression equation and a given value of x. Before studying these concepts, you need to understand the three types of variation about a regression line.

To find the total variation, the explained variation, and the unexplained variation about a regression line, you must first calculate the **total deviation**, the **explained deviation**, and the **unexplained deviation** for each ordered pair (x_i, y_i) in a data set. These deviations are shown in the figure.

Total deviation = $y_i - \bar{y}$

Explained deviation = $\hat{y}_i - \bar{y}$

Unexplained deviation = $y_i - \hat{y}_i$

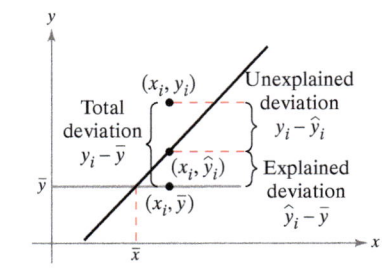

After calculating the deviations for each data point (x_i, y_i), you can find the **total variation**, the **explained variation**, and the **unexplained variation**.

> **DEFINITION**
>
> The **total variation** about a regression line is the sum of the squares of the differences between the y-value of each ordered pair and the mean of y.
>
> Total variation = $\Sigma(y_i - \bar{y})^2$
>
> The **explained variation** is the sum of the squares of the differences between each predicted y-value and the mean of y.
>
> Explained variation = $\Sigma(\hat{y}_i - \bar{y})^2$
>
> The **unexplained variation** is the sum of the squares of the differences between the y-value of each ordered pair and each corresponding predicted y-value.
>
> Unexplained variation = $\Sigma(y_i - \hat{y}_i)^2$
>
> The sum of the explained and unexplained variations is equal to the total variation.
>
> Total variation = Explained variation + Unexplained variation

As its name implies, the *explained variation* can be explained by the relationship between x and y. The *unexplained variation* cannot be explained by the relationship between x and y and is due to other factors, such as sampling error, coincidence, or lurking variables. (Recall from Section 4.1 that lurking variables are variables that have an effect on the variables being studied but are not included in the study.)

Picturing the World

Janette Benson (Psychology Department, University of Denver) performed a study relating the age at which infants crawl (in weeks after birth) with the average monthly temperature six months after birth. Her results are based on a sample of 414 infants. Benson believes that the reason for the correlation of temperature and crawling age is that parents tend to bundle infants in more restrictive clothing and blankets during cold months. This bundling doesn't allow the infant as much opportunity to move and experiment with crawling.

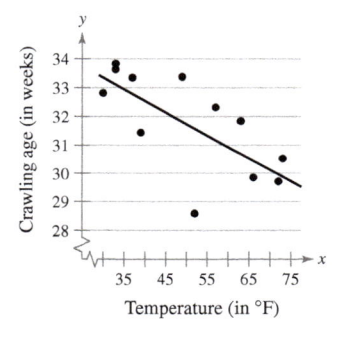

The correlation coefficient is $r \approx -0.701$. What percent of the variation in the data can be explained? What percent is due to other factors, such as sampling error, coincidence, or lurking variables?

The Coefficient of Determination

You already know how to calculate the correlation coefficient r. The square of this coefficient is called the **coefficient of determination**. It can be shown that the coefficient of determination is equal to the ratio of the explained variation to the total variation.

DEFINITION

The **coefficient of determination** r^2 is the ratio of the explained variation to the total variation. That is,

$$r^2 = \frac{\text{Explained variation}}{\text{Total variation}}.$$

It is important that you interpret the coefficient of determination correctly. For instance, if the correlation coefficient is $r = 0.900$, then the coefficient of determination is

$$r^2 = (0.900)^2$$
$$= 0.810.$$

This means that 81% of the variation in y can be explained by the relationship between x and y. The remaining 19% of the variation is unexplained and is due to other factors, such as sampling error, coincidence, or lurking variables.

EXAMPLE 1

Finding the Coefficient of Determination

The correlation coefficient for the gross domestic products and carbon dioxide emissions data is

$r \approx 0.874$.   See Example 4 in Section 4.1.

Find the coefficient of determination. What does this tell you about the explained variation of the data about the regression line? about the unexplained variation?

SOLUTION

The coefficient of determination is

$$r^2 \approx (0.874)^2$$
$$\approx 0.764.$$ Round to three decimal places.

Interpretation About 76.4% of the variation in the carbon dioxide emissions can be explained by the relationship between the gross domestic products and carbon dioxide emissions. About 23.6% of the variation is unexplained and is due to other factors, such as sampling error, coincidence, or lurking variables.

TRY IT YOURSELF 1

The correlation coefficient for the Old Faithful data is

$r \approx 0.979$.   See Example 5 in Section 4.1.

Find the coefficient of determination. What does this tell you about the explained variation of the data about the regression line? about the unexplained variation?

Answer: Page A8

The Standard Error of Estimate

When a $\hat{y}$-value is predicted from an x-value, the prediction is a point estimate. You can construct an interval estimate for $\hat{y}$, but first you need to calculate the **standard error of estimate.**

> **DEFINITION**
>
> The **standard error of estimate** s_e is the standard deviation of the observed y_i-values about the predicted $\hat{y}$-value for a given x_i-value. It is given by
>
> $$s_e = \sqrt{\frac{\Sigma(y_i - \hat{y}_i)^2}{n-2}}$$
>
> where n is the number of pairs of data.

From this formula, you can see that the standard error of estimate is the square root of the unexplained variation divided by $n - 2$. So, the closer the observed y-values are to the predicted $\hat{y}$-values, the smaller the standard error of estimate will be.

> **GUIDELINES**
>
> **Finding the Standard Error of Estimate s_e**
>
> | In Words | In Symbols |
> |---|---|
> | 1. Make a table that includes the five column headings shown at the right. | $x_i, y_i, \hat{y}_i, (y_i - \hat{y}_i), (y_i - \hat{y}_i)^2$ |
> | 2. Use the regression equation to calculate the predicted y-values. | $\hat{y}_i = mx_i + b$ |
> | 3. Calculate the sum of the squares of the differences between each observed y-value and the corresponding predicted y-value. | $\Sigma(y_i - \hat{y}_i)^2$ |
> | 4. Find the standard error of estimate. | $s_e = \sqrt{\dfrac{\Sigma(y_i - \hat{y}_i)^2}{n-2}}$ |

Instead of the formula used in Step 4, you can also find the standard error of estimate using the formula

$$s_e = \sqrt{\frac{\Sigma y^2 - b\Sigma y - m\Sigma xy}{n-2}}.$$

This formula is easy to use if you have already calculated the slope m, the y-intercept b, and several of the sums. For instance, consider the gross domestic products and carbon dioxide emissions data (see Example 4 in Section 4.1 and Example 1 in Section 4.2). To use the alternative formula, note that the regression equation for these data is $\hat{y} = 199.535x + 56.036$ and the values of the sums are $\Sigma y^2 = 3{,}312{,}080.89$, $\Sigma y = 5129.7$, and $\Sigma xy = 14{,}350.74$. So, using the alternative formula, the standard error of estimate is

$$s_e = \sqrt{\frac{\Sigma y^2 - b\Sigma y - m\Sigma xy}{n-2}}$$

$$= \sqrt{\frac{3{,}312{,}080.89 - (56.036)(5129.7) - (199.535)(14{,}350.74)}{10-2}}$$

$$\approx 141.932.$$

EXAMPLE 2

Finding the Standard Error of Estimate

The regression equation for the gross domestic products and carbon dioxide emissions data is

$\hat{y} = 199.535x + 56.036.$ See Example 1 in Section 4.2.

Find the standard error of estimate.

SOLUTION

Use a table to calculate the sum of the squared differences of each observed y-value and the corresponding predicted y-value.

x_i	y_i	$\hat{y}_i$	$y_i - \hat{y}_i$	$(y_i - \hat{y}_i)^2$
1.8	604.4	415.199	189.201	35,797.0184
1.3	434.2	315.4315	118.7685	14,105.95659
2.4	544.0	534.92	9.08	82.4464
1.5	370.4	355.3385	15.0615	226.8487822
3.9	742.3	834.2225	−91.9225	8,449.746006
2.1	340.5	475.0595	−134.5595	18,106.25904
0.9	232.0	235.6175	−3.6175	13.08630625
1.4	262.3	335.385	−73.085	5,341.417225
3.0	441.9	654.641	−212.741	45,258.73308
4.6	1157.7	973.897	183.803	33,783.54281
				$\Sigma = 161,165.0546$

Unexplained variation

When $n = 10$ and $\Sigma (y_i - \hat{y}_i)^2 = 161,165.0546$ are used, the standard error of estimate is

$$s_e = \sqrt{\frac{\Sigma (y_i - \hat{y}_i)^2}{n - 2}}$$

$$= \sqrt{\frac{161,165.0546}{10 - 2}}$$

$$\approx 141.935.$$

Interpretation   The standard error of estimate of the carbon dioxide emissions for a specific gross domestic product is about 141.935 million metric tons.

TRY IT YOURSELF 2

A researcher collects the data shown below and concludes that there is a significant relationship between the amount of radio advertising time (in minutes per week) and the weekly sales of a product (in hundreds of dollars).

Radio ad time, x	15	20	20	30	40	45	50	60
Weekly sales, y	26	32	38	56	54	78	80	88

Find the standard error of estimate. Use the regression equation

$\hat{y} = 1.405x + 7.311.$

Answer: Page A8

Prediction Intervals

Recall from Section 4.1 that one of the requirements for calculating a correlation coefficient is that the two variables x and y have a bivariate normal distribution. Two variables have a **bivariate normal distribution** when for any fixed values of x the corresponding values of y are normally distributed, and for any fixed values of y the corresponding values of x are normally distributed.

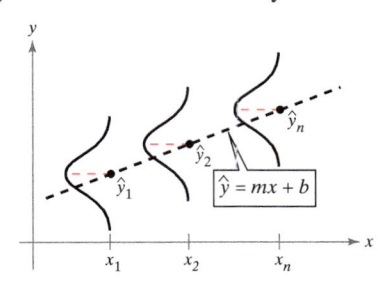

Bivariate Normal Distribution

Because regression equations are determined using random samples of paired data and because x and y are assumed to have a bivariate normal distribution, you can construct a **prediction interval** for the true value of y. To construct the prediction interval, use a t-distribution with $n - 2$ degrees of freedom.

DEFINITION

Given a linear regression equation $\hat{y} = mx + b$ and x_0, a specific value of x, a **c-prediction interval** for y is $\hat{y} - E < y < \hat{y} + E$ where

$$E = t_c s_e \sqrt{1 + \frac{1}{n} + \frac{n(x_0 - \bar{x})^2}{n\Sigma x^2 - (\Sigma x)^2}}.$$

The point estimate is $\hat{y}$ and the margin of error is E. The probability that the prediction interval contains y is c (the level of confidence), assuming that the estimation process is repeated a large number of times.

GUIDELINES

Constructing a Prediction Interval for y for a Specific Value of x

In Words	In Symbols
1. Identify the number n of pairs of data and the degrees of freedom.	d.f. $= n - 2$
2. Use the regression equation and the given x-value to find the point estimate $\hat{y}$.	$\hat{y}_i = mx_i + b$
3. Find the critical value t_c that corresponds to the given level of confidence c.	Use Table 5 in Appendix B.
4. Find the standard error of estimate s_e.	$s_e = \sqrt{\dfrac{\Sigma(y_i - \hat{y}_i)^2}{n - 2}}$
5. Find the margin of error E.	$E = t_c s_e \sqrt{1 + \dfrac{1}{n} + \dfrac{n(x_0 - \bar{x})^2}{n\Sigma x^2 - (\Sigma x)^2}}$
6. Find the left and right endpoints and form the prediction interval.	Left endpoint: $\hat{y} - E$ Right endpoint: $\hat{y} + E$ Interval: $\hat{y} - E < y < \hat{y} + E$

Study Tip

The formulas for s_e and E use the quantities $\Sigma(y_i - \hat{y}_i)^2$, $(\Sigma x)^2$, and Σx^2. Use a table to calculate these quantities.

EXAMPLE 3

Constructing a Prediction Interval

Using the results of Example 2, construct a 90% prediction interval for the carbon dioxide emissions when the gross domestic product is $2.8 trillion. What can you conclude?

SOLUTION

Because $n = 10$, there are d.f. $= 10 - 2 = 8$ degrees of freedom. Using the regression equation

$$\hat{y} = 199.535x + 56.036$$

and

$$x = 2.8$$

the point estimate is

$$\hat{y} = 199.535x + 56.036$$
$$= 199.535(2.8) + 56.036$$
$$= 614.734.$$

From Table 5, the critical value is $t_c = 1.860$ and from Example 2, $s_e \approx 141.935$. From Example 4 in Section 4.1, you found that $\Sigma x = 22.9$ and $\Sigma x^2 = 65.49$. Also, $\bar{x} = 2.29$. Using these values, the margin of error is

$$E = t_c s_e \sqrt{1 + \frac{1}{n} + \frac{n(x_0 - \bar{x})^2}{n\Sigma x^2 - (\Sigma x)^2}}$$

$$\approx (1.860)(141.935)\sqrt{1 + \frac{1}{10} + \frac{10(2.8 - 2.29)^2}{10(65.49) - (22.9)^2}}$$

$$\approx 279.382.$$

Using $\hat{y} = 614.734$ and $E \approx 279.382$, the prediction interval is constructed as shown.

Left Endpoint	Right Endpoint
$\hat{y} - E \approx 614.734 - 279.382$	$\hat{y} + E \approx 614.734 + 279.382$
$= 335.352$	$= 894.116$

$$335.352 < y < 894.116$$

Interpretation You can be 90% confident that when the gross domestic product is $2.8 trillion, the carbon dioxide emissions will be between 335.352 and 894.116 million metric tons.

TRY IT YOURSELF 3

Using the results of Example 2, construct a 95% prediction interval for the carbon dioxide emissions when the gross domestic product is $4 trillion. What can you conclude?

Answer: Page A8

For x-values near $\bar{x}$, the prediction interval for y becomes narrower. For x-values further from $\bar{x}$, the prediction interval for y becomes wider. (This is one reason why the regression equation should not be used to predict y-values for x-values outside the range of the observed x-values in the data.) For instance, consider the 90% prediction intervals for y in Example 3 shown at the left. The range of the x-values is $0.9 \leq x \leq 4.6$. Notice how the confidence interval bands curve away from the regression line as x gets closer to 0.9 or to 4.6.

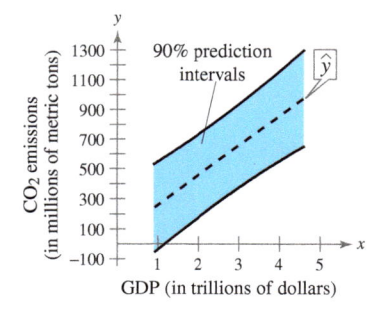

4.3 EXERCISES

For Extra Help: **MyLab Statistics**

Building Basic Skills and Vocabulary

Graphical Analysis *In Exercises 1–3, use the figure.*

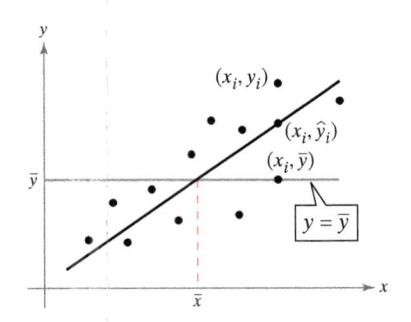

1. Describe the total variation about a regression line in words and in symbols.

2. Describe the explained variation about a regression line in words and in symbols.

3. Describe the unexplained variation about a regression line in words and in symbols.

4. The coefficient of determination r^2 is the ratio of which two types of variations? What does r^2 measure? What does $1 - r^2$ measure?

5. What is the coefficient of determination for two variables that have perfect positive linear correlation or perfect negative linear correlation? Interpret your answer.

6. Two variables have a bivariate normal distribution. Explain what this means.

In Exercises 7–10, use the value of the correlation coefficient r to calculate the coefficient of determination r^2. What does this tell you about the explained variation of the data about the regression line? about the unexplained variation?

7. $r = 0.465$

8. $r = -0.328$

9. $r = -0.957$

10. $r = 0.881$

Using and Interpreting Concepts

Finding the Coefficient of Determination and the Standard Error of Estimate *In Exercises 11–20, use the data to (a) find the coefficient of determination r^2 and interpret the result, and (b) find the standard error of estimate s_e and interpret the result.*

11. **Stock Offerings** The numbers of initial public offerings of stock issued and the total proceeds of these offerings (in millions of dollars) for 12 years are shown in the table. The equation of the regression line is $\hat{y} = 104.965x + 14{,}093.666$. *(Source: University of Florida)*

Number of offerings, x	316	485	382	79	70	67
Proceeds, y	34,314	64,906	64,876	34,241	22,136	10,068

Number of offerings, x	183	168	162	162	21	43
Proceeds, y	31,927	28,593	30,648	35,762	22,762	13,307

12. **Earnings of Men and Women** The table shows the median annual earnings (in dollars) of male and female workers from 10 states in a recent year. The equation of the regression line is $\hat{y} = 1.005x - 10{,}770.313$.
 (Source: U.S. Census Bureau)

Median annual earnings of male workers, x	50,976	46,763	46,934	41,092	47,960
Median annual earnings of female workers, y	40,214	36,834	36,841	31,110	40,173

Median annual earnings of male workers, x	43,829	47,092	51,628	46,123	61,666
Median annual earnings of female workers, y	32,096	35,753	41,690	33,443	50,802

13. **Goals Allowed and Points** The table shows the number of goals allowed and the total points earned (2 points for a win and 1 point for an overtime or shootout loss) by the 14 Western Conference teams in the 2016–2017 National Hockey League season. The equation of the regression line is $\hat{y} = -0.573x + 220.087$. *(Source: ESPN)*

Goals allowed, x	213	208	218	224	256	262	278
Points, y	109	106	99	94	87	79	48

Goals allowed, x	200	212	201	221	205	260	243
Points, y	105	103	99	94	86	70	69

14. **Trees** The table shows the heights (in feet) and trunk diameters (in inches) of eight trees. The equation of the regression line is $\hat{y} = 0.479x - 24.086$.

Height, x	70	72	75	76	85	78	77	82
Trunk diameter, y	8.3	10.5	11.0	11.4	14.9	14.0	16.3	15.8

15. **STEM Employment and Mean Wage** The table shows the percentage of employment in STEM (science, technology, engineering, and math) occupations and mean annual wage (in thousands of dollars) for 16 industries. The equation of the regression line is $\hat{y} = 1.153x + 46.374$. *(Source: U.S. Bureau of Labor Statistics)*

Percentage of employment in STEM occupations, x	10.5	15.8	1.6	11.0	8.4	1.1	23.7	7.0
Mean annual wage, y	63.3	73.1	51.3	49.6	54.8	46.2	70.4	67.4

Percentage of employment in STEM occupations, x	1.0	34	16.7	3.7	4.8	1.0	1.4	8.4
Mean annual wage, y	45.0	77.6	79.6	36.7	52.4	51.0	39.2	57.4

16. **Voter Turnout** The Australian voting age populations (in millions) and the number of votes cast (in millions) for the democratic elections for nine election years are shown in the table. The equation of the regression line is $\hat{y} = 0.8194x + 1.842$. *(Source: Institute for Democracy and Electoral Assistance)*

Voting age population, x	18.1	17.4	16.2	15.7	15.0
Votes cast in elections, y	16.5	16.2	15.1	14.9	14.1

Voting age population, x	14.3	14.0	13.5	13.0
Votes cast in elections, y	13.6	13.3	12.9	12.4

17. **Wheat** The table shows the quantity of wheat (in millions of kilograms per year) produced by India and the quantity of wheat (in millions of kilograms per year) exported by India for seven years. The equation of the regression line is $\hat{y} = 0.249x - 19023$. *(Source: IndexMundi)*

Produced, x	69355	75807	78570	80679	80804	86874	94882
Exported, y	94	49	23	58	72	891	6824

18. **Fund Assets** The table shows the total assets (in billions of dollars) of individual retirement accounts (IRAs) and federal defined benefit (DB) plans for ten years. The equation of the regression line is $\hat{y} = 0.140x + 453.959$. *(Source: Investment Company Institute)*

IRAs, x	4748	3681	4488	5029	5153
Federal DB plans, y	978	1033	1095	1161	1230

IRAs, x	5785	6819	7292	7329	7850
Federal DB plans, y	1270	1370	1438	1512	1595

19. **New-Vehicle Sales** The table shows the numbers of new-vehicle sales (in thousands) in the United States for Ford and General Motors for 11 years. The equation of the regression line is $\hat{y} = 1.624x - 747.304$. *(Source: NADA Industry Analysis Division)*

New-vehicle sales (Ford), x	3107	2848	2502	1942	1656	1905
New-vehicle sales (General Motors), y	4457	4068	3825	2956	2072	2211

New-vehicle sales (Ford), x	2111	2206	2435	2418	2549
New-vehicle sales (General Motors), y	2504	2596	2786	2935	3082

20. New-Vehicle Sales The table shows the numbers of new-vehicle sales (in thousands) in the United States for Toyota and Honda for 11 years. The equation of the regression line is $\hat{y} = 0.460x + 410.839$. *(Source: NADA Industry Analysis Division)*

New-vehicle sales (Toyota), x	2260	2543	2621	2218	1770	1764
New-vehicle sales (Honda), y	1463	1509	1552	1429	1151	1231

New-vehicle sales (Toyota), x	1645	2083	2236	2374	2499
New-vehicle sales (Honda), y	1147	1423	1525	1541	1587

Constructing and Interpreting a Prediction Interval *In Exercises 21–30, construct the indicated prediction interval and interpret the results.*

21. Proceeds Construct a 95% prediction interval for the proceeds from initial public offerings in Exercise 11 when the number of offerings is 450.

22. Earnings of Women Construct a 95% prediction interval for the median annual earnings of female workers in Exercise 12 when the median annual earnings of male workers is $45,637.

23. Points Construct a 90% prediction interval for total points earned in Exercise 13 when the number of goals allowed by the team is 250.

24. Trees Construct a 90% prediction interval for the trunk diameter of a tree in Exercise 14 when the height is 80 feet.

25. Mean Wage Construct a 99% prediction interval for the mean annual wage in Exercise 15 when the percentage of employment in STEM occupations is 13% in the industry.

26. Voter Turnout Construct a 99% prediction interval for number of votes cast in Exercise 16 when the voting age population is 15 million.

27. Wheat Construct an 80% prediction interval for the quantity of wheat exported by India in Exercise 17 when the quantity of wheat produced by India is 99,000 million kilograms per year.

28. Total Assets Construct a 90% prediction interval for the total assets in federal defined benefit plans in Exercise 18 when the total assets in IRAs is $6200 billion.

29. New-Vehicle Sales Construct a 95% prediction interval for new-vehicle sales for General Motors in Exercise 19 when the number of new vehicles sold by Ford is 2628 thousand.

30. New-Vehicle Sales Construct a 99% prediction interval for new-vehicle sales for Honda in Exercise 20 when the number of new vehicles sold by Toyota is 2359 thousand.

Old Vehicles *In Exercises 31–34, use the figure shown at the left.*

31. Scatter Plot Construct a scatter plot of the data. Show $\bar{y}$ and $\bar{x}$ on the graph.

32. Regression Line Find and draw the regression line.

33. Coefficient of Determination Find the coefficient of determination r^2 and interpret the results.

34. Error of Estimate Find the standard error of estimate s_e and interpret the results.

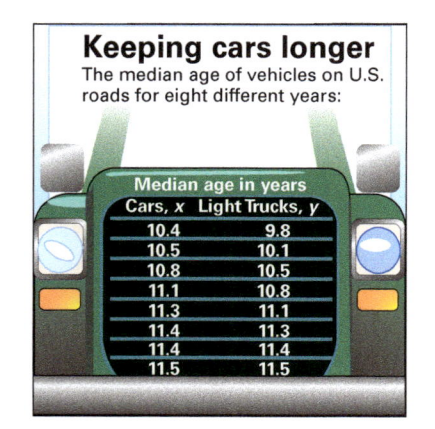

Keeping cars longer
The median age of vehicles on U.S. roads for eight different years:

Median age in years

Cars, x	Light Trucks, y
10.4	9.8
10.5	10.1
10.8	10.5
11.1	10.8
11.3	11.1
11.4	11.3
11.4	11.4
11.5	11.5

(Source: Polk Co., IHS Automotive)

FIGURE FOR EXERCISES 31–34

Extending Concepts

Hypothesis Testing for Slope *When testing the slope M of the regression line for the population, you usually test that the slope is 0, or H_0: $M = 0$. A slope of 0 indicates that there is no linear relationship between x and y. To perform the t-test for the slope M, use the standardized test statistic*

$$t = \frac{m}{s_e}\sqrt{\Sigma x^2 - \frac{(\Sigma x)^2}{n}}$$

with $n - 2$ degrees of freedom. Then, using the critical values found in Table 5 in Appendix B, make a decision whether to reject or fail to reject the null hypothesis. You can also use the LinRegTTest feature on a TI-84 Plus to calculate the standardized test statistic as well as the corresponding P-value. If $P \leq \alpha$, then reject the null hypothesis. If $P > \alpha$, then do not reject H_0.

In Exercises 35 and 36, test the claim and interpret the results in the context of the problem. If convenient, use technology.

35. The table shows the weights (in pounds) and the numbers of hours slept in a day by a random sample of infants. Test the claim that $M \neq 0$. Use $\alpha = 0.01$.

Weight, x	8.1	10.2	9.9	7.2	6.9	11.2	11	15
Hours slept, y	14.8	14.6	14.1	14.2	13.8	13.2	13.9	12.5

36. The table shows the ages (in years) and salaries (in thousands of dollars) of a random sample of engineers at a company. Test the claim that $M \neq 0$. Use $\alpha = 0.05$.

Age, x	25	34	29	30	42	38	49	52	35	40
Salary, y	57.5	61.2	59.9	58.7	87.5	67.4	89.2	85.3	69.5	75.1

Confidence Intervals for y-Intercept and Slope *You can construct confidence intervals for the y-intercept B and slope M of the regression line $y = Mx + B$ for the population by using the inequalities below.*

y-intercept B: $b - E < B < b + E$

$$\text{where } E = t_c s_e \sqrt{\frac{1}{n} + \frac{\bar{x}^2}{\Sigma x^2 - \frac{(\Sigma x)^2}{n}}} \text{ and}$$

slope M: $m - E < M < m + E$

$$\text{where } E = \frac{t_c s_e}{\sqrt{\Sigma x^2 - \frac{(\Sigma x)^2}{n}}}$$

The values of m and b are obtained from the sample data, and the critical value t_c is found using Table 5 in Appendix B with $n - 2$ degrees of freedom.

In Exercises 37 and 38, construct the indicated confidence intervals for B and M using the gross domestic products and carbon dioxide emissions data found in Example 2.

37. 95% confidence interval

38. 99% confidence interval

4.4 Multiple Regression

What You Should Learn

▶ How to use technology to find and interpret a multiple regression equation, the standard error of estimate, and the coefficient of determination

▶ How to use a multiple regression equation to predict y-values

Finding a Multiple Regression Equation ■ Predicting y-Values

Finding a Multiple Regression Equation

In many instances, a better prediction model can be found for a dependent (response) variable by using more than one independent (explanatory) variable. For instance, a more accurate prediction for the carbon dioxide emissions discussed in previous sections might be made by considering the number of cars as well as the gross domestic product. Models that contain more than one independent variable are multiple regression models.

> **DEFINITION**
>
> A **multiple regression equation** for independent variables $x_1, x_2, x_3, \ldots, x_k$ and a dependent variable y has the form
>
> $$\hat{y} = b + m_1 x_1 + m_2 x_2 + m_3 x_3 + \cdots + m_k x_k$$
>
> where $\hat{y}$ is the predicted y-value for given x_i values and b is the y-intercept. The y-intercept b is the value of $\hat{y}$ when all x_i are 0. Each coefficient m_i is the amount of change in $\hat{y}$ when the independent variable x_i is changed by one unit and all other independent variables are held constant.

Because the mathematics associated with multiple regression is complicated, this section focuses on how to use technology to find a multiple regression equation and how to interpret the results.

Tech Tip

Detailed instructions for using Minitab and Excel to find a multiple regression equation are shown in the technology manuals that accompany this text.

EXAMPLE 1

Finding a Multiple Regression Equation

A researcher wants to determine how employee salaries at a company are related to the length of employment, previous experience, and education. The researcher selects eight employees from the company and obtains the data shown in the table.

Employee	Salary (in dollars), y	Employment (in years), x_1	Experience (in years), x_2	Education (in years), x_3
A	57,310	10	2	16
B	57,380	5	6	16
C	54,135	3	1	12
D	56,985	6	5	14
E	58,715	8	8	16
F	60,620	20	0	12
G	59,200	8	4	18
H	60,320	14	6	17

Use Minitab to find a multiple regression equation that models the data.

Study Tip

In Example 1, it is important that you interpret the coefficients m_1, m_2, and m_3 correctly. For instance, if x_2 and x_3 are held constant and x_1 increases by 1, then y increases by $364. Similarly, if x_1 and x_3 are held constant and x_2 increases by 1, then y increases by $228. If x_1 and x_2 are held constant and x_3 increases by 1, then y increases by $267.

SOLUTION

Enter the y-values in C1 and the x_1-, x_2-, and x_3-values in C2, C3, and C4, respectively. Select "Regression▶Regression▶Fit Regression Model" from the *Stat* menu. Using the salaries as the response variable and the remaining data as the predictors, you should obtain results similar to the display shown.

MINITAB

Regression Analysis: Salary, y versus x1, x2, x3

Model Summary

S	R-sq	R-sq(adj)
659.490	94.38%	90.17%

Coefficients

Term	Coef	SE Coef	T-Value	P-Value
Constant	49764 — b	1981	25.12	0.000
x1	364.4 — m_1	48.3	7.54	0.002
x2	228 — m_2	124	1.84	0.140
x3	267 — m_3	147	1.81	0.144

Regression Equation

Salary, y = 49764 + 364.4 x1 + 228 x2 + 267 x3

The regression equation is $\hat{y} = 49{,}764 + 364x_1 + 228x_2 + 267x_3$.

TRY IT YOURSELF 1

A statistics professor wants to determine how students' final grades are related to the midterm exam grades and number of classes missed. The professor selects 10 students and obtains the data shown in the table.

Student	Final grade, y	Midterm exam, x_1	Classes missed, x_2
1	81	75	1
2	90	80	0
3	86	91	2
4	76	80	3
5	51	62	6
6	75	90	4
7	44	60	7
8	81	82	2
9	94	88	0
10	93	96	1

Use technology to find a multiple regression equation that models the data.

Answer: Page A8

Minitab displays much more than the regression equation and the coefficients of the independent variables. For instance, it also displays the standard error of estimate, denoted by S, and the coefficient of determination, denoted by R-Sq. In Example 1, $S = 659.490$ and R-$Sq = 94.38\%$. So, the standard error of estimate is $659.49. The coefficient of determination tells you that 94.38% of the variation in y can be explained by the multiple regression model. The remaining 5.62% is unexplained and is due to other factors, such as sampling error, coincidence, or lurking variables.

Picturing the World

In a lake in Finland, 159 fish of 7 species were caught and measured for weight G (in grams), length L (in centimeters), height H, and width W (H and W are percents of L). The regression equation for G and L is

$G = -491 + 28.5L$,
$r \approx 0.925$, $r^2 \approx 0.855$.

When all four variables are used, the regression equation is

$G = -712 + 28.3L + 1.46H + 13.3W$,
$r \approx 0.930$, $r^2 \approx 0.865$.

(Source: Journal of Statistics Education)

Predict the weight of a fish with the following measurements: $L = 40$, $H = 17$, and $W = 11$. How do your predictions vary when you use a single variable versus many variables? Which do you think is more accurate?

Predicting *y*-Values

After finding the equation of the multiple regression line, you can use the equation to predict *y*-values over the range of the data. To predict *y*-values, substitute the given value for each independent variable into the equation, then calculate $\hat{y}$.

EXAMPLE 2

Predicting *y*-Values Using Multiple Regression Equations

Use the regression equation

$$\hat{y} = 49{,}764 + 364x_1 + 228x_2 + 267x_3$$

found in Example 1 to predict an employee's salary for each set of conditions.

1. 12 years of current employment
   5 years of previous experience
   16 years of education

2. 4 years of current employment
   2 years of previous experience
   12 years of education

3. 8 years of current employment
   7 years of previous experience
   17 years of education

SOLUTION

To predict each employee's salary, substitute the values for x_1, x_2, and x_3 into the regression equation. Then calculate $\hat{y}$.

1. $\hat{y} = 49{,}764 + 364x_1 + 228x_2 + 267x_3$
    $= 49{,}764 + 364(12) + 228(5) + 267(16)$
    $= 59{,}544$

    The employee's predicted salary is $59,544.

2. $\hat{y} = 49{,}764 + 364x_1 + 228x_2 + 267x_3$
    $= 49{,}764 + 364(4) + 228(2) + 267(12)$
    $= 54{,}880$

    The employee's predicted salary is $54,880.

3. $\hat{y} = 49{,}764 + 364x_1 + 228x_2 + 267x_3$
    $= 49{,}764 + 364(8) + 228(7) + 267(17)$
    $= 58{,}811$

    The employee's predicted salary is $58,811.

TRY IT YOURSELF 2

Use the regression equation found in Try It Yourself 1 to predict a student's final grade for each set of conditions.

1. A student has a midterm exam score of 89 and misses 1 class.
2. A student has a midterm exam score of 78 and misses 3 classes.
3. A student has a midterm exam score of 83 and misses 2 classes.

Answer: Page A8

4.4 EXERCISES

For Extra Help: MyLab Statistics

Building Basic Skills and Vocabulary

Predicting y-Values *In Exercises 1–4, use the multiple regression equation to predict the y-values for the values of the independent variables.*

1. **Cauliflower Yield** The equation used to predict the annual cauliflower yield (in pounds per acre) is

   $$\hat{y} = 24{,}791 + 4.508x_1 - 4.723x_2$$

   where x_1 is the number of acres planted and x_2 is the number of acres harvested. *(Adapted from United States Department of Agriculture)*

   (a) $x_1 = 36{,}500, x_2 = 36{,}100$
   (b) $x_1 = 38{,}100, x_2 = 37{,}800$
   (c) $x_1 = 39{,}000, x_2 = 38{,}800$
   (d) $x_1 = 42{,}200, x_2 = 42{,}100$

2. **Sorghum Yield** The equation used to predict the annual sorghum yield (in bushels per acre) is

   $$\hat{y} = 80.1 - 20.2x_1 + 21.2x_2$$

   where x_1 is the number of acres planted (in millions) and x_2 is the number of acres harvested (in millions). *(Adapted from United States Department of Agriculture)*

   (a) $x_1 = 5.5, x_2 = 3.9$
   (b) $x_1 = 8.3, x_2 = 7.3$
   (c) $x_1 = 6.5, x_2 = 5.7$
   (d) $x_1 = 9.4, x_2 = 7.8$

3. **Black Cherry Tree Volume** The volume (in cubic feet) of a black cherry tree can be modeled by the equation

   $$\hat{y} = -52.2 + 0.3x_1 + 4.5x_2$$

   where x_1 is the tree's height (in feet) and x_2 is the tree's diameter (in inches). *(Source: Journal of the Royal Statistical Society)*

   (a) $x_1 = 70, x_2 = 8.6$
   (b) $x_1 = 65, x_2 = 11.0$
   (c) $x_1 = 83, x_2 = 17.6$
   (d) $x_1 = 87, x_2 = 19.6$

4. **Elephant Weight** The equation used to predict the weight of an elephant (in kilograms) is

   $$\hat{y} = -4016 + 11.5x_1 + 7.55x_2 + 12.5x_3$$

   where x_1 represents the girth of the elephant (in centimeters), x_2 represents the length of the elephant (in centimeters), and x_3 represents the circumference of a footpad (in centimeters). *(Source: Field Trip Earth)*

   (a) $x_1 = 421, x_2 = 224, x_3 = 144$
   (b) $x_1 = 311, x_2 = 171, x_3 = 102$
   (c) $x_1 = 376, x_2 = 226, x_3 = 124$
   (d) $x_1 = 231, x_2 = 135, x_3 = 86$

Using and Interpreting Concepts

Finding a Multiple Regression Equation *In Exercises 5 and 6, use technology to find (a) the multiple regression equation for the data shown in the table, (b) the standard error of estimate, and (c) the coefficient of determination. Interpret the results.*

5. **Used Cars** The table shows the prices (in dollars), age (in years), and mileage (in thousands of miles) of eight pre-owned Honda Civic Sedans.

Price, y	Age, x_1	Mileage, x_2
9454	6	91.2
10,920	5	77.1
13,929	3	45.1
14,604	2	37.7
11,500	4	52.1
15,308	2	34.7
14,500	3	35.6
14,878	3	21.6
8000	9	87.9

6. **Shareholder's Equity** The table shows the net sales (in billions of dollars), total assets (in billions of dollars), and shareholder's equities (in billions of dollars) for Wal-Mart for six years. *(Adapted from Wal-Mart Stores, Inc.)*

Shareholder's equity, y	Net sales, x_1	Total assets, x_2
71.3	443.9	193.4
76.3	465.6	202.9
76.3	473.1	204.5
81.4	482.2	203.5
80.5	478.6	199.6
77.8	481.3	198.8

Extending Concepts

Adjusted r^2 *The calculation of the coefficient of determination r^2 depends on the number of data pairs and the number of independent variables. An adjusted value of r^2 based on the number of degrees of freedom is calculated using the formula*

$$r^2_{adj} = 1 - \left[\frac{(1-r^2)(n-1)}{n-k-1} \right]$$

where n is the number of data pairs and k is the number of independent variables.

In Exercises 7 and 8, calculate r^2_{adj} and determine the percentage of the variation in y that can be explained by the relationships between variables according to r^2_{adj}. Compare this result with the one obtained using r^2.

7. Calculate r^2_{adj} for the data in Exercise 5.

8. Calculate r^2_{adj} for the data in Exercise 6.

USES AND ABUSES

Statistics in the Real World

Uses

Correlation and Regression Correlation and regression analysis can be used to determine whether there is a significant relationship between two variables. When there is, you can use one of the variables to predict the value of the other variable. For instance, educators have used correlation and regression analysis to determine that there is a significant correlation between a student's SAT score and the grade point average from a student's freshman year at college. Consequently, many colleges and universities use SAT scores of high school applicants as a predictor of the applicant's initial success at college.

Abuses

Confusing Correlation and Causation The most common abuse of correlation in studies is to confuse the concepts of correlation with those of causation (see page 192). Good SAT scores do not cause good college grades. Rather, there are other variables, such as good study habits and motivation, that contribute to both. When a strong correlation is found between two variables, look for other variables that are correlated with both.

x	1	0	−1	0
y	0	1	0	−1

Considering Only Linear Correlation The correlation studied in this chapter is linear correlation. When the correlation coefficient is close to 1 or close to −1, the data points can be modeled by a straight line. It is possible that a correlation coefficient is close to 0 but there is still a strong correlation of a different type. Consider the data listed in the table at the left. The value of the correlation coefficient is 0. However, the data are perfectly correlated with the equation $x^2 + y^2 = 1$, as shown in the figure at the left.

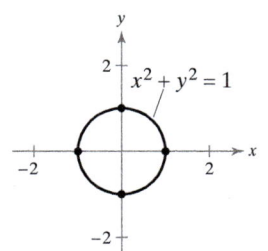

Ethics

When data are collected, all of the data should be used when calculating statistics. In this chapter, you learned that before finding the equation of a regression line, it is helpful to construct a scatter plot of the data to check for outliers, gaps, and clusters in the data. Researchers cannot use only those data points that fit their hypotheses or those that show a significant correlation. Although eliminating outliers may help a data set coincide with predicted patterns or fit a regression line, it is unethical to amend data in such a way. An outlier or any other point that influences a regression model can be removed only when it is properly justified.

In most cases, the best and sometimes safest approach for presenting statistical measurements is with and without an outlier being included. By doing this, the decision as to whether or not to recognize the outlier is left to the reader.

EXERCISES

1. ***Confusing Correlation and Causation*** Find an example of an article that confuses correlation and causation. Discuss other variables that could contribute to the relationship between the variables.

2. ***Considering Only Linear Correlation*** Find an example of two real-life variables that have a nonlinear correlation.

4 Chapter Summary

What Did You Learn?	Example(s)	Review Exercises
Section 4.1		
▶ How to construct a scatter plot and how to find a correlation coefficient $$r = \frac{n\Sigma xy - (\Sigma x)(\Sigma y)}{\sqrt{n\Sigma x^2 - (\Sigma x)^2}\sqrt{n\Sigma y^2 - (\Sigma y)^2}}$$	1–5	1–4
▶ How to test a population correlation coefficient ρ using a table and how to perform a hypothesis test for a population correlation coefficient ρ $$t = \frac{r}{\sqrt{\frac{1-r^2}{n-2}}}$$	6, 7	5–8
Section 4.2		
▶ How to find the equation of a regression line $$\hat{y} = mx + b$$ $$m = \frac{n\Sigma xy - (\Sigma x)(\Sigma y)}{n\Sigma x^2 - (\Sigma x)^2}$$ $$b = \bar{y} - m\bar{x} = \frac{\Sigma y}{n} - m\frac{\Sigma x}{n}$$	1, 2	9–12
▶ How to predict y-values using a regression equation	3	9–12
Section 4.3		
▶ How to find and interpret the coefficient of determination $$r^2 = \frac{\text{Explained variation}}{\text{Total variation}}$$	1	13–18
▶ How to find and interpret the standard error of estimate for a regression line $$s_e = \sqrt{\frac{\Sigma(y_i - \hat{y}_i)^2}{n-2}} = \sqrt{\frac{\Sigma y^2 - b\Sigma y - m\Sigma xy}{n-2}}$$	2	17, 18
▶ How to construct and interpret a prediction interval for y $$\hat{y} - E < y < \hat{y} + E, \quad E = t_c s_e \sqrt{1 + \frac{1}{n} + \frac{n(x_0 - \bar{x})^2}{n\Sigma x^2 - (\Sigma x)^2}}$$	3	19–24
Section 4.4		
▶ How to use technology to find and interpret a multiple regression equation, the standard error of estimate, and the coefficient of determination $$\hat{y} = b + m_1 x_1 + m_2 x_2 + m_3 x_3 + \cdots + m_k x_k$$	1	25, 26
▶ How to use a multiple regression equation to predict y-values	2	27, 28

4 Review Exercises

Section 4.1

In Exercises 1–4, (a) display the data in a scatter plot, (b) calculate the sample correlation coefficient r, and (c) describe the type of correlation and interpret the correlation in the context of the data.

1. The numbers of pass attempts and passing yards for seven professional quarterbacks for a recent regular season *(Source: National Football League)*

Pass attempts, x	610	545	567	552	432	486	403
Passing yards, y	4428	4240	4090	3877	3554	3401	2710

2. The numbers of wildland fires (in thousands) and wildland acres burned (in millions) in the United States for eight years *(Source: National Interagency Coordinate Center)*

Fires, x	78.8	72.0	74.1	67.8	47.6	63.3	68.2	67.7
Acres, y	5.9	3.4	8.7	9.3	4.3	3.6	10.1	5.5

3. The intelligence quotient (IQ) scores and brain sizes, as measured by the total pixel count (in thousands) from an MRI scan, for nine female college students *(Adapted from Intelligence)*

IQ score, x	138	140	96	83	101	135	85	77	88
Pixel count, y	991	856	879	865	808	791	799	794	894

4. The annual per capita sugar consumptions (in kilograms) and the average numbers of cavities of 11- and 12-year-old children in seven countries

Sugar consumption, x	2.1	5.0	6.3	6.5	7.7	8.7	11.6
Cavities, y	0.59	1.51	1.55	1.70	2.18	2.10	2.73

In Exercises 5–8, use Table 11 in Appendix B, or perform a hypothesis test using Table 5 in Appendix B to make a conclusion about the correlation coefficient.

5. Refer to the data in Exercise 1. At $\alpha = 0.05$, is there enough evidence to conclude that there is a significant linear correlation between the data? (Use the value of r found in Exercise 1.)

6. Refer to the data in Exercise 2. At $\alpha = 0.05$, is there enough evidence to conclude that there is a significant linear correlation between the data? (Use the value of r found in Exercise 2.)

7. Refer to the data in Exercise 3. At $\alpha = 0.01$, is there enough evidence to conclude that there is a significant linear correlation between the data? (Use the value of r found in Exercise 3.)

8. Refer to the data in Exercise 4. At $\alpha = 0.01$, is there enough evidence to conclude that there is a significant linear correlation between the data? (Use the value of r found in Exercise 4.)

Section 4.2

In Exercises 9–12, find the equation of the regression line for the data. Then construct a scatter plot of the data and draw the regression line. (Each pair of variables has a significant correlation.) Then use the regression equation to predict the value of y for each of the x-values, if meaningful. If the x-value is not meaningful to predict the value of y, explain why not. If convenient, use technology.

9. The average number (in thousands) of milk cows and the amounts (in billions of pounds) of milk produced in the United States for eight years *(Source: U.S. Department of Agriculture)*

Milk cows, x	9202	9123	9199	9237
Milk produced, y	189.2	192.9	196.3	200.6

Milk cows, x	9224	9257	9314	9328
Milk produced, y	201.2	206.1	208.6	212.4

(a) $x = 9080$ cows (b) $x = 9230$ cows
(c) $x = 9250$ cows (d) $x = 9300$ cows

10. The average times (in hours) per day spent watching television for men and women for 10 years *(Source: U.S. Bureau of Labor Statistics)*

Men, x	2.80	2.88	3.01	3.10	2.94
Women, y	2.36	2.38	2.55	2.56	2.53

Men, x	2.99	3.07	2.98	3.05	3.02
Women, y	2.53	2.61	2.57	2.61	2.56

(a) $x = 2.85$ hours (b) $x = 2.97$ hours
(c) $x = 3.04$ hours (d) $x = 3.13$ hours

11. The ages (in years) and the numbers of hours of sleep in one night for seven adults

Age, x	35	20	59	42	68	38	75
Hours of sleep, y	7	9	5	6	5	8	4

(a) $x = 16$ years (b) $x = 25$ years
(c) $x = 85$ years (d) $x = 50$ years

12. The engine displacements (in cubic inches) and the fuel efficiencies (in miles per gallon) of seven automobiles

Displacement, x	170	134	220	305	109	256	322
Fuel efficiency, y	29.5	34.5	23.0	17.0	33.5	23.0	15.5

(a) $x = 86$ cubic inches (b) $x = 198$ cubic inches
(c) $x = 289$ cubic inches (d) $x = 407$ cubic inches

Section 4.3

In Exercises 13–16, use the value of the correlation coefficient r to calculate the coefficient of determination r^2. What does this tell you about the explained variation of the data about the regression line? about the unexplained variation?

13. $r = -0.450$
14. $r = -0.937$
15. $r = 0.642$
16. $r = 0.795$

In Exercises 17 and 18, use the data to (a) find the coefficient of determination r^2 and interpret the result, and (b) find the standard error of estimate s_e and interpret the result.

17. The table shows the combined city and highway fuel efficiency (in miles per gallon gasoline equivalent) and top speeds (in miles per hour) for nine hybrid and electric cars. The regression equation is $\hat{y} = -0.465x + 139.433$. *(Source: Car and Driver)*

Fuel efficiency, x	114	95	120	105	107	116	118	68	84
Top speed, y	80	103	78	85	92	88	92	105	101

18. The table shows the cooking areas (in square inches) of 18 gas grills and their prices (in dollars). The regression equation is $\hat{y} = 2.335x - 853.278$. *(Source: Lowe's)*

Area, x	650	669	529	725	844	445	669	844	740
Price, y	149	699	499	374	1599	187	1299	899	374

Area, x	529	450	644	600	575	998	529	265	530
Price, y	599	399	499	269	299	1999	519	99	109

In Exercises 19–24, construct the indicated prediction interval and interpret the results.

19. Construct a 90% prediction interval for the amount of milk produced in Exercise 9 when there are an average of 9275 milk cows.

20. Construct a 90% prediction interval for the average time women spend per day watching television in Exercise 10 when the average time men spend per day watching television is 3.08 hours.

21. Construct a 95% prediction interval for the number of hours of sleep for an adult in Exercise 11 who is 45 years old.

22. Construct a 95% prediction interval for the fuel efficiency of an automobile in Exercise 12 that has an engine displacement of 265 cubic inches.

23. Construct a 99% prediction interval for the top speed of a hybrid or electric car in Exercise 17 that has a combined city and highway fuel economy of 90 miles per gallon equivalent.

24. Construct a 99% prediction interval for the price of a gas grill in Exercise 18 with a usable cooking area of 900 square inches.

Section 4.4

In Exercises 25 and 26, use technology to find (a) the multiple regression equation for the data shown in the table, (b) the standard error of estimate, and (c) the coefficient of determination. Interpret the result.

25. The table shows the carbon monoxide, tar, and nicotine content, all in milligrams, of 14 brands of U.S. cigarettes. *(Source: Federal Trade Commission)*

Carbon monoxide, y	Tar, x_1	Nicotine, x_2
15	16	1.1
17	16	1.0
11	10	0.8
12	11	0.9
14	13	0.8
16	14	0.8
14	16	1.2
16	16	1.2
10	10	0.8
18	19	1.4
17	17	1.2
11	12	1.0
10	9	0.7
14	15	1.2

26. The table shows the numbers of acres planted, the numbers of acres harvested, and the annual yields (in pounds) of spinach for five years. *(Source: United States Department of Agriculture)*

Yield, y	Acres planted, x_1	Acres harvested, x_2
15,200	36,400	35,000
18,600	35,400	32,900
17,900	34,400	32,300
18,600	38,500	36,600
16,000	36,400	35,680

In Exercises 27 and 28, use the multiple regression equation to predict the y-values for the values of the independent variables.

27. An equation that can be used to predict fuel economy (in miles per gallon) for automobiles is

$$\hat{y} = 41.3 - 0.004x_1 - 0.0049x_2$$

where x_1 is the engine displacement (in cubic inches) and x_2 is the vehicle weight (in pounds).

(a) $x_1 = 305, x_2 = 3750$ (b) $x_1 = 225, x_2 = 3100$
(c) $x_1 = 105, x_2 = 2200$ (d) $x_1 = 185, x_2 = 3000$

28. Use the regression equation found in Exercise 25.

(a) $x_1 = 10, x_2 = 0.7$ (b) $x_1 = 15, x_2 = 1.1$
(c) $x_1 = 13, x_2 = 1.0$ (d) $x_1 = 9, x_2 = 0.8$

4 Chapter Quiz

Take this quiz as you would take a quiz in class. After you are done, check your work against the answers given in the back of the book.

For Exercises 1–8, use the data in the table, which shows the average annual salaries (both in thousands of dollars) for secondary and elementary school teachers, excluding special and vocational education teachers, in the United States for 11 years. *(Source: Bureau of Labor Statistics)*

Secondary school teachers, x	Elementary school teachers, y
51.2	48.7
52.5	50.0
54.4	52.2
55.2	53.2
56.0	54.3
56.8	55.3
57.8	56.1
58.3	56.3
59.3	56.8
60.4	57.7
61.4	59.0

1. Construct a scatter plot for the data. Do the data appear to have a positive linear correlation, a negative linear correlation, or no linear correlation? Explain.
2. Calculate the correlation coefficient r and interpret the result.
3. Test the significance of the correlation coefficient r that you found in Exercise 2. Use $\alpha = 0.05$.
4. Find the equation of the regression line for the data. Draw the regression line on the scatter plot that you constructed in Exercise 1.
5. Use the regression equation that you found in Exercise 4 to predict the average annual salary of elementary school teachers when the average annual salary of secondary school teachers is $52,500.
6. Find the coefficient of determination r^2 and interpret the result.
7. Find the standard error of estimate s_e and interpret the result.
8. Construct a 95% prediction interval for the average annual salary of elementary school teachers when the average annual salary of secondary school teachers is $52,500. Interpret the results.
9. **Stock Price** The equation used to predict the stock price (in dollars) at the end of the year for a restaurant chain is

    $$\hat{y} = -86 + 7.46x_1 - 1.61x_2$$

    where x_1 is the total revenue (in billions of dollars) and x_2 is the shareholders' equity (in billions of dollars). Use the multiple regression equation to predict the y-values for the values of the independent variables.

    (a) $x_1 = 27.6, x_2 = 15.3$ (b) $x_1 = 24.1, x_2 = 14.6$
    (c) $x_1 = 23.5, x_2 = 13.4$ (d) $x_1 = 22.8, x_2 = 15.3$

4 Chapter Test

Take this test as you would take a test in class.

1. **Net Sales** The equation used to predict the net sales (in millions of dollars) for a fiscal year for a clothing retailer is

   $$\hat{y} = 23{,}769 + 9.18x_1 - 8.41x_2$$

   where x_1 is the number of stores open at the end of the fiscal year and x_2 is the average square footage per store. Use the multiple regression equation to predict the y-values for the values of the independent variables.

   (a) $x_1 = 1057, x_2 = 3698$ (b) $x_1 = 1012, x_2 = 3659$
   (c) $x_1 = 952, x_2 = 3601$ (d) $x_1 = 914, x_2 = 3594$

   For Exercises 2–9, use the data in the table, which shows the average annual salaries (both in thousands of dollars) for librarians and postsecondary library science teachers in the United States for 12 years. *(Source: Bureau of Labor Statistics)*

Librarians, x	Library science teachers, y
49.1	56.6
50.9	57.6
52.9	59.7
54.7	61.6
55.7	64.3
56.4	67.0
57.0	70.0
57.2	70.8
57.6	73.3
58.1	72.4
58.9	73.0
59.9	72.3

2. Construct a scatter plot for the data. Do the data appear to have a positive linear correlation, a negative linear correlation, or no linear correlation? Explain.

3. Calculate the correlation coefficient r and interpret the result.

4. Test the significance of the correlation coefficient r that you found in Exercise 3. Use $\alpha = 0.01$.

5. Find the equation of the regression line for the data. Draw the regression line on the scatter plot that you constructed in Exercise 2.

6. Use the regression equation that you found in Exercise 5 to predict the average annual salary of postsecondary library science teachers when the average annual salary of librarians is $56,000.

7. Find the coefficient of determination r^2 and interpret the result.

8. Find the standard error of estimate s_e and interpret the result.

9. Construct a 99% prediction interval for the average annual salary of postsecondary library science teachers when the average annual salary of librarians is $56,000. Interpret the results.

REAL STATISTICS REAL DECISIONS — Putting it all together

Acid rain affects the environment by increasing the acidity of lakes and streams to dangerous levels, damaging trees and soil, accelerating the decay of building materials and paint, and destroying national monuments. The goal of the Environmental Protection Agency's (EPA) Acid Rain Program is to achieve environmental health benefits by reducing the emissions of the primary causes of acid rain: sulfur dioxide and nitrogen oxides.

You work for the EPA and you want to determine whether there is a significant correlation between the average concentrations of sulfur dioxide and nitrogen dioxide.

EXERCISES

1. **Analyzing the Data**

   (a) The data in the table show the annual averages of the daily maximum concentrations of sulfur dioxide (in parts per billion) and nitrogen dioxide (in parts per billion) for 12 years. Construct a scatter plot of the data and make a conclusion about the type of correlation between the average concentrations of sulfur dioxide and nitrogen dioxide.

   (b) Calculate the correlation coefficient r and verify your conclusion in part (a).

   (c) Test the significance of the correlation coefficient found in part (b). Use $\alpha = 0.05$.

   (d) Find the equation of the regression line for the average concentrations of sulfur dioxide and nitrogen dioxide. Add the graph of the regression line to your scatter plot in part (a). Does the regression line appear to be a good fit?

   (e) Can you use the equation of the regression line to predict the average concentration of nitrogen dioxide given the average concentration of sulfur dioxide? Why or why not?

   (f) Find the coefficient of determination r^2 and the standard error of estimate s_e. Interpret your results.

2. **Making Predictions**

   Construct a 95% prediction interval for the average concentration of nitrogen dioxide when the average concentration of sulfur dioxide is 28 parts per billion. Interpret the results.

Average sulfur dioxide concentration, x	Average nitrogen dioxide concentration, y
75.6	56.3
74.9	55.9
68.9	54.9
64.7	53.2
59.0	52.2
50.8	48.0
46.3	47.5
37.9	47.9
36.7	44.8
30.5	45.9
31.9	46.9
25.3	44.6

(Source: Environmental Protection Agency)

TECHNOLOGY

MINITAB | **EXCEL** | **TI-84 PLUS**

Nutrients in Breakfast Cereals

U.S. Food and Drug Administration

The U.S. Food and Drug Administration (FDA) requires nutrition labeling for most foods. Under FDA regulations, manufacturers are required to list the amounts of certain nutrients in their foods, such as calories, sugar, fat, and carbohydrates. This nutritional information is displayed in the "Nutrition Facts" panel on the food's package.

The table shows the nutritional content below for one cup of each of 21 different breakfast cereals.

- C = calories
- S = sugar in grams
- F = fat in grams
- R = carbohydrates in grams

C	S	F	R
100	12	0.5	25
130	11	1.5	29
100	1	2	20
130	15	2	31
130	13	1.5	29
120	3	0.5	26
100	2	0	24
120	10	0	29
150	16	1.5	31
110	4	0	25
110	12	1	25
150	15	0	36
160	15	1.5	35
150	12	2	29
150	15	1.5	29
110	6	1	23
190	19	1.5	45
100	3	0	23
120	4	0.5	23
120	11	1.5	28
130	5	0.5	29

EXERCISES

1. Use technology to draw a scatter plot of the (x, y) pairs in each data set.
   - (a) (calories, sugar)
   - (b) (calories, fat)
   - (c) (calories, carbohydrates)
   - (d) (sugar, fat)
   - (e) (sugar, carbohydrates)
   - (f) (fat, carbohydrates)

2. From the scatter plots in Exercise 1, which pairs of variables appear to have a strong linear correlation?

3. Use technology to find the correlation coefficient for each pair of variables in Exercise 1. Which has the strongest linear correlation?

4. Use technology to find an equation of a regression line for each pair of variables.
   - (a) (calories, sugar)
   - (b) (calories, carbohydrates)

5. Use the results of Exercise 4 to predict each value.
   - (a) The sugar content of one cup of cereal that has 120 calories
   - (b) The carbohydrate content of one cup of cereal that has 120 calories

6. Use technology to find the multiple regression equations of each form.
   - (a) $C = b + m_1 S + m_2 F + m_3 R$
   - (b) $C = b + m_1 S + m_2 R$

7. Use the equations from Exercise 6 to predict the calories in 1 cup of cereal that has 7 grams of sugar, 0.5 gram of fat, and 31 grams of carbohydrates.

Extended solutions are given in the technology manuals that accompany this text.
Technical instruction is provided for Minitab, Excel, and the TI-84 Plus.

APPENDIX B

Table 4—Standard Normal Distribution

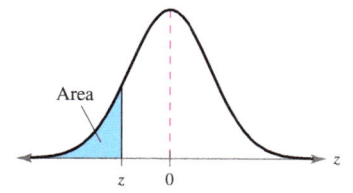

z	.09	.08	.07	.06	.05	.04	.03	.02	.01	.00
−3.4	.0002	.0003	.0003	.0003	.0003	.0003	.0003	.0003	.0003	.0003
−3.3	.0003	.0004	.0004	.0004	.0004	.0004	.0004	.0005	.0005	.0005
−3.2	.0005	.0005	.0005	.0006	.0006	.0006	.0006	.0006	.0007	.0007
−3.1	.0007	.0007	.0008	.0008	.0008	.0008	.0009	.0009	.0009	.0010
−3.0	.0010	.0010	.0011	.0011	.0011	.0012	.0012	.0013	.0013	.0013
−2.9	.0014	.0014	.0015	.0015	.0016	.0016	.0017	.0018	.0018	.0019
−2.8	.0019	.0020	.0021	.0021	.0022	.0023	.0023	.0024	.0025	.0026
−2.7	.0026	.0027	.0028	.0029	.0030	.0031	.0032	.0033	.0034	.0035
−2.6	.0036	.0037	.0038	.0039	.0040	.0041	.0043	.0044	.0045	.0047
−2.5	.0048	.0049	.0051	.0052	.0054	.0055	.0057	.0059	.0060	.0062
−2.4	.0064	.0066	.0068	.0069	.0071	.0073	.0075	.0078	.0080	.0082
−2.3	.0084	.0087	.0089	.0091	.0094	.0096	.0099	.0102	.0104	.0107
−2.2	.0110	.0113	.0116	.0119	.0122	.0125	.0129	.0132	.0136	.0139
−2.1	.0143	.0146	.0150	.0154	.0158	.0162	.0166	.0170	.0174	.0179
−2.0	.0183	.0188	.0192	.0197	.0202	.0207	.0212	.0217	.0222	.0228
−1.9	.0233	.0239	.0244	.0250	.0256	.0262	.0268	.0274	.0281	.0287
−1.8	.0294	.0301	.0307	.0314	.0322	.0329	.0336	.0344	.0351	.0359
−1.7	.0367	.0375	.0384	.0392	.0401	.0409	.0418	.0427	.0436	.0446
−1.6	.0455	.0465	.0475	.0485	.0495	.0505	.0516	.0526	.0537	.0548
−1.5	.0559	.0571	.0582	.0594	.0606	.0618	.0630	.0643	.0655	.0668
−1.4	.0681	.0694	.0708	.0721	.0735	.0749	.0764	.0778	.0793	.0808
−1.3	.0823	.0838	.0853	.0869	.0885	.0901	.0918	.0934	.0951	.0968
−1.2	.0985	.1003	.1020	.1038	.1056	.1075	.1093	.1112	.1131	.1151
−1.1	.1170	.1190	.1210	.1230	.1251	.1271	.1292	.1314	.1335	.1357
−1.0	.1379	.1401	.1423	.1446	.1469	.1492	.1515	.1539	.1562	.1587
−0.9	.1611	.1635	.1660	.1685	.1711	.1736	.1762	.1788	.1814	.1841
−0.8	.1867	.1894	.1922	.1949	.1977	.2005	.2033	.2061	.2090	.2119
−0.7	.2148	.2177	.2206	.2236	.2266	.2296	.2327	.2358	.2389	.2420
−0.6	.2451	.2483	.2514	.2546	.2578	.2611	.2643	.2676	.2709	.2743
−0.5	.2776	.2810	.2843	.2877	.2912	.2946	.2981	.3015	.3050	.3085
−0.4	.3121	.3156	.3192	.3228	.3264	.3300	.3336	.3372	.3409	.3446
−0.3	.3483	.3520	.3557	.3594	.3632	.3669	.3707	.3745	.3783	.3821
−0.2	.3859	.3897	.3936	.3974	.4013	.4052	.4090	.4129	.4168	.4207
−0.1	.4247	.4286	.4325	.4364	.4404	.4443	.4483	.4522	.4562	.4602
−0.0	.4641	.4681	.4721	.4761	.4801	.4840	.4880	.4920	.4960	.5000

Critical Values

Level of Confidence c	z_c
0.80	1.28
0.90	1.645
0.95	1.96
0.99	2.575

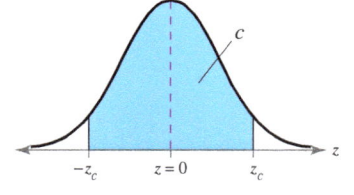

Table A-3, pp. 681–682 from *Probability and Statistics for Engineers and Scientists*, 6e by Walpole, Myers, and Myers. Copyright 1997. Pearson Prentice Hall, Upper Saddle River, N.J.

Table 4—Standard Normal Distribution (continued)

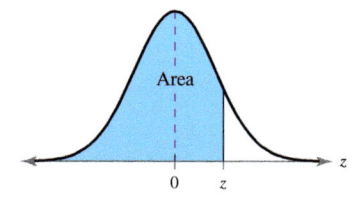

z	.00	.01	.02	.03	.04	.05	.06	.07	.08	.09
0.0	.5000	.5040	.5080	.5120	.5160	.5199	.5239	.5279	.5319	.5359
0.1	.5398	.5438	.5478	.5517	.5557	.5596	.5636	.5675	.5714	.5753
0.2	.5793	.5832	.5871	.5910	.5948	.5987	.6026	.6064	.6103	.6141
0.3	.6179	.6217	.6255	.6293	.6331	.6368	.6406	.6443	.6480	.6517
0.4	.6554	.6591	.6628	.6664	.6700	.6736	.6772	.6808	.6844	.6879
0.5	.6915	.6950	.6985	.7019	.7054	.7088	.7123	.7157	.7190	.7224
0.6	.7257	.7291	.7324	.7357	.7389	.7422	.7454	.7486	.7517	.7549
0.7	.7580	.7611	.7642	.7673	.7704	.7734	.7764	.7794	.7823	.7852
0.8	.7881	.7910	.7939	.7967	.7995	.8023	.8051	.8078	.8106	.8133
0.9	.8159	.8186	.8212	.8238	.8264	.8289	.8315	.8340	.8365	.8389
1.0	.8413	.8438	.8461	.8485	.8508	.8531	.8554	.8577	.8599	.8621
1.1	.8643	.8665	.8686	.8708	.8729	.8749	.8770	.8790	.8810	.8830
1.2	.8849	.8869	.8888	.8907	.8925	.8944	.8962	.8980	.8997	.9015
1.3	.9032	.9049	.9066	.9082	.9099	.9115	.9131	.9147	.9162	.9177
1.4	.9192	.9207	.9222	.9236	.9251	.9265	.9279	.9292	.9306	.9319
1.5	.9332	.9345	.9357	.9370	.9382	.9394	.9406	.9418	.9429	.9441
1.6	.9452	.9463	.9474	.9484	.9495	.9505	.9515	.9525	.9535	.9545
1.7	.9554	.9564	.9573	.9582	.9591	.9599	.9608	.9616	.9625	.9633
1.8	.9641	.9649	.9656	.9664	.9671	.9678	.9686	.9693	.9699	.9706
1.9	.9713	.9719	.9726	.9732	.9738	.9744	.9750	.9756	.9761	.9767
2.0	.9772	.9778	.9783	.9788	.9793	.9798	.9803	.9808	.9812	.9817
2.1	.9821	.9826	.9830	.9834	.9838	.9842	.9846	.9850	.9854	.9857
2.2	.9861	.9864	.9868	.9871	.9875	.9878	.9881	.9884	.9887	.9890
2.3	.9893	.9896	.9898	.9901	.9904	.9906	.9909	.9911	.9913	.9916
2.4	.9918	.9920	.9922	.9925	.9927	.9929	.9931	.9932	.9934	.9936
2.5	.9938	.9940	.9941	.9943	.9945	.9946	.9948	.9949	.9951	.9952
2.6	.9953	.9955	.9956	.9957	.9959	.9960	.9961	.9962	.9963	.9964
2.7	.9965	.9966	.9967	.9968	.9969	.9970	.9971	.9972	.9973	.9974
2.8	.9974	.9975	.9976	.9977	.9977	.9978	.9979	.9979	.9980	.9981
2.9	.9981	.9982	.9982	.9983	.9984	.9984	.9985	.9985	.9986	.9986
3.0	.9987	.9987	.9987	.9988	.9988	.9989	.9989	.9989	.9990	.9990
3.1	.9990	.9991	.9991	.9991	.9992	.9992	.9992	.9992	.9993	.9993
3.2	.9993	.9993	.9994	.9994	.9994	.9994	.9994	.9995	.9995	.9995
3.3	.9995	.9995	.9995	.9996	.9996	.9996	.9996	.9996	.9996	.9997
3.4	.9997	.9997	.9997	.9997	.9997	.9997	.9997	.9997	.9997	.9998

Table 5—t-Distribution

d.f.	Level of confidence, c	0.80	0.90	0.95	0.98	0.99
	One tail, α	0.10	0.05	0.025	0.01	0.005
	Two tails, α	0.20	0.10	0.05	0.02	0.01
1		3.078	6.314	12.706	31.821	63.657
2		1.886	2.920	4.303	6.965	9.925
3		1.638	2.353	3.182	4.541	5.841
4		1.533	2.132	2.776	3.747	4.604
5		1.476	2.015	2.571	3.365	4.032
6		1.440	1.943	2.447	3.143	3.707
7		1.415	1.895	2.365	2.998	3.499
8		1.397	1.860	2.306	2.896	3.355
9		1.383	1.833	2.262	2.821	3.250
10		1.372	1.812	2.228	2.764	3.169
11		1.363	1.796	2.201	2.718	3.106
12		1.356	1.782	2.179	2.681	3.055
13		1.350	1.771	2.160	2.650	3.012
14		1.345	1.761	2.145	2.624	2.977
15		1.341	1.753	2.131	2.602	2.947
16		1.337	1.746	2.120	2.583	2.921
17		1.333	1.740	2.110	2.567	2.898
18		1.330	1.734	2.101	2.552	2.878
19		1.328	1.729	2.093	2.539	2.861
20		1.325	1.725	2.086	2.528	2.845
21		1.323	1.721	2.080	2.518	2.831
22		1.321	1.717	2.074	2.508	2.819
23		1.319	1.714	2.069	2.500	2.807
24		1.318	1.711	2.064	2.492	2.797
25		1.316	1.708	2.060	2.485	2.787
26		1.315	1.706	2.056	2.479	2.779
27		1.314	1.703	2.052	2.473	2.771
28		1.313	1.701	2.048	2.467	2.763
29		1.311	1.699	2.045	2.462	2.756
30		1.310	1.697	2.042	2.457	2.750
31		1.309	1.696	2.040	2.453	2.744
32		1.309	1.694	2.037	2.449	2.738
33		1.308	1.692	2.035	2.445	2.733
34		1.307	1.691	2.032	2.441	2.728
35		1.306	1.690	2.030	2.438	2.724
36		1.306	1.688	2.028	2.434	2.719
37		1.305	1.687	2.026	2.431	2.715
38		1.304	1.686	2.024	2.429	2.712
39		1.304	1.685	2.023	2.426	2.708
40		1.303	1.684	2.021	2.423	2.704
45		1.301	1.679	2.014	2.412	2.690
50		1.299	1.676	2.009	2.403	2.678
60		1.296	1.671	2.000	2.390	2.660
70		1.294	1.667	1.994	2.381	2.648
80		1.292	1.664	1.990	2.374	2.639
90		1.291	1.662	1.987	2.368	2.632
100		1.290	1.660	1.984	2.364	2.626
500		1.283	1.648	1.965	2.334	2.586
1000		1.282	1.646	1.962	2.330	2.581
∞		1.282	1.645	1.960	2.326	2.576

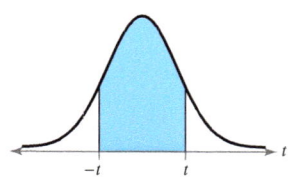

c-confidence interval

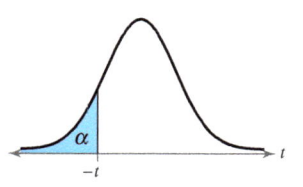

Left-tailed test

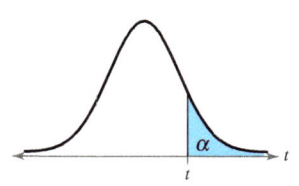

Right-tailed test

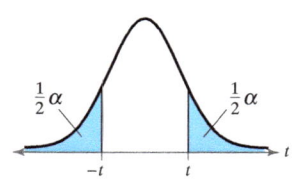

Two-tailed test

The critical values in Table 5 were generated using Excel.

TRY IT YOURSELF ANSWERS

Chapter 1

Section 1.1

1. The population consists of the responses of all ninth to twelfth graders in the United States. The sample consists of the responses of the 1501 ninth to twelfth graders in the survey. The sample data set consists of 1215 ninth to twelfth graders who said leaders today are more concerned with their own agenda than with achieving the overall goals of the organization they serve and 286 ninth to twelfth graders who did not say that.
2. a. Population parameter, because the total spent on employees' salaries, $5,150,694, is based on the entire company.
   b. Sample statistic, because 43% is based on a subset of the population.
3. a. The population consists of the responses of all U.S. adults, and the sample consists of the responses of the 1000 U.S. adults in the study.
   b. The part of this study that represents the descriptive branch of statistics involves the statement "three out of four adults will consult with their physician or pharmacist and only 8% visit a medication-specific website [when they have a question about their medication]."
   c. A possible inference drawn from the study is that most adults consult with their physician or pharmacist when they have a question about their medication.

Section 1.2

1. The city names are nonnumerical entries, so these are qualitative data. The city populations are numerical entries, so these are quantitative data.
2. (1) Ordinal, because the data can be put in order.
   (2) Nominal, because no mathematical computations can be made.
3. (1) Interval, because the data can be ordered and meaningful differences can be calculated, but it does not make sense to write a ratio using the temperatures.
   (2) Ratio, because the data can be ordered, meaningful differences can be calculated, the data can be written as a ratio, and the data set contains an inherent zero.

Section 1.3

1. This is an observational study.
2. There is no way to tell why the people quit smoking. They could have quit smoking as a result of either chewing the gum or watching the DVD. The gum and the DVD could be confounding variables. To improve the study, two experiments could be done, one using the gum and the other using the DVD. Or just conduct one experiment using either the gum or the DVD.
3. *Sample answer:* Assign numbers 1 to 79 to the employees of the company. Use the table of random numbers and obtain 63, 7, 40, 19, and 26. The employees assigned these numbers will make up the sample.
4. (1) The sample was selected by using the students in a randomly chosen class. This is cluster sampling.
   (2) The sample was selected by numbering each student in the school, randomly choosing a starting number, and selecting students at regular intervals from the starting number. This is systematic sampling.

Chapter 2

Section 2.1

1.

Class	Frequency, f
14–20	8
21–27	15
28–34	14
35–41	7
42–48	4
49–55	3

2.

Class	Frequency, f	Midpoint	Relative frequency	Cumulative frequency
14–20	8	17	0.1569	8
21–27	15	24	0.2941	23
28–34	14	31	0.2745	37
35–41	7	38	0.1373	44
42–48	4	45	0.0784	48
49–55	3	52	0.0588	51
	$\Sigma f = 51$		$\Sigma \dfrac{f}{n} = 1$	

Sample answer: The most common range of points scored by winning teams is 21 to 27. About 14% of the winning teams scored more than 41 points.

A6 Quantitative Analysis: Interpreting Numerical Data

3. Points Scored by Winning Super Bowl Teams

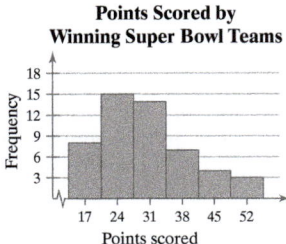

Sample answer: The most common range of points scored by winning teams is 21 to 27. About 14% of the winning teams scored more than 41 points.

4. Points Scored by Winning Super Bowl Teams

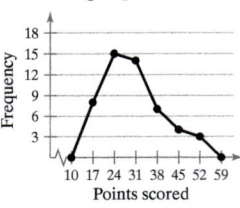

Sample answer: The frequency of points scored increases up to 24 points and then decreases.

5. Points Scored by Winning Super Bowl Teams

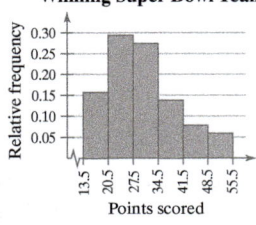

6. Points Scored by Winning Super Bowl Teams

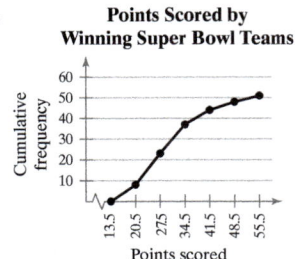

7.

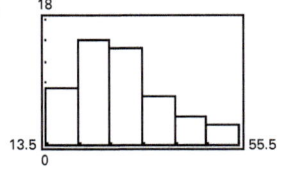

Section 2.2

1.
```
1 | 4 6 6 6 7                    Key: 1|4 = 14
2 | 0 0 0 1 1 1 3 3 4 4 4 4 6 7 7 7 7 7 8 9
3 | 0 1 1 1 1 2 2 3 4 4 4 4 5 5 5 7 8 8 9
4 | 2 3 6 8 9
5 | 2 5
```

Sample answer: Most of the winning teams scored between 20 and 39 points.

2.
```
1 | 4                            Key: 1|4 = 14
1 | 6 6 6 7
2 | 0 0 0 1 1 1 3 3 4 4 4 4
2 | 6 7 7 7 7 7 8 9
3 | 0 1 1 1 1 2 2 3 4 4 4 4
3 | 5 5 5 7 8 8 9
4 | 2 3
4 | 6 8 9
5 | 2
5 | 5
```

Sample answer: Most of the winning teams scored from 20 to 35 points.

3. Points Scored by Winning Super Bowl Teams

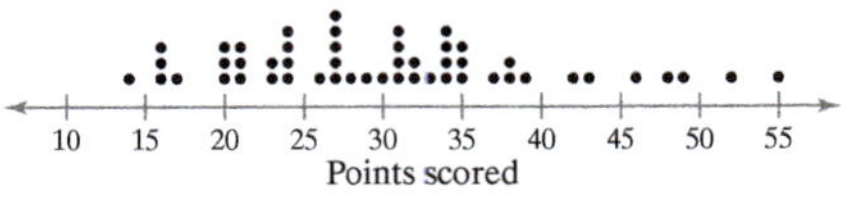

Sample answer: Most of the points scored by winning teams cluster between 20 and 40.

4. Earned Degrees Conferred in 1990
- Doctoral 5.4%
- Master's 17.0%
- Bachelor's 54.2%
- Associate's 23.5%

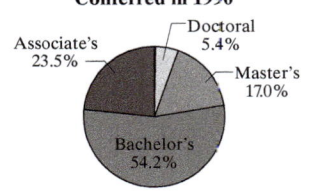

From 1990 to 2014, as percentages of the total degrees conferred, associate's degrees increased by 2.9%, bachelor's degrees decreased by 5.1%, master's degrees increased by 2.8%, and doctoral degrees decreased by 0.7%.

5. Causes of BBB Complaints

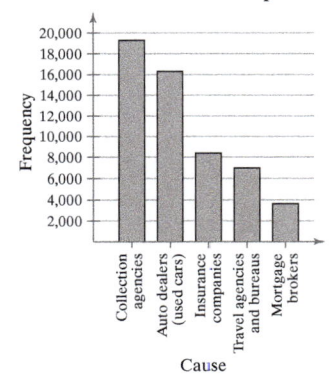

Collection agencies are the greatest cause of complaints.

6.

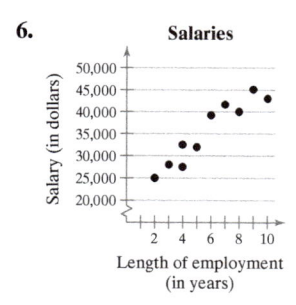

Salaries

It appears that the longer an employee is with the company, the greater the employee's salary.

7.

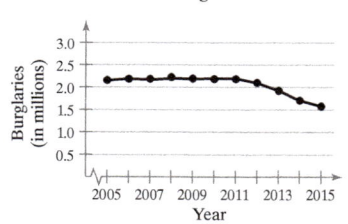

Burglaries

Sample answer: The number of burglaries remained about the same until 2012 and then decreased through 2015.

Section 2.3

1. About 30.2 2. 30 3. 28.5 4. 27 5. "some"
6. $\bar{x} \approx 21.6$; median $= 21$; mode $= 20$
   The mean in Example 6 ($\bar{x} \approx 23.8$) was heavily influenced by the entry 65. Neither the median nor the mode was affected as much by the entry 65.
7. About 2.6
8. About 30.0; This is very close to the mean found using the original data set.

Section 2.4

1. 35, or $35,000; The range of the starting salaries for Corporation B, which is $35,000, is much larger than the range of Corporation A.
2. $\sigma^2 \approx 110.3$; $\sigma \approx 10.5$, or $10,500
3. $s^2 \approx 177.1$; $s \approx 13.3$ 4. $\bar{x} \approx 19.8$; $s \approx 7.8$
5. *Sample answer:* 7, 7, 7, 7, 7, 13, 13, 13, 13, 13 6. 34.13%
7. At least 75% of Iowa's population is between 0 and 86.3 years old. Because $80 < 86.3$, an age of 80 lies within two standard deviations of the mean. So, the age is not unusual.
8. $\bar{x} = 1.7$; $s \approx 1.5$
   Both the mean and sample standard deviation decreased slightly.
9. $\bar{x} \approx 195.5$; $s \approx 169.5$
   Both the mean and sample standard deviation increased.
10. Los Angeles: $CV \approx 47.2\%$
    Dallas: $CV \approx 39.4\%$
    The office rental rates are more variable in Los Angeles than in Dallas.

Section 2.5

1. $Q_1 = 23$, $Q_2 = 30$, $Q_3 = 35$
   About one-quarter of the winning scores were 23 points or less, about one-half were 30 points or less, and about three-quarters were 35 points or less.
2. $Q_1 = 23.5$, $Q_2 = 30$, $Q_3 = 41$
   About one-quarter of these universities charge tuition of $23,500 or less, about one-half charge $30,000 or less, and about three-quarters charge $41,000 or less.
3. IQR $= 12$; 55 is an outlier.
4. **Points Scored by Winning Super Bowl Teams**

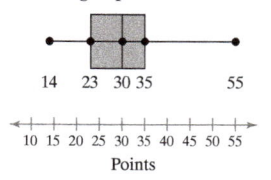

   About 50% of the winning scores were between 23 and 35 points. About 25% of the winning scores were less than 23 points. About 25% of the winning scores were greater than 35 points.
5. 19.5; About 10% of the winning scores were 19 points or less.
6. 28th percentile
7. For $60, $z = -1.25$.
   For $71, $z = 0.125$.
   For $92, $z = 2.75$.
8. Man: $z = -3.3$; Woman: $z \approx -1.7$
   The z-score for the 5-foot-tall man is 3.3 standard deviations below the mean. This is a very unusual height for a man. The z-score for the 5-foot-tall woman is 1.7 standard deviations below the mean. This is among the typical heights for a woman.

Chapter 3

Section 3.1

1. 20.9 2. 0.8 hour
3. (20.1, 21.7); This confidence interval is wider than the one found in Example 3.
4. (20.6, 21.5); (20.5, 21.6); (20.4, 21.7); As the confidence level increases, so does the width of the interval.
5. (22.4, 23.4) [*Tech:* (22.5, 23.4)]; Because of the larger sample size, the confidence interval is slightly narrower.
6. 37; Because of the larger margin of error, the sample size needed is smaller.

Section 3.2

1. 1.721 2. (157.6, 166.4); (154.6, 169.4)
3. (9.08, 10.42); (8.94, 10.56); The 90% confidence interval is slightly narrower.
4. Use a t-distribution because σ is not known and the population is normally distributed.

Section 3.3
1. 15% 2. (0.14, 0.16) 3. (0.454, 0.546)
4. (1) 1692 (2) 400

Section 3.4
1. 42.557, 17.708
2. Population variance: (0.98, 2.36), (0.91, 2.60)
   Standard deviation: (0.99, 1.54), (0.96, 1.61)

Chapter 4
Section 4.1
1.

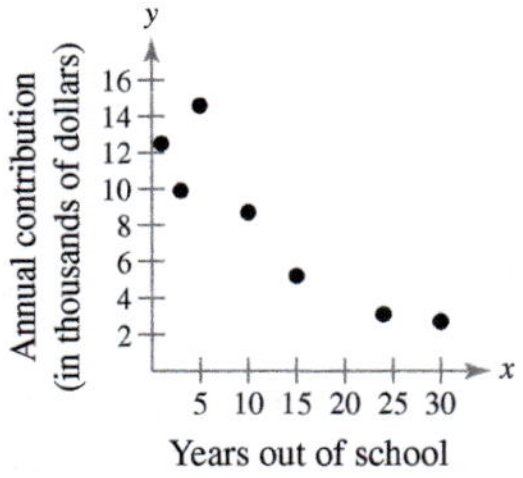

It appears that there is a negative linear correlation. As the number of years out of school increases, the annual contribution tends to decrease.

2.

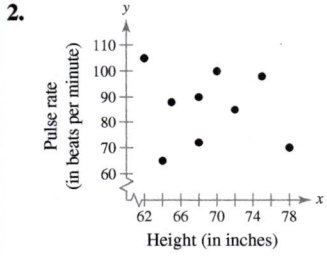

It appears that there is no linear correlation between height and pulse rate.

3.

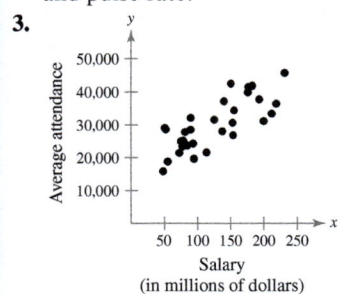

It appears that there is a positive linear correlation. As the team salary increases, the average attendance per home game tends to increase.

4. Because r is close to -1, this suggests a strong negative linear correlation. As the number of years out of school increases, the annual contribution tends to decrease.
5. 0.775; Because r is close to 1, this suggests a strong positive linear correlation. As the team salaries increase, the average attendance per home game tends to increase.
6. $|r| \approx 0.908 > 0.875$; The correlation is significant.
   There is enough evidence at the 1% level of significance to conclude that there is a significant linear correlation between the number of years out of school and the annual contribution.
7. There is enough evidence at the 1% level of significance to conclude that there is a significant linear correlation between the salaries and average attendances per home game for the teams in Major League Baseball.

Section 4.2
1. $\hat{y} = -0.380x + 12.876$
2. $\hat{y} = 108.022x + 16,586.282$
3. (1) 58.645 minutes (2) 75.120 minutes

Section 4.3
1. 0.958; About 95.8% of the variation in the times is explained. About 4.2% of the variation is unexplained.
2. 6.218
3. $477.553 < y < 1230.799$
   You can be 95% confident that when the gross domestic product is $4 trillion, the carbon dioxide emissions will be between 477.553 and 1230.799 million metric tons.

Section 4.4
1. $\hat{y} = 46.385 + 0.540x_1 - 4.897x_2$
2. (1) 90 (2) 74 (3) 81

ODD ANSWERS

Chapter 1

Section 1.1 (page 8)

1. A sample is a subset of a population.
3. A parameter is a numerical description of a population characteristic. A statistic is a numerical description of a sample characteristic.
5. False. A statistic is a numerical description of a sample characteristic.
7. True
9. False. A population is the collection of *all* outcomes, responses, measurements, or counts that are of interest.
11. Sample, because the collection of 95 shopkeepers is a subset of the population of 550 shopkeepers in the commercial complex.
13. Population, because it is a collection of the heights of each of the athlete participating in the Summer Olympics.
15. Sample, because the collection of the 10 patients is a subset of the population of 50 patients at the clinic.
17. Population, because it is a collection of all the gamers' scores in the tournament.
19. Sample, because the collection of the top 10 taxpayers is a subset within the population of the country's total tax payers.
21. Population: Parties of registered voters
    Sample: Parties of registered voters who respond to a survey
23. Population: Ages of adults in the United States who own automobiles
    Sample: Ages of adults in the United States who own Honda automobiles
25. Population: Collections of the responses of all U.S. adults
    Sample: Collection of the responses of the 1020 U.S. adults surveyed
    Sample data set: 42% of adults who said they trust their political leaders and 58% who said they did not
27. Population: Collection of the influenza immunization status of all adults in the United States
    Sample: Collection of the influenza immunization status of the 3301 U.S. adults surveyed
    Sample data set: 39% of U.S. adults who received an influenza vaccine and 61% who did not
29. Population: Collection of the average hourly billing rates of all U.S. law firms
    Sample: Collection of the average hourly billing rates for partners of the 159 U.S. law firms surveyed
    Sample data set: The average hourly billing rate for partners of 159 U.S. law firms is $604.
31. Population: Collection of the blood donations collected globally
    Sample: Collection of the 112.5 million blood donations collected globally
    Sample data set: 50% of the donors who belong to high-income countries and 50% who do not
33. Population: Collection of the 1000 mutual funds listed on a recognized stock exchange
    Sample: Collection of the 134 mutual funds of the 1000 mutual funds listed on a recognized stock exchange
    Sample data set: Best mutual funds out of the 134 mutual funds listed on a recognized stock exchange
35. Population Parameter. Forty out of 500 total students is a numerical description of the students who received a C grade.
37. Sample Statistic. The value two million is a numerical description of a sample of civilian casualties during World War II.
39. Population Parameter. The entire population of employees working in the organization has been reviewed.
41. Sample statistic. The value 80% is a numerical description of a sample of U.S. adults.
43. The statement "50% are collected from high-income countries" is an example of descriptive statistics. Using inferential statistics, you may conclude that an association exists between income and the number of blood donations in a country.
45. Answers will vary.
47. The inference may incorrectly imply that exercise increases a person's cognitive ability. The study shows a slower decline in cognitive ability, not an increase.
49. (a) The sample is the results on the standardized test by the participants in the study.
    (b) The population is the collection of all the results of the standardized test.
    (c) The statement "the closer that participants were to an optimal sleep duration target, the better they performed on a standardized test" is an example of descriptive statistics.
    (d) Individuals who obtain optimal sleep will be more likely to perform better on a standardized test than they would without optimal sleep.

Section 1.2 (page 15)

1. Nominal and ordinal
3. False. Data at the ordinal level can be qualitative or quantitative.
5. False. More types of calculations can be performed with data at the interval level than with data at the nominal level.
7. Qualitative, because breeds of horses are attributes.
9. Quantitative, because blood pressure levels are numerical measurements.
11. Qualitative, because colors are attributes.
13. Quantitative, because weight is a numerical measurement.
15. Ordinal. Data can be arranged in order, but the differences between data entries are not meaningful.

17. Nominal. No mathematical computations can be made, and data are categorized using numbers.
19. Ordinal. Data can be arranged in order, but the differences between data entries are not meaningful.
21. Horizontal: Nominal; Vertical: Ratio
23. Horizontal: Nominal; Vertical: Ratio
25. (a) Ordinal   (b) Ratio   (c) Nominal   (d) Interval
27. Quantitative. Ratio. A ratio of two data entries can be formed, so one data entry can be expressed as a multiple of another.
29. Qualitative. Ordinal. Data can be arranged in order, but the differences between data entries are not meaningful.
31. Qualitative. Ordinal. Data can be arranged in order, but the differences between data entries are not meaningful.
33. An inherent zero is a zero that implies "none." Answers will vary.

Section 1.3   (page 26)

1. In an experiment, a treatment is applied to part of a population and responses are observed. In an observational study, a researcher measures characteristics of interest of a part of a population but does not change existing conditions.
3. In a random sample, every member of the population has an equal chance of being selected. In a simple random sample, every possible sample of the same size has an equal chance of being selected.
5. False. A placebo is a fake treatment.
7. False. Using stratified sampling guarantees that members of each group within a population will be sampled.
9. False. A systematic sample is selected by ordering a population in some way and then selecting members of the population at regular intervals.
11. Observational study. The study does not apply a treatment to the adults.
13. Experiment. The study applies a treatment (different photographs) to the subjects.
15. Answers will vary.   **17.** Answers will vary.
19. (a) The experimental units are the 500 females ages 25 to 45 years old who suffer from migraine headaches. The treatment is the new drug used to treat migraine headaches.
(b) A problem with the design is that the sample is not representative of the entire population because only females ages 25 to 45 were used. To increase validity, use a stratified sample.
(c) For the experiment to be double-blind, neither the subjects nor the company would know whether the subjects are receiving the drug or the placebo.
21. *Sample answer:* Treatment group: Lewis, Dennis, Jennifer, Ronald, Edgar, Kate, Lara, William, and Raj. Control group: Alice, Edwin, Mercer, Bill, Zoya, Bertha, Ahmed, Harry, and Arthur.
A random number generator was used.
23. Cluster sampling is used because the constituency is divided into areas, and 12 areas are then entirely selected. A possible source of bias is that problems of the residents of one area might be different from that of the other area.
25. Cluster sampling is used because the disaster area is divided into grids, and 30 grids are then entirely selected. A possible source of bias is that certain grids may have been much more severely damaged than others.
27. Simple random sampling is used because each house number has an equal chance of being selected, and all samples of 1638 house numbers have an equal chance of being selected. The sample is unbiased.
29. Sampling, because the population of mobile phone purchasers is too large for their most popular model of mobile phone to be easily recorded. Random sampling would be advised because it would be easy to select mobile phone purchasers randomly and then record their most popular model of mobile phones.
31. The question is biased because it already suggests that eating whole-grain foods improves your health. The question could be rewritten as "How does eating whole-grain foods affect your health?"
33. The question is biased because it already suggests that listening to music while studying increases the chances of retention. The question could be rewritten as "Does listening to music while studying have an effect on retention?"
35. Answers will vary.
37. Open Question
Advantage: Allows respondent to express some depth and shades of meaning in the answer. Allows for new solutions to be introduced.
Disadvantage: Not easily quantified and difficult to compare surveys.
Closed Question
Advantage: Easy to analyze results.
Disadvantage: May not provide appropriate alternatives and may influence the opinion of the respondent.

Section 1.3 Activity   (page 29)

1. Answers will vary. The list contains one number at least twice.
2. The minimum is 1, the maximum is 731, and the number of samples is 8. Answers will vary.

Uses and Abuses for Chapter 1   (page 30)

1. Answers will vary.   **2.** Answers will vary.

Review Exercises for Chapter 1   (page 32)

1. Population: Collection of the responses of all U.S. adults
Sample: Collection of the responses of the 4787 U.S. adults who were sampled
Sample data set: 15% of adults who use ride-hailing applications and 85% who do not

3. Population: Collection of the responses of all U.S. adults
   Sample: Collection of the responses of the 2223 U.S. adults who were sampled
   Sample data set: 62% of adults who would encourage a child to pursue a career as a video game developer or designer and 38% who would not
5. Population parameter. The value $22.7 million is a numerical description of the total infrastructure-strengthening investments.
7. Parameter. The 12 students minoring in math is a numerical description of all physics majors at a university.
9. The statement "62% would encourage a child to pursue a career as a video game developer or designer" is an example of descriptive statistics. An inference drawn from the sample is that a majority of people encourage children to pursue a career as a video game developer or designer.
11. Quantitative, because ages are numerical measurements.
13. Quantitative, because revenues are numerical measurements.
15. Interval. The data can be ordered and meaningful differences can be calculated, but it does not make sense to say that 84 degrees is 1.05 times as hot as 80 degrees.
17. Nominal. The data are qualitative and cannot be arranged in a meaningful order.
19. Experiment. The study applies a treatment (drug to treat hypertension in patients with obstructive sleep apnea) to the subjects.
21. *Sample answer:* The subjects could be split into male and female and then be randomly assigned to each of the five treatment groups.
23. Simple random sampling is used because random telephone numbers were generated and called. A potential source of bias is that telephone sampling only samples individuals who have telephones, who are available, and who are willing to respond.
25. Cluster sampling is used because each district is considered a cluster and every pregnant woman in a selected district is surveyed. A potential source of bias is that the selected districts may not be representative of the entire area.
27. Stratified sampling is used because the population is divided by religious groups and then 50 voters are randomly selected from each religious group.
29. Answers will vary.

Quiz for Chapter 1   (page 34)

1. Population: Collection of the school performance of all Korean adolescents
   Sample: Collection of the school performance of the 359,264 Korean adolescents in the study
2. (a) Sample statistic. The value 52% is a numerical description of a sample of U.S. adults.
   (b) Population parameter. The 90% of members that approved the contract of the new president is a numerical description of all Board of Trustees members.
   (c) Sample statistic. The value 25% is a numerical description of a sample of small business owners.
3. (a) Qualitative, because debit card personal identification numbers are labels and it does not make sense to find differences between numbers.
   (b) Quantitative, because final scores are numerical measurements.
4. (a) Ordinal, because badge numbers can be ordered and often indicate seniority of service, but no meaningful mathematical computation can be performed.
   (b) Ratio, because one data entry can be expressed as a multiple of another.
   (c) Ordinal, because data can be arranged in order, but the differences between data entries make no sense.
   (d) Interval, because meaningful differences between entries can be calculated but a zero entry is not an inherent zero.
5. (a) Observational study. The study does not attempt to influence the responses of the subjects and there is no treatment.
   (b) Experiment. The study applies a treatment (multivitamin) to the subjects.
6. Randomized block design
7. (a) Convenience sampling, because all of the people sampled are in one convenient location.
   (b) Systematic sampling, because every tenth machine part is sampled.
   (c) Stratified sampling, because the population is first stratified and then a sample is collected from each stratum.
8. Convenience sampling. People at campgrounds may be strongly against air pollution because they are at an outdoor location.

Real Statistics—Real Decisions for Chapter 1   (page 36)

1. (a)–(b) Answers will vary.
   (c) *Sample answer:* Use surveys.
   (d) *Sample answer:* You may take too large a percentage of your sample from a subgroup of the population that is relatively small.
2. (a) *Sample answer:* Qualitative, because questions will ask for demographics and the sample questions have nonnumerical categories.
   (b) *Sample answer:* Nominal and ordinal, because the results can be put in categories and the categories can be ranked.
   (c) Sample   (d) Statistics
3. (a) *Sample answer:* Sample includes only members of the population with access to the Internet.
   (b) Answers will vary.

Chapter 2

Section 2.1 (page 41)

1. Organizing the data into a frequency distribution may make patterns within the data more evident. Sometimes it is easier to identify patterns of a data set by looking at a graph of the frequency distribution.
3. Class limits determine which numbers can belong to each class. Class boundaries are the numbers that separate classes without forming gaps between them.
5. The sum of the relative frequencies must be 1 or 100% because it is the sum of all portions or percentages of the data.
7. False. Class width is the difference between lower or upper limits of consecutive classes.
9. False. An ogive is a graph that displays cumulative frequencies.
11. Class width = 8; Lower class limits: 9, 17, 25, 33, 41, 49, 57; Upper class limits: 16, 24, 32, 40, 48, 56, 64
13. Class width = 15; Lower class limits: 17, 32, 47, 62, 77, 92, 107, 122; Upper class limits: 31, 46, 61, 76, 91, 106, 121, 136
15. (a) 11
    (b) and (c)

Class	Midpoint	Class boundaries
0–10	5	−0.5–10.5
11–21	16	10.5–21.5
22–32	27	21.5–32.5
33–43	38	32.5–43.5
44–54	49	43.5–54.5
55–65	60	54.5–65.5
66–76	71	65.5–76.5

17.

Class	Frequency, f	Midpoint	Relative frequency	Cumulative frequency
0–10	188	5	0.15	188
11–21	372	16	0.30	560
22–32	264	27	0.22	824
33–43	205	38	0.17	1029
44–54	83	49	0.07	1112
55–65	76	60	0.06	1188
66–76	32	71	0.03	1220
	$\Sigma f = 1220$		$\Sigma \dfrac{f}{n} = 1$	

19. (a) 7
    (b) Greatest frequency: about 300
        Least frequency: about 10
    (c) 10
    (d) *Sample answer:* About half of the employee salaries are between $50,000 and $69,000.
21. Class with greatest frequency: 506–510
    Classes with least frequency: 474–478
23. (a) Class with greatest relative frequency: 35–36 centimeters
        Class with least relative frequency: 39–40 centimeters
    (b) Greatest relative frequency ≈ 0.25
        Least relative frequency ≈ 0.01
    (c) *Sample answer:* From the graph, 0.25 or 25% of females have a fibula length between 35 and 36 centimeters.
25. (a) 75   (b) 158.5–201.5 pounds
27. (a) 47   (b) 287.5 pounds   (c) 40   (d) 6
29.

Class	Frequency, f	Midpoint	Relative frequency	Cumulative frequency
8–12	5	10	0.22	5
13–17	8	15	0.33	13
18–22	8	20	0.33	21
23–27	2	25	0.08	23
28–32	1	30	0.04	24
	$\Sigma f = 24$		$\Sigma \left(\dfrac{f}{n}\right) = 1$	

Classes with greatest frequency: 13–17, 18–22
Class with least frequency: 28–32

31.

Class	Frequency, f	Midpoint	Relative frequency	Cumulative frequency
985–1288	3	1136.5	0.1429	3
1289–1592	6	1440.5	0.2857	9
1593–1896	2	1744.5	0.0952	11
1897–2200	4	2048.5	0.1905	15
2201–2504	2	2352.5	0.0952	17
2505–2808	4	2656.5	0.1905	21
	$\Sigma f = 21$		$\Sigma \left(\dfrac{f}{n}\right) = 1$	

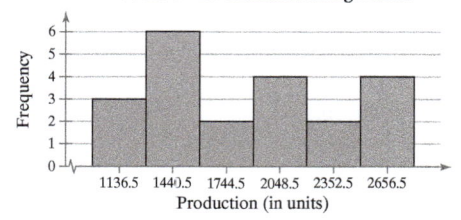

Sample answer: The graph shows that the production is evenly distributed between 1745 units to 2657 units.

33.

Class	Frequency, f	Mid-point	Relative frequency	Cumulative frequency
2–4	9	3	0.31	9
5–7	10	6	0.33	19
8–10	4	9	0.13	23
11–13	1	12	0.03	24
14–16	3	15	0.10	27
17–19	2	18	0.07	29
20–22	0	21	0.00	29
23–25	1	24	0.03	30
	$\Sigma f = 30$		$\Sigma \left(\dfrac{f}{n}\right) = 1$	

Response Times for Males

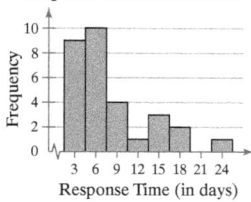

Sample answer: The graph shows that the response time is evenly distributed between 9 to 18 days or 2 to 7 days.

35.

Class	Frequency, f	Midpoint	Relative frequency	Cumulative frequency
42–46	4	44	0.0889	4
47–51	11	49	0.2444	15
52–56	14	54	0.3111	29
57–61	9	59	0.2000	38
62–66	4	64	0.0889	42
67–71	3	69	0.0667	45
	$\Sigma f = 45$		$\Sigma \dfrac{f}{n} = 1$	

Ages of U.S. Presidents at Inauguration

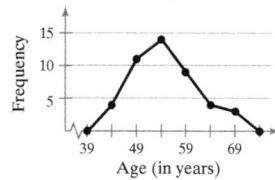

Sample answer: The graph shows that the number of U.S. presidents who were 52 or older at inauguration was twice as many as those who were 51 and younger.

37.

Class	Frequency, f	Midpoint	Relative frequency	Cumulative frequency
1–2	7	1.5	0.19	7
3–4	6	3.5	0.17	13
5–6	14	5.5	0.39	27
7–8	4	7.5	0.11	31
9–10	5	9.5	0.14	36
	$\Sigma f = 36$		$\Sigma \left(\dfrac{f}{n}\right) = 1$	

Taste Test Ratings

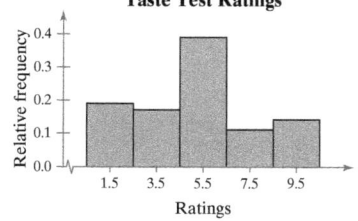

Class with greatest relative frequency: 5–6
Class with least relative frequency: 7–8

39.

Class	Frequency, f	Midpoint	Relative frequency	Cumulative frequency
401–420	10	410.5	0.36	10
421–440	5	430.5	0.18	15
441–460	4	450.5	0.14	19
461–480	5	470.5	0.18	24
481–500	4	490.5	0.14	28
	$\Sigma f = 28$		$\Sigma \left(\dfrac{f}{n}\right) = 1$	

Weights of Polar Bears

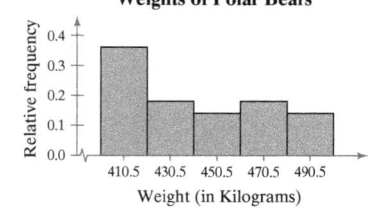

Class with greatest relative frequency: 401–420
Classes with least relative frequency: 441–460 and 481–500

41.

Class	Frequency, f	Midpoint	Relative frequency	Cumulative frequency
49–54	4	51.5	0.11	4
55–60	12	57.5	0.34	16
61–66	8	63.5	0.23	24
67–72	6	69.5	0.17	30
73–78	3	75.5	0.09	33
79–84	2	81.5	0.06	35
	$\Sigma f = 35$		$\Sigma\left(\dfrac{f}{n}\right) = 1$	

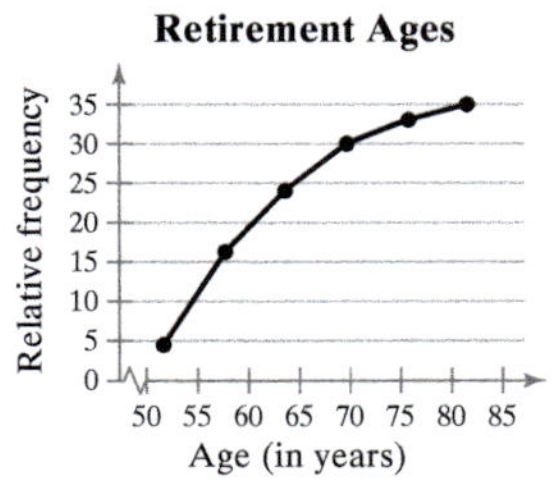

Retirement Ages

Location of the greatest increase in frequency: 55–60

43. (a)

Class	Frequency, f	Midpoint	Relative frequency	Cumulative frequency
2–6	5	4	0.2083	5
7–11	10	9	0.4167	15
12–16	6	14	0.2500	21
17–21	2	19	0.0833	23
22–26	0	24	0.0000	23
27–31	1	29	0.0417	24
	$\Sigma f = 24$		$\Sigma\left(\dfrac{f}{n}\right) = 1$	

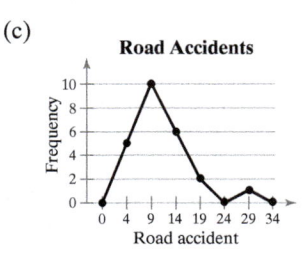

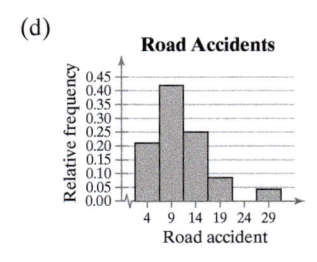

(b) Road Accidents (c) Road Accidents (d) Road Accidents (e) Road Accidents

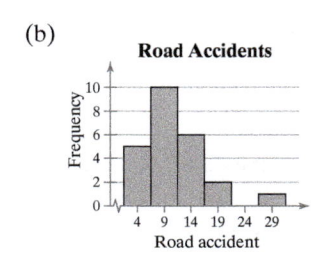

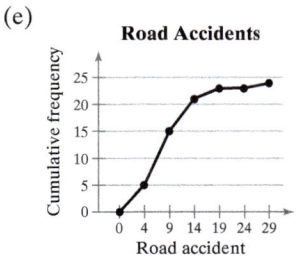

45. (a) Daily Withdrawals

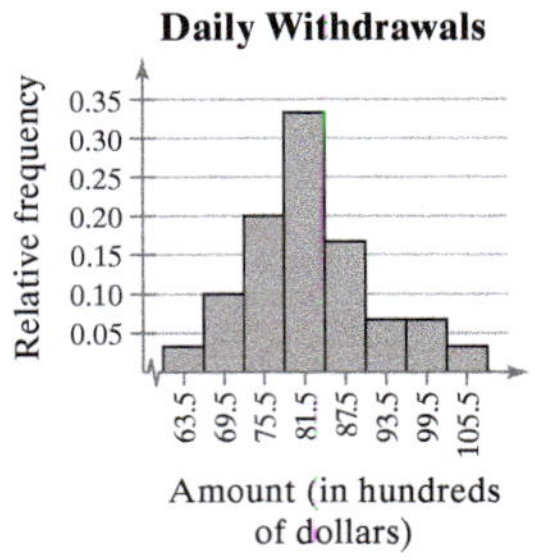

(b) 16.7%, because the sum of the relative frequencies for the last three classes is 0.167.

(c) $9700, because the sum of the relative frequencies for the last two classes is 0.10.

47. Histogram (5 Classes) Histogram (10 Classes) Histogram (20 Classes)

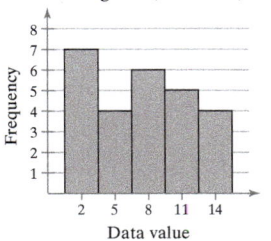

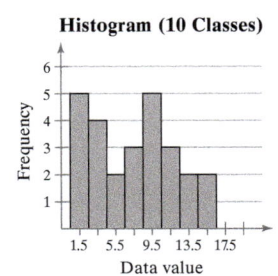

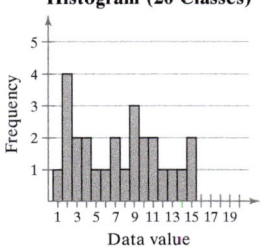

In general, a greater number of classes better preserves the actual values of the data set but is not as helpful for observing general trends and making conclusions. In choosing the number of classes, an important consideration is the size of the data set. For instance, you would not want to use 20 classes if your data set contained 20 entries. In this particular example, as the number of classes increases, the histogram shows more fluctuation. The histograms with 10 and 20 classes have classes with zero frequencies. Not much is gained by using more than five classes. Therefore, it appears that five classes would be best.

Section 2.2   (page 64)

1. Quantitative: stem-and-leaf plot, dot plot, histogram, scatter plot, time series chart
   Qualitative: pie chart, Pareto chart
3. Both the stem-and-leaf plot and the dot plot allow you to see how data are distributed, to determine specific data entries, and to identify unusual data values.
5. b   6. d   7. a   8. c
9. 27, 32, 41, 43, 43, 44, 47, 47, 48, 50, 51, 51, 52, 53, 53, 53, 54, 54, 54, 54, 55, 56, 56, 58, 59, 68, 68, 68, 73, 78, 78, 85
   Max: 85; Min: 27

11. 13, 13, 14, 14, 14, 15, 15, 15, 15, 15, 16, 17, 17, 18, 19
Max: 19; Min: 13

13. *Sample answer:* Facebook has the most users, and Pinterest has the least. Tumblr and Instagram have about the same number of users.

15. *Sample answer:* The Texter is the least popular driver. The Left-Lane Hog is tolerated more than the Tailgater. The Speedster and the Drifter have the same popularity.

17. Humidity (in percentages)

18	6	Key: 18|6 = 18.6
19	2 4 6 6 9	
20	1 5 8 8 8	
21	0 3 4 5 6 8	
22	5 6 8	

Sample answer: Most of the days had a humidity level of 19.9% to 21.8%.

19. Runs scored

7	0 0 1 3 3 5 5 7 8 8 9	Key: 7|0 = 70
8	1 2 5 6 7 8	
9	0 0 1 1 4 8 9	

Sample answer: Most runs scored by the batsman were in the 70s.

21. Incomes (in millions) of Highest Paid Tech CEOs

1	3 3 4 4 4 5 5 6 7	Key: 1|3 = 13T
	8 9 9 9 9	
2	0 0 0 0 2 2 5 5 5	
	8 8	
3	2 3 3	
4	1 1	

Sample Answer: Most of the highest-paid tech CEOs have an income of $13 million to $22 million.

23.

Sample answer: Blood glucose level tends to be between 94 and 101 milligrams per deciliter.

25. Student Loan Borrowers by Balance Owed in Fourth Quarter 2015

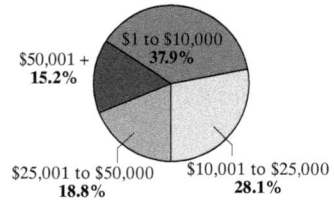

$1 to $10,000: 37.9%
$10,001 to $25,000: 28.1%
$25,001 to $50,000: 18.8%
$50,001+: 15.2%

Sample answer: The majority of student loan borrowers owe $25,000 or less.

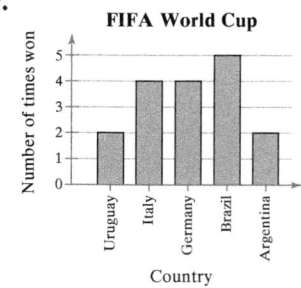

27. FIFA World Cup

Sample answer: Brazil won the FIFA World Cup the most number of times out of the five countries and Uruguay and Argentina won the least number of times.

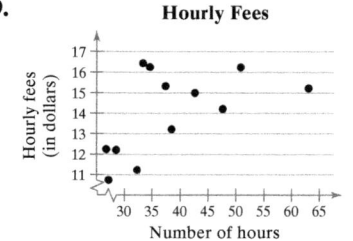

29. Hourly Fees

Sample answer: It appears that there is a slight positive relation between fees and hours of coaching.

31. Engineering Degrees

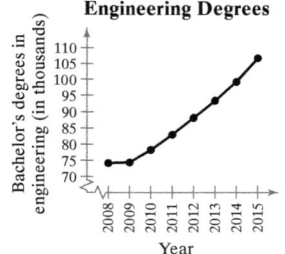

Sample answer: The number of bachelor's degrees in engineering conferred in the U.S. has increased from 2008 to 2015.

33. Heights (in inches)

7	2 2 4	Key: 7|2 = 72
7	5 5 5 5 6	
8	1 1 2 2 2 4	
8		

The dot plot helps you see that the data are clustered from 72 to 76 and 81 to 84, with 75 being the most frequent value. The stem-and-leaf plot helps you see that most values are 75 or greater.

35. Favorite Season of U.S. Adults Ages 18 and Older

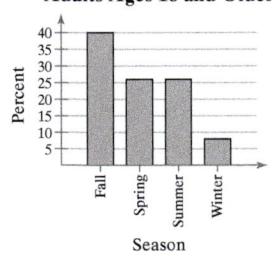

The pie chart helps you to see the percentages as parts of a whole, with fall being the largest. It also shows that while fall is the largest percentage, it makes up less than half of the pie chart. That means that a majority of U.S. adults ages 18 and older prefer a season other than fall. This means it would not be a fair statement to say that most U.S. adults ages 18 and older prefer fall. The Pareto chart helps you to see the rankings of the seasons.

37. (a) The graph is misleading because the large gap from 0 to 90 makes it appear that the sales for the 3rd quarter are disproportionately larger than the other quarters.
(b) Sales for Company A

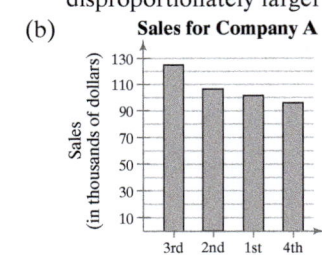

39. (a) The graph is misleading because the angle makes it appear as though the 3rd quarter had a larger percent of sales than the others, when the 1st and 3rd quarters have the same percent.
(b) Sales for Company B

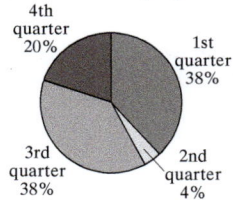

41. (a) At Law Firm A, the lowest salary was $90,000 and the highest salary was $203,000. At Law Firm B, the lowest salary was $90,000 and the highest salary was $190,000. There are 30 lawyers at Law Firm A and 32 lawyers at Law Firm B.
(b) At Law Firm A, the salaries are clustered at the far ends of the distribution range. At Law Firm B, the salaries are spread out.

43. (a) 2 | 6   Key: 2|6 = 26
       3 | 1
       4 | 0 4 4 5 6 7 9 9
       5 | 5 5 5
       6 | 3 4 4
       7 | 0 1 2 2

(b) dot plot from 25 to 70

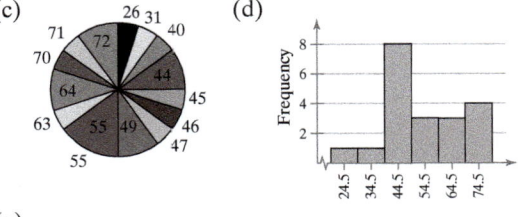

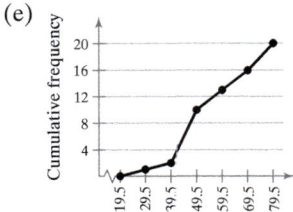

(c) pie chart with values 26, 31, 40, 44, 45, 46, 47, 55, 49, 55, 63, 64, 72, 71, 70

(d) frequency histogram

(e) cumulative frequency ogive

Sample answer: The stem-and-leaf plot, dot plot, frequency histogram, and ogive display the data best because the data is quantitative.

Section 2.3 (page 76)

1. True **3.** True **5.** *Sample answer:* 1, 2, 2, 2, 3
7. *Sample answer:* 2, 5, 7, 9, 35
9. The shape of the distribution is skewed right because the bars have a "tail" to the right.
11. The shape of the distribution is uniform because the bars are approximately the same height.
13. (11), because the distribution of values ranges from 1 to 12 and has (approximately) equal frequencies.
14. (9), because the distribution has values in the thousands and is skewed right due to the few vehicles that have much higher mileages than the majority of the vehicles.
15. (12), because the distribution has a maximum value of 90 and is skewed left due to a few students scoring much lower than the majority of the students.
16. (10), because the distribution is approximately symmetric and the weights range from 80 to 160 pounds.
17. $\bar{x} \approx 24.8$; median $= 24.5$; mode $= 24, 26$
19. $\bar{x} \approx 37.52$; median $= 34$; mode $= 28$; The mode does not represent the center of the data set because they are small values compared to the rest of the data.
21. $\bar{x} \approx 49.8$; median $= 50.5$; mode $= 51$
23. $\bar{x} \approx 7.4$; median $= 6$; mode $= 6$
25. $\bar{x} = 14.3$; median $= 9$; mode $=$ none; The mode cannot be found because no data entry is repeated. The mean does not represent the center of the data set because it is influenced by the outlier of 42.

27. $\bar{x}$ is not possible; median is not possible; mode = "Search and buy online"; The mean and median cannot be found because the data are at the nominal level of measurement.
29. $\bar{x}$ is not possible; median is not possible; mode = "Junior"; The mean and median cannot be found because the data are at the nominal level of measurement.
31. $\bar{x} \approx 29.2$; median = 30.5; mode = 23, 34
33. $\bar{x} \approx 19.5$; median = 20; mode = 15
35. Cluster around 275–425
37. Mode, because the data are at the nominal level of measurement.
39. Mean, because the distribution is symmetric and there are no outliers.
41. 79 **43.** $612.73 **45.** 84 **47.** 81.5
49. 26.178 kilometers per hour **51.** 37.02 years old
53.

Class	Midpoint, x	Frequency, f
127–161	144	7
162–196	179	6
197–231	214	3
232–266	249	3
267–301	284	1

Hospital Beds

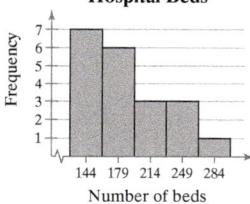

[Histogram with bars at midpoints 144, 179, 214, 249, 284 showing frequencies 7, 6, 3, 3, 1]

Positively skewed

55.

Class	Midpoint, x	Frequency, f
40–45	42.5	7
46–51	48.5	10
52–57	54.5	4
58–63	60.5	4
64–69	66.5	5

Weights of Females

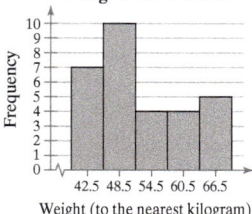

[Histogram with bars at midpoints 42.5, 48.5, 54.5, 60.5, 66.5 showing frequencies 7, 10, 4, 4, 5]

Positively skewed

57. (a) $\bar{x} \approx 20$, median = 20.3
(b) $\bar{x} \approx 19.875$, median = 20.1
(c) Median

59. The data are skewed right.
A = mode, because it is the data entry that occurred most often.
B = median, because the median is to the left of the mean in a skewed right distribution.
C = mean, because the mean is to the right of the median in a skewed right distribution.

61. Increase one of the three-credit B classes to an A. The three-credit class is weighted more than the two-credit classes, so it will have a greater effect on the grade point average.

63. (a) Mean, because Car A has the highest mean of the three.
(b) Median, because Car B has the highest median of the three.
(c) Mode, because Car C has the highest mode of the three.

65. (a) $\bar{x} \approx 49.2$; median = 46.5
(b) **Test Scores**

```
1 | 1 3      Key: 3|6 = 36
2 | 2 8
3 | 6 6 6 7 7 7 8
4 | 1 3 4 6 7 ——— mean
5 | 1 1 1 3
6 | 1 2 3 4      median
7 | 2 2 4 6
8 | 5
9 | 0
```

(c) Positively skewed

Section 2.3 Activity (page 83)

1. The distribution is symmetric. The mean and median both decrease slightly. Over time, the median will decrease dramatically and the mean will also decrease, but to a lesser degree.

2. Neither the mean nor the median can be any of the points that were plotted. Because there are 10 points in each region, the mean will fall somewhere between the two regions. By the same logic, the median will be the average of the greatest point between 0 and 0.75 and the least point between 20 and 25.

Section 2.4 (page 95)

1. The range is the difference between the maximum and minimum values of a data set. The advantage of the range is that it is easy to calculate. The disadvantage is that it uses only two entries from the data set.

3. The units of variance are squared. Its units are meaningless (example: dollars^2). The units of standard deviation are the same as the data.

5. When calculating the population standard deviation, you divide the sum of the squared deviations by N, then take the square root of that value. When calculating the sample standard deviation, you divide the sum of the squared deviations by $n - 1$, then take the square root of that value.

7. Similarity: Both estimate proportions of the data contained within k standard deviations of the mean.
   Difference: The Empirical Rule assumes the distribution is approximately symmetric and bell-shaped and Chebychev's Theorem makes no such assumption.
9. Approximately 35, or $35,000
11. (a) 67.8   (b) 130.8
13. Range = 13; $\mu \approx 5.83$; $\sigma^2 \approx 16.36$; $\sigma \approx 4.04$
15. Range = 8; $\bar{x} = 18$; $s^2 \approx 4.7$; $s \approx 2.2$
17. The data set in (a) has a standard deviation of 2.4 and the data set in (b) has a standard deviation of 5 because the data in (b) have more variability.
19. Company A; An offer of $36,000 is within two standard deviations from the mean of Company A's starting salaries, which makes it likely. The same offer is three standard deviations of the mean of Company B's starting salaries, which makes the offer unlikely.
21. (a) Greatest sample standard deviation: (ii)
       Data set (ii) has more entries that are farther away from the mean.
       Least sample standard deviation: (iii)
       Data set (iii) has more entries that are close to the mean.
    (b) The three data sets have the same mean, median, and mode, but have a different standard deviation.
    (c) Estimates will vary; (i) $s \approx 1.1$; (ii) $s \approx 1.3$; (iii) $s \approx 0.8$
23. (a) Greatest sample standard deviation: (i)
       Data set (i) has more entries that are farther away from the mean.
       Least sample standard deviation: (iii)
       Data set (iii) has more entries that are close to the mean.
    (b) The three data sets have the same mean, median, and mode, but have a different standard deviation.
    (c) Estimates will vary; (i) $s \approx 9.6$; (ii) $s \approx 9.0$; (iii) $s \approx 5.1$
25. Sample answer: 3, 3, 3, 7, 7, 7
27. Sample answer: 12, 12, 12, 12, 12
29. 68%   31. (a) 51   (b) 17
33. 78, 76, and 82 are unusual; 82 is very unusual because it is more than 3 standard deviations from the mean.
35. 53
37. At least 75% of the student heights are from 117 to 133 centimeters.
39.

x	f	xf	$x - \bar{x}$	$(x - \bar{x})^2$	$(x - \bar{x})^2 f$
0	10	0	−3.08	9.4864	94.864
1	12	12	−2.08	4.3264	51.9168
2	9	18	−1.08	1.1664	10.4976
3	2	6	−0.08	0.0064	0.0128
4	2	8	0.92	0.8464	1.6928
5	3	15	1.92	3.6864	11.0592
6	1	6	2.92	8.5264	8.5264
7	4	28	3.92	15.3664	61.4656
8	2	16	4.92	24.2064	48.4128
9	5	45	5.92	35.0464	175.232
	$n = 50$	$\Sigma xf = 154$			$\Sigma(x - \bar{x})^2 f = 463.38$

$\bar{x} \approx 3.08$, $s \approx 3.076$

41.

Class	x	f	xf
15,000–17,499	16,249.5	9	146,245.5
17,500–19,999	18,749.5	10	187,495
20,000–22,499	21,249.5	16	339,992
22,500–24,999	23,749.5	11	261,244.5
25,000 or more	26,249.5	6	157,497
		$n = 52$	$\Sigma xf = 1,092,474$

$x - \bar{x}$	$(x - \bar{x})^2$	$(x - \bar{x})^2 f$
−4759.62	22,653,982.54	203,885,842.9
−2259.62	5,105,882.54	51,058,825.4
240.38	57,782.54	924,520.64
2740.38	7,509,682.54	82,606,507.94
5240.38	27,461,582.54	164,769,495.20
		$\Sigma(x - \bar{x})^2 f = 503,245,192.1$

$\bar{x} \approx \$21,009.12$; $s \approx \$3141.27$

43.

x	f	xf	$x - \bar{x}$	$(x - \bar{x})^2$	$(x - \bar{x})^2 f$
1	2	2	−1.9	3.61	7.22
2	18	36	−0.9	0.81	14.58
3	24	72	0.1	0.01	0.24
4	16	64	1.1	1.21	19.36
	$n = 60$	$\Sigma xf = 174$			$\Sigma(x - \bar{x})^2 f = 41.4$

$\bar{x} \approx 2.9$; $s \approx 0.8$

45. $CV_{\text{Denver}} \approx 9.7\%$, $CV_{\text{LA}} \approx 8.8\%$
    Salaries for entry level architects are more variable in Denver than in Los Angeles.
47. $CV_{\text{ages}} \approx 13.3\%$, $CV_{\text{heights}} \approx 3.5\%$
    Ages are more variable than heights for all members of the 2016 Women's U.S. Olympic swimming team.
49. $CV_{\text{males}} \approx 6.81\%$, $CV_{\text{females}} \approx 3.84\%$
    Weights are more variable for males than for females.
51. (a) Answers will vary.   (b) $s \approx 2.2$
    (c) They are the same.
53. (a) $\bar{x} \approx 42.1$; $s \approx 5.6$ (b) $\bar{x} \approx 44.3$; $s \approx 5.9$
    (c) 3.5, 3, 3, 4, 4, 2.75, 4.25, 3.25, 3.25, 3.5, 3.25, 3.75, 3.5, 4.17
    $\bar{x} \approx 3.5$; $s \approx 0.47$
    (d) When each entry is multiplied by a constant k, the new sample mean is $k \cdot x$, and the new sample standard deviation is $k \cdot s$.
55. (a) $P \approx -2.61$
       The data are skewed left.
    (b) $P \approx 4.12$
       The data are skewed right.
    (c) $P = 0$
       The data are symmetric.
    (d) $P = 1$
       The data are skewed right.
    (e) $P = -3$
       The data are skewed left.

Section 2.4 Activity (page 102)

1. When a point with a value of 15 is added, the mean remains constant or changes very little, and the standard deviation decreases. When a point with a value of 20 is added, the mean is raised and the standard deviation increases.
2. To get the largest standard deviation, plot four of the points at 30 and four of the points at 40.
   To get the smallest standard deviation, plot all of the points at the same number. That way, each $x - \bar{x}$ is 0, so the standard deviation will be 0.

Section 2.5 (page 111)

1. The talk is longer in length than 75% of the lectures in the series.
3. The student scored higher than 89% of the students who took the Fundamentals of Engineering exam.
5. The interquartile range of a data set can be used to identify outliers because data entries that are greater than $Q_3 + 1.5(\text{IQR})$ or less than $Q_1 - 1.5(\text{IQR})$ are considered outliers.
7. True
9. False; An outlier is any number above $Q_3 + 1.5(\text{IQR})$ or below $Q_1 - 1.5(\text{IQR})$.
11. (a) $Q_1 = 41, Q_2 = 46, Q_3 = 48$ (b) IQR = 7   (c) 65
13. Min = 0, $Q_1 = 2, Q_2 = 5, Q_3 = 8$, Max = 10
15. (a) Min = 45, $Q_1 = 52, Q_2 = 49, Q_3 = 65$, Max = 79
    (b) 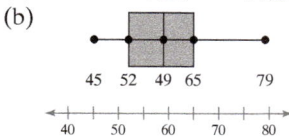
17. (a) Min = 1, $Q_1 = 4.5, Q_2 = 6, Q_3 = 7.5$, Max = 9
    (b) 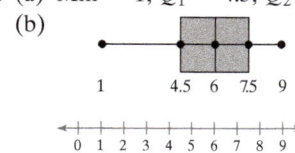
19. None. The data are not skewed or symmetric.
21. Skewed left. Most of the data lie to the right on the box plot.
23. Extra Classes
25. Hours Worked in a Month
27. (a) 2 hours   (b) 50%   (c) 75%
29. About 158; About 70% of quantitative reasoning scores on the Graduate Record Examination are less than 158.
31. About 8th percentile; About 8% of quantitative reasoning scores on the Graduate Record Examination are less that 140.
33. 40th percentile
35. 28, 35, 38, 40, 41, 41, 42, 43, 43, 43, 44, 45, 47, 47, 48, 50, 50, 50, 53, 54, and 54.
37. **Depatment of Motor Vehicles Wait Times**
39. About 85th percentile
41. $A \rightarrow z = -1.43$
    $B \rightarrow z = 0$
    $C \rightarrow z = 2.14$
    A z-score of 2.14 would be unusual.
43. Not unusual; The z-score is 0.94, so the age of 31 is about 0.94 standard deviation above the mean.
45. Not unusual; The z-score is -0.27, so the age of 27 is about 0.27 standard deviation below the mean.
47. Unusual; The z-score is -2.39, so the age of 20 is about 2.39 standard deviations below the mean.
49. (a) For 1250, $z = 2.5$; For 1175, $z = 1.75$;
       For 950, $z = -0.5$
       The lady bug with a life span of 1250 days has an unusually long life span.
    (b) For 1150, about 93rd percentile;
       For 910, about 18th percentile;
       For 845, about 6th percentile
51. Robert Duvall: $z \approx 1.07$; Jack Nicholson: $z \approx -0.32$; The age of Robert Duvall was about 1 standard deviation above the mean age of Best Actor winners, and the age of Jack Nicholson was less than 1 standard deviation below the mean age of Best Supporting Actor winners. Neither actor's age is unusual.
53. John Wayne: $z \approx 2.10$; Gig Young: $z \approx 0.41$; The age of John Wayne was more than 2 standard deviations above the mean age of Best Actor winners, which is unusual. The age of Gig Young was less than 1 standard deviation above the mean age of Best Supporting Actor winners, which is not unusual.
55. 5
57. (a) The distribution of Concert 1 is symmetric. The distribution of Concert 2 is skewed right. Concert 1 has less variation.
    (b) Concert 2 is more likely to have outliers because it has more variation.
    (c) Concert 1, because 68% of the data should be between ± 16.3 of the mean.
    (d) No, you do not know the number of songs played at either concert or the actual lengths of the songs.

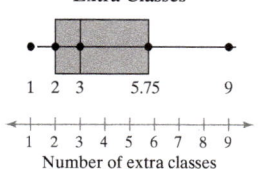

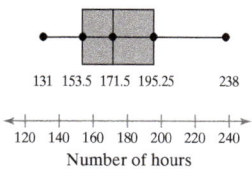

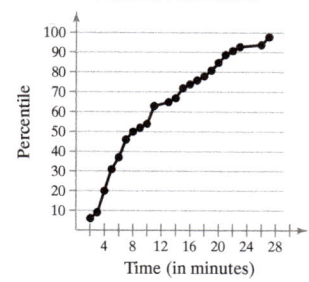

59. (a) 24, 2 (b)

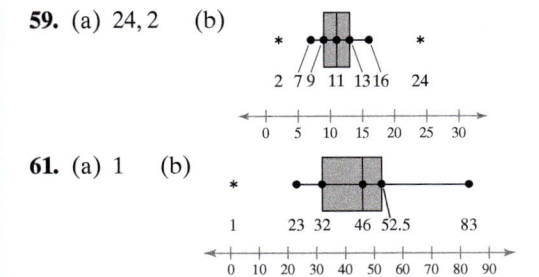

61. (a) 1 (b)

63. Answers will vary.

Uses and Abuses for Chapter 2 (page 116)

1. Answers will vary.
2. No, it is not ethical because it misleads the consumer to believe that drinking red wine is more effective at preventing heart disease than it may actually be.

Review Exercises for Chapter 2 (page 118)

1.

Class	Midpoint	Class boundaries
26–31	28.5	25.5–31.5
32–37	34.5	31.5–37.5
38–43	40.5	37.5–43.5
44–49	46.5	43.5–49.5
50–55	52.5	49.5–55.5

Frequency, f	Relative frequency	Cumulative frequency
5	0.25	5
4	0.20	9
6	0.30	15
3	0.15	18
2	0.10	20
$\Sigma f = 20$	$\Sigma \frac{f}{n} = 1$	

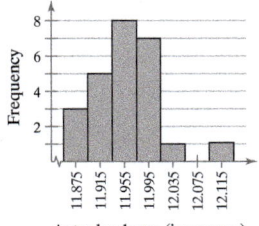

3. Liquid Volume 12-oz Cans

5.

Class	Midpoint	Frequency, f
79–93	86	9
94–108	101	12
109–123	116	5
124–138	131	4
139–153	146	2
154–168	161	1
		$\Sigma f = 33$

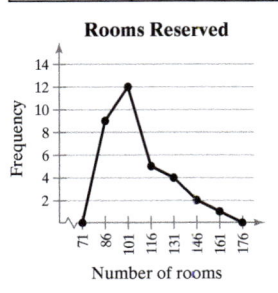

Rooms Reserved

7. Pollution Indices of U.S. Cities

```
2 | 2 3 8 8        Key: 2|2 = 22
3 | 2 3 6 8 8 9 9
4 | 1 1 3 6 9
5 | 0 3 4 6 7
6 | 3 5 5
```

Sample answer: Most U.S. cities have a pollution index from 32 to 57.

9. College Students' Activities and Time Use

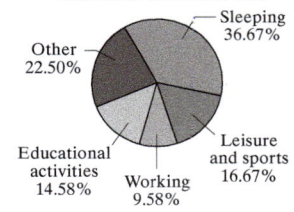

Sleeping 36.67%, Other 22.50%, Educational activities 14.58%, Working 9.58%, Leisure and sports 16.67%

Sample answer: Full-time university and college students spend the least amount of time working.

11. Heights of Buildings

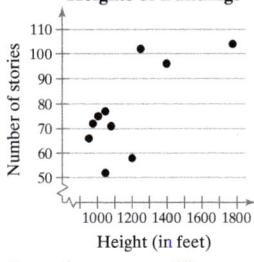

Sample answer: The number of stories appears to increase with height.

13. $\bar{x} = 29.5$; median $= 29.5$; mode $= 29.5$
15. 82.45   **17.** 38.4   **19.** Skewed right   **21.** Skewed right
23. Mean; When a distribution is skewed right, the mean is to the right of the median.
25. Range $= 8$; $\mu \approx 81$; $\sigma^2 \approx 5.92$; $\sigma \approx 2.43$
27. Range $= \$1262$; $\bar{x} \approx \$1106.27$; $s^2 \approx 182714.35$; $s \approx \$427.45$

29. $13 and $23   **31.** 15 students
33. $\bar{x} \approx 2.5$; $s \approx 1.2$
35. $CV_A \approx 28.96\%$; $CV_B \approx 20.2\%$
Dividends are more variable for Company A than Company B.
37. Min $= 16$, $Q_1 = 25$, $Q_2 = 35$, $Q_3 = 56$, Max $= 136$
39. Model 2017 Vehicle Fuel Economies

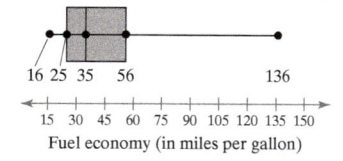

41. 7 inches   **43.** 85%
45. Not unusual; The z-score is 1.97, so a towing capacity of 16,500 pounds is about 1.97 standard deviations above the mean.
47. Unusual; The z-score is 2.60, so a towing capacity of 18,000 pounds is about 2.60 standard deviations above the mean.

Quiz for Chapter 2   (page 122)

1. (a)

Class	Midpoint	Class boundaries
101–112	106.5	100.5–112.5
113–124	118.5	112.5–124.5
125–136	130.5	124.5–136.5
137–148	142.5	136.5–148.5
149–160	154.5	148.5–160.5

Frequency, f	Relative frequency	Cumulative frequency
3	0.11	3
11	0.41	14
8	0.30	22
3	0.11	25
2	0.07	27

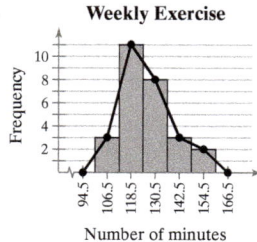

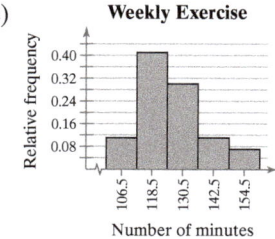

(b) Weekly Exercise

(c) Weekly Exercise

(d) Skewed right

(e) Weekly Exercise

(f) Weekly Exercise (in minutes)

```
10 | 1 8         Key: 10|8 = 108
11 | 1 4 6 7 8 9 9
12 | 0 0 3 3 4 7 7 8
13 | 0 1 1 2 5 9 9
14 | 2
15 | 0 7
```

(g) Weekly Exercise

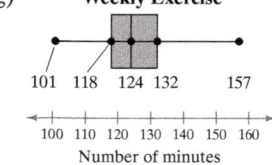

2. $\bar{x} \approx 126.1$; $s \approx 13.0$

3. (a) Elements with Known Properties

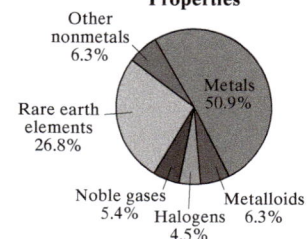

(b) Elements with Known Properties

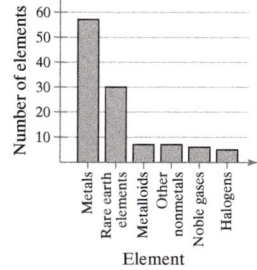

4. (a) $\bar{x} \approx 1016.4$; median $= 1019$; mode $= 1100$; The mean or median best describes a typical salary because there are no outliers.
(b) Range $= 666$; $s^2 \approx 47{,}120.9$; $s \approx 217.1$
(c) $CV \approx 21.4\%$

5. $150,000 and $210,000

6. (a) Unusual; The z-score is 3, so a new home price of $225,000 is about 3 standard deviations above the mean.
   (b) Unusual; The z-score is −6.67, so a new home price of $80,000 is about 6.67 standard deviations below the mean.
   (c) Not unusual; The z-score is 1.33, so a new home price of $200,000 is about 1.33 standard deviations above the mean.
   (d) Unusual; The z-score is −2.2, so a new home price of $147,000 is about 2.2 standard deviations below the mean.

7. **Wins for Each MLB Team**

   59, 71, 82.5, 89, 103
   Number of wins

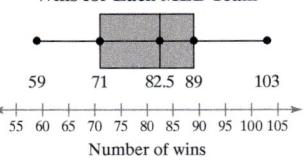

Real Statistics—Real Decisions for Chapter 2 (page 124)

1. (a) Find the average cost of renting an apartment for each area and do a comparison.
   (b) The mean would best represent the data sets for the four areas of the city.
   (c) Area A: $\bar{x} = \$1131.58$
       Area B: $\bar{x} = \$998.33$
       Area C: $\bar{x} = \$991.58$
       Area D: $\bar{x} = \$1064.17$

2. (a) Construct a Pareto chart, because the data are quantitative and a Pareto chart positions data in order of decreasing height, with the tallest bar positioned at the left.
   (b) **Cost of Monthly Rent per Area**
   (c) Yes. From the Pareto chart, you can see that Area A has the highest average cost of monthly rent, followed by Area D, Area B, and Area C.

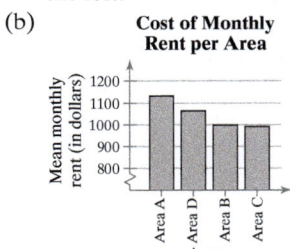

3. *Sample answer:*
   (a) You could use the range and sample standard deviation for each area.
   (b)
Area A	Area B
range = $467	range = $474
$s \approx \$138.45$	$s \approx \$163.11$

Area C	Area D
range = $518	range = $560
$s \approx \$164.51$	$s \approx \$156.26$

   (c) No. Area A has the lowest range and standard deviation, so the rents in Areas B–D are more spread out. There could be one or two inexpensive rents that lower the means for these areas. It is possible that the population means of Areas B–D are close to the populations mean of Area A.

4. (a) Answers will vary.
   (b) Location, weather, population

Cumulative Review for Chapters 1–2 (page 128)

1. Systematic sampling is used because every fortieth toothbrush from each assembly line is tested. It is possible for bias to enter into the sample if, for some reason, an assembly line makes a consistent error.

2. Simple random sampling is used because each telephone number has an equal chance of being dialed, and all samples of 1090 phone numbers have an equal chance of being selected. The sample may be biased because telephone sampling only samples those individuals who have telephones, who are available, and who are willing to respond.

3. **Workplace Fraud**

4. Parameter. The median salary is based on all marketing account executives.

5. Statistic. The percent, 88%, is based on a subset of the population.

6. (a) 95%
   (b) For $93,500, $z \approx 4.67$; For $85,600, $z \approx -0.6$; For $82,750, $z \approx -2.5$.
       The salaries of $93,500 and $82,750 are unusual.

7. Population: Collection of opinions of all college and university admissions directors and enrollment officers.
   Sample: Collection of opinions of the 339 college and university admission directors and enrollment officers surveyed.

8. Population: Reasons for pain reliever use of all Americans ages 12 or older
   Sample: Reasons for pain reliever use of the 67,901 Americans ages 12 or older surveyed

9. Experiment. The study applies a treatment (digital device) to the subjects.

10. Observational study. The study does not attempt to influence the responses of the subjects.

11. Quantitative; Ratio

12. Qualitative; Nominal

13. (a) **Tornadoes by State**

    0, 2, 10, 32, 99
    Number of tornadoes

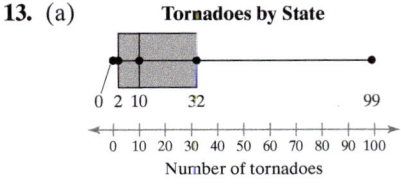

    (b) Skewed right

14. 88.9

15. (a) $\bar{x} \approx 5.49$; median $= 5.4$; mode $=$ none; Both the mean and the median accurately describe a typical American alligator tail length.
(b) Range $= 4.1$; $s^2 \approx 2.34$; $s \approx 1.53$

16. (a) An inference drawn from the study is that the life expectancies for Americans will continue to increase or remain stable.
(b) This inference may incorrectly imply that Americans will have higher life expectancies in the future.

17.

Class	Midpoint	Class boundaries
0–8	4	−0.5–8.5
9–17	13	8.5–17.5
18–26	22	17.5–26.5
27–35	31	26.5–35.5
36–44	40	35.5–44.5
45–53	49	44.5–53.5
54–62	58	53.5–62.5
63–71	67	62.5–71.5

Frequency, f	Relative frequency	Cumulative frequency
20	0.500	20
7	0.175	27
6	0.150	33
1	0.025	34
2	0.050	36
1	0.025	37
2	0.050	39
1	0.025	40

18. Skewed right

19.

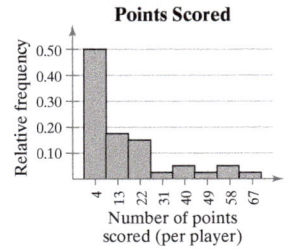

Montreal Canadiens Points Scored

Class with greatest frequency: 0–8
Classes with least frequency: 27–35, 45–53, and 63–71

Chapter 3

Section 3.1 (page 139)

1. You are more likely to be correct using an interval estimate because it is unlikely that a point estimate will exactly equal the population mean.

3. d; As the level of confidence increases, z_c increases, causing wider intervals.

5. 1.28   **7.** 1.15   **9.** −0.47   **11.** 1.76   **13.** 1.861

15. 0.192   **17.** c   **18.** d   **19.** b   **20.** a

21. (12.0, 12.6)   **23.** (9.7, 11.3)   **25.** $E = 1.4$, $\bar{x} = 13.4$

27. $E = 0.17$, $\bar{x} = 1.88$ **29.** 126   **31.** 7

33. $E = 1.95$, $\bar{x} = 28.15$

35. (58.57, 59.89); (58.44, 60.02)
With 90% confidence, you can say that the population mean price is between $58.57 and $59.89. With 95% confidence, you can say that the population mean price is between $58.44 and $60.02. The 95% CI is wider.

37. (6.98, 13.46); (6.46, 14.08)
With 90% confidence, you can say that the population mean rainfall is between 6.98 and 13.46 millimeters. With 95% confidence, you can say that the population mean rainfall is between 6.36 and 14.08 millimeters. The 95% CI is wider.

39. Yes; The margin of error is small ($E = 0.67$).

41. Yes; The right endpoint of the 95% CI is 14.08.

43. (a) An increase in the level of confidence will widen the confidence interval and the less certain you can be about a point estimate.
(b) An increase in the sample size will narrow the confidence interval because it decreases the standard error.
(c) An increase in the population standard deviation will widen the confidence interval because small standard deviations produce more precise intervals, which are smaller.

45. (151.5, 193.9); (139.5, 205.9)
With 90% confidence, you can say that the population mean quantity is between 151.5 and 193.9 milligrams. With 99% confidence, you can say that the population mean quantity is between 139.5 and 205.9 milligrams. The 99% CI is wider.

47. 89

49. (a) 66 servings
(b) No; Yes; The 95% CI is (28.252, 29.748). If the population mean is within 3% of the sample mean, then it falls outside the CI. If the population mean is within 0.3% of the sample mean, then it falls within the CI.

51. (a) 7 cans
(b) Yes; The 90% CI is (127.3, 128.2) and 128 ounces falls within that interval.

53. (a) 74 balls
(b) Yes; The 99% CI is (27.360, 27.640) and there are amounts less than 27.6 inches that fall within that interval.

55. *Sample answer:* A 99% CI may not be practical to use in all situations. It may produce a CI so wide that it has no practical application.

57. (a) 0.707 (b) 0.949 (c) 0.962 (d) 0.975
  (e) 0.711 (f) 0.937 (g) 0.964 (h) 0.979
  The finite population correction factor approaches 1 as the sample size decreases and the population size remains the same.
  The finite population correction factor approaches 1 as the population size increases and the sample size remains the same.

59. *Sample answer:*

$E = \dfrac{z_c \sigma}{\sqrt{n}}$ Write the original equation.

$E\sqrt{n} = z_c \sigma$ Multiply each side by $\sqrt{n}$.

$\sqrt{n} = \dfrac{z_c \sigma}{E}$ Divide each side by E.

$n = \left(\dfrac{z_c \sigma}{E}\right)^2$ Square each side.

Section 3.2 (page 149)

1. 1.833 **3.** 2.947 **5.** 2.664 **7.** 0.686 **9.** (10.9, 14.1)
11. (4.1, 4.5) **13.** $E = 3.7, \bar{x} = 18.4$ **15.** $E = 9.5, \bar{x} = 74.1$
17. 6.0; (29.5, 41.5); With 95% confidence, you can say that the population mean commute time is between 29.5 and 41.5 minutes.
19. 153.83; (372.67, 680.33); With 95% confidence, you can say that the population mean cell phone price is between $372.67 and $680.33.
21. 6.4; (29.1, 41.9); With 95% confidence, you can say that the population mean commute time is between 29.1 and 41.9 minutes. This confidence interval is slightly wider than the one found in Exercise 17.
23. Yes **25.** (a) 1185 (b) 168.1 (c) (1034.3, 1335.7)
27. (a) 7.49 (b) 1.64 (c) (6.28, 8.70) **29.** No
31. (a) 278,430 (b) 56,769 (c) (253,813.07, 303,046.93)
33. No
35. Use a *t*-distribution because σ is unknown and $n \geq 30$. (26.0, 29.4); With 95% confidence, you can say that the population mean BMI is between 26.0 and 29.4.
37. Neither distribution can be used because $n < 30$ and the mileages are not normally distributed.
39. Yes; Half the sample mean is 0.202, which falls within the confidence interval.
41. No; They are not making good tennis balls because the *t*-value for the sample is $t = 10$, which is not between $-t_{0.99} = -2.797$ and $t_{0.99} = 2.797$.

Section 3.2 Activity (page 152)

1–2. Answers will vary.

Section 3.3 (page 159)

1. False. To estimate the value of *p*, the population proportion of successes, use the point estimate $\hat{p} = x/n$.
3. 0.060, 0.940 **5.** 0.650, 0.350

7. $E = 0.014, \hat{p} = 0.919$ **9.** $E = 0.042, \hat{p} = 0.554$
11. (0.573, 0.607); (0.570, 0.610)
  With 90% confidence, you can say that the population proportion of U.S. adults who say they have made a New Year's resolution is between 57.3% and 60.7%. With 95% confidence, you can say it is between 57.0% and 61.0%. The 95% confidence interval is slightly wider.
13. (0.663, 0.737)
  With 99% confidence, you can say that the population proportion of U.S. adults who say they think police officers should be required to wear body cameras while on duty is between 66.3% and 73.7%.
15. (0.030, 0.031)
17. (a) 601 adults (b) 451 adults
  (c) Having an estimate of the population proportion reduces the minimum sample size needed.
19. (a) 752 adults (b) 295 adults
  (c) Having an estimate of the population proportion reduces the minimum sample size needed.
21. Yes; It falls within both confidence intervals.
23. No; The minimum sample size needed is 451 adults.
25. United States: (0.282, 0.358)
  Canada: (0.177, 0.243)
  France: (0.215, 0.285)
  Japan: (0.459, 0.541)
  Australia: (0.103, 0.157)
27. (a) Expect to stay at first employer for 3 or more years: (0.670, 0.710)
  Completed an apprenticeship or internship: (0.660, 0.700)
  Employed in field of study: (0.629, 0.671)
  Feel underemployed: (0.488, 0.532)
  Prefer to work for a large company: (0.125, 0.155)
  (b) Expect to stay at first employer for 3 or more years: (0.663, 0.717)
  Completed an apprenticeship or internship: (0.653, 0.707)
  Employed in field of study: (0.623, 0.677)
  Feel underemployed: (0.481, 0.539)
  Prefer to work for a large company: (0.120, 0.160)
29. (0.666, 0.734) is approximately a 98.1% CI.
31. (0.68, 0.74) is approximately a 96.3% CI.
33. (0.45, 0.49) is approximately a 98.3% CI.
  (0.51, 0.55) is approximately a 98.3% CI.
35. If $n\hat{p} < 5$ or $n\hat{q} < 5$, the sampling distribution of $\hat{p}$ may not be normally distributed, so z_c cannot be used to calculate the confidence interval.

37.

$\hat{p}$	$\hat{q}=1-\hat{p}$	$\hat{p}\hat{q}$	$\hat{p}$	$\hat{q}=1-\hat{p}$	$\hat{p}\hat{q}$
0.0	1.0	0.00	0.45	0.55	0.2475
0.1	0.9	0.09	0.46	0.54	0.2484
0.2	0.8	0.16	0.47	0.53	0.2491
0.3	0.7	0.21	0.48	0.52	0.2496
0.4	0.6	0.24	0.49	0.51	0.2499
0.5	0.5	0.25	0.50	0.50	0.2500
0.6	0.4	0.24	0.51	0.49	0.2499
0.7	0.3	0.21	0.52	0.48	0.2496
0.8	0.2	0.16	0.53	0.47	0.2491
0.9	0.1	0.09	0.54	0.46	0.2484
1.0	0.0	0.00	0.55	0.45	0.2475

$\hat{p}=0.5$ gives the maximum value of $\hat{p}\hat{q}$.

Section 3.3 Activity (page 163)

1–2. Answers will vary.

Section 3.4 (page 168)

1. Yes **3.** $\chi_R^2=14.067, \chi_L^2=2.167$
5. $\chi_R^2=32.852, \chi_L^2=8.907$
7. $\chi_R^2=52.336, \chi_L^2=13.121$
9. (a) (7.33, 20.89) (b) (2.71, 4.57)
11. (a) (755, 2401) (b) (27, 49)
13. (a) (0.1615, 0.5136) (b) (0.4018, 0.7167)
With 90% confidence, you can say that the population variance is between 0.1615 and 0.5136, and the population standard deviation is between 0.4018 and 0.7167 centimeters.
15. (a) (181.50, 976.54) (b) (13.47, 31.25)
With 99% confidence, you can say that the population variance is between 181.50 and 976.54, and the population standard deviation is between 13.47 and 31.25 thousand dollars.
17. (a) (5.46, 45.70) (b) (2.34, 6.76)
With 99% confidence, you can say that the population variance is between 5.46 and 45.70, and the population standard deviation is between 2.34 and 6.76 days.
19. (a) (128, 492) (b) (11, 22)
With 95% confidence, you can say that the population variance is between 128 and 492, and the population standard deviation is between 11 and 22 grains per gallon.
21. (a) (0.0986, 0.3137) (b) (0.314, 0.560)
With 90% confidence, you can say that the population variance is between 0.0986 and 0.3137, and the population standard deviation is between 0.314 and 0.560 hours.
23. (a) (12.8, 57.1) (b) (3.6, 7.6)
With 99% confidence, you can say that the population variance is between 12.8 and 57.1, and the population standard deviation is between 3.6 and 7.6 minutes.
25. No, because all of the values in the confidence interval are greater than 0.35.
27. No, because 0.50 is contained in the class interval.
29. *Sample answer:* Unlike a confidence interval for a population mean or proportion, a confidence interval for a population variance does not have a margin of error. The left and right endpoints must be calculated separately.

Uses and Abuses for Chapter 3 (page 170)

1–2. Answers will vary. **3.** (a) No (b) Yes

Review Exercises for Chapter 3 (page 172)

1. (a) 119.05 (b) 6.5
3. (112.6, 125.6); With 90% confidence, you can say that the systolic blood pressure mean is between 112.6 and 125.6 mmHg.
5. $E=6.125, \bar{x}=36.375$ **7.** 38 people **9.** 1.796
11. 1.341 **13.** 5.96
15. 1.39
17. (146, 184); With 90% confidence, you can say that the population mean height is between 146 and 184 feet.
19. (a) 0.720, 0.280 (b) (0.697, 0.743); (0.692, 0.747)
(c) With 90% confidence, you can say that the population proportion of U.S. adults who say they want the U.S. to play a leading or major role in global affairs is between 69.7% and 74.3%. With 95% confidence, you can say it is between 69.2% and 74.7%. The 95% confidence interval is slightly wider.
21. (a) 0.530, 0.470 (b) (0.513, 0.547); (0.509, 0.551)
(c) With 90% confidence, you can say that the population proportion of U.S. adults who think antibiotics are effective against viral infections is between 51.3% and 54.7%. With 95% confidence, you can say it is between 50.9% and 55.1%. The 95% confidence interval is slightly wider.
23. No; It falls outside both confidence intervals.
25. (a) 385 adults (b) 335 adults
(c) Having an estimate of the population proportion reduces the minimum sample size needed.
27. $\chi_R^2=23.685, \chi_L^2=6.571$ **29.** $\chi_R^2=32.852, \chi_L^2=8.907$
31. (a) (185.1, 980.8) (b) (13.6, 31.3)
With 95% confidence, you can say that the population variance is between 185.1 and 980.8, and the population standard deviation is between 13.6 and 31.3 knots.

Quiz for Chapter 3 (page 174)

1. (a) 2.598 (b) 0.123
(c) (2.475, 2.721); With 95% confidence, you can say that the population mean winning time is between 2.475 and 2.721 hours.
(d) No; It falls outside the confidence interval.
2. 42 champions

3. (a) $\bar{x} = 6.61$, $s \approx 3.38$
   (b) (4.65, 8.57); With 90% confidence, you can say that the population mean amount of time is between 4.65 and 8.57 minutes.
   (c) (4.79, 8.43); With 90% confidence, you can say that the population mean amount of time is between 4.79 and 8.43 minutes. This confidence interval is narrower than the one in part (b).
4. (109,990, 156,662); With 95% confidence, you can say that the population mean annual earnings is between $109,990 and $156,662.
5. Yes
6. (a) 0.740
   (b) (0.717, 0.763); With 90% confidence, you can say that the population proportion of U.S. adults who say that the energy situation in the United States is very or fairly serious is between 71.7% and 76.3%.
   (c) No; The values fall outside the confidence interval.
   (d) 798 adults
7. (a) (5.41, 38.08)
   (b) (2.32, 6.17); With 95% confidence, you can say that the population standard deviation is between 2.32 and 6.17 minutes.

Real Statistics—Real Decisions for Chapter 3 (page 176)

1. (a) Yes, there has been a change in the mean concentration level because the confidence interval for Year 1 does not overlap the confidence interval for Year 2.
   (b) No, there has not been a change in the mean concentration level because the confidence interval for Year 2 overlaps the confidence interval for Year 3.
   (c) Yes, there has been a change in the mean concentration level because the confidence interval for Year 1 does not overlap the confidence interval for Year 3.
2. The concentrations of cyanide in the drinking water have increased over the three-year period.
3. The width of the confidence interval for Year 2 may have been caused by greater variation in the levels of cyanide than in other years, which may be the result of outliers.
4. Increase the sample size.
5. Answers will vary.
   (a) *Sample answer:* The sampling distribution of the sample means was used because the "mean concentration" was used. The sample mean is the most unbiased point estimate of the population mean.
   (b) *Sample answer:* No, because typically σ is unknown. They could have used the sample standard deviation.

Chapter 4

Section 4.1 (page 193)

1. Increase; Decrease
3. The sample correlation coefficient r measures the strength and direction of a linear relationship between two variables; $r = -0.932$ indicates a stronger correlation because $|-0.932| = 0.932$ is closer to 1 than $|0.918| = 0.918$.
5. A table can be used to compare r with a critical value, or a hypothesis test can be performed using a t-test.
7. H_0: $\rho = 0$ (no significant correlation)
   H_a: $\rho \neq 0$ (significant correlation)
   Reject the null hypothesis if t is in the rejection region.
9. Strong negative linear correlation
11. No linear correlation
13. Explanatory variable: Amount of water consumed
    Response variable: Weight loss
15. c; You would expect a positive linear correlation between age and income.
16. d; You would not expect age and height to be correlated.
17. b; You would expect a negative linear correlation between age and balance on student loans.
18. a; You would expect the relationship between age and body temperature to be fairly constant.
19. *Sample answer:* People who can afford more valuable homes will live longer because they have more money to take care of themselves.
21. *Sample answer:* Ice cream sales are higher when the weather is warm and people are outside more often. This is when homicides rates go up as well.
23. (a) [scatter plot: Vocabulary size vs Age (in years)]
    (b) 0.979
    (c) Strong positive correlation; As age increases, the number of words in children's vocabulary tends to increase.
    (d) There is enough evidence at the 1% level of significance to conclude that there is a significant linear correlation between children's ages and number of words in their vocabulary.

25. (a)

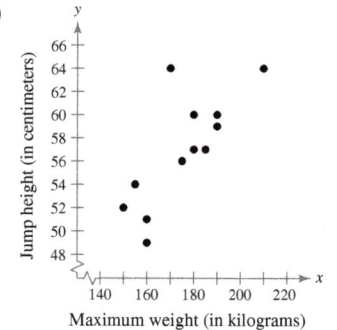

(b) 0.756
(c) Strong positive linear correlation; As the maximum weight for one repetition of a half squat increases, the jump height tends to increase.
(d) There is enough evidence at the 1% level of significance to conclude that there is a significant linear correlation between maximum weight for one repetition of a half squat and jump height.

27. (a)

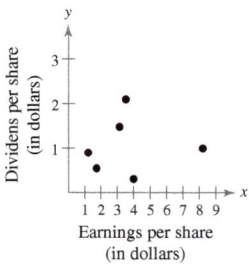

(b) 0.061
(c) No linear correlation; The earnings per share for the companies do not appear to be related to their dividends per share.
(d) There is not enough evidence at the 1% level of significance to conclude that there is a significant linear correlation between earning per share for the companies and their dividends per share.

29. The correlation coefficient gets stronger, going from $r \approx 0.979$ to $r \approx 0.985$.

31. The correlation coefficient gets weaker, going from $r \approx 0.756$ to $r \approx 0.666$.

33. There is not enough evidence at the 1% level of significance to conclude that there is a significant linear correlation between vehicle weight and the variability in braking distance on a dry surface.

35. There is enough evidence at the 5% level of significance to conclude that there is a significant linear correlation between the maximum weight for one repetition of a half squat and the jump height.

37. $r \approx -0.975$; The correlation coefficient remains unchanged when the x-values and y-values are switched.

Section 4.1 Activity (page 197)

1–4. Answers will vary.

Section 4.2 (page 202)

1. A residual is the difference between the observed y-value of a data point and the predicted y-value on the regression line for the x-coordinate of the data point. A residual is positive when the data point is above the line, negative when the point is below the line, and zero when the observed y-value equals the predicted y-value.

3. Substitute a value of x into the equation of a regression line and solve for $\hat{y}$.

5. The correlation between variables must be significant.

7. b   **8.** a   **9.** e   **10.** c   **11.** f
12. d   **13.** b   **14.** c   **15.** d   **16.** a
17. $\hat{y} = 0.486x - 15.057$

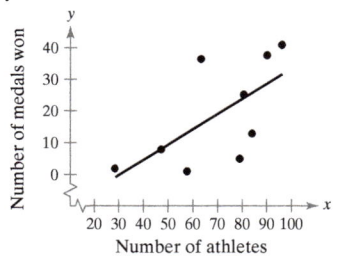

(a) 21 medals   (b) 24 medals
(c) 26 medals
(d) It is not meaningful to predict the value of y for $x = 120$ because $x = 120$ is outside the range of the original data.

19. $\hat{y} = 4.974x + 49.994$

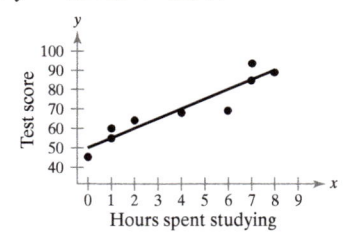

(a) 67   (b) 75
(c) 87
(d) It is not meaningful to predict the value of y for $x = 14$ because $x = 14$ is outside the range of the original data.

21. $\hat{y} = -2.044x + 520.668$

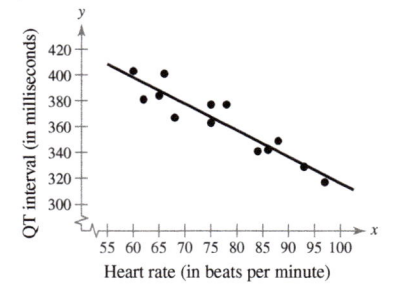

(a) It is not meaningful to predict the value of y for $x = 120$ because $x = 120$ is outside the range of the original data.
(b) 384 milliseconds   (c) 337 milliseconds
(d) 351 milliseconds

23. $\hat{y} = 2.979x + 52.476$

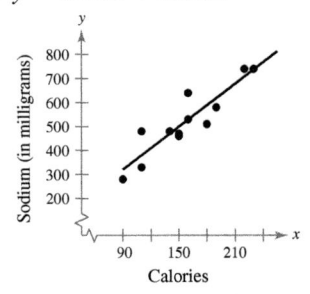

(a) 559 milligrams (b) 350 milligrams
(c) It is not meaningful to predict the value of y for $x = 260$ because $x = 260$ is outside the range of the original data.
(d) 678 milligrams

25. $\hat{y} = 1.870x + 51.360$

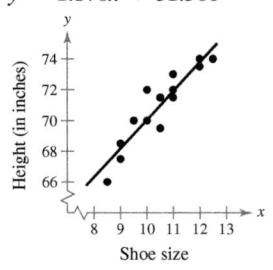

(a) 72.865 inches (b) 66.320 inches
(c) It is not meaningful to predict the value of y for $x = 15.5$ because $x = 15.5$ is outside the range of the original data.
(d) 70.060 inches

27. Strong positive linear correlation; As the years of experience of the registered nurses increase, their salaries tend to increase.

29. No, it is not meaningful to predict a salary for a registered nurse with 28 years of experience because $x = 28$ is outside the range of the original data.

31. (a) $\hat{y} = -4.297x + 94.200$

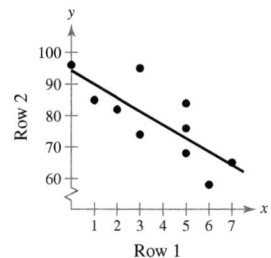

(b) $\hat{y} = -0.141x + 14.763$

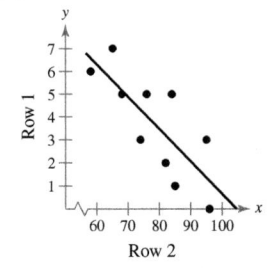

(c) The slope of the line keeps the same sign, but the values of m and b change.

33. (a) $\hat{y} = 0.139x + 21.024$
(b) 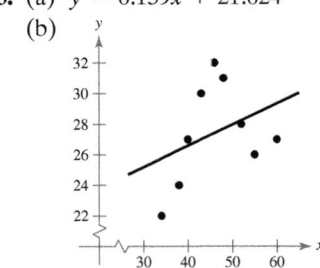
(c) Residual
(d) The residual plot shows a pattern because the residuals do not fluctuate about 0. This implies that the regression line is not a good representation of the relationship between the two variables.

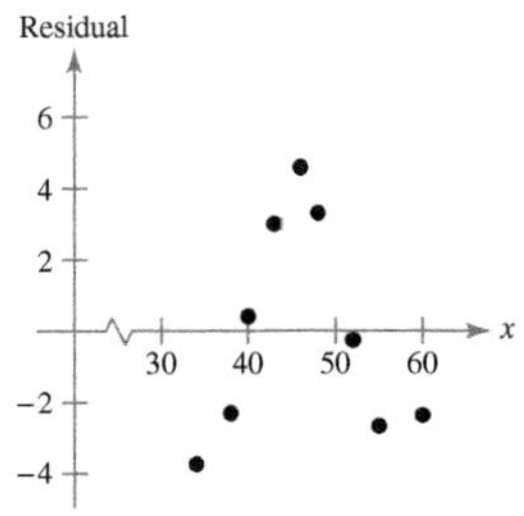

35. (a) 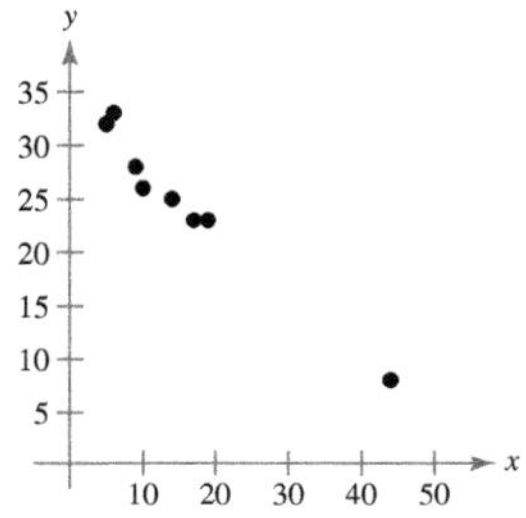
(b) The point $(44, 8)$ may be an outlier.
(c) The point $(44, 8)$ is not an influential point because the slopes and y-intercepts of the regression lines with the point included and without the point included are not significantly different.

37. $\hat{y} = 654.536x - 1214.857$

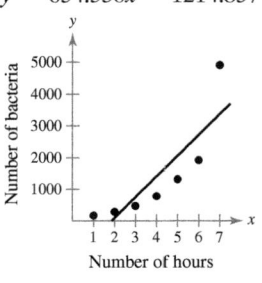

39. $y = 93.028(1.712)^x$

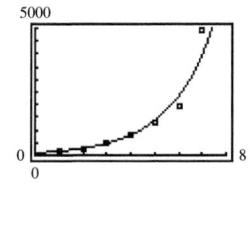

41. $\hat{y} = -78.929x + 576.179$

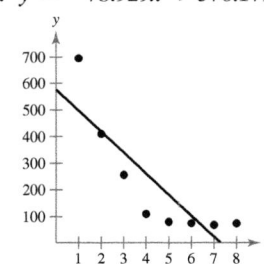

43. $y = 782.300x^{-1.251}$

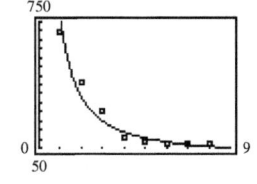

45. $y = 25.035 + 19.599 \ln x$

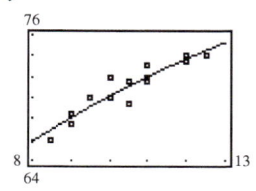

47. The logarithmic equation is a better model for the data. The graph of the logarithmic equation fits the data better than the regression line.

Section 4.2 Activity (page 308)

1–4. Answers will vary.

Section 4.3 (page 316)

1. The total variation is the sum of the squares of the differences between the y-values of each ordered pair and the mean of the y-values of the ordered pairs, or $\Sigma(y_i - \bar{y})^2$.

3. The unexplained variation is the sum of the squares of the differences between the observed y-values and the predicted y-values, or $\Sigma(y_i - \hat{y}_i)^2$.

5. Two variables that have perfect positive or perfect negative linear correlation have a correlation coefficient of 1 or −1, respectively. In either case, the coefficient of determination is 1, which means that 100% of the variation in the response variable is explained by the variation in the explanatory variable.

7. 0.216; About 21.6% of the variation is explained. About 78.4% of the variation is unexplained.

9. 0.916; About 91.6% of the variation is explained. About 8.4% of the variation is unexplained.

11. (a) 0.798; About 79.8% of the variation in proceeds can be explained by the relationship between the number of offerings and proceeds, and about 20.2% of the variation is unexplained.
(b) 8054.328; The standard error of estimate of the proceeds for a specific number of offerings is about 8,054,328,000.

13. (a) 0.729; About 72.9% of the variation in points earned can be explained by the relationship between the number of goals allowed and points earned, and about 27.1% of the variation is unexplained.
(b) 9.438; The standard error of estimate of the points earned for a specific number of goals allowed is about 9.438.

15. (a) 0.651; About 65.1% of the variation in mean annual wages can be explained by the relationship between percentages of employment in STEM occupations and mean annual wages, and about 34.9% of the variation is unexplained.
(b) 8.141; The standard error of estimate of the mean annual wages for a specific percentage of employment in STEM occupations is about $8141.

17. (a) 0.642; About 64.2% of the variation in the quantity of wheat exported can be explained by the relationship between the quantity of wheat produced and the quantity exported, and about 35.8% of the variation is unexplained.
(b) 1653.623; The standard error of estimate of the quantity of wheat exported for a specific quantity of wheat produced is about 1,653,623,000 kilograms per year.

19. (a) 0.816; About 81.6% of the variation in the new-vehicle sales of General Motors can be explained by the relationship between the new-vehicle sales of Ford and General Motors, and about 18.4% of the variation is unexplained.
(b) 346.341; The standard error of estimate of the new-vehicle sales of General Motors for a specific amount of new-vehicle sales of Ford is about 346,341 new vehicles.

21. $40{,}083.251 < y < 82{,}572.581$
You can be 95% confident that the proceeds will be between $40,083,251,000 and $82,572,581,000 when the number of initial offerings is 450 issues.

23. $59.009 < y < 94.665$
You can be 90% confident that the total points earned will be between 59 and 95 when the number of goals allowed is 250.

25. $36.264 < y < 86.462$
You can be 99% confident that the mean annual wage will be between $36,264 and $86,462 when the percentage of employment in STEM occupations is 13% in the industry.

27. $2209.419 < y < 9046.581$
You can be 80% confident that the quantity of wheat exported will be in between 2209.419 and 9046.581 million kilograms when the quantity of wheat produced is 99,000 million kilograms per year.

29. $2684.712 < y < 4356.424$
You can be 95% confident that the new-vehicle sales of General Motors will be between 2,684,712 and 4,356,424 when the new-vehicle sales of Ford are 2,628,000.

31.

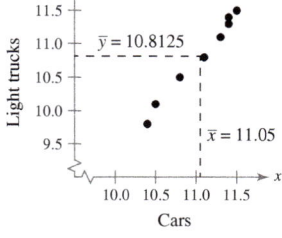

33. 0.987; About 98.7% of the variation in the median ages of light trucks can be explained by the relationship between the median ages of cars and light trucks, and about 1.3% of the variation is unexplained.

35. Fail to reject H_0. There is not enough evidence at the 1% level of significance to support the claim that there is a linear relationship between weight and number of hours slept.

37. $-175.836 < B < 287.908$; $108.928 < M < 290.142$

Section 4.4 (page 324)

1. (a) 18,832.7 pounds per acre
   (b) 18,016.4 pounds per acre
   (c) 17,350.6 pounds per acre
   (d) 16,190.3 pounds per acre
3. (a) 7.5 cubic feet
   (b) 16.8 cubic feet
   (c) 51.9 cubic feet
   (d) 62.1 cubic feet
5. (a) $\hat{y} = 17,899 - 606.58x_1 - 52.9x_2$
   (b) 564.314   (c) 0.966
   The standard error of estimate of the predicted price given specific age and milage of pre-owned Honda Civic Sedans is about $564.31. The multiple regression model explains about 96.6% of the variation.
7. 0.955; About 95.5% of the variation in y can be explained by the relationship between variables; $r^2_{adj} < r^2$.

Uses and Abuses for Chapter 4 (page 326)

1–2. Answers will vary.

Review Exercises for Chapter 4 (page 328)

1. (a) 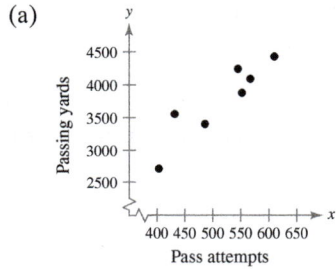
   (b) 0.917
   (c) Strong positive linear correlation; As the number of pass attempts increase, the number of passing yards tends to increase.
3. (a) 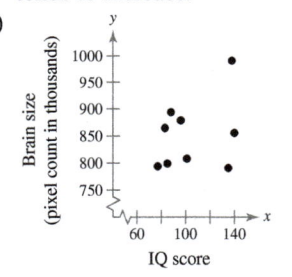
   (b) 0.338
   (c) Weak positive linear correlation; The IQ does not appear to be related to the brain size.
5. There is enough evidence at the 5% level of significance to conclude that there is a significant linear correlation between a quarterback's pass attempts and passing yards.
7. There is not enough evidence at the 1% level of significance to conclude that there is a significant linear correlation between IQ and brain size.

9. $\hat{y} = 0.106x - 781.327$

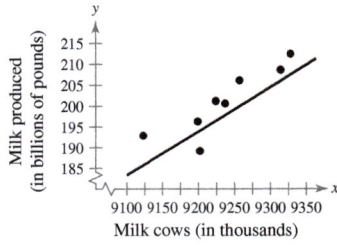

   (a) It is not meaningful to predict the value of y for $x = 9080$ because $x = 9080$ is outside the range of the original data.
   (b) 197.053 billions of pounds
   (c) 199.173 billions of pounds
   (d) 204.473 billions of pounds
11. $\hat{y} = -0.086x + 10.450$

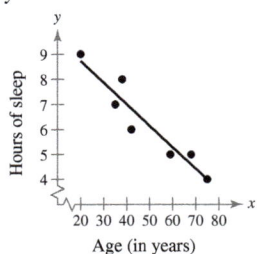

    (a) It is not meaningful to predict the value of y when $x = 16$ because $x = 16$ is outside the range of the original data.
    (b) 8.3 hours
    (c) It is not meaningful to predict the value of y when $x = 85$ because $x = 85$ is outside the range of the original data.
    (d) 6.15 hours
13. 0.203; About 20.3% of the variation is explained. About 79.7% of the variation is unexplained.
15. 0.412; About 41.2% of the variation is explained. About 58.8% of the variation is unexplained.
17. (a) 0.690; About 69.0% of the variation in top speed for hybrid and electric cars can be explained by the relationship between their fuel efficiencies and top speeds, and about 31.0% of the variation is unexplained.
    (b) 5.851; The standard error of estimate of the top speed for hybrid and electric cars for a specific fuel efficiency is about 5.851 miles per hour.
19. $193.364 < y < 210.282$
    You can be 90% confident that the amount of milk produced will be between 193.364 billion pounds and 210.282 billion pounds when the average number of cows is 9275.
21. $4.866 < y < 8.294$
    You can be 95% confident that the hours slept will be between 4.866 and 8.294 hours for an adult who is 45 years old.
23. $75.349 < y < 119.817$
    You can be 99% confident that the top speed of a hybrid or electric car will be between 75.349 and 119.817 miles per hour when the combined city and highway fuel efficiency is 90 miles per gallon equivalent.

25. (a) $\hat{y} = 3.6738 + 1.2874x_1 - 7.531x_2$
(b) 0.710; The standard error of estimate of the predicted carbon monoxide content given specific tar and nicotine contents is about 0.710 milligram.
(c) 0.943; The multiple regression model explains about 94.3% of the variation in y.

27. (a) 21.705 miles per gallon
(b) 25.21 miles per gallon
(c) 30.1 miles per gallon
(d) 25.86 miles per gallon

Quiz for Chapter 4   (page 332)

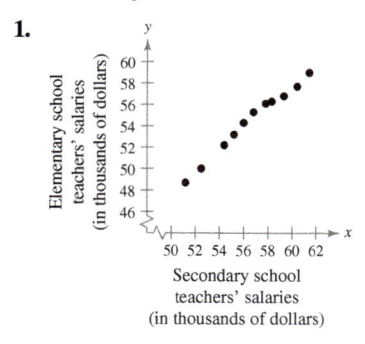

1.

The data appear to have a positive linear correlation. As x increases, y tends to increase.

2. 0.992; Strong positive linear correlation; As the average annual salaries of secondary school teachers increase, the average annual salaries of elementary school teachers tend to increase.

3. Reject H_0. There is enough evidence at the 5% level of significance to conclude that there is a significant linear correlation between the average annual salaries of secondary school teachers and the average annual salaries of elementary school teachers.

4. $\hat{y} = 0.997x - 1.960$

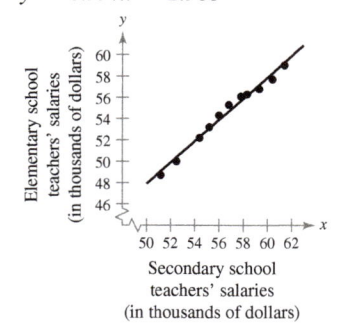

5. $50,382.50

6. 0.984; About 98.4% of the variation in the average annual salaries of elementary school teachers can be explained by the relationship between the average annual salaries of secondary school teachers and elementary school teachers, and about 1.6% of the variation is unexplained.

7. 0.422; The standard error of estimate of the average annual salaries of elementary school teachers for a specific average annual salary of secondary school teachers is about $422.

8. $49.311 < y < 51.455$
You can be 95% confident that the average annual salary of elementary school teachers will be between $49,311 and $51,455 when the average annual salary of secondary school teachers is $52,500.

9. (a) $95.26   (b) $70.28   (c) $67.74   (d) $59.46

Real Statistics—Real Decisions for Chapter 4   (page 334)

1. (a)

It appears that there is a positive linear correlation. As the annual average of the daily maximum sulfur dioxide concentration increases, the annual average of the daily maximum nitrogen dioxide concentration tends to increase.

(b) 0.966; There is a strong positive linear correlation.
(c) There is enough evidence at the 5% level of significance to conclude that there is a significant linear correlation between annual averages of the daily maximum concentrations of sulfur dioxide and nitrogen dioxide.
(d) $\hat{y} = 0.234x + 38.081$

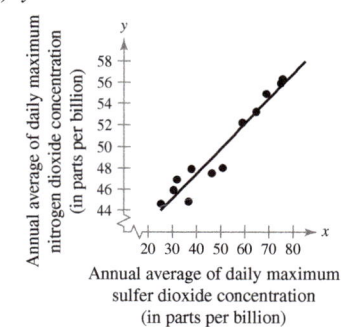

(e) Yes, for x-values that are within the range of the data set.
(f) $r^2 \approx 0.934$; About 93.4% of the variation in nitrogen dioxide concentrations can be explained by the variation in sulfur dioxide concentrations, and about 6.6% of the variation is unexplained.
$s_e \approx 1.178$; The standard error of estimate of the annual averages of the daily maximum concentration of nitrogen dioxide for a specific annual average of the daily maximum concentration of sulfur dioxide is about 1.178 parts per billion.

2. $41.733 < y < 47.533$
You can be 95% confident that the annual average of the daily maximum nitrogen dioxide concentration will be between 41.733 and 47.533 parts per billion when the annual average of the daily maximum sulfur dioxide concentration is 28 parts per billion.